LITERARY IMPOSTORS

LITERARY IMPOSTORS

Canadian Autofiction of the Early Twentieth Century

ROSMARIN HEIDENREICH

McGill-Queen's University Press
Montreal & Kingston • London • Chicago

ISBN 978-0-7735-5453-5 (cloth)
ISBN 978-0-7735-5454-2 (paper)
ISBN 978-0-7735-5528-0 (ePDF)
ISBN 978-0-7735-5529-7 (ePUB)

Legal deposit third quarter 2018
Bibliothèque nationale du Québec

Printed in Canada on acid-free paper that is 100% ancient forest free (100% post-consumer recycled), processed chlorine free

This book has been published with the help of a grant from the Université de Saint-Boniface.

Funded by the Government of Canada | Financé par le gouvernement du Canada | Canada | Canada Council for the Arts | Conseil des arts du Canada

We acknowledge the support of the Canada Council for the Arts, which last year invested $153 million to bring the arts to Canadians throughout the country.

Nous remercions le Conseil des arts du Canada de son soutien. L'an dernier, le Conseil a investi 153 millions de dollars pour mettre de l'art dans la vie des Canadiennes et des Canadiens de tout le pays.

Library and Archives Canada Cataloguing in Publication

Heidenreich, Rosmarin Elfriede, author
Literary impostors: Canadian autofiction of the early twentieth century / Rosmarin Heidenreich.

Includes bibliographical references and index.
Issued in print and electronic formats.
ISBN 978-0-7735-5453-5 (hardcover). – ISBN 978-0-7735-5454-2 (softcover). – ISBN 978-0-7735-5528-0 (ePDF). – ISBN 978-0-7735-5529-7 (ePUB)

1. Canadian prose literature (English) – 20th century – History and criticism. 2. Creative nonfiction, Canadian (English). 3. Autobiography. 4. Literary forgeries and mystifications – History – 20th century. 5. Impostors and imposture in literature. 6. Impersonation in literature. 7. Authors, Canadian (English) – 20th century – Biography. I. Title.

PS8185.A88H45 2018 C810'.9492 C2018-901703-1
C2018-901704-X

This book was typeset by Marquis Interscript in 10.5/13 Sabon.

For Paul

Contents

Illustrations

Acknowledgments

Primary biographical research is arduous, time- and resource-consuming work. It would have been impossible to write this book, centred on six very different authors, had there not been reliable published biographical material available on which to base my account of their lives: Donald B. Smith's excellent biographies of Long Lance and Grey Owl, Diana Birchall's moving biography of her grandmother, Winnifred Eaton/Onoto Watanna, and three mutually complementary biographies of Ernest Dufault/Will James. All biographical writing, however, is essentially open-ended, and as previously unknown aspects of a subject's life and work are brought to light, the subject's identitary image may shift significantly. Thus Klaus Martens's discoveries regarding the life of Felix Paul Greve/Frederick Philip Grove have necessitated a reassessment of some of the observations of D.O. Spettigue, the Canadian scholar who first identified Greve as Grove and wrote about the author's life in Canada and Europe. In the case of Annette White-Parks's biography of Edith Eaton/Sui Sin Far, some elements, in particular the characterization of the author's literary production, have been contradicted by Mary Chapman's recovery of a trove of Edith Eaton/Sui Sin Far stories not taken into account by White-Parks. I am most indebted to Mary Chapman for letting me read her manuscript before it was published, giving me the opportunity to revise my own work on Edith Eaton before my manuscript entered the editorial process.

I'm extremely grateful to Donald B. Smith for reading and commenting on my chapters on Long Lance and Grey Owl, to Diana Birchall for reading and commenting on my chapter on the Eaton sisters, and to Philip Heidenreich, Roger Léveillé, Doug Parker, Paul

Paterson, and Doug Whiteway for reading early drafts of the manuscript and for offering support and encouragement as well as suggestions and critical feedback. Stephanie Heidenreich read not only the early drafts, but virtually all the subsequent versions as well. Her comments and suggestions were enormously helpful to me in the overall shaping of the manuscript.

Many thanks to Daniel Beaulieu, reference librarian at the Université de Saint-Boniface, for his help in obtaining elusive and hard-to-access materials. I would like to thank Madeleine Samuda, his predecessor, for putting me onto the story of Will James. Discussions with my colleague Paul Morris regarding the scope and structure of the manuscript were most helpful, as was his concrete advice. I am grateful to the Université de Saint-Boniface for the sabbatical leave that made it possible to undertake this project, as well as for a financial grant that helped bring it to its conclusion.

Warm thanks are also due to Diana Birchall, Klaus Martens, and André Cousineau for making photographs from their own collections available for inclusion in this book.

I owe a huge debt of gratitude to my editor Mark Abley, who wisely and patiently guided my manuscript throughout the various stages of the editorial process. One could not wish for a more helpful, insightful, and knowledgeable editor.

Finally, I would like to thank my husband, Paul Paterson, for his interest in the project, and for his support, encouragement, and patience.

The idea of writing this book sprang from a combination of circumstances. It was Régine Robin's splendid book on European autofiction (*Le Golem de l'écriture: De l'autofiction au Cybersoi*), my reading of which coincided with my immersion into Frederick Philip Grove's complicated intertwining of fact and fiction for an essay I was writing, that suggested to me the idea of assembling the stories of some of Canada's best-known "literary impostors" – writers who, like Grove, had constructed new identities – and examining their lives and works through the lens of autofiction.

I am indebted to my parents for my first encounter with one of my subjects. They visited the Groves in Simcoe, with me in tow as a toddler, shortly before Grove died, and maintained a friendship with Catherine Grove after his death. In the 1990s I had occasion to meet Grove's son Leonard and his wife Mary. I later interviewed Len (now deceased) in Toronto in connection with this book.

Over the years that I have been researching their lives and writings, the six highly diverse authors discussed in the pages that follow have become living figures in my imagination. They are all, literally and in every sense, larger than life.

LITERARY IMPOSTORS

Introduction

The early twentieth century saw the emergence of a number of critically praised "autobiographical" literary works by high-profile Canadian authors, which were subsequently found – to the shock of critics and readers alike, and in some cases long after the authors' deaths – to be fabrications, or works in which fact and fiction were inextricably interwoven. What is even more extraordinary is that all but one of the writers who produced them assumed false identities which they lived out, largely unchallenged, in their everyday lives, concealing or even obliterating their true pasts. In fact the very purpose of these writers' "autobiographies" seemed to be, at least in part, to authenticate their self-constructed identities. The writers to be examined in this book thus represent an extreme form of what is known as *autofiction* (texts that are both fictional and autobiographical), in that they not only wrote in the voices of their invented new identities, but actually performed them, "becoming," in their everyday lives, the figures they had themselves created.

Literary Impostors explores the intriguing stories – both the "true" and the invented versions – of six famous late colonial writers, who assumed and for the most part lived out self-created identities: Felix Paul Greve alias Frederick Philip Grove, Archie Belaney alias Grey Owl, Ernest Dufault alias Will James, Sylvester Long alias Chief Buffalo Child Long Lance, Winnifred Eaton alias Onoto Watanna, and Edith Eaton alias Sui Sin Far. It analyzes their lives and literary works, examining the external circumstances and inner impulses that drove them to assume alien identities, and shows how these assumed identities were linked to their respective (actual) pasts. It also demonstrates how both their "true" and their self-created identities are revealed in their "autobiographies" as well as in some of their other literary works, and discusses the consequences of living out their assumed identities on their personal lives.

The deception that most of these writers undertook was not fraudulent in the sense in which the term is usually understood. These writers, in essence, re-invented themselves to "become" who and what they felt they really were. Their self-re-engenderment was, in many ways, an emancipatory process that freed them from the constraints of a biographical identity that they rejected, and that they wished, for various reasons, to leave behind. In this sense, they were all "passing," for as Elaine K. Ginsberg has pointed out, the term can be used to apply not only to racial passing, but "to disguises of other [non-racial] elements of an individual's presumed 'natural' or 'essential' identity."[1] While it is the phenomenon of self-reinvention in the sense of self-engenderment that represents the overarching theoretical principle, in four of these cases racial passing plays a significant role. The relevant chapters therefore discuss in some detail the role of racial identity in motivating these writers to "become someone else," and analyze the significance of racial issues and "passing" as they manifest themselves in the writers' autofictional works.

The lives and works of the authors discussed in this book can be seen as extreme forms of "identity performance," a kind of self-representation that can involve double, multiple, or assumed identities,[2] examples of which are found throughout Canadian literary history. There was, for example, the poet Pauline Johnson, daughter of a Mohawk chief and an English mother, who around the turn of the century gave performances of her poetry in which she appeared in European dress for the first half of the program, and changed into Indian attire for the second half, during which she spoke as an Indian princess.[3] Métis icon Howard Adams wrote a (seemingly uncompleted) "autobiography," with parallel and alternate depictions of events, partly in his own voice and partly in the voice of an alter ego, variously named Tony Parker or Tony Bruce.[4] There have also been elaborate literary hoaxes. One involved a writer calling himself Tuesday Lobsang Rampa, who said he had grown up in Tibet and claimed to have acquired the identity of a Tibetan lama by means of an operation involving the insertion of a "third eye."[5] Rampa, whose real name was Cyril Henry Hoskin, was in fact the son of an English plumber. Hoskin/Rampa spent the latter part of his life in Canada, first on the east coast and then in Vancouver, ending up in Calgary, where he died in 1981. Another, more recent literary hoax involved Montreal poet David Solway, who claimed to have discovered a Greek poet called Andreas Karavis, publishing poetry by "Karavis" that Solway said he had translated into English. In fact, Karavis was Solway's own invention.[6] Nevertheless such role-playing rarely extended to the writers' private lives, although in the case of the Quebec writer Hubert Aquin the assumed identity straddled the distinction between the literary persona and biographical identity. In the 1960s and 1970s, Aquin not only "performed," in his everyday life, various aspects of the ambiguous identities he had created in his novels, but also (re)enacted the death by suicide of one of them, namely H. de Heutz, the double-agent protagonist of Aquin's most famous novel, *Prochain épisode*.[7]

The writers profiled in this book have in common two elements that set them apart from those who "wrote" or periodically "performed" alternate identities: they all wrote "autobiographies" and, with the exception of Edith Eaton, they were, to varying degrees, "impostors" insofar as they actually lived out their invented *personae* in everyday life, effectively concealing and ultimately effacing their true identities. It is these two elements that stand at the centre of the examination that follows, of their work and lives.

The assumption of a new identity by Felix Paul Greve (1879–1948) alias Frederick Philip Grove upon his immigration to Canada was motivated by a troubled past: he had served a prison term for fraud in his native Germany, and was burdened by an unsurmountable financial debt upon his release. These problematic circumstances, compounded by the scandal of his running off with the wife of a distinguished architect, had cut him off from the elite social circles in which he had moved as a promising young student and subsequently as a talented writer and translator. His assumption of a new identity in Canada was dictated, in part, by expediency, but it was also motivated by the protean and narcissistic inclinations that had begun to manifest themselves in his personality even in Europe. His best known work is his "autobiography," suggestively titled *In Search of Myself*.

Ernest Dufault (1892–1945) was the son of a French-Canadian family that had been established in Quebec for generations. His running away to the West at the age of fifteen was driven by a burning desire to experience the western frontier. Inspired by romantic accounts of the Wild West of legend, he "became" the cowboy he had always felt he was. As a cowboy, illustrator, and movie stunt man he assumed a new identity under the name of Will James, supposedly born in

Montana. He subsequently became known as an author in the Western genre, and many of his books, including the "autobiographical" *Lone Cowboy*, were made into Hollywood films.

The story of Archie Belaney (1888–1938) and his metamorphosis into the Indian Grey Owl[8] was the realization of a cherished childhood fantasy, but it also offered an escape from the stigmatization of being raised – parentless but not orphaned – by two maiden aunts in Hastings, England, in a genteel middle-class household that he found stifling. He internalized his new identity to the point of claiming the role of spokesperson and advocate not only for the Indians, but, above all, for the wilderness that had sustained them for centuries. Archie Belaney had fantasized about being an Indian and begun to invent and organize activities and games about Indians as a schoolboy. But there was another motive to invent a new persona for himself: the trauma of being abandoned by a father who had gone to America and was said to be living among the Indians of the southwestern United States. The humiliations of parental abandonment and the boredom of conventional middle-class life in Hastings could best be effaced by living out a life of adventure in the New World, eclipsing, as the Indian Grey Owl, even the peripatetic life of his much-admired father.

Just as intriguing is the story of the man who called himself Chief Buffalo Child Long Lance (1890–1932), who was born in Winston-Salem, North Carolina, as Sylvester Long, of mixed Black, white, Cherokee, and Croatan[9] origins. Given the stringent racial segregation that prevailed in the southern United States at that time, Sylvester Long had every reason to escape the indignities of being designated as "coloured" and to carve out a new life for himself. He was too dark-skinned to pass as white, but he had the straight black hair of an Indian, which allowed him to assume the identity of a full-blooded Cherokee and then that of a western Plains Indian, an identity which he sought to authenticate as a journalist who wrote about Plains Indians "from the inside," and, ultimately, a best-selling "autobiography" titled *Long Lance*, in which he recounted the story of a boy growing up as a Blood Indian in southern Alberta. As Dufault/Will James had "become" the quintessential cowboy of the Wild West, Long Lance "became" a professional Indian, whose career culminated in his celebrated "autobiography" and in his playing a starring role in the Hollywood film *The Silent Enemy*, meant to depict life among the Indians before contact with Europeans.

Edith (1865–1914) and Winnifred Eaton (1875–1954), who grew up in Montreal as the daughters of an English father and a Chinese mother, are considered to be the first writers of Asian–North American fiction, Edith publishing under the Chinese name Sui Sin Far, Winnifred under the Japanese pseudonym Onoto Watanna. While both Eaton sisters adopted alien personae in an attempt to come to terms with their identity as Chinese half-castes, the case of Edith Eaton alias Sui Sin Far differs from those of the other writers portrayed in this study as, apart from using a pseudonym, she never attempted to conceal her racial or biographical identity. Her autobiographical essay "Leaves from the Mental Portfolio of an Eurasian" constitutes a more or less authentic if selective account of her life. Some of her stories, however, are highly autofictional, as they represent latent desires and predispositions on the part of her protagonists that can be readily attributed to the author herself. In these stories, Edith reinvents herself by creating an alternate identity that she inscribes in her fiction, one that, as an alter ego of her protagonists, she can vicariously live out. Edith did at times present herself as being Chinese. Writing under the Chinese pseudonym Sui Sin Far, she defiantly challenged the then-prevailing image (and status) of the Chinese by consistently privileging the Chinese side of her identity.

Her sister Winnifred adopted the persona of a Japanese, a minority viewed much more favourably in America (at least until the Second World War). During most of her career as a writer, she used the Japanese pseudonym Onoto Watanna, and presented herself publicly as being Japanese. In her own (anonymously published) "autobiographical" memoir *Me: A Book of Remembrance*, she evades the racial issue by leaving the heroine's racial background undesignated, thus marking her, for North American and European readers, as white by default. In the latter part of her career, however, Winnifred gave up her Japanese persona, and lived out the rest of her life without making any attempt to conceal her origins.

It is significant that all six writers saw themselves as "Other" early on in their lives. Even in Europe, Felix Paul Greve had created a sort of composite persona for which he drew on certain attributes of his fellow students from wealthy and influential families as well as on those of the figures he admired in the artistic *bohème*. In the case of Ernest Dufault, this sense of Otherness began to reveal itself in his earliest childhood. But unlike the protean impulses that characterized Greve/Grove's multiple transformations, Ernest Dufault's vision of his true self could not have been more clearly or unambiguously defined: he was a lone cowboy who would bring the frontier West alive once again. Archie Belaney's fantasy of living the life of an Indian in the wilderness manifested itself from young boyhood, when he invented not only games involving Indians, but also an alternate identity: far from being the abandoned child of uncaring and selfish parents, he was really, he said, the son of a daring adventurer father and an Apache mother who had met in the Wild West. Sylvester Long resisted the "coloured" identity by which he was designated early on, his multiple racial origins enabling him to claim the socially less stigmatizing identity of a Plains Indian. As for the Eaton sisters, their autobiographical writings reveal an early tendency to see themselves as possessing unique talents, as being somehow destined to make their mark as artists. This sense of having been endowed with special gifts that set them apart represented the reverse side of their stigmatized racial identity, which in fact set them apart as socially marginal and legally unentitled.

It is important to point out that among the writers to be discussed here, these self-reinventions manifested themselves in different ways. Three of them – Archie Belaney, Sylvester Long, and Ernest Dufault – began progressively to construct and live out their fictitious identities long before they began writing, and their "autobiographical" works can be seen, above all, as a way to authenticate and document the identities *they had already assumed*. The case of the Eaton sisters as well as that of Frederick Philip Grove is different insofar as it appears that they constructed their new identities largely *through their writing*. Although Greve/Grove, who came from humble origins, had played the role of a wealthy landowner's son from his university days onward, it was in his "autobiographical" Canadian works that he created the multi-faceted persona that would come to define him as a writer in Canada. However, what connects these very different writers from entirely dissimilar backgrounds, regardless of their respective immediate motives in assuming their new identities, is their overwhelming impulse to reinvent themselves – to re-engender themselves, so to speak – in the identities that they felt dwelt within them. While, as we shall see, external circumstances played a crucial role in the assumption of two fictive identities – those of Grove and Long Lance – the biographies of Archie Belaney and Ernest Dufault reveal less tangible elements that would seem to motivate their metamorphoses into, respectively, Grey Owl and Will James. The Eaton sisters, stigmatized by their Chinese heritage and traumatized by their half-caste status, took diverging paths, Edith choosing to assert the Chinese part of her identity, Winnifred assuming the persona of a Japanese lady with aristocratic antecedents.

The self-inventions of the North American writers to be examined in this study had their origins in widely disparate circumstances. The common element in their respective biographies is that they were, roughly speaking, contemporaries, who lived at a time when immigration to the New World – or migration within it – offered unlimited possibilities of self-reinvention. At the turn of the twentieth century, documentation of one's identity was based largely on the claims of the immigrants or migrants themselves. (Passports or other formal identification documents did not come into general use until after the First World War.) The late colonial era thus represented a time and space that made possible the kind of biographical imposture to be discussed here.

What enabled these writers to live out their fictive identities was the fact that – as immigrants or migrants – they moved from densely populated centres to thinly settled areas in western North America, where verification of the identities they presented would have been difficult if not impossible. Manitoba was still very much a pioneer society when Greve/Grove took up teaching in small rural communities in that province. So was Alberta, when Long/Long Lance was writing his stories about Indian communities there, and when Winnifred Eaton took up residence in Calgary. Even San Francisco and Seattle, at the time when Edith Eaton was living there as a writer, were just beginning to develop into major cities. In the years following the Gold Rush, which saw a huge influx of immigrants to those areas, it would not have been difficult to "disappear," or to assume another identity, especially in the cities' Chinatowns. The southwestern United States, Dufault/Will James's ultimate destination, was frontier country, as was the wilderness of northern Ontario and northern Quebec, where Archie Belaney/Grey Owl first established himself as a trapper.

Thus in the cases to be examined, the creation of a new identity, an Other Self, seems to be marked by the subject's entering a new geographical and/or sociocultural space, particularly when ties with the one formerly inhabited have been ruptured, be it by choice, chance, or necessity. The creation of a palimpsestic identity, the re-creation of one's self, is very much a part of the immigrant or pioneer experience. In North America this self-reinvention has tended to take the form of either mere embellishment of one's personal past, or a recasting of one's identity and social role by using the freedom and the resources available to immigrants entering the New World. The artistic expression of such self-reinvention in colonial literature is hardly a surprising phenomenon. But the extensions of identity claimed by five of the six writers discussed here go beyond mere embellishment: they represent intriguing instances of *passages à l'acte*, in which the deliberately created fictitious selves come to determine the sociobiographical existence of their creators.

THE EMERGENCE OF AUTOFICTION AS A GENRE

The six Canadian authors portrayed here occupy a unique place in the emergence of autofiction as a definable genre. Unlike some of their successors, such as Roland Barthes, or predecessors, such as Jean-Jacques Rousseau, it is unlikely that any of them were aware that their self-reinventions could be seen as a calling into question of what constitutes identity, although there is a glimmering of such awareness in some of Frederick Philip Grove's "autobiographical" works. Thus he writes, towards the end of *In Search of Myself*: "The life which is peculiar to me consists in letting other lives work themselves out within that, to me entirely mysterious, entity which is known to others by my name ... I have often doubted whether there is anything that I can legitimately call 'I.'"[10] What all six authors illustrate, in their "autobiographical" writings, is the latent transformational power of writing to create not only "new worlds," but new identities that could actually be lived out by their creators.

For while the re-invention of the Self is a fantasy shared by virtually everyone, it has been most closely realized by writers.[11] In creating a world of fiction, an Other world, an Other reality, the writer acts as an *alter deus*, creator of an *altera natura*. It is an old idea: as an *alter deus*, creator of a fictive world, the writer is, indeed, omnipotent and protean, the actor playing all the parts in the realization of the visions, dreams, fears, and desires that reside within the Self in the multiple characters, events, landscapes represented in the work of fiction. It is the virtual Selves that inhabit the writer (or that he or she comes to inhabit) that give him or her the ability to write from different perspectives, as an Other.

Traditionally, the hallmark of the work of art was its "wholeness," the artist's creation of (the illusion of) an entire "world," but one that was hermetically separated from the reality surrounding it. The paradigm shift that created a permeable zone in which fiction and reality could readily intersect came about in the late nineteenth and early twentieth centuries, which saw a tendency of literary texts to deliberately draw attention to their own fictionality. In the works of writers as diverse as Marcel Proust (*À la Recherche du temps perdu*), Oscar Wilde (*The Picture of Dorian Gray*), Franz Kafka (*The Metamorphosis*), and Virginia Woolf (*Orlando*; *Jacob's Room*), to name only a few, the reality principle that had constituted an incontrovertible rule of narrative fiction was called into question, resulting in a fracturing of the narrative voice: the narrative perspective could no longer be unambiguously situated with regard to the characters or events portrayed.

Accompanying this increasing ambiguity in narrative texts was the foregrounding of themes such as fragmented identity and self-alienation, which have come to dominate literary writing in modernist and postmodernist genres. The resulting trend toward textual self-allusiveness and narrative self-reflection has been variously explained by the emergence of theoretical concepts derived from psychoanalysis, existentialist philosophy, and phenomenology; by the geographic and emotional dislocations caused by the two world wars; and by the fact that realism as a genre, by the turn of the twentieth century, seemed to have exhausted itself. One intriguing aspect of the emergence of these inward-looking literary genres problematizing identity has been an examination of what happens in the process of writing itself, with the omniscient narrator being replaced by multiple narrative voices (sometimes deliberately contradictory), or by deliberately unreliable ones.

While prose fiction writers have alluded to the problem of narrative voice since the emergence of the novel as a genre, for example by using an epistolary form or by creating distance to the fictional reality in the form of "dear reader" asides, the implications of assuming an alien persona (in creating a narrative voice, by definition not identical to that of the biographical author) for the writer's own identity began to manifest themselves more and more self-consciously in the nineteenth century. The focus on the Self as Other has become increasingly self-reflexive, occurring in the form of pronounced doubles, *Doppelgänger*, and alter egos. John Keats used the image of the chameleon to describe the multiplicity and fragmentation of the author's persona. Jean-Jacques Rousseau dramatized this schism in his dialogue, *Rousseau juge de Jean-Jacques*, and, much later, Roland Barthes demonstrated it in his autobiography, *Roland Barthes par Roland Barthes.*

The latter is an example of the development of a genre that has arisen even more recently, that of *autofiction*, a term introduced in 1977 by French writer Serge Doubrovsky to designate texts that are both fictional and autobiographical, and that focus on the inevitable cleavage between the subject (the Self), the protagonist, and the narrative voice. In the act of writing, the subject adopts a narrative persona in the form of a narrative voice which can never duplicate the subject's own consciousness, if only due to the inevitable selectivity of narration. The subject/writer of autofiction often remains unaware of the subjectivity of his or her perceptions, of the tricks of memory, and of the workings of the subconscious. In the act of writing, the identity of the subject is necessarily fragmented and altered.

In writing about the resulting alienation of their assumed identities from their biographical ones, writers of autofiction are in a sense "staging" their lives, and, in some cases, actually remain unaware that the "truth" they seek to communicate about themselves often diverges from the "truth" created by their own texts. Hence the connection that is often made between the writing of autofiction and the psychoanalytical process.[12] It is the porousness of the line between fiction and (auto)biography that characterizes the work of autofiction writers. In such cases, Rimbaud's famous pronouncement *"Je" est un autre* refers to more than an aesthetic principle designating the Otherness of the literary voice. The blurring of the distinction between the biographical and the fictional that is the hallmark of autofiction has, in some cases, led to the phenomenon of writers creating and living out identities not their own, and can be documented in European literature, for example in the assumed identity of Austrian novelist Joseph Roth or that of French novelist Romain Gary.[13]

This actual living-out of the lives – the "I-s" – the writer has him/herself created is determined, essentially, by two conditions. One consists of problematic elements in the writer's actual biography. The other is an unusually strong disposition, at once protean and narcissistic, to break out of the constraints of a given identity, to actually live, as the omnipotent creator, the lives one has fictitiously engendered. Literary sociologist Régine Robin defines this in spatial terms:

"To occupy all the places is the dream of every novelist, every poet, every artist – in fact it is everyone's dream. To bring the others whom I carry within me into play, to transform myself into another, to let every possibility of becoming-other run its course, to become one's own fictive being, or rather to experience in the text the fictiveness of identity – there are so many powerful temptations, almost within our grasp, that are currently emerging in the area of fiction."[14]

As Robin points out, this transformation of the Self into another can result in an almost pathological fragility, the identity of the (biographical) author deconstructing or dissolving to the point where it is no longer distinguishable from the created persona this former "identity" (the biographical author) has itself engendered. Such a case is impressively illustrated in the will left by Ernest Dufault/Will James, in which he made an inadvertent slip, bequeathing all his belongings not to his brother, Auguste Dufault, as he had intended, but to "Ernest Dufault," that is, to himself.[15] The Self, then, has been disassembled, with disparate parts superimposed on the previously existing "structure."

It is the "original" or "biographical" Self that has created or engendered the new composite entity, or persona, consistent with Nietzsche's famous exhortation: "Become who you are!" The boundaries between the "original" and the "assumed" identity dissolve to become indefinable and, to the subjects themselves, at times indistinguishable. What leads some writers to cross the line between their own realities and the fictions they invented is a question that straddles poetics, biography, and psychoanalysis. A number of studies on this subject point out that the double or multiple lives lived out by such figures result in an identitary instability or fragility that threatens the Self, or rather the intactness of that identity, a condition that may be precipitated by the constant need to authenticate the assumed biography.[16] This instability becomes even more pronounced when the subject migrates to an unfamiliar socio-geographic setting, especially when the migration involves the adoption of a new language. All six of the writers discussed in this book changed countries, and two of them adopted new languages consistent with their professed identities.

A NOTE ON AUTOFICTION AND AUTO/BIOGRAPHY

The term *autofiction*, coined by Serge Doubrovsky in his autobiographical novel *Fils* (1977),[17] is commonly used by French critics and theorists, but rarely found in theoretical or critical works written in English, which tend to use the broader composite term *auto/biography* to include all forms of life-writing, and indeed all self-narration. The explosive growth in the number of published autobiographies, memoirs, and diaries since the 1970s and 1980s, and the increasing popularity of life-writing, once considered marginal by literary critics and theorists, has given rise to an unprecedented interest in auto/biographical scholarship.[18] The literature generated by theorists and critics of auto/biography has resulted in a reconceptualization of self-narration that has spilled over into fields such as sociology, psychology, gender studies, and ethics. In fact, a number of concepts developed by scholars of auto/biography have been derived from studies in these fields, such as Erving Goffman's *The Presentation of Self in Everyday Life* (1959) and *Stigma: Notes on the Management of Spoiled Identity* (1963), Teresa De Lauretis's *Technologies of Gender* (1987), Judith Butler's "Performative Acts and Gender Constitution" (1988), and Paul John Eakin's *The Ethics of Life Writing* (2004), to name a few. The focus on identity as performance has informed a great many of the recent studies that examine the phenomenon of imposture in autobiographical writing, particularly as it manifests itself in racial passing.[19]

Because of its more restrictive usage and definition, I have nevertheless chosen to use the term *autofiction* (rather than *auto/biography*) in this study, as the term is centred on the inscription of self-invented identity in the form of fiction and above all fictive "autobiography." The term thus seems to lend itself to the representation of the lives, the self-invented lives, and the fictive "autobiographies" that together constitute the subject of this book.

It must be pointed out, however, that even in the French context, where the term *autofiction* is specifically circumscribed, critics and theorists have tended to focus on different aspects of the concept designated by the term, and its usage varies accordingly.

In its broadest sense, autofiction refers to texts that are both autobiographical and fictional. For Doubrovsky himself, autofiction is a post-Freudian phenomenon that gives voice to the multiplicity of "selves," the elusiveness of what constitutes the "self," to the inchoate mix of perceived reality, fantasy, desire, and repression, and above all to the selectivity and transformation of memory that constitutes the human condition. In his novel *Le livre brisé*, he writes: "When I try to remember, I (re)invent myself … I am a fictive being." ("Si j'essaie de me remémorer, je m'invente … Je suis un être fictive.")[20] For Doubrovsky, autofiction is closely linked to psychoanalysis, and particularly associated with traumatic events.

While most theorists agree that autofiction represents a break with the "autobiographical pact," a term used by Philippe Lejeune to describe autobiographical writings,[21] characterized by the fact that author, narrator, and hero are one and the same as well as by the "authenticity" or "sincerity" of the autobiographical work, they diverge considerably in terms of the elements on which they focus in defining the genre.

Thus for example Arnaud Genon observes that according to most definitions, the term is used to refer to texts in which the author-narrator imagines "a life," indeed often inventing multiple lives that have no referents in reality.[22] Vincent Colonna sees autofiction as a fabrication of the Self, in which the writer stands at the centre of the text, as is the case in an autobiography, but transforms his or her identity in an invented narrative that disregards verisimilitude.[23] Philippe Vilain suggests that autofiction often involves the encoding or disguising of real events in the narrative, using strategies of displacement, or adding fictional elements to factual referents.[24] For Chloé Delaume, the writing of autofiction represents a "suicide" of the Self as he/she was prior to his/her "self-reinvention," abandoning the old self in order to become someone else, and re-writing the self as a fictional character.[25] Régine Robin sees the re-invention of the self as manifested in autofictional texts as emerging from a narcissistic desire to "play all the parts," "to occupy all the places" – as the crossing of a porous line that separates the writer, the narrator, and the characters.[26]

In the present study, I use the term *autofiction* to designate the fictionalization of the self, in which the writers (re)invent their own lives by assuming new identities, in most cases effacing their true pasts. In the lives of writers living out identities not their own, there often seems to come a point where the line that separates the writer, the narrator, and the fictitious characters is not only blurred, but, in some cases, all but disappears. Frederick Philip Grove sums up the resulting sense of self-alienation in one of his diaries: "I hardly know who the F.P.G. is who is compact of contradictions."[27]

All the writers under discussion here, not just Greve/Grove, reinvented their lives; all of them were – to paraphrase the title of Grove's "autobiography" – "in search of themselves," on a quest to live out the identities that they felt dwelt within them.

1

Felix Paul Greve/Frederick Philip Grove: Being and Becoming

> One's real life is so often the life that one does not lead.
>
> Oscar Wilde

FELIX PAUL GREVE / FREDERICK PHILIP GROVE

In the early 1970s, the exposure of Frederick Philip Grove's past landed like a bombshell in the Canadian literary establishment.

The cultivated writer with aristocratic manners who called himself Frederick Philip Grove had arrived in Canada as an immigrant in 1912, and soon established himself as a country schoolteacher by profession and a writer by vocation. He became celebrated for his epic novels depicting life on the Canadian prairies, and also published three "autobiographical" works, which were generally accepted as authentic if thinly disguised accounts of the author's life.[1]

But until 1973 when Douglas O. Spettigue published his research on Grove's European years, the truth about his past was known only to his wife Catherine. Until Spettigue published his findings,[2] most Canadians knew Grove only as a distinguished prairie novelist, the first to portray the conflicts and hardships of what was still essentially a pioneer society.

While Grove's contribution to Canadian literature was widely recognized, he was generally regarded as staid and conventional, and even stodgy and pompous, by some contemporaries who came to know him personally, not a few of whom also qualified him as arrogant and patronizing towards the culture of the country that had welcomed him.[3] This latter perception was partially grounded in the persona that Grove had created in his "autobiographical" works, where he claimed to possess genteel, quasi-aristocratic, and extremely wealthy antecedents, and to have been associated in Europe with an international social elite as well as with leading figures of the European literary avant-garde. In these "autobiographical" works he explained his reduced circumstances in Canada by claiming that the family's wealth had been lost due to a sudden reversal of fortunes, and that, like other young men of similar background, he had been forced to make a new start elsewhere. It was likely the discrepancy between Grove's claims, on the one hand, to a past rooted in the sophisticated European *haute bourgeoisie* and free-thinking artistic *bohème* and, on the other hand, the judgmental, *petit bourgeois* morals and values to which he seemed to subscribe in his Canadian works as well as in his personal life in Canada that contributed to the stir when Spettigue revealed the turbulent and scandalous events that had led to Grove's coming to Canada. It suddenly became clear that this discrepancy reflected the conflict between two highly divergent value systems, both of which Grove had internalized and both of which played themselves out in his works: that of a European social and artistic elite, to which Grove claimed to belong, with its tolerance for flamboyance and unconventionality, and that of his true lower-middle-class background, which prized conventionality and moral rectitude above all things.

Spettigue's research threw all Grove's Canadian writings into a new light, revealing that Grove's accounts of his past life were a mixture of *Dichtung und Wahrheit*, fact and fiction, which scholars interested in Grove have been trying to disentangle ever since. What Spettigue found was that although it was true that Felix Paul Greve (Grove's real name) had been a German writer and translator who was associated with the leading literary movements of *fin de siècle* Europe, his personal background was a far cry from the glamorous antecedents with which he had endowed himself in his works. He was the child of a troubled lower-middle-class family whose parents' dysfunctional relationship ended in divorce, the father abandoning the family when Felix was thirteen. Despite these inauspicious circumstances, Felix, helped by his ambitious mother and a teacher who took an interest in him, was able to enter university, where he passed himself off as the son of a wealthy landowner and where he made advantageous contacts, some of which led to associations with members of Germany's social elite as well as with leading artists and writers. Due to these associations, as well as his literary translations and other publications, by the early 1900s he had come to play a significant role in the German literary establishment.

But by 1909, when Felix Paul Greve faked a suicide and surfaced in America under a new identity, namely that of Frederick Philip Grove, allegedly of genteel Scottish-Swedish descent, he was a desperate young man fleeing not only his creditors but also a society that had turned against him after he had served a prison term for fraud. Given the circumstances with which he was confronted in Europe, it is hardly surprising that he, like others in similar positions, sought to make a fresh start in America, the land of opportunity.

REINVENTION OF THE SELF

At the beginning of the twentieth century, America offered unique possibilities of *rifacimento*,[4] the reinvention of the individual through the myths and paradigms that were specific to a society that was still trying to define itself. Although Greve would have been unaware of Archie Belaney's self-reincarnation as the Indian Grey Owl, or the mythologizing of the painter Tom Thomson as the lonely woodsman of the north, he would have been familiar with the popular ideas of the period with regard to the purity of nature and unspoiled wilderness as well as with the image of the pioneer settler or that of the immigrant who rises to fame and fortune after years of toil as a migrant worker or menial labourer. It can be argued that these archetypes of the New World played a significant role in Greve's self-reinvention, and that his account of his early years in North America was the product of many such narratives combined.

What is extraordinary about his story is that his self-reinvention was driven as much by an overwhelming desire to refuse the constraints of his given identity and "become someone else" as by the catastrophic circumstances under which he left Europe. It was in Grove's Canadian life that he was able to live out a multiplicity of roles far more diverse than the persona he had adopted earlier, from his student days on, in Europe.

The only son of an unhappy marriage, born into extremely modest circumstances – his father had been a farm manager in Pomerania before moving the family to Hamburg and becoming a tram conductor – he seems to have felt early on that he was destined for higher things. Given the rigidly hierarchical structure that characterized German society at the turn of the last century, it was clear that his pursuit of the kind of life he desired and felt he was destined for would require considerable embellishment of his antecedents. His childhood was marked by the stigma of poverty and divorced parents, and there were other emotional scars to be concealed: the trauma of his father's brutality and abandonment, and his mother's death, which coincided with his entering Bonn University. This latter event seems to have been, for Greve, a catastrophe, emotionally no less than materially. The apartment in Hamburg was given up, and Felix was now without a permanent home and entirely on his own.

The romantic fantasies of wealth and high birth of a young boy growing up in the indignity of an impecunious household ridden with domestic strife may have been nourished by those of an ambitious mother, who herself had been at least exposed to the kind of domestic and social refinements described in Grove's autobiographical works. In *In Search of Myself*, for instance, Grove talks about his nurse's stories, which, in the light of Spettigue's reading of this period of Felix Paul Greve's life, may have actually been his mother's. These stories always began: "Once upon a time there was a little boy." The made-up and embellished stories that followed, Grove says, "dominated my inner life" to the point that "to this day I cannot distinguish my actual memories from the reflected ones."[5]

The discrepancy between Grove/Greve's youthful fantasies and his actual problematic childhood manifests itself throughout his work, both fictional and "autobiographical." The subject-hero-narrator of Grove's *œuvre* compensates for his deprived childhood, re-creating and making real the fantasies, dreams, illusions, aspirations, and deeply rooted cultural images that the author carried within him. Self-creation, self-invention as an Other, allows the writer to distance himself from the determinations of the socio-biographical reality and to make its deficiencies, fragmentations, absences, and lacks tolerable, manageable, controllable.

Greve's self-engenderment began when he left Hamburg after his mother's death. Now free of any compromising familial attachments, Greve took his enrolment at Bonn University, where his background was unknown, as an opportunity to reinvent himself as the son of a monied and quasi-aristocratic family. He soon joined a prestigious fraternity, where his aristocratic manners and expensive tastes, acquired by his association with his classmates at the elite *Gymnasium* he had attended in Hamburg and likely encouraged by his mother, effectively concealed how socially and financially disadvantaged he was compared with his wealthy and well-connected fraternity brothers.

Greve's membership in the Rhenus fraternity did more than open doors for him socially. It also presented an opportunity for sexual exploration and sexual conquest. Within the fraternity, his impeccable taste and manners along with his tall, fair good looks soon led to a close association along homoerotic lines with some of his fraternity brothers, notably Herman Kilian, son of a wealthy, distinguished, internationally connected family from Leipzig.

Greve was also friendly with another fraternity brother, Hans Lomberg, who had joined the fraternity at the same time as Greve and Kilian. After a fraternity outing on the Rhine, which both Kilian and Greve seem to have attended, Lomberg, an excellent swimmer, went missing, and his body was found weeks later in the river. Officially, the circumstances of Lomberg's death remained a mystery, but soon after the funeral Kilian was expelled from the fraternity, the first member in the club's history to be thus punished, and Greve withdrew his membership. If voluntary, his decision to leave must have been difficult, given the status he had acquired through his association with Rhenus, of which he had been the respected and well-liked president.

There are strong indications that Kilian's romantic attachment to Greve played a role in Lomberg's death.[6] But his admiration for Greve also manifested itself in financial gifts and generous loans, the last of which was for the sum of 10,000 marks (the equivalent of approximately $300,000 American today).

In 1900, having left the university, Greve, with his wide range of academic interests, mainly in literature, languages, and the then-fashionable field of archaeology, had begun to publish essays, poems, and academic papers, and now saw himself as an emerging writer and academic. With his excellent social and academic contacts, he soon found access to the literary and artistic circles that orbited around writers such as the brooding German symbolist poet Stefan George and the French modernist André Gide. In the exclusive salons of Munich and Berlin, Greve successfully maintained the aura of wealth and high birth that he had cultivated at university.

From his university days and onward, Greve constructed an identity that situated him in the dominant social class and at the forefront of the prestigious cultural avant-garde of his time. To create this new identity as the son of a wealthy, cultured family, he drew on antecedents of his Bonn fraternity friend Herman Kilian, whose grandfather Rutherfurd became Grove's "great-uncle Rutherford" in *In Search of Myself*. Another source was Harry Count Kessler, an alumnus of the *Gymnasium* Greve had attended in Hamburg, whose family associated with the *crème de la crème* of German society, including

Figure 1.1 Greve (on the pushcart) in androgynous mermaid pose with fraternity brothers, acting out a charade, circa 1898. The figure holding a footstool as if he were strumming a harp may be Lomberg. According to Martens, the charade represents the River Rhine with its waterfalls (depicted by the figure holding a large enamel jug as if he were pouring from it) and the Loreley, acted out by Greve in mermaid pose, with Lomberg (?) accompanying the mermaid's song on a harp. (See Klaus Martens, *F.P. Grove in Europe and Canada: Translated Lives*, 41.)

Chancellor Count Bismarck and Emperor Wilhelm I, and whose memoirs Grove likely drew on in describing his (entirely fictitious) travels with his mother. Grove's descriptions of his European antecedents as recounted in *A Search for America* and *In Search of Myself* were clearly inspired by the Kilian and Kessler families, whom he had come to know – or to know about – during his student days in Bonn.[7]

But Greve/Grove's needs went beyond "correcting" what he perceived to be deficiencies in his biography. As Régine Robin has pointed out, autofictional authors are driven as much by narcissistic impulses as by protean ones.[8] In Grove the narcissistic element manifested itself in his perception that he stood (or should stand) at the very top of the social hierarchy, as part of an elite which at the turn of the nineteenth century was determined on the one hand by distinguished antecedents, social acceptance, wealth, and the cultivated tastes supposedly accompanying them, and, on the other, by an avant-gardistic *bohème* associated with sexual freedom, artistic innovation, and, in theory, the challenging of the hierarchical norms of *bourgeois* institutions. For the most part these seemingly opposing social forces were in reality by no means contradictory, as young Felix Paul Greve was to discover.

While initially he was phenomenally successful in his self-reinvention as an independently wealthy, well-bred young man, one who showed promising signs of embarking on a brilliant literary career, his luck turned when he ran off with Else Endell, the wife of August Endell, an *art nouveau* architect who had been a part of the artistic circles in which Felix now moved.

It was the financial security Greve was enjoying as a result of Kilian's huge loan that enabled him to go off to Italy with Else. Kilian, enraged and jealous, took his revenge by summoning Greve to Bonn under a pretext and having him arrested for fraud, of which Greve was duly convicted and for which he served a year's prison term.[9] His distinguished literary associates were quick to turn against him, although this was due less, it seems, to his "scandalous liaison" than because of the exposure of Greve's modest social background and lack of financial means. His first German novel, *Fanny Essler*, a *roman à clef* in which he criticized and ridiculed individual members of German literary salons, further contributed to his ostracization.

His reaction to having to serve time in prison had been one of resignation and, somewhat inexplicably, a certain *equanimitas*: from Wilhelmstrasse 19, the address of the Bonn city jail, he maintained an active correspondence with his publishers regarding honoraria owed him and future translation projects. Confident that after his release his life would continue as before, he was plotting a course that would, or so he must have thought, lead him to a successful career as one of Germany's foremost writers and translators. For Greve, the quick and unceremonious abandonment by his literary friends was sudden and seemingly totally unexpected.

Cast off by his literary friends, ostracized and abandoned by his university associates, stigmatized by his jail record, the only resources on which he could draw after his release were the literary interests he had cultivated in his university years and later in the salons of Munich and Berlin, and his phenomenal gift for languages. He became a literary translator – indeed, the most prolific and ground-breaking German translator of his time, producing dozens of translations of works by famous French and British authors. But his vulnerability due to the circumstances in which he found himself, heavily indebted and in no position to negotiate favourable terms with his publishers, entrapped him in a life of ceaseless toil for little reward, a bleak future from which there seemed to be no escape. Despairing of ever repaying the enormous debt he had incurred and stigmatized by his prison sentence, five years after his release from prison he faked a suicide and made his way to North America.

When he finally left Europe, leaving Else, who had divorced her husband to marry him, behind, he left a suicide note. Felix Paul Greve was officially dead. The Grove legend of a European *jeunesse dorée*, which situated its author at the centre of the leading intellectual and aesthetic movements of the turn of the century, began with Felix Paul Greve's reincarnation as Frederick Philip Grove, "travelling author," who disembarked in the port of Montreal, Canada, in 1909.

To say that there were compelling reasons, financial and personal, for Felix Paul Greve to discard his old European identity and to assume a new one on entering the New World is an understatement. But the problematic circumstances in which he found himself on leaving Europe and arriving in Canada hardly explain the extravagance with which he describes his youthful past. All three of the "autobiographical" works – *Over Prairie Trails*, *In Search of Myself*, and *A Search for America* – dwell at great length on the magnificent seaside estate, complete with innumerable servants, of the author's childhood, the genteel recreational pursuits of his parents, their brilliant social connections, and the luxurious around-the-world travel of the subject himself, the source of all of which is the family's apparently inexhaustible inherited wealth.

If as a university student in Germany Felix Paul Greve had found it necessary to invent a distinguished background for himself to gain access to the prestigious circles in which he felt he belonged, Frederick Philip Grove the immigrant writer further embroidered the illustrious identity he had claimed in Europe. The self-created legend of Grove as the indulged son of a wealthy, cultured landowner dynasty as recounted in his Canadian works was inspired by narcissistic fantasies, a crucial element of which is that he saw his true origins as an accident of birth. As E.D. Blodgett puts it, "The compensation for Greve's lack of luck was to find a way of inventing himself, that is, to become a fiction in which he was the author."[10]

The works Grove published in Canada show that he was no mere social climber. The self-reinvention he undertook in his Canadian "autobiographical" writings goes beyond his role-playing as a dashing gentleman who moved in the top echelons of European society. The protean impulse in Greve/Grove consists in nothing less than the desire for omnipotence, the ultimate manifestation of which is self-engenderment. It is clear that Grove's phantom doubles, in the endlessly multifaceted personae created in the "autobiographical" works (and, to some degree, in the novels) were motivated by his desire to "occupy all the places,"[11] to play all the roles, and Grove appears, throughout his autobiographical works, in a multiplicity of them. He is the privileged only son, heir-apparent to a fortune and an estate, and then the picaresque hero who, through no fault of his own, experiences a dramatic reversal of fortune and loses all, and is forced by circumstances to create, literally, a new life for himself. In his European youth he is, by turns, an archaeologist, a comparative philologist, a poet-writer, and a world traveller. He is the avant-garde bohemian of the "great cities of Europe," in particular the young man who espouses the sexual mores, or absence thereof, of artistic circles – in the wake of writers such as Oscar Wilde, George, and Gide – of which he is a part. The rupture with this former life, this cultural background, cannot be more dramatic (or "romantic"). In North America, he becomes a farmer, a farmhand, a hobo, a waiter, a salesman, and finally a teacher and writer, a judgmental middle-aged moralist, the narrator of the prairie novels, whose point of view at times verges on the primness of the conventional *petit bourgeois* that Else recognizes in him even as he is living out his scandalous affair with her.

Reluctant to relinquish the rich memories of a European youth marked by his association with ground-breaking philosophical and aesthetic movements and the social and moral principles accompanying them, Greve/Grove is at the same time seduced by the man-of-action picaresque, including its values and ethos, that characterize the New World at the turn of the century, various incarnations of which populate his Canadian novels: the self-made man who founds a dynasty and wrests a fortune from the virgin hostile land; the existential freedom of the hobo who rides the rail cars; the self-made industrialist who, in creating his own dynastic wealth, is laying an economic cornerstone for the development of a great nation as well as assuring a livelihood – *noblesse oblige* – for his community; and finally the teacher, the mentor, who enlightens the minds and frees the spirits of the children of the pioneers who are at work building a new society. Above all, he becomes the writer, the man of letters, who will single-handedly articulate the vision and the experience of being and becoming that characterize the pioneer existence.

Between these two extreme poles, one represented by an overbred European social elite, the (supposed) absence of taboos of its artistic avant-garde, and its complicated aesthetic sensibilities, the other by the rawness, the absence of a past, and the puritan pioneer life that characterize the immigrant experience, Greve/Grove is irresistibly drawn to both as to powerful magnets. The protean urge to "occupy all the places," to live out the fantasies of omniscience and omnipotence that he carries within himself, is expressed in various passages throughout the autobiographical works. The synthesis of these two opposing value systems is made possible by the omnipotence of the artist as *alter deus*, by the cultural mediation of one who knows both the self-reflective European world and the pragmatic North American one, and, above all, by the intellectual who understands the metaphysical implications of it all.

One of the most revealing passages in this regard can be found in *In Search of Myself*. The perspectival vantage point is that of God and the prophets:

> I could truthfully call my knowledge of the pioneering section of the west of the North-American continent unique. At a glance I could survey the prairie country from Kansas to Saskatchewan or Alberta; and at a thought I could evaluate, in my own way of course, the implications of pioneer life. I, the cosmopolitan, had fitted myself to be the spokesman of a race – not necessarily a race in the ethnographic sense; in fact, not at all in that sense; rather in the sense of a stratum of society which cross-sectioned all races, consisting of those who, in no matter what climate, at no matter what time, feel the impulse of starting anew, from the ground up, to fashion a new world which might serve as the breeding-place of a civilization to come. These people, the pioneers, reaffirmed me in my conception of what often takes the form of a tragic experience; the age-old conflict between human desire and the stubborn resistance of nature. Order must arise out of chaos; the wilderness must be tamed. No matter where I looked, then as today, I failed to see that the task of recording that struggle of man with nature had ever adequately been done … To record that struggle seemed to be my task.[12]

The "task" is, indeed, daunting: to fashion a coherent and meaningful narrative – or epic – describing the diversity of the pioneer people and the lives they lead, and the multiplicity of their nomadic pasts. Walter Pache has followed up W.J. Keith's suggestion that the lonely traveller of *Over Prairie Trails* is a "distinctly modern-day Ulysses,"[13] a reading which the book, with its references to the narrator's peripatetic wanderings, bears out. But in an unmistakable allusion to the Homeric epic, and in formulaic language that further underlines the evocation, Grove explodes the restrictions of the *Odyssey* and its Mediterranean setting to encompass the entire world: "I have lived in southern countries, and I have travelled rather far for a single lifetime. Like an epic stretch my memories into dim and ever receding pasts. The Southern Cross is no strange sight to my eyes. I have slept in the desert close to my horse, and I have walked on Lebanon. I have cruised in the seven seas and seen the white marvels of ancient cities reflected in the waves of incredible blueness."[14]

Grove as Odysseus, ever-returning? "So I came home to the north. On days like this, I should like once more to fly out and see the tireless wave and the unconquerable rock."[15] But the narrator of *Over Prairie Trails* is also a self-described Moses, who "sees" but cannot enter (return to?) this promised land of "ancient cities," a coded reference to the European cities he has left behind: "I should like to see them from afar and dimly only – as Moses saw the promised land."[16]

Greve's chameleon nature and the narcissistic and protean impulses that drove him were recognized by some of his literary associates long before he undertook his definitive change of identity in America. That the young Felix Paul Greve had a strong predisposition to present himself as someone other than who he was was recognized by the writers André Gide and Thomas Mann as well as by his wife Else.

André Gide, whom Greve visited in Paris immediately after his release from prison, saw through Greve's role-playing and was so intrigued with it that he recorded their conversation *verbatim* in his journal, subsequently publishing an account of their meeting titled "Conversation avec un Allemand quelques années avant la guerre."[17] This "conversation" revolves around a debate about life versus art. Gide privileges art, equating it with *faire agir* ("causing action"). Greve declares that he prefers "life," equating it with *agir* ("acting"), asserting that he is driven by the will to act: "Action ... that's what I want, yes, the most extreme action – extreme to the point of murder."[18]

Gide, however, takes the position of the artist who, in manipulating his characters, "causes action" rather than acting himself: "I'm afraid, you understand, of compromising myself. I mean, of limiting, by what I do, what I could do. Of the idea that because I've done *this*, I could no longer do *that*, this is what I find intolerable. I prefer to *cause action* rather than to act myself."[19] For Gide, it is art rather than life that bestows the protean gift of ultimate freedom from the constraints of personal identity.

In responding, Greve accuses Gide of contradicting his own exhortation to pursue life rather than art, invoking the teachings of Ménalque in Gide's *Nourritures terrestres* to justify his desire to live out the multiplicity of human experience: "Throw away my book; say to yourself that it is only *one* of the thousands of postures in life. Look for your own."[20] But in justifying his position, Greve also warns Gide of his, Greve's, "lies," which consist in consciously creating an appearance of reality or "truth," representing an ironic identicality between the illusion of reality (the "lie") and reality itself (the "truth"). Greve's "lying" is an act of mimesis, so to speak, in which he represents himself: "I must warn you, Monsieur Gide, that I lie constantly ... I feel the same need to lie and take the same satisfaction in lying as other people do in telling the truth ... For example: when someone hears a sudden noise right next to him, he turns his head ... I don't! Or if I turn it, I do so deliberately: I'm lying."[21]

Greve is here clearly invoking "The Decay of Lying," an essay published in the form of a "conversation" in Oscar Wilde's *Intentions* in 1891, which Greve had translated into German in 1902. Greve's claim to be "always lying" is a manifestation of breath-taking narcissism, implying that his entire life, down to the most banal act, is in effect art, following Wilde's contention that even for the ancient Greeks, "what at first had been merely a natural instinct [such as turning the head upon hearing a noise?] was elevated to a self-conscious science," and that the "highest development" of such lying is "Lying in Art."[22]

That Gide recognized the narcissistic impulses underlying Greve's extreme statements is evidenced not only in the sly evocation of Wilde's essay, by titling his piece about Greve a "conversation," but also in the fact that in some of his later novels he presents figures that are modelled after the *jeune Allemand* of the "Conversation." In *Les Caves du Vatican*, for instance, the protean and narcissistic Lafcadio figure is unmistakeably an alter ego of Felix Paul Greve.[23] Gide's recognition of Greve's narcissism and protean hubris was based solely on Greve's intense performance during their first encounter in Paris and on the letters Greve had sent him in the course of their extensive correspondence.[24] There had been no further contact between the two men after Greve's "suicide," and there is no indication that Gide ever read Greve's German novels or any of Grove's Canadian works. For Grove, however, who followed Gide's brilliant career from Canada, Gide would remain a determining influence, ultimately inspiring Grove to write his "autobiography," *In Search of Myself*, possibly as a reaction to a comprehensive biography of his distinguished friend that had appeared a few years previous to the publication of Grove's account of his own life.

That Thomas Mann, however, *had* certainly read not only Greve's two German novels but also at least some of Grove's Canadian writings, including the "autobiographical" ones, is evident in Mann's last published work, *The Confessions of Felix Krull, Confidence Man (The Early Years)*,[25] which is clearly modelled mainly on Felix Paul Greve and his multiple self-created personae. Mann's parodic novel depicts Greve as a narcissistic impostor from his very birth, suggesting that like André Gide, Mann, too, saw through Grove/Greve's role-playing early on.[26]

It is doubtful that any source connected with Greve/Grove, extant or yet to be discovered, throws as much light on the chameleon aspects of Greve's personality as Else's autobiography. She describes him, first of all, as an impressive, enigmatic presence, a strong personality, a man of extraordinary intellectual powers. He is also glamorous, stylishly dressed, and seems wealthy. A few quotations from Else's autobiography present the general idea: "Mr. Felix was surrounded by a glamour of mysterious wealth – so that wellintentioned [*sic*] people believed him to be a millionaire – and the others – who knew as little as the first – declared him to be a cardsharp."[27]

While Else accuses her lover of lying out of his own self-interest, she recognizes the aesthetic dimensions of this trait, observing that the roles he assumed went beyond the intellectual and the literary. In the following quotation, she is expressing her doubt as to Felix's truthfulness in telling her he has to return to Bonn (from Palermo, where the couple were staying) for "money reasons." Even in this pragmatic context, it is clear that she sees a deeper motivation for Felix's lies: "I had – until now – not the slightest suspicion of this governing trait in his nature that, together with his deepest ambition – to succeed in life, using his industry, brilliant qualities – *honestly* – gave a dangerous combination. In good times this lie urge he used for spiritual satisfaction not always unmixed with practical benefits on the side. When conditions became tipsy he developed swindler qualities."[28]

Else's accounts of Felix Paul Greve reveal a man who in Jungian terms has remained unindividuated, narcissistic – "a man who liked to love only himself ... He becomes a mere outward driving force by restless neurasthenic ambition – infertile within himself";[29] and "all was pride's pretence – and he was *not* the one he wanted to be! He was a fake – the most honest and sparkling that could be – believing in himself."[30]

FPG AND ELSE ENDELL

If the work of André Gide and Felix Paul Greve's relationship with the author were to become determining elements in young Greve's self-definition as an artist, a sort of bar against which he measured himself even as the mature Canadian writer known as Fredrick Philip Grove, it was his affair and subsequent marriage with Else Endell that constituted the definitive turning point in his personal life, leading to his ostracization by his former associates in Germany and culminating in his clandestine departure from Europe.

When they first met in a Munich salon in 1903, Else, although recently married, already had a reputation for promiscuity, having had affairs with a number of artists she had met in German avant-garde circles.[31] Although at their first meeting Greve, characteristically aloof, showed himself proud and distant, Else was instantly seduced by his elegant appearance suggesting wealth and breeding, and by his mysterious and erotic aura.[32]

Else's relationship with her husband had proven to be unsatisfactory sexually, and his impecunious circumstances at the time must have been a further strain on the marriage. While Greve's elegant appearance and the erotic appeal he exuded no doubt seduced Else, according to her memoir, it was his air of mystery, his "veiledness," and his cool, formal distance that proved irresistible.

But it soon became clear that Felix Paul Greve was equally smitten. Not long after the meeting in Munich he visited the Endells, who were living in Berlin, and subsequently relocated there. It was his first sexual encounter with Else that led him to abandon his homosexual relationship with Kilian, with whom he had undertaken a romantic trip the same year. The relationship between the two men seems to have been serious and passionate on both sides. From their trip Greve wrote a euphoric postcard, stating that he and Kilian were "virtually reeling in ecstasy."[33] He had also dedicated a collection of poems to Kilian.[34]

Else, who had always been the pursuer in her previous affairs, including with Endell (it was she who proposed marriage to him), characteristically took the initiative in her first sexual encounter with Greve, an encounter that would prove an epiphanic experience for both. Irene Gammel, Else's biographer, sees the account of the protagonist's seduction by Mrs Broegler in *Settlers of the Marsh* as relating the effect of Greve's first sexual intimacies with Else. She cites a passage from the book: "My own overpowering experience with Mrs. Broegler … saved me from becoming involved [with homosexuals] in any sense whatever. If I had not always been so, I had become definitely, finally heterosexual."[35] Gammel points out that "[e]ven the random details – the dinner, the after-dinner champagne, the husband going to bed, her first sexual move, her childlessness, her sexual shamelessness – all correspond point by point to Else's profile and to [her] memoir account."[36] After this sexual encounter with Else, Greve's relationship with Kilian was abruptly and irrevocably ended.

Endell had agreed to Else's taking a lover[37] – she would have had Greve in mind – and about one month after Else and Felix's first sexual encounter, which took place in the Endells' house on Christmas Eve 1902, both Endells and Greve left together for Italy, where Felix and Else registered in hotels as a couple. The two soon sent Endell off on his own, in a state of shock and despair from which he would not soon recover.

After Greve's sudden return to Bonn at Kilian's behest, Else was left on her own in Italy, where she took a series of lovers before returning to Germany in May 1904 to reunite with Greve upon his release from prison. The two lovers spent a nomadic three years, living for brief periods in Wollerau, near Zurich, in Étaples, on the Normandy coast, and at various addresses in Berlin, before they finally married in 1907 (Else had been divorced from her first husband in 1904). It was during this period that Felix Paul Greve published his two German novels as well as a series of poems, all centring around Else.

His first novel, *Fanny Essler* (1905), is a thinly disguised account of the life of Else Endell née Plötz, beginning with her escape from her dysfunctional family on the Baltic. The story follows her from her acting and chorus-girl days in Berlin to her short-lived marriage and her fateful meeting with her "prince," with whom she goes abroad. The "prince" (the Greve figure), although he fulfills her every wish, remains unattainable emotionally, and the novel ends rather abruptly with the heroine's death of malaria while the couple are visiting Lisbon.

As both Klaus Martens and Irene Gammel point out, the novel fulfilled the purpose of exposing the hypocrisy of the salon cliques of Munich and Berlin as well as the inadequacies of some of their individual members, constituting a form of revenge for their abandonment of Greve, who, until he ran off with Else and served time in prison, had been one of their own. To this extent, *Fanny Essler* is indeed a *roman à clef*, the biographical accuracy of which can be ascertained not only with regard to the encoded characters who figure in it but also from the degree to which the characters and events depicted in it coincide with Else's memoir. At the same time, Greve was eager to establish himself as a writer as well as a translator, and Else's story offered "the material," as she puts it, for a novel that lent itself to the naturalistic treatment Greve was interested in at the time, with only one perspective and little or no narrative commentary. "The method is all mine, and it is a method without commentary; a textual editing without annotations," he wrote to Gide in a letter dated 1 July 1905.[38]

Greve began writing the novel in prison, completing it during his and Else's sojourn in Switzerland. Both Greve and Else acknowledged that it was a collaborative project, Else insisting that it was "dictated by me as far as *material* was concerned – it was *my life* and persons out of my life – he did the executive part of the business – giving the thing a conventional shape and dress."[39] Greve, for his part, acknowledges Else's role in more oblique terms in a letter to André Gide: "I am no longer just *one* person, I am *three*: 1.) M. Felix Paul Greve; 2.) Mme Else Greve; 3.) Mme Fanny Essler."[40] This playful description of his multiple roles and identities in fact refers not only to the novel *Fanny Essler* but also to a series of poems, signed "Fanny Essler," that appeared in the German journal *Die Freistatt* in issues published in 1904 and 1905. Both the novel, which according to Greve's letter to Gide was originally intended to be published as Else's autobiography and signed "Fanny Essler," and the poems appearing under that name were collaborative projects, based on texts that Else had actually written herself and that Greve had subsequently shaped into a more conventional form.[41]

This "collaboration," in which the division of labour between Else and Greve appears to be one of Else providing the content and Greve recasting it in its final and published version, has significant implications with regard to the couple's relationship. For one thing, Else's comments in her memoir about their collaborative projects reveal that Else herself had literary ambitions, and had produced a body of writing of her own. Both Else and Felix are listed as writers (*Schriftsteller*) in the Berlin Directory between 1904 and 1909.[42] Although four of the seven "Fanny Essler" poems are atmospheric nature descriptions that bear the stamp of Greve's rewriting along the lines of Stefan George's sensuous lyric poetry, obliterating Else's original versions, three of them constitute a "portrait" of Greve and are clearly written from Else's perspective, depicting Greve's inaccessibility and coldness, his "masks," and his latent violence.[43]

Although the three "portrait" poems were no doubt as heavily edited by Greve with regard to the "form" as the other four, they reveal Else's talent for rendering the telling detail as well as the originality and resolute honesty in her writing. Both qualities would characterize her later daring avant-gardistic work as "Baroness Elsa" in New York, and contrasted dramatically with Felix's authorial "masks" and adherence to literary conventions of the day.

That Felix's and Else's approaches to writing were diametrical opposites must have manifested itself during their "collaboration." Did Greve recognize the originality and uncompromising "truth" expressed in his wife's writings as potentially eclipsing the impact of his own conventional literary efforts? If so, was this recognition a factor in his decision to desert Else? Did he see her as a potential literary rival?

Else's repeated claims in her memoir that it was she who contributed the "material" for Greve's German works and that he merely cast it in a conventional (more marketable?) form suggest that she considered Greve's publication of his two German novels an appropriation of her own work and, arguably, that she saw the novels as an exploitation of her life story.

FANNY ESSLER

Become who you are.
Nietzsche

Greve's treatment of Else's biography in the two German novels foregrounds another, even more significant aspect of their relationship, this one revealing the degree to which Else had become an alter ego of Felix Paul Greve. Certain elements in Else's background are shaped to resemble those that had governed his own life as a youth – growing up in a dysphoric household in provincial eastern Germany, the father's brutality, and the yearning to escape.

Although the German protagonists are female and modelled after Else, their experiences and feelings are portrayed in such a way as to reveal significant parallels to those of Greve himself. Fanny Essler's relationship with her "prince," the Reelen character, evokes Herman Kilian's seduction of Felix Paul Greve, and Greve's initiation into a life of luxury and privilege the tram conductor's son had never known. The impoverished Fanny's "rescue" by her wealthy suitor marks a turning point in her life that promises to bestow upon her all the social and material advantages as well as the admiration, the emotional attachment, and the erotic pleasures of an ardent lover, as had been the case in Greve's relationship with Kilian. In *Fanny Essler*, Reelen/Greve becomes Kilian as well as Fanny, whom Reelen/Kilian indulges as Kilian had indulged Greve.

But Greve's identification with Fanny/Else goes beyond biographical parallels. Certain traits in the Else figure in the novel *Fanny Essler* closely resemble those found in its author. In the novel he is not only inscribing elements of his own life story, but also attributing his own narcissistic and protean fantasies to Fanny, the Else character. Fanny's decision to flee her home and her dysfunctional family is motivated not only by her desire to escape an autocratic father, or to seek adventure in Berlin, but also by her longing to be omnipresent: "And that feeling overcame her of wanting to be everywhere at once, a feeling that most people, including Fanny at that moment, think can be stilled by moving somewhere else."[44]

Greve/Grove's own quest for acknowledgment, for recognition, his desire to be "chosen," which was evident to his European colleagues and would later manifest itself in his Canadian fiction and in his "autobiographical" work, is echoed in Fanny Essler's longing – expressed by the omniscient narrator – for the "prince" who will "recognize" her, and will liberate her from a mundane and needy existence: "Far, very far away, a vision would once again appear: that of the saviour who came down, as if from heaven, that of the prince who could and must rescue her!"[45]

As in Grove's own life, in *Fanny Essler* the desire for self-realization that at times appears as a narcissistic need for omnipotence and status is thwarted by the lack of money. The means to the desired end – financial success and public recognition – is to be sought in artistic circles: "If she succeeded in making the leap, then she knew that she belonged to the artists, that she had to look for her prince in that group of people, and that it would come true: she would be successful because she wanted to hold on to it tenaciously! And finally she told herself, almost arrogantly, if I could only find enough money to live on, then I'd go anywhere."[46]

As he would continue to do in his Canadian works, Greve as autofictional author is playing a multiplicity of roles: that of Fanny/Else, an alter ego; that of Reelen/Greve himself, playing the role that Kilian had played in Greve's life; and finally that of the narrator, whose ironic distance, possibly inspired by Greve's admiration of Flaubert (whose correspondence he was translating into German at the time), is undercut by the authenticity of feeling of the protagonist, whenever she speaks in her "own" (i.e. Greve's) voice.

When Fanny repeatedly expresses regret at the mistakes she has made in her former life, including her choice of unsuitable partners and her chorus-girl past, her "prince" exhorts her not to confuse her "past" with "herself." Fanny's dramatic rupture with her past and her becoming what she is, he suggests, are in fact determined and made possible by that past: "all of that had to be, in order for you to become what you are now … it's good that all of that took place because it shaped you into who you are."[47] The rationale he offers for dealing with the disparate realities of past and present is that the Self must be split off from one's past to "become" who one "is."

This sense of fatedness, of having to live one's life to become oneself, is expressed even more explicitly in a subsequent passage, where Reelen, in response to Fanny's expressions of self-disgust, says: "You don't have to be disgusted with your*self* but only with the *path* you took … You're always just confusing your*self* with your past."[48]

According to Reelen's precepts in *Fanny Essler*, the Self can be re-formed and the past re-written by selective obliteration, blurring the boundaries between past and present identity, a project so successfully carried out by Frederick Philip Grove in his Canadian "autobiographical" novels and in his new life in Canada. In *Fanny Essler*, the result of this process of transformation is the feeling of being, literally, beside oneself. Fanny describes this feeling in concrete terms as she, the unloved daughter raised in a modest provincial household, sits with her "prince" in a box in the Paris opera, listening to Wagner's *Meistersinger*: "Suddenly she saw herself in retrospect, through her former eyes, the eyes of times gone by, when she was still the 'little girl,' sitting here as she now was ... And she nearly became jealous of herself."[49] Fanny's sudden vision of herself as two different, simultaneously present personae, as the Self she was and the Self she has become, seems to express the author's own awareness of his "doubleness," in which one Self recognizes the other. That he recognized himself as a double and indeed a composite figure, including elements of Else, in *Fanny Essler* is suggested in his 1 July 1905 letter to Gide, when he says, speaking of the novel: "on rereading it, I saw with great astonishment that it was I (*c'était Moi*) who had written it."[50]

THE FATHER AS KAISER

In his second German novel, *Maurermeister Ihles Haus*, Greve focuses on Else's early life from childhood to young adulthood, but it is less a coming-of-age novel than an exposé of the physical and psychological abuse that Richard Ihle, modelled after Else's father, Adolf Plötz, inflicts upon his wife and his two daughters. As actually happened in the Plötz family, in the novel, when the girls are in their early teens, their mother becomes "odd," and ends up in a mental institution where she dies a few years later. The father then marries a tyrannical and controlling spinster, causing Suse Ihle, the Else figure, to seek to escape from her unhappy home by accepting the advances of the unprepossessing but socially superior Konsul Blume, whom she despises. It is with this decision of Suse's to accept Blume that the novel ends.

Like *Fanny Essler*, *Maurermeister Ihles Haus* may be based on Else's story, but it, too, contains a number of elements that reappear in Grove's Canadian novels and in his "autobiographical" accounts. The most obvious of these is Richard Ihle's autocratic and bullying character, which evokes Frederick Philip Grove's descriptions of authoritarian father figures in *Fruits of the Earth* and *Our Daily Bread*, and also the depiction of his own father in *In Search of Myself* and *A Search for America*.

The theme of the oppressive and remote father who withholds his affection, approval, and very presence from his child reflects the realities of Felix Paul Greve's own youth. In *Maurermeister Ihles Haus*, his treatment of the father-child relationship exposes the unworthiness of a father who closely resembles his own. The Else figure of Suse, like her counterpart Fanny Essler in his first novel, has been given the same type of father figure whose tyranny he had endured in his own deprived childhood. Else, in many ways, it seems, had become an alter ego of the author.

An intriguing aspect of this symbiotic relationship is Suse's veneration of the *Kaiser*, whose death she bitterly mourns when it is announced at her school. She closely associates the *Kaiser* with her father:

> Master Mason Ihle rarely talked about himself. Suse had always seen him as a figure of towering strength who wielded enormous power. Until she was about nine, her father was the incarnation of a father: all fathers, she thought, were like him, though perhaps not as powerful as royalty. Proud of her father in his absence, fear of him whenever he was present; those were the two emotions that characterized her relationship with her father. She knew that her father wielded influence in the town and was also popular, and townspeople, masons, draymen and so on were eager to serve him. Her father came right after the king.[51]

Although the powerful and unpredictable father figure of Richard Ihle inspires fear and dread in his daughter when she is in his presence, from a distance she admires and venerates him, almost as she had the *Kaiser*. When the family physician sends Ihle to the spa of Bad Ems to cure his catarrh, Suse looks forward to the freedom she anticipates during his prolonged absence. At the same time his departure to Bad Ems, a destination which had been favoured by the *Kaiser*, enhances her father's stature in Suse's eyes, and indeed, according to the narrator, it heightens the prestige of her entire family in the eyes of the townsfolk: "the *Kaiser* had often gone to Ems … the next day everyone at school knew, and Herr Ihle was somehow connected in an almost personal way with the dead monarch: Ihle's going to Ems was considered almost an act of piety, a kind of accomplishment: Suse's status was greatly enhanced in everyone's eyes."[52]

The passage describing Ihle's departure for Bad Ems is also significant in this context because it explicitly expresses Suse's yearning for a benevolent father figure, and above all her need for her father's approval, however obliquely transmitted. As he bids his family farewell, Ihle exhorts his daughters to write to him while he is absent: "Both Suse and Lotte were glad when the farewells were over. But Suse's joy was strongly tinged with other emotions. She was moved by her father's parting words. She had the impression that her father had been trying to show kindness for once and that he was ashamed of it – well, if only you were like that! she thought … She was pleased that it was important to him to receive letters from his daughters."[53]

Suse's highly emotional reaction to the *Kaiser*'s death is particularly significant when considered as a vicarious expression of the author's own quest for a father worthy of the affection and respect of his yearning child. The *Kaiser*'s death and Suse's grief in response to it are described in minute detail, and, although neither has any relevance to the plot itself, their description fills approximately twelve pages of the novel. In a particularly telling passage, the description of the *Kaiser* as seen through the eyes of the young Suse evokes an image of the Judeo-Christian deity: he is a distant higher being, an old man with a white beard, in whom Suse sees a resemblance to her own father: "it seemed to her that the *Kaiser* wore a beard like her father's, but without evoking the dread of a real father."[54]

Suse's naïve transference of her affection and loyalty from the unworthy figure of her father to the remote and almost mythical figure of the benevolent *Kaiser* represents a theme that will recur in several variants in subsequent works by Frederick Philip Grove, notably in *The Adventure of Leonard Broadus*, which ends with young Leonard receiving the explicitly expressed approval of the king in a scene reminiscent of the archaic patriarchal blessing. That Greve developed this theme, to which he would return again in his Canadian work, in his early German novel is an eloquent indicator of the degree to which he was traumatized by his relationship with his own abusive and mostly absent father, and his need to mitigate this trauma.

THE PARTING OF WAYS

Since their reunion in Germany, relations between Else and Felix had been turbulent. Although the couple's sexual passion remained, Else reverted to her aggressive capriciousness and Greve became increasingly cold and distant. Greve announced to André Gide as early as 1904 that he wanted to leave Else, but also confessed that he could not live without her.[55] The last few years in Europe were marked by increasing financial constraints and social isolation, although Greve was pursuing his own literary projects as well as producing literary translations at a Herculean rate. In summer of 1909, in a state of desperation at ever being able to repay his huge debt to Kilian and to re-establish his career in Europe, Greve faked his death by drowning, re-emerging in America under a new identity.

The news of Greve's "suicide," transmitted by Else, seems to have been received with scepticism by his main publisher, who declared "advances made to Greve to be a special honorarium, should her husband be alive or dead."[56] A year later, Else travelled to America to join her husband in their new home on Eagle's Creek near Sparta, Kentucky.

Although the early years in America are the least-documented period in the life of both Felix and Else, there is evidence that the couple owned or leased a small farm near Sparta, and that Greve (as "Fred Grove") worked as a schoolteacher in the town.[57] What seems evident is that the relationship between Felix and Else completely unravelled during the Kentucky years. Gammel, basing her speculation on Else's memoir and on her poetry from that time, suggests that there may even have been domestic violence.[58]

In late 1911, Greve/Grove abandoned Else in Kentucky. We pick up his trail again late in 1912, in Manitoba, Canada, where he becomes a schoolteacher and, in 1914, marries a young Mennonite teaching colleague, Catherine Wiens, decorous, self-contained, "virginal" – the very antithesis of the flamboyant Else. The Groves have a daughter, Phyllis May, who dies of a ruptured appendix at age twelve. Years later, in Ottawa, shortly before moving to Simcoe, Ontario, the couple have a second child, a son, Arthur Leonard.

Grove's new life in Canada, although fraught with hardships, was, at least outwardly, familial and orderly by the time the couple moved to Simcoe, and it was here that he produced a large body of enduring literary works, including the "autobiographical" *In Search of Myself*. Yet memories of Else still loomed large: her alter egos have been identified in a number of Grove's Canadian novels, and, on his deathbed, Grove, attended by his Canadian wife, is said to have cried out for Else.[59]

What led Greve/Grove to abandon Else (rather than seeking a conventional divorce), making sure she would have no way of tracking his whereabouts, leaving her destitute and helpless in Kentucky? The answer likely lies in Else's volcanic temperament, verging on madness, and perhaps, as Gammel suggests, in the fact that Else was beginning once again to show signs of asserting herself as an artist in her own right by writing poetry.

BARONESS ELSA

There is no indication that there was any contact between Greve and his wife after he abandoned her in Kentucky, nor that either of them ever knew what had become of the other. After her husband's desertion, Else somehow made her way to New York and into the art scene of Greenwich Village, where she soon became associated with the very centre of the literary and artistic avant-garde, ultimately becoming the acknowledged queen of New York dada.

Intimately connected with the avant-garde circles of Germany's salons, exposed to the major contemporary literary movements of all of Europe through her liaison with Greve/Grove, Else, as a writer herself, would seem to have been well-equipped to make her way in New York's literary world. But the assets she had acquired through her extraordinary life were offset by daunting handicaps: "I spoke no English, had no working skills, was arrogant, and was considered crazy," she says in marginal notes made on one of her sheets of poetry. Abandoned and destitute, she married the German Baron von Freytag-Loringhofen, who was then living in New York but soon returned to Germany to serve as an officer in World War I. He committed suicide after the war.

In her new life in New York, Else (who had anglicised the spelling of her name and was known in New York as Elsa) managed to turn her marginality into an advantage. She made an indelible impression wherever she appeared, devising elaborate costumes for herself, at one point shaving and lacquering her head, donning tomato can brassieres, and ornamenting herself with teaspoon earrings and coal scuttle hats. She made her body her canvas, and with her witty, allusive costumes, which were often visual puns, and her equally idiosyncratic poetry, she represented quintessential features of the dada movement.

That she was a powerful influence on the American modernist avant-garde of the early twentieth century is well documented: she was promoted by Margaret Anderson and Jane Heap, editors of the *Little Review*, who in spite of mounting opposition from the literary establishment published Elsa's sexually explicit and esoterically encoded poems. Other staunch supporters were writers as diverse as Djuna Barnes and Ernest Hemingway. Berenice Abbott and Man Ray produced photographic portraits of Elsa in her stunning costumes; Ezra Pound praised "Elsa Kassandra, 'the baroness/von Freytag,'" in his *Cantos*; and William Carlos Williams said he drank "pure water from her spirit."[60]

Although Else gained prominence in the New York arts scene as a poet, model, and performance artist, she remained poor. In spite of his title and family connections, the Baron had been destitute, and "the Baroness," as she was now known, subsisted on the meagre fees she earned from modelling in art studios and on hand-outs from artists and supporters. The originality and intensity of her own art may have won her a prominent place in the memoirs of many famous artists and writers as well as the undisputed title of New York dada queen, but it did not earn her any money. When many of her American benefactors established themselves in Europe, her poverty became desperate. A campaign for donations from artists and writers enabled her to return to Europe. She went first to Berlin and then to Paris, where she died in her apartment of gas asphyxiation, possibly a suicide.

There is some evidence to suggest that Else was mentally unstable. Even in the early years in New York, she "lived in total disorder ... with an assortment of animals, mostly mangy dogs and cats."[61] Gammel observes that at one point, Else manifested an "unusual sympathy with rats and cockroaches, later even feeding rats in her flat,"[62] a sympathy she may have developed in the jails of New York, for "the Baroness was routinely incarcerated, mostly for stealing in department stores like Woolworth's and Wannamaker's, as she purloined items she needed for her very existence, for her poverty was excruciating."[63]

Yet there was an aesthetic quality to this squalor, which reminded visual artist George Biddle of Brancusi's studio in Paris. It is also Biddle who describes Else's sexual pursuit as traumatizing, in part due to her physical neglect: "as I stood there, partly in admiration yet cold with horror, she stepped over close to me so that I smelt her filthy body."[64]

The Baroness's mental state is alluded to again and again in documents of the time. Jane Heap, defending the Baroness against a critic's accusation that she is a "mad woman," categorically repudiates the statement: "When a person has created a state of consciousness which is madness and adjusts (designs and executes) every form and aspect of her life to fit this state there is no disorder anywhere."[65]

It cannot be denied that the Baroness's sexual aggressiveness and relentless pursuit of her prey must have been tinged with a kind of madness, at least in the perception of those being pursued. The writer William Carlos Williams, one of the men she sought to conquer, was physically afraid of her to the point of buying a punching bag and practising in order to be able to defend himself against her assaults. What is more, he "listed all the men who were afraid of her. The American poet and insurance executive Wallace Stevens (1879–1955), who lived in Hartford, Connecticut, had admired her artistic dress and timidly told her so – but feared her pursuit, and was afraid to go 'below 14th Street for several years whenever he came to the city.' Similarly, the Lithuanian American sculptor William Zorach (1887–1966) found the Baroness 'crawl out naked under his bed' one night, refusing to return home until he accompanied her."[66]

Greve/Grove would have been thoroughly familiar with Else's volatile personality and the aggressiveness she was capable of. These attributes of hers likely explain not only his desertion, but also, to no small degree, his continued clandestinity in Canada. Indeed, it is possible that when Else dispatched her friend Berenice Abbott, who was moving from New York to Paris, on a mission to André Gide, to give him a package that contained three copies of *The Little Review* (presumably containing works by the Baroness) as well as a letter proposing that Gide support her in Paris,[67] Else was also trying to re-establish contact with the husband who had abandoned her. Frederick Philip Grove, settled in his new life in Canada, may have feared being found by Else even more than having his true identity exposed and being called to account by his former European associates.

THE "FUNDAMENTAL FLAW"

Yet Else continued to haunt him. Else-like figures occur in a number of his Canadian novels, flamboyant seductresses such as Clara Vogel in *Settlers of the Marsh* and Mrs Broegler in *Fruits of the Earth*, who prey on the novels' young and idealistic male protagonists, threatening to destroy their lives.

It is in *The Yoke of Life* that Grove's obsession with Else and his sense that their relationship was both fated and doomed manifests itself most clearly. In this coming-of-age novel, Lydia Hausman, the

Else figure, unlike the more worldly Clara Vogel and Mrs Broegler (who have both been married and have a "past"), is, at the outset, portrayed as an innocent farm girl. When the novel opens, she resembles the naïve and guileless Else Plötz (and her alter ego Fanny Essler), arriving in Berlin from provincial Pomerania before becoming a chorus girl and promiscuous woman of the world. *The Yoke of Life* sheds a great deal of light on the relationship between Greve and Else due to the fact that the protagonist Len Sterner, a figure who resembles Grove, explicitly articulates the nature of his obsession with the farm girl Lydia and the destructive, self-alienating effect of their relationship.[68]

Chaste and idealistic in its early stages, Len's relationship with Lydia undergoes a profound change while he is working in a remote lumber camp, separated from the rest of society (and of course from Lydia), circumstances that parallel Greve's "seclusion" while serving his prison term and his separation from Else, who is in Italy and who, like Lydia, is obliged to fend for herself financially as best she can (Lydia becomes a prostitute). It is not difficult to imagine Greve languishing in a Bonn prison and, knowing that his Else was no shrinking violet when it came to sex, being preoccupied with the thoughts and feelings he attributes to his protagonist Len Sterner. Like Greve in prison, Len is marking time at the camp as though serving a sentence: he counts the days he must remain there, "glad with every morning's five-o'clock bell that the tale of those which remained was diminished by another unit."[69]

Virtually imprisoned in the remote camp, Len feels, reading Lydia's letters, that he doesn't really know her, and "a new, carnal, and jealous element stole into his thought of her, intensely disquieting."[70] This "less exalted" vision of Lydia, together with a feeling that the relationship, in which he had formerly seen "a deification of things within himself," gives way to carnal passion, and the "mysteries between them" only intensify Lydia's seductiveness and Len's desire to possess her.[71]

Len feels that his own "purity" is defiled by Lydia's defilement, and that his despising of her, later in the novel, once he learns the truth about her, causes him to despise himself. Although he senses that she is drawing him into an abyss, he "knew that in this girl, for better or for worse, he had met his fate: for ever after she would obsess him."[72] These lines, filled with intensity and momentous implication, were written by Frederick Philip Grove decades after Felix Paul Greve had abandoned Else. In them, it is not difficult to detect the voice of the author.

If one accepts this as a premise, Len's subsequent wondering about her ("Was she lost to him?"[73]) and, later in the novel, his determination to find her, opens up the intriguing possibility that in this novel, which ends with the lovers' joint suicides, Grove was "rewriting" his and Else's story, acknowledging that it had not ended as it should have. This disturbing recognition is one of hindsight, and it springs "from the hidden knowledge that in his reconstruction of the past there was a fundamental flaw."[74] Was Grove fantasizing about what Else might have become when he describes Len finding Lydia, in dubious company, gaudily dressed and cheaply made up, a contemporary version of "the sphinx and the women of Babylon"?[75] Would a suicide by drowning, with Else, like Len and Lydia's double suicide, have "corrected" the "flaw" in his "reconstruction of the past"? Or does the "fundamental flaw" lie in Grove's inability to obliterate Else from his life, making his metamorphosis from Felix Paul Greve to Frederick Philip Grove forever incomplete?

The phrase used to describe Len's brooding over Lydia reads like an allusion to the "reconstruction of the past" Frederick Philip Grove had undertaken so successfully in creating his new identity in Canada. That Greve/Len sees the "flaw" in the ending of the relationship with Lydia/Else as being "fundamental" indicates the enormity of his mistake. Years after he had left her, and in fact even as he lay dying, Grove could not erase Else from his life, and his attempt to do so had, in some measure, resulted only in creating a void, an incompleteness in himself, that would always make his new, his "reconstructed" identity hollow and vulnerable, lacking an essential piece.

Len recognizes that his life is inextricably bound up with Lydia's, and it is this bond that transforms him, not only alienating him from his family and his past, but also stymying his ambitions for the future. This recognition that his passion for Lydia has destroyed his life is all the more bitter as it is accompanied by the realization that the bond between them cannot be broken.

Lydia is part of his fate, the unbreakable bond with her a part of "that force which rules our lives," the "force" that makes him sever his connection with the past "forever."[76] Although Len "scorns and despises" Lydia,[77] he realizes that she is a part of him, and that in despising her, he despises the world and himself. Without Lydia, who is an integral part of himself, "there was nothing left to work for, to live for; there was no sense in being alive, in going on with no matter what."[78]

The author Grove's inability (or unwillingness?) to sever entirely his connections with his own past, which he re-inscribes again and again in his works, is bound up with the sense of fatedness he shares with his protagonist Len Sterner, namely that "some other power had taken command and hurled him out of his orbit into a different world."[79] As we shall see in the next chapter, in *A Search for America* and in *In Search of Myself*, Grove expressed in the first person this feeling of being driven by forces beyond his control, forces that he situated in the circumstances that led him to break so dramatically with his European past. (The "autobiographical" novels, however, contain no Else-like figures – Else remains absent, rendering the "forces" driving the narrator curiously abstract.)

In *The Yoke of Life* these "forces" are associated with and, one might say, personified in the Else-like figure of Lydia. From the perspective of the Grove-like figure of Len, it is the obsession with her that brings about the catastrophe. This novel is the Canadian work in which Grove acknowledges and most explicitly describes the nature of his bond with Else, attributing the irreversible turn his life has taken to the "forces" that govern his relationship with her. What he was never able to acknowledge was the fact that these "forces" were rooted, ultimately, within himself, in his own narcissism, in the overwhelming desire to recreate himself, forces that had become manifest well before he had met Else.

2

In Search of Frederick Philip Grove

L'art est un mensonge qui dit la vérité.
Jean Cocteau

RECONFIGURING THE PAST IN GROVE'S AUTOFICTION

The two novels Felix Paul Greve had published in Germany, *Fanny Essler* and *Maurermeister Ihles Haus*, contain a number of autofictional elements, superimposed on the narratives that purportedly recount the background and the experiences of the young Else Endell née Plötz. Thus the characterization of Else/Fanny/Suse's tyrannical father also represents a literary representation of Greve's own authoritarian and abusive father; some aspects of the erotic relationship between Fanny and her "prince" are a reconfiguration of Felix Paul Greve's passionate affair with his erstwhile lover Herman Kilian; in Fanny and Suse's fervent desire to "become someone else" and to begin another life "elsewhere," it can be argued that Greve was inscribing his own longing and his own ambitions to reinvent himself in literary works that supposedly portrayed his lover Else, in the process constructing a feminine persona that constituted an alter ego of the author.

In Frederick Philip Grove's Canadian works, the autofictional elements are even more pronounced, with figures and events from the author's European youth transposed into the fictional reality of his novels set in the New World. In the "autobiographical" works, *A Search for America*, *In Search of Myself*, and *Over Prairie Trails*, Grove recreates his past to assume an identity in which he can ultimately triumph over the misfortunes, injustices, and sheer bad luck he experienced in his actual past life (including what he considers his unfortunate and unsuitable antecedents). He constructs this new persona by conflating the personal characteristics, achievements, and above all the backgrounds and social circumstances of former European associates, either claiming them as his own, or attributing them, in various displacements, to figures close to him, such as his father and mother.

The "autobiographical" works reflect the duality of the author's identity in a kind of self-dialogue, at times revealing the identitary dislocation – in fact, a sort of dissolving – of the self in whose voice the narrator is speaking. At the same time, in the later "autobiographical" works, *A Search for America* and *In Search of Myself*, the author comes close to disclosing his "real" identity – not as the son of a problematic and impoverished family, but as the talented and promising man of letters he actually was before leaving Europe, and as whom his European associates had known him.

ENGENDERING THE FATHER

It is not surprising that one of the most remarkable features of Felix Paul Greve's self-reinvention lies in the multiple and diverse manifestations of the father figure: Carl Eduard Greve, rural estate manager turned streetcar conductor, hardly fits into his ambitious son's fantasies of privileged birth and breeding. In his "reconstruction" of his past, Felix Paul Greve's claiming of a wealthy and distinguished family background represents not only a first step in the creation of a new persona for *himself*, but also involves the engendering, so to speak, of his own father: the abusive, ineffectual, socially unpresentable, and, above all, absent father is replaced by an overwhelmingly powerful, authoritarian, patriarchal figure who looms large in the "autobiographical" writings of Frederick Philip Grove, and whose "death" is in fact the pivotal event that ushers in the narrator's reversal of fortunes and rupture with the past. In creating his new persona, Greve/Grove invents a father whose image authenticates the distinguished biography he claims, but who can also be given the negative attributes that justify his son's rejection of him.

The father's abandonment of the son, and his subsequent absence, is nothing short of traumatic psychologically. D.O. Spettigue speculated early on that it was the absence of the father in Greve's own life that gave rise to the multiple mentors and patriarchal dynastic father figures in his German novels as well as in Grove's Canadian ones. Spettigue also argues that Felix's homelessness after his mother's death constitutes a lack, an absence, that let the material image of the family house take on an almost emblematic importance in the novels of the young Greve as well as in those of the mature Grove.[1]

Grove's father figures are derived from two oppositional paternal archetypes, one being the authoritarian patriarch, the other represented in a series of benevolent mentors, surrogate fathers, and, in a very few cases, actual fathers. These two paternal archetypes play determining roles in Grove's construction of his biographical legend. The depiction of the oppressive father is cathartic: the socially powerful, respected, and admired father is exposed as a brutal and and malevolent domestic tyrant, whose abusiveness and inaccessibility has nefarious and even catastrophic consquences for the family, especially the children. On the other hand, the psychological trauma of domestic abuse and abandonment of the son is compensated for and to a degree mitigated by the presence of the benevolent mentor/surrogate father figures, who provide the acknowledgment and approval of which the son has been deprived by his own father. That this acknowledgment is sought from the highest possible authority in two of Greve/Grove's works reflects another aspect of the narcissism inherent in Grove's creation of his new persona. The narcissistic fantasy of obtaining the praise and recognition of the ultimate patriarchal authority, namely the reigning monarch, a fantasy which remains vague and implicit in *Maurermeister Ihles Haus*, becomes reality in *The Adventure of Leonard Broadus*, where the importance of the king's approval eclipses even that offered by Leonard's exemplary father.

In real life, the young Felix Paul Greve's solution in dealing with his problematic father is to deny his existence. School documents from Hamburg indicate that Felix described his mother as a widow.[2] In his first encounter with André Gide (1904) Felix describes his father as a wealthy industrialist from Mecklenburg and declares him to be dead. Grove's "autobiographical" novels, however, acknowledge the father's oppressive presence: in *In Search of Myself*, written years later in Canada, the depiction of his father as an enormously wealthy estate owner who brutalizes his son represents a kind of settling of scores, and the fact that it is the father who is abandoned by the son and his complicit mother[3] can be read as another manifestation of the son's revenge.

Grove's portrayal of his mother, however, is as contrafactual as that of his father: while the impoverished Bertha Greve kept a boarding house in a dubious area of Hamburg to earn a living, in *In Search of Myself* she is depicted as a high society matron who plays an important role in her son's upbringing, which consists mainly of extensive travel and of exposing him to the social elites of the capitals of Europe. The void left by the absent father is to a certain degree filled by the paternal interest shown in him by his mother's various associates, whom she introduces to her son as "uncles" at her glamorous *soirées*. This (partial) compensation for the father's absence, however, remained fictional. In young Felix's real life, the abandonment by his ineffectual, unsupportive, and brutal father constituted a lack, a social and emotional deprivation, creating a need that demanded to be met. It is small wonder that young Felix was predisposed to identify so passionately with the mentors he encountered at school and later at university, a number of whom appear in his Canadian works as surrogate fathers who are associated with or supplant his own father. These father figures either extravagantly praise "the son" or awe and inspire him as role models owing to their exotic travels, their intellectual interests, or their physical prowess.

It is likely the predominant mentor figure of his school days, the classicist Friedrich Schultess, instrumental in awarding Felix prizes, awards, and generous university stipends, who is referred to when the ageing Grove writes: "I shall never forget what a revered teacher said to me ... '...You are sure to leave your mark on whatever you choose. Genius is bound to win.' ... His estimation of my gifts and powers still whispers with subtle flattery."[4]

The attentions lavished on Felix by his "revered teacher" may, however, have been less than altruistic. If, as Klaus Martens implies, there was a homosexual relationship between student and mentor, this experience would have indelibly marked Felix's subsequent relationships with older, more influential, and in some cases famous men, notably Stefan George and André Gide. Given Schultess's teaching area, which would presumably have included Plato's dialogues, Greve's relationship with Schultess might also have been a factor in Felix's abiding fascination with Oscar Wilde, whose praise of "Greek love" and whose imprisonment for homosexuality were subjects of public controversy in intellectual circles at the time. Martens points out that after Felix graduated from his school and left Hamburg to pursue his studies, he returned to visit Schultess twice a year. What is more, while "Greve was demonstrably in Italy ... Schultess took, for the first time in his career, a four-and-a-half month vacation – 'a trip to the South.'"[5]

Three other figures in Greve's life give rise to surrogate father figures in the "autobiographical" works. One is "Uncle Jakobsen," no doubt inspired by a man named August Jakobsen with whom Greve's mother had been associated after her husband's departure. Jakobsen, depicted in *In Search of Myself* as an impressive athlete and expert sailor who takes the young protagonist out in his boat, disappears from the scene with the death of the boy's mother. His portrayal in the "autobiography" is likely a composite that conflates some of the features of two other surrogate father figures whom Greve later encountered at university, when he joined a fraternity.

The fencing fraternity ARC Rhenus focused strongly on its rowing-club, in which Felix was active. Its gymnastic trainer was Theo Thiel, "a widely travelled, adventurous medical doctor and an older mentor much beloved by Rhenus members," who cultivated a circle that met socially in his home, a circle that in many respects resembled a "family" of which the young Felix soon became a part.[6]

The other "father figure" from this period was the intrepid traveller and adventurer Robert von Kraft, a Rhenus alumnus who had business interests in Asia. He was an imposingly tall figure with a powerful build, whom Felix met at a Rhenus Christmas party. Grove's accounts of his exotic travels in *In Search of Myself* are very likely based on accounts he heard whilst a student at Bonn. Furthermore, in his "autobiography" Grove ascribes physical attributes of the much-venerated Thiel and von Kraft to his own father. When Grove ostensibly describes his father exercising on the ancestral estate, he is actually conflating the gymnastic feats of Thiel with the physical attributes of von Kraft: "He [his father] could readily perform what he called the 'giants' turn' ... To do it, he jumped clear of the ground, firmly grasping the bar, which was perhaps set at a height of eight feet. Swinging back and forth a few times, he suddenly gathered for a supreme effort and went over in a complete circle, four, five times, and gracefully at that – a not inconsiderable feat for a man weighing 225 pounds."[7]

Greve's membership in Rhenus provided him with more than a "family" in the form of fraternity brothers and mentor figures who supplanted his absent father. Just as a number of these figures would be appropriated to construct certain features of his own assumed identity in the mature Frederick Philip Grove's "autobiographical" works, the fraternity house and its well-kept grounds would come to represent the "family home" which must have meant so much to the homeless Felix Paul Greve. Martens has demonstrated that Grove's description of "Castle Thurow," the family's "ancestral estate," borrowed significant elements from the Rhenus fraternity's boathouse.[8] In *In Search of Myself* Grove portrays his "childhood home" as a large, impressive structure surrounded by treed lawns, all the components of the building, the interiors and the grounds, being described in great detail, and all of them corresponding closely to the Rhenus boathouse, including the waterfront location, with the difference that "Castle Thurow" faced not the River Rhine but the Baltic Sea.[9]

It is in the boys' story *The Adventure of Leonard Broadus*[10] that the implications of the archetypal father figures as well as the emblematic importance of the "family home" fully emerge. The father figure in *Leonard Broadus* is the benevolent patriarch of a spacious, comfortable family home – located near water. Father Broadus builds his son a raft, which young Leonard uses to nab an intruder who threatens the Broaduses. This heroic deed not only makes his father proud: in a dramatic *dénouement*, it also earns Leonard praise and reward from the ultimate patriarchal authority figure, the king himself.

The idyllic, solidly anchored family represented in the Broaduses could not be more different from that of Felix Paul Greve, a family constantly on the move, with Felix growing up in various remote rural regions of eastern Germany and then, after the father's desertion, in dubious areas of the port city of Hamburg. Everyday life in the Broadus family resembles that of the Groves in Simcoe, Ontario, and indeed the fictitious Leonard's raft adventure may have been inspired by a raft Grove had actually built for his son Leonard.[11] Yet like Grove's "autobiographical" writings, *Leonard Broadus* contains telling traces of the former Felix Paul Greve's life in Europe, the disastrous aspects of which are not only made harmless, but transformed into peripatetic events that let the protagonist emerge as a larger-than-life hero rather than as the victim of catastrophe.

The water mishap as described in *Leonard Broadus* is characteristic of Frederick Philip Grove's strategy of displacement and recontextualization of events from his European past, in which the most traumatic memories are inevitably the most radically transformed. As we have seen in the entirely contrafactual descriptions of his father, features of the most disturbing figures and events in Greve's troubled past are often turned into their opposites or entirely omitted as the mature Frederick Philip Grove (re)writes his life. A death by water that must have been a traumatic event for young Greve has no counterpart in these works: the incident on the Rhine in which Felix's fraternity brother Lomberg, an expert swimmer and rower, drowns under mysterious circumstances involving Herman Kilian, Greve's ardent admirer (and future nemesis), and possibly Greve himself.

In *Leonard Broadus*, young Leonard nearly drowns when his raft is swept away in the current, in itself a metaphor for fate that is particularly apt to describe Felix Paul Greve's falling victim to events over which, as he seems to have seen it, he had no control. But in Grove's boys' tale, catastrophe is averted, and the raft becomes the vehicle for Leonard's heroic deeds, leading to the capture of robbers who invade the Broadus home, a substantial financial reward, and, ultimately, "recognition" by and immediate proximity to the visiting royal couple, the king and queen.

The only adventure story destined for a youthful readership in Grove's literary corpus, *Leonard Broadus* would seem to have been written with his own son Leonard in mind. What makes the tale significant in our context is the fact that the adventure and the "heroic deed" are all but eclipsed by the royal acknowledgment that constitutes Leonard's reward.

The Adventure of Leonard Broadus was far from being inspired by casual circumstance. By his own admission, Grove had been planning such a work for years, and, what is more, the king was always destined to play a role in it. In a letter to Lorne Pierce he writes: "In order to distract myself, I took up an old plan: that of a juvenile which I had planned for years. I had the idea, long before it took place, to weave the king's visit into it. It will be finished in about a month. On account of that visit of the king, it will be imperative, from a commercial point of view, to bring the book out this year, at least in Canada."[12]

A few weeks later he writes to Pierce again about the book: "Now I have let a very few people read this Ms. as it was being written. Every single one, a youngster among them, pronounced it a thriller. It was written to be one, of course. I set out to write what would have delighted my heart at the age of twelve. I believe I also mentioned that, since I wove the visit of the king into the yarn, I consider it imperative that the book should appear this fall: that visit makes it a selling point. There is still one chapter to write: I cannot write till the king has gone through Hamilton day after tomorrow."[13]

The importance Grove attached to the king's visit as playing a crucial part in what, even without it, would have been a lively boys' adventure story, cannot be explained in terms of the "commercial" reasons he invokes in the 29 May letter to Pierce. As he himself asserts in the same letter, he had laid plans for the story, including the king's role in it, long before the royal visit to Canada was announced.

The key to the dramatic scene in which the king and queen bestow "richly deserved praise" upon Leonard may lie buried deep in Grove's European past. Leonard's acknowledgment by the ultimate patriarchal authority, the king, not only compensates for young Felix Paul Greve's deprivation of paternal approval, it also fulfils his narcissistic desire to situate himself in proximity to the very top of the social elite. In his Canadian "autobiographical" writings, Grove endows himself with the aristocratic and even royal connections he would have witnessed or heard about through his fraternity brothers and members of other, even more prestigious fraternities. However, the fantasy of being associated with "the highest in the land" manifested itself long before the dramatic events that had interrupted his promising European career and that had led to his self-reinvention in Canada.

Even as a student in Bonn, Felix Paul Greve had taken extraordinary steps to associate himself with the royal family, strongly indicating that his hubris and narcissism manifested itself long before he undertook his definitive change of identity. As first-in-charge of his fraternity, he became the president of the executive committee responsible for organizing public celebrations for the emperor's birthday, a position he must have worked hard to achieve, as Martens points out: Rhenus, Greve's fraternity, had never before played a prominent part in these festivities.[14] By convincing his fraternity brothers that Rhenus should participate, and that he himself should be the one to act as master of ceremonies, Greve created the opportunity to earn public acknowledgment and praise in his honouring of the epitome of German patriarchy, the *Kaiser*. Thus, in Bonn's impressive *Beethoven Halle*, Greve, dressed in the ceremonial fraternity uniform, presides over an event featuring, if not the *Kaiser* in person, a "large painting that depicted the *Kaiser* mounted on horseback with his entourage."[15] The event was a resounding success, and Greve must have found gratifying the fact that the festivities, in which he seems to have played his role well, were written up favourably in the local press as well as in the fraternity bulletin. For the young man of inauspicious background, whose own father was anything but a benign and worthy authority figure, his successfully played role in celebrating the birthday of the emperor, the ultimate benevolent patriarch, must have seemed a confirmation of the legitimacy of his aspirations, his acknowledgment as a worthy "son."

Leonard Broadus's "recognition" by the king and queen as well as by his own parents thus represents fulfilment of Greve's ultimate ambitions, palliation of his greatest trauma. For Leonard's "recognition" takes a homely, nominally familial form as well as a ceremonial one, and for Leonard it is nothing short of a life-altering epiphany. Having been acknowledged for his heroic deed by the queen, Leonard is subsequently acknowledged and rewarded by the king himself: "It is a great pleasure for me to be able to hand you this cheque, my boy. I am sure the money was richly earned. We are all proud of you.' ... As he [Leonard] passed through the crowded lobby and through the masses thronging the square in front of the hotel, he felt his very body had changed and consisted now of a different substance from mere flesh, bone, and sinew; as if he had gone through fire and come out tempered; and he knew, with the knowledge that comes from the heart, not the mind, that he would feel tempered throughout life."[16]

The fictional Leonard Broadus has a real-life counterpart in Leonard Grove: the hero of Grove's novel not only bears the name of the author's son, his adventures begin on a raft which, like Leonard Grove's, was built for him by his father. Life in the Broadus family closely resembles that of the Grove family in their home on Lake Simcoe. That the capture of the robbers by young Leonard, a fitting *dénouement* for a "juvenile" novel, is eclipsed by acts of royal recognition of the sort that its author had always craved suggests that Leonard Broadus represents an autofictional protagonist in whom the figures of Felix Paul Greve, Frederick Philip Grove, and his own son are conflated. The patriarchal "blessing" Grove here seems to be bestowing on his son (by way of his fictional counterpart Leonard Broadus, for whom the king's expression of approval is life-changing) encompasses the author himself.

Thus in *Leonard Broadus* the "recognition" of the king and queen and the intimacy of their dialogue with the Broaduses become an autofictional realization of Greve/Grove's life-long fantasy of personal proximity to royalty, at the same time vicariously fulfilling the desire for patriarchal acknowledgment that drove the young Greve in Germany as it did the mature Grove in Canada. The words "We are all proud of you," spoken by the king, express the ultimate patriarchal approval that Felix Paul Greve had been denied in his own youth and that he had pursued tirelessly ever since, even as the mature Canadian writer who penned them in *The Adventure of Leonard Broadus*.

DROPPING CLUES, AND THE ANDRÉ GIDE CONNECTION

I believe I have hidden myself fairly well.
Frederick Philip Grove, *In Search of Myself*

In his introduction to the 1971 edition of *A Search for America*, Stanley McMullin observes that the work "has generally been treated as thinly disguised autobiography."[17] One is tempted to replace "thinly disguised" with "encoded," for in fact the book contains so many references – chronologically and geographically displaced and recontextualized though they may be – to Greve/Grove's past that it was this work, together with the purportedly autobiographical *In Search of Myself*, that enabled biographers to begin to piece together the story of the man who called himself Frederick Philip Grove. Indeed, Grove acknowledges as much in the "Author's Note to the Fourth Edition" of *A Search for America*: "In every single part fact and fiction are inextricably interwoven ... Why, so I have been asked, did I choose a pseudonym for my hero? Well, while a pseudonym ostensibly dissociates the author from his creation, it gives him at the same time an opportunity to be even more personal than, in the conditions of our present-day civilization, it would be either safe or comfortable to be were he speaking in the first person, unmasked."[18]

In *In Search of Myself*, Grove was to go further. In the prologue to the "autobiography," Grove hinted more explicitly at his hidden past. First published as an essay in 1940, the "Prologue" describes a journey through the Ontario wilderness, the main narrative alternating with reflections on his European past. The journey frame itself is metaphorical: the road on which the narrator is travelling grows progressively worse until finally he is forced to stop, as the road has been completely washed away.[19]

What triggers his reflections during this involuntary interruption of his journey is a book he has received from a recent visitor. It is the biography of a "young Frenchman," who in Europe had been one of the narrator's "intimates." Reading this biography that portrays the "young Frenchman" as a world-renowned writer has driven home to the narrator that his own literary efforts, undertaken in the remoteness of western Canada, have met with only modest success. Comparing his friend's life and work with his own, he sees himself as a failure: "Like a flash of lightning it had struck me that, to earn the distinction of seeing his biography published within his lifetime, he [the 'young Frenchman'] must have achieved things which had focused on him the eyes of a world, a living world full of fire and enthusiasm as any world had ever been – whereas I, only slightly his junior, in spite of often titanic endeavour, had lived and worked in obscurity, giving expression, at the best, to a few, a very few mirrorings of life in the raw such as it had been my lot to witness."[20]

The narrator resolves to "explain" his failure, namely to recount the circumstances that have brought his once promising life and literary career to a standstill (symbolized in the prologue by the washed-out road). Although he feels that he has no audience to whom to address his account, he decides that the attempt to make himself heard must be made, and that his intended audience will be the "young Frenchman," now a man of seventy or more: "Whether he ever read the explanation, what did it matter? There would be others, if not today, then ten decades from now. The only thing that did matter, as far as I was concerned, was the fact that the attempt had been made. The rest I must leave to the gods ... That night I sat down to begin, with an avowedly autobiographic purpose, the story of MY LIFE AS A WRITER IN CANADA."[21]

Grove's memories of his friendship with the "young Frenchman," whom Spettigue correctly identified as André Gide, contain several clues as to the latter's identity: the references to translations of his works that had appeared in many languages (Felix Paul Greve had translated six of them into German), meetings of the two friends in Paris, one such encounter being a dinner in one of that city's "great, famous restaurants," a hint to the setting of Gide's "Conversation avec un Allemand quelques années avant la guerre," and finally the time frame of the publication of the "Frenchman's" biography. Jean Hytier's biography of André Gide was published in 1938. In 1940, Grove refers to it as "recent."

Although Grove acknowledges that the "young Frenchman" had been one of the "determining influences in overcoming my own immaturities,"[22] his reminiscences reveal the same hubris and narcissism exhibited elsewhere in the "autobiography": he exaggerates the intimacy of their friendship, claiming they had been "inseparable," so much so that friends had referred to them as "Castor and Pollux." Grove goes so far as to claim that the attitude of the older writer had been that of "a mentor coaching one of whom great things were expected, things greater than those within his own reach."[23]

Grove himself describes his initial response to the biography as one of shock: "I had turned dumbly back to my desk; and shaking with excitement, I had let myself sink into the chair by the shaded lamp.

With trembling fingers I had reached for the book … opening it at the last pages where I expected to find a bibliography. The bibliography was there; and it was put together with obvious care and completeness."[24] It is clear that Grove was looking for his own name. What must have distressed Grove about Gide's biography was that nowhere was there mention of the role Felix Paul Greve had played as Gide's translator or, on a personal level, as his friend, "one of the most interesting figures I have ever encountered," as Gide put it in a letter to Greve. Klaus Martens is likely right when he points out that "the troubling impact of Hytier's Gide biography was less a result of the Frenchman's worldwide reputation than simply the absence of his, 'Grève's,' role in it. If his former existence had been erased from the world in which he lived, then not even discovery (or rediscovery) would be possible."[25]

When Grove, with "trembling fingers," opened Hytier's biography of André Gide, he had good reason to assume that the name "Grève" (Gide's spelling of the name in his letters to Greve) would occur in it. Thanks to a friend who was a university librarian and who brought him books, Grove had been following Gide's career from Canada even before reading the biography. He would have recognized himself not only in the "Conversation avec un Allemand quelques années avant la guerre" (1924), but also as the model for certain characters in two of Gide's fictional works, *Les Caves du Vatican* (1922) and *Les Faux-monnayeurs* (1925). That "Grève" played an important role in Gide's life is documented not only in the "Conversation" and the lively and in parts very personal correspondence between the two men, but also in Gide's *Journal* (1949), which was not published until after Grove's death.

Gide's description of their very first meeting in Paris, which he noted in the journal entry on which he would base the "Conversation," reveals that the encounter was as significant to Gide as it was to Greve, and begins with Gide recording the intensity of his anticipation of it: "As I entered the hotel lobby, looking about, I immediately saw this clean-shaven face, pale, as though it had been bleached [unbeknownst to Greve, Gide was aware that Greve had just been released from prison], this extremely tall body for whom all seats are too low … I ardently wished it might be Greve. It was he."[26]

If *In Search of Myself* was inspired by memories of Gide, the "young Frenchman," for Gide, too, the relationship with Greve was far from forgotten, although there had been no contact between the two men after 1909, shortly before Greve's leaving Europe. Twenty-eight years after their first encounter, Gide remained haunted by the respective roles assumed by the two writers in the "Conversation." In a journal entry written in 1932, Gide reflects on one of the phrases he himself had used at that first memorable meeting: "'I prefer to cause action rather than to act.' No, this phrase was not a 'slip.' The astonishing thing is that Greve, in responding to it, simply recited the teachings of my *Nourritures* back to me. In assuming my stance, he had cornered me. In the end, I managed to evade the issue."[27]

Gide's fascination with the "jeune Allemand" endured long after the two men had lost contact with one another. The figure of Felix Paul Greve emerges not only in various journal entries and in the non-fictional "conversation" that Gide had published in 1924. Greve/Grove must also have recognized himself in several of Gide's fictional works, notably in the character of Lafcadio in *Les Caves du Vatican*, and in certain passages in *Les Faux-monnayeurs*.

Gide scholar George D. Painter pointed out early on that Lafcadio was at least partially modelled on Greve.[28] Like Greve, Lafcadio is not only exceptionally tall, he is also handsome and blond. But the resemblances Lafcadio bears to Greve manifest themselves in a variety of other, equally significant ways in Gide's novel: Lafcadio's obscure origins, his fastidious tastes, his association with maritime settings. Furthermore, in his meeting with Julius de Baraglioul, Lafcadio, like Greve in his first encounter with Gide, declares his father to be dead, and as is the case in Greve's account, the father's role is assumed by a series of "uncles," who strongly resemble those who appear in *In Search of Myself*.[29] When Julius de Baraglioul (a novelist, generally considered to be an alter ego of the author, André Gide) pays a visit to Lafcadio in the latter's poor bohemian flat, he sees before him "a young handsome blond man who was watching him, smiling."[30] Julius is captivated.

The resemblances between the fictional Lafcadio and the biographical Greve also serve to dramatize manifestations of Gide's own (virtual) multiple identities, and the bond Gide had felt with Greve from the moment the two had first met. In *Les Caves du Vatican*, Lafcadio, who "acts" and commits the ultimate *acte gratuit*, is the illegitimate half-brother of the novelist Julius de Baraglioul, who "causes action." While Lafcadio, who is "of obscure Eastern European origins," bears a number of the features of Greve, it is easy, as Gide scholar Claude Martin has pointed out, to recognize in Julius de Baraglioul a mask of his author. The fraternal bond between these two characters in the novel further suggests that both Julius and Lafcadio, the Greve-like figure, can be read as alter egos of Gide himself.

In this context it is therefore significant that Gide initially thought of making Lafcadio, the character resembling Greve, rather than Édouard (who, like Julius de Baraglioul of *Les Caves du Vatican*, is a novelist and a character generally resembling Gide), the narrator of his new novel. In the opening sentence of his *Journal des Faux-monnayeurs* we read: "For two days I have been wondering whether I should have Lafcadio narrate my novel."[31] In Gide's mind, the figures of Lafcadio and Édouard have merged, both characterized by their constant metamorphoses. As Claude Martin succinctly puts it, in *Les Faux-monnayeurs*, Narcissus becomes Proteus.[32]

But if Greve appears, in various disguises, in Gide's works, allusions to Gide, although far more oblique than those in *In Search of Myself*, occur in a number of Grove's writings as well. The incident of the counterfeiters in *A Search for America* is one example.

Gide's *Counterfeiters* (*Les Faux-monnayeurs*) was published in 1925. It was much commented upon by contemporary critics due to the complexity of its *mises en abyme*, the most significant of which is that Édouard, the main character, is a novelist who is writing a novel called *Les Faux-monnayeurs*. In it he reflects on the disguises and the falseness in the lives of people around him. Early on in Gide's novel, Édouard is confronted with a youthful band of actual counterfeiters, the children of the hypocritical *bourgeois* he is writing about – a "coincidence" he finds disconcerting. But Édouard is also constantly wrestling with his own demons, notably with the authenticity of his own identity. As Ernst Robert Curtius puts it in his lengthy review of Gide's novel, "For Édouard, the word 'authenticity' has lost its meaning, because his Self is constantly changing. It can happen that in the evening he no longer recognizes the being that he was in the morning."[33] The irony of Édouard's quest for authenticity, to discover the truth that lies behind the multiple forms of human disguise, expressed from a perspective that can be so closely associated with Gide's own, would hardly have been lost on Grove, a writer living under an assumed identity, who had presumably already recognized himself not only in the "Conversation" but also in the Lafcadio of *Les Caves du Vatican*. That the counterfeit episode in *A Search for America* represents a response (perhaps an ironic rebuttal?) to Gide's novel is not unlikely.

Grove's *A Search for America* appeared in 1927, two years after Gide's *Counterfeiters* (*Les Faux-monnayeurs*). A chapter suggestively titled "The Issue Is Obscured" is devoted entirely to a description of the hero's encounter with a group of counterfeiters. It begins with Phil Branden's attempt to orient himself in New York, and his references to the famous landmarks of Manhattan, as he wanders about, appear as parodic equivalents of the Paris landmarks that occur in the opening chapter of *Les Faux-monnayeurs*. The action describes Branden's falling in with a group of hard-drinking gambling men, none of whom, as it turns out, is what he seems. Branden is drawn into a poker game and wins the pot, but the money is counterfeit, and when he tries to use it, he is arrested. The episode, and particularly the ensuing dialogue with the detective, can be read as a response to Gide's recently published novel.

In *A Search for America*, the detective assures Branden that if he didn't know the money was counterfeit, he will not be punished, but cautions him: "your story has got to be straight." "My story," replies Branden, "is straight enough. I want to make a confession. It's lucky that I was the victim and not the crook."[34] Grove's prefatory "Author's Note," in which he points out that "every event in the story was lived through; but only a very few events … had taken place in the years with which the book deals," can be easily linked to Felix Paul Greve's European past, including the time he spent in prison due to Kilian's machinations. In the counterfeit chapter Branden describes his experiences with the justice system in some detail. Branden's remark that it was lucky that he was the victim and not the crook may be read as a vindication, a claim that Greve's imprisonment had been unjust. The counterfeit episode in *A Search for America*, an oblique allusion to Gide's *Faux-monnayeurs* and to Greve alias Grove's recognition of himself in the novel, may also represent a coded message destined for Gide, even though Grove would hardly have assumed that this message would reach its intended recipient.

Grove must have found the impulse to respond to what he surely recognized as a representation of himself in *Les Faux-monnayeurs* (and in *Les Caves du Vatican*) to be irresistible, yet he could not reveal himself. His prefatory note to *A Search for America* can be read as a disguised response to Gide, written in the same vein and with the same intention as his preface to *In Search of Myself*.

The relationship with André Gide was as crucial for Frederick Philip Grove as it had been for Felix Paul Greve. Not only does Gide precipitate the writing of *In Search of Myself*, he is the ultimately intended reader of Grove's other "autobiographical" works – the reader the author has in mind, although he knows Gide will likely never read them; Gide is also, in his desire to live multiple lives, an alter ego of the author. In positing Gide as his interlocutor (which Grove does implicitly in *A Search for America* and explicitly in *In Search of Myself*), Grove is inscribing Gide as his alter ego into his own autofiction. Grove's self-narratives represent a continuation of the dialogue with "the young Frenchman" whom he sees as being in many ways a virtual version of himself. That Gide, for his part, also recognized aspects of himself in "Grève" and pursued their initial "conversation" in his journals and in some of his novels must have been, for Grove, at once gratifying and – given his continued clandestinity – frustrating.

This frustration may explain why, in *In Search of Myself* (1947), Grove dropped clues that would make it possible to reconstruct his past. He had reached a point where he was ready to reveal himself, and he would do so by way of oblique reference to his old friend, now an illustrious author. With this "autobiographical" work, he was deliberately marking a trail that would lead to the discovery of his true identity. Although it was Spettigue's identification of André Gide as being the "young Frenchman" in Grove's account that led to the discovery, Grove likely also envisaged another famous European writer as a potential recipient of its encoded message. Grove's taking up contact with the famous writer Thomas Mann when the latter was living in Princeton was another sign that he was now intent on "making himself heard."

His decision to establish contact with the eminent writer was probably motivated by two factors. First of all, at the time he wrote to Mann (presumably in German, as Mann's response is written in that language), Grove was working on the manuscript of the "autobiography" that would have brought back vivid memories not only of his association with Gide but of other aspects of his previous life in Europe. That the two men knew each other in Munich can be assumed with some certainty, given the content of Mann's *Confessions of Felix Krull, Confidence Man*, in which the author's intimate familiarity with Greve's story is evident, not only in the obvious parallels between the lives of Felix Paul Greve and the fictional (anti)hero Felix Krull, but also in the specificity of certain telling details.[35] Furthermore, when he contacted Mann, Grove had himself become an established literary figure in Canada. In sending Mann his latest novel, *Two Generations*, and announcing that *A Search for America* was to follow, Grove was letting Mann know that he, too, had "arrived."

That Grove was now ready to reveal himself is also suggested by his references to another work he had produced. In letters written in 1940 to Lorne Pierce, he alludes to a manuscript titled "Felix Powell's Career."[36] The title itself is significant in this regard, for "Powell" is a phonetic approximation of the German pronunciation of Greve's middle name, Paul. We can assume that this manuscript contained a more explicit and less "thinly disguised" account of his life than *A Search for America* or *In Search of Myself*: Grove's wife Catherine, already deeply unhappy about the revelations in *In Search of Myself*,[37] burned the Felix Powell manuscript in 1969.[38] Grove had called it "the most powerful thing I have ever written."[39]

A SEARCH FOR AMERICA

In retrospect, it seems clear that Grove had always wanted to be "found," and that he had written at least some of his works with that possibility in mind. If *In Search of Myself* was written with an "avowedly autobiographic purpose," Grove's much earlier novel, *A Search for America*, is also strewn with biographical clues as to the hidden identity of its author, as Grove coyly admits in his "Author's Preface." In *A Search for America*, which describes the protagonist Phil Branden's life after coming to America as an immigrant, the headings that structure the narrative reflect a more complicated trajectory, one that can be seen, as Grove surely intended to be recognized at some point, to encompass the desperate situation of the author – his social disgrace and inability to continue his literary career after serving his prison term – before coming to America, as well as his peripatetic experiences as an immigrant.

The first section of the novel, "The Descent," is purportedly set in America, but it would seem to be inspired by the circumstance of Greve's having hit rock bottom during his last years in Europe. The protagonist is described as being at the nadir of his existence, living a life over which he has lost all control, in which all external forces seem hostile. Phil Branden's summing up of his state of mind readily translates into the despair Felix Paul Greve must have felt when he found himself shunned and abandoned by his former associates: "I lived, as it were, on the sea-level; I had the perspective of the frog: above him, all things loom."[40]

"The Relapse," the section following "The Descent," reveals a similar encoding, the fictional timeline corresponding to Grove's difficult beginnings in North America. It recounts the dashing of Phil Branden's hopes for a better life, and his inability to establish himself in the New World. When read in parallel to Grove's painful start in North America, this section represents the problematic sojourn in Sparta, Kentucky, and the pain of forced clandestinity, alluding to Greve/Grove's need for concealment, to go underground, to bury himself, so to speak: "I had felt as if I were chained underground, full of an overpowering yearning to get back to the surface, the life of real men, the light. Now I was very near to a desire to bury myself, to hide away from the view of all those who had their definite place in the work of the world."[41]

If Greve/Grove is "dead" (after faking his suicide) and so must now "bury" himself, his "death" and "burial" – going underground – are an opportunity to reinvent himself, to be reborn, so to speak. In a subsequent subterranean image, the "burial" is transformed from an image evoking death to an organic process necessary to bring forth new life, a period of gestation, as it were. The protagonist is planting – or rather transplanting – himself in a sort of parthenogenesis: "to find, in this labyrinth of roads, and fields, rocks and soils, that spot of humus where I could take root *in order to grow*. I had so far accepted myself, my innermost I, as something *that was* ... I suddenly saw myself as a mere germ, as a seed that wanted to be planted. I realized that I was nothing finished; that there were still possibilities of growth in me. But, unless I found the soil in which I could grow, I was bound to perish."[42]

The subterranean image is succeeded by an aquatic one, in which the author seems to be alluding to his supposed suicide by drowning as an act necessary to be (re)born: Phil Branden, now in New York, goes to the sea-shore, where he suddenly realizes "that the beach on which I was sitting consisted of myriads and millions of shells, thrown up by the waves from the deep, from their home, here to die, to be ground to pieces by the wash of the surf ... yes, I was such a shell thrown on these shores, in the process of being ground to pieces and fragments, in order to furnish the soil for others to stand on and maybe to thrive on."[43]

In a sort of dramatization of his "taking root" in new soil and his "rebirth" into his new identity in America, the narrator casts off his European wardrobe and also the books he has brought with him to America, books that had "formed his inner self." Both the clothes and the books represent extensions of himself, his divesting himself of them an abandonment of his former "shell," a stripping away of his old identity.

These images of gestation and (re)birth are expanded in Phil Branden's description of a train journey undertaken while he is working as a book salesman, a journey during which feels as if he is "passing through [America] as if I were rolling along through an underground corridor,"[44] a metaphor for the descending fetal movement immediately preceding birth. The journey evokes two other significant train trips undertaken by Felix Paul Greve: one is the trip from Italy back to Bonn, which ends in his arrest, and the other is the train journey he must have undertaken when he abandoned Else in Kentucky. Conflated in Phil Branden's account of his sales trip, the narrator expresses thoughts that no doubt preoccupied Felix Paul Greve on those two fateful earlier trips: "The trip was a fiery ordeal. I was in Purgatory or in worse than that."[45] Then: "I did not arrive at any very definite conclusion during that trip in the train. Yet, I remember, there was some vague idea of 'breaking away.'"[46] And: "I dimly felt a desire to do something, to get away from things, to simplify them, to remodel myself and my life."[47]

The third section of the novel, titled "The Depths," corresponds, in the chronology of Greve/Grove's life, to the period when he abandons Else. The trauma of this "breaking away" would have affected Greve profoundly: like his despised father, he is abandoning his wife, and like his father, he is becoming a failure. It is this period of his life that Grove most carefully conceals: "The narrative must ... lose some of its connections; transitions will be missing; apparent contradictions will crop up; feelings, thoughts which are hard to reconcile."[48]

As must have been the case for Greve, when the consequences of his "breaking away" begin to sink in, Branden feels that he has once again sunk to the lowest point of human existence: "By and by the consciousness of what I have done obtrudes. I laugh; but a sob mingles into the laugh. It seems so simple – all I have done is to walk out of a great city. But it means that I have left the society of man. I am an outcast – something closely resembling those dreaded beings which

I have thought of with a shudder: anarchists. I am alone; I stand against the world."[49]

Emerging from the "depths" in the final section, "The Level," Branden begins to affirm his new life, his new identity. He feels "a craving for peace with society,"[50] a sense of mission and destiny combined: "I knew now that whenever I chose to leave the life that I was leading, I could do so. I saw the gate which led out of the wilderness into the garden of civilization where I, too, might be useful in exterminating weeds and maybe even in planting the trees which would bear fruit."[51] As he heads north, towards his "destiny," which turns out to be to become a school teacher and writer in Canada, he is aware that his "rebirth," his (re)creation of himself in America, has all but obliterated the Self that was: "Odd combinations of words, idle plays of my brain, kept floating through my mind and sometimes wove themselves into disconnected lines of verse. Some of them recur to me even now, at this belated hour, as I try to re-visualize myself, walking along those roads into the setting sun. Others merely peep up through the darkening oblivion which has settled like a cloak over the details of my life."[52]

DISSOLUTION OF THE SELF: WHO IS "I"?

The fragmentation of the self into multiple identities, a sense of being inhabited by "otherness," of being outside one's self – these sensations are common to many writers of autofiction. The writing process implies the exploration of alterity, of alien identities, an exploration that can lead to the discovery of latent fantasies and predispositions within the writers themselves. The articulation of these latencies through fictional characters permits their creators vicariously to "live out" hidden or virtual identitary aspects of themselves.

In the case of autofictional writers who assume self-created identities in real life, the porous line that separates the writer, the narrator, and the characters is actually breached, the creative impulse giving rise to what Élisabeth Bizouard has termed *auto-engendrement*, or self-(re)creation. She calls this phenomenon totipotentiality (*totipotentialité*): "Totipotentiality involves for the most part people who suffer from the feeling that they do not exist. The object of their totipotentiality is self-creation, in order to give birth to themselves. They gradually become what they have made themselves out to be."[53]

Grove's "autobiographical" works contain numerous passages suggesting that Bizouard's observations apply to his "self-engenderment," and that the process began when he was very young. In *In Search of Myself*, Grove describes stories told to him as a child, stories that always began: "Once upon a time there was a little boy." Little Felix's identification with these made-up stories was different from that of most children, both in its intensity and in its long-term effects. Grove's description of his reaction to these childhood stories as blurring the boundaries between the real and the imaginary is one of many signs that his creation of his new persona represented a far more complex and problematic transformation of the Self than was dictated by expediency in beginning a new life and assuming a new identity when he came to North America. In his "autobiographical" works, Frederick Philip Grove crossed the line that separates the numinous extensions of the author (the double, the alter ego) as manifested in fiction from the sociobiographical identity determining his everyday existence. To what degree he was in control of this more far-reaching process, one that seems to have resulted in the partial obliteration of his past self, is by no means clear.

In *A Search for America*, the narrator and protagonist Phil Branden seems to recognize his own hubris in seeking the omniscience that would allow him to recreate himself and his past in a form corresponding to his own self-image: "To master nothing less than all human knowledge was for my ambition – or, had I better say, for my conceit? – no more than the preliminary to swinging the earth out of its orbit and readjusting, while improving upon, the creator's work."[54]

Phil Branden keenly feels the irrevocability of creating a new life for himself in America: "Here I was in a different world. Here I stood on my own feet. Whatever I might have to go through, if I achieved something, no matter how little, it would be my own achievement; I must be I."[55] But just as keenly, he feels the ambiguity and sense of disorientation resulting from his new identity: "I was the same and not the same."[56] And: "I had lost a thread leading out of the past into the present, a guiding clue; I felt disquieted."[57]

Throughout Grove's "autobiographical" works, one finds references to a disquieting sense of disorientation, an inability to discern between the fictive and the imaginary, the opacity of the past and its relation to the present, the co-incidence of what is written and what is lived. These references suggest that Grove, in his self-reinvention, was indeed driven by "forces" (within himself?) that were "beyond his control." But there are also passages in the same "autobiographical" texts, as well as in earlier writings from Germany, in which he denies the deliberateness of his "self-engenderment," which in itself suggests that his self-recreation was undertaken in full consciousness of its implications. Some of the most striking statements in this regard can be found in Felix Paul Greve's essay *Randarabesken zu Oscar Wilde*, published by J.C.C. Bruns in 1903, where Greve tries to reconcile Wilde's life with his literary work. These statements point to an awareness of his own self-engenderment as well as to the protean hubris of the writer as ultimate creator: "Ah, who writes life? ... Where does [Wilde] end his little remote tale-telling, and start, perhaps without knowing it himself, to raise his hand toward the deed? ... And finally, what is the deception based on: I am equal to God, I can do anything?"[58]

When Greve wrote the *Randarabesken* he was in prison in Bonn, and in spring of the same year he used an alias – F.C. Gerden – for the first time. Under the circumstances, he had every reason to "tell remote tales," to assume a new identity, and there is every evidence, from the subsequent suicide note to the modalities he negotiated for payment of his translations subsequent to his disappearance, that his re-incarnation in Canada, complete with a "legend" of his past, was planned, deliberate. But there are also indications, particularly in the Canadian "autobiographical" works, that this "legend," this re-created Self, in which he could realize all his youthful fantasies, had taken on a life of its own, beyond its author's conscious control.

In *A Search for America*, the narrator expresses the self-alienation resulting from the sense that his actions have been dictated not by himself, but by some other force: "Sometimes I realize to my amazement that the life I am dealing with has been my own. I honestly try to understand why I did this or that; and I do not succeed. I can only say, I did it. Something seemed to push and move me on."[59] "[P]rocesses were at work which were to remould me, which were to make me into something new, something different from what I had been, something less artificial. I felt as if I were in the hands of powers beyond my own or any human control."[60]

The shadow side of this all-powerful, protean, and self-created role of the writer who plays all the parts in the world he himself creates, who becomes his own fiction, is that it results in a discontinuity, a dangerous existence in which the very Self risks dissolution. Towards the end of *In Search of Myself*, Grove, by now living in relative financial security in his own home in Simcoe, Ontario, reflects on the price humanity pays for even modest material comforts. His reflections on this topic lead to an excursus in which, typically, Grove seems in complete narrative control. (In fact, like much of Grove's writing, the passage has a strongly didactic tone.) In the light of his true biography, however, it becomes highly illuminating in that the writer (unconsciously?) effaces all boundaries between the Self and the Other: "The life which is peculiar to me consists in letting other lives work themselves out within that, to me entirely mysterious, entity which is known to others by my name ... I have often doubted whether there is anything that I can legitimately call 'I.'"[61] These statements encapsulate what Régine Robin considers to be the hallmark of autofiction: "to say 'I' and not be able to say it, to say 'I' without knowing what exactly this utterance refers to."[62]

Grove had "found his identity" in his prairie life, Malcolm Ross had written in his introduction to *Over Prairie Trails*: "Here ... is the portrait of a man; over these lonely trails Grove, always in search of himself, for once found himself."[63] Indeed, with the metaphoric potency of its nature descriptions and in the way the narrator situates himself within them, the book has been seen above all as an account of the narrator's "quest" and self-examination. In the face of the implacable, primeval forces of nature, the superimposed identities of the "I" of Grove's autobiographical works seem at times stripped away: "Nature strips down our pretences with a relentless finger, and we stand, bare of disguises, as helpless failures," says the narrator.[64] The concept of Nature as a force that strips man of the pretences, of the "masks," of civilization is a romantic one, and one that Grove the European immigrant no doubt found appealing.

But notwithstanding the narrator's descriptions of the awesome grandeur of nature as an irresistible primeval force, the overriding representation of the Self in *Over Prairie Trails* is one of self-alienation, disorientation, and lack of control over the forces that determine his thoughts and actions as well as the physical journey. In the chapter entitled "Fog," the outer world with its topographical and man-made landmarks disappears. The scene is ghostly: the magpies' mocking laughter accompanies the traveller as he passes through the "Finnish woods," where a small thin voice comes floating out of the fog. The lonely voyager is the archetypal outsider. As he passes the farmhouses that, like all the other landmarks, have disappeared in the fog, the narrator sees in his mind's eye people sitting around their firesides or in the lamplight, secure and protected, as he passes by: "But between those people and myself a curtain had fallen – no sign of their presence, no faintest gleam of their light and warmth! They did not know of the stranger passing outside."[65] When the narrator asks "But where was I?"[66] the question is a metaphysical one. As in the prologue to *In Search of Myself*, the difficulties met with on the journey "over prairie trails" metaphorically describe not only individual features of the narrator's life in Canada, but in fact his entire past.[67] The narrator's musings culminate in a profound sense of self-alienation and helplessness: "the feeling of estrangement, as it were – as if I were not myself, but looking on from the outside of the adventure of somebody who was yet I – the feeling of other-worldliness ... a feeling of having been carried beyond my depth where I could not swim –"[68]

Was Grove in control of his self-engenderment? Or was he really "beyond his depth"?

As with his childhood stories, in which "actual memories" and "reflected ones" converge, the narrator of the autobiographical works often seems genuinely to have "lost sight of himself," of his true identity. In *In Search of Myself*, in describing the (fictional) trip to Russia with his "great-uncle Rutherford," the narrator observes that he cannot give detailed descriptions of what he has seen: "It is all over fifty years ago, and I kept no records of any kind ... like the face of Europe my memory is a palimpsest on which writing has overlaid writing."[69]

The obliteration of reality by time, by memory, by movement, like the obliteration of the palimpsest, where writing overlays writing, becomes an emblem of the dissolution of the narrator's identity. In *Over Prairie Trails*, the motion of the traveller's journey through the open landscape transforms reality, resulting in a sort of *trompe l'œil*: "The distance seems to stand still, while the foreground rushes past you ... In that case there are two points which speed along: you yourself, in a race with you, the distance. You can go many miles before the horizon changes. But between it and yourself the foreground is rushed back like a ribbon ... So it is truly in life. My childhood seems as near to me now as it was when I was twenty – nearer, I sometimes think; but the years of my early manhood have rushed by like that ribbon and are half swallowed by oblivion."[70]

In the light of Greve's re-creation of himself in Canada (of which Else would have been unaware), Else's autobiography provides what can only be described as startling insights regarding her one-time lover and husband. For throughout her autobiography, she reiterates that the problem with Felix Paul Greve was that *he didn't know himself*, that he was other than how he saw himself, that he was oblivious to the fact that he was not a true artist. In fact, Else was a perceptive critic: the degree to which her assessment, between the lines, coincides with the main tenor of criticism of Greve/Grove's novels, both English and German – that his prose is overwritten, that his characters tend to lack credibility – is astonishing: "*Mr. Felix ...* this resplendent young man of my stirring desire ... He made – in spite of his intelligence – the mistake of thinking himself 'an artist!' *How is that possible – I don't know!* he was *just the opposite of it!* But that was the only way it seems – he *could* account for his brilliancy. Which shows, for his intelligence, an amazing lack of observation, selfanalysis [*sic*] and intellect."[71]

It is Else who presciently and succinctly formulates the dilemma – the tragedy – of the self-engenderer whose "falseness," whose lack of self-knowledge, of self-identity, condemns him to the loss of his "soul": "This he will never live down ... within himself – hence he must murder his soul or perish on it."[72]

Is the "soul," as Else calls it, "lost" in a palimpsestic identity such as Greve/Grove's? Or does it grow to encompass many? What is at issue is the question of the nature of identity in a philosophical-metaphysical sense: when does the "I" become an Other? In his book on conceptions of identity Stéphane Ferret illustrates the difficulty in an analogy to the mythical story of Theseus's ship: "The vessel in which Theseus departed and returned was a galleon with thirty oars, which the Athenians preserved until the Time of Demetrios of Phaleron, constantly removing old pieces of wood from it, as they rotted, and replacing them with new ones; so that ever since, in philosophical disputes, [the status of] things that are added to, to determine whether they are the same or become other [things], this galleon was always alleged to present [the position of] doubt, because while some maintained that it was the same original vessel, others insisted that it was not."[73]

Although some of Grove's essays and miscellaneous writings that were never published during his lifetime suggest that he was well aware of the existential ambiguity resulting from his altered identity and all that it entailed, others suggest the "amnesia" and self-obliteration expressed in some passages in his "autobiographical" works. What is more, Grove's reflections suggest that even the protean persona he has created through his writing has not lived up to the – impossible – goals he has set for himself. His sense of failure in spite of "heroic efforts," which he invokes in his "autobiographical" works and notably in the prologue to *In Search of Myself*, leads to a poignant self-assessment, one in which he points to the discrepancy between what he set out to be and what he has actually achieved. His essay "Rebels All" begins thus: "I have lived through half a century and look back upon my life. Has it been anything extraordinary? Hardly. And yet, in thought as well as in actual range it has probably encompassed more than the lives of most men do."[74]

While the irony of this opening, for the reader, need not be underlined, it is entirely possible that Grove, who felt his achievements had fallen far short of what he might have done, did not intend his statements ironically. With regard to his fabricated identity, Else's perceptive observations – that he set out to attain impossibly high goals and, above all, that he did not know himself – are borne out again and again in Grove's work, both in his fictional and non-fictional writing. In *Settlers of the Marsh*, Niels Lindstedt, generally acknowledged to be one of the author's closest doubles, reflects: "Are there in us unsounded depths of which we do not know ourselves? Can things outside us sway us in such a way as to change our very nature? Are we we?"[75]

And in his diary, Grove in his own voice, musing over the mystery of his own identity, significantly uses his initials to refer to himself: "I hardly know who the F.P.G. is who is compact of contradictions."[76]

At the end of *In Search of Myself*, the mature Grove draws up a balance-sheet of the life he has lived: the constant financial worry; the disappointment of insufficient income from his books; the ambitious plans for books that were never written. "Was it worth it?" he asks. His spontaneous response to the question echoes with the euphoria of Felix Paul Greve's past freedom and desire for lives unlived: "Suppose I went out on the road once more, leaving wife and child? Suppose I merged myself once more in the life which is that of the unemployed ... I could see myself sitting by the roadside, jotting down thoughts or imaginations that have come to me. I should taste once more the triumph of creation, the utter triumph of the pangs of birth; and I should *grow* inwardly as nothing can make a man grow except the vicarious living of scores of other lives."[77]

In the end, however, the mature author Frederick Philip Grove, a husband and father settled in a comfortable, conventional life in Canada, ends his "autobiography" on a note of ironic ambiguity: "But, after all, there are things which a man does not do. As I have said, this is an argument against material progress; but it is an argument only; it is not the verdict."[78]

3

Archie Belaney alias Wa-Sha-Quon-Asin, or Grey Owl

We know Wa-Sha-Quon-Asin is not born of us, and we say nothing.
For us it is of no importance. We do not waste our words
but save them, because we know in this struggle of generations
they are our strongest medicine. This man flies for us true and
sharp, and we are thankful he has chosen our side.

Armand Garnet Ruffo

ARCHIE BELANEY ALIAS GREY OWL

Among the Canadian writers who assumed self-invented identities and then proceeded to live them out, the case of the naturalist and conservationist who called himself Grey Owl is no doubt the best known.

He claimed that his father was a Scotsman who had served under the command of Colonel Cody, the famous "Buffalo Bill"; that his mother was an Apache princess; and that he, Grey Owl, had been adopted by the Ojibwa. In fact, Grey Owl's real name was Archie Belaney, and he had emigrated to Canada from Hastings, England, where he had been raised in an upper-middle-class household by his two unmarried aunts because they considered his mother, who had been a child-bride of fifteen when he was born, unfit to raise him. His father had been forced to leave England when Archie was a young child: after having been educated at private schools and given all social and career advantages, George Belaney had become a wastrel and an alcoholic, and had failed in numerous business endeavours.

The seeds for the metamorphosis of Archibald Belaney into Grey Owl were sown during his schooldays in Hastings, where he was taunted about the conspicuous and unsatisfactorily explained absence of both his parents. Archie's building of the legend of his mixed-blood identity began when he told friends and schoolmates that his father was in the United States with his mother, the daughter of an Apache chieftain, and travelled with Buffalo Bill's famous Wild West Show.

The English schoolboy who wanted to be an Indian realized his ambitions beyond his wildest dreams. In the course of his short life (he died in 1938 at the age of forty-nine), Archie Belaney alias Grey Owl produced four books on life in the Canadian wilderness, written from the perspective of a Native woodsman, trapper, and conservationist best-known for his efforts to preserve the beaver, the national symbol of Canada, which was then threatened by extinction. Although all of his books were best-sellers, Grey Owl's fame was based mainly on his public persona. He appeared in films depicting him and his Iroquois wife Anahareo with their beaver, and he gave charismatic lecture-performances, in which, with the authority of the Indian who was at home there, he spoke passionately as an advocate of the Canadian wilderness. In the words of one critic, Grey Owl, with his exotic image as an authentic Indian, had acquired the status of a pop star,[1] not only in Canada, but also in Britain where, during one of his lecture tours, he was invited for tea at Buckingham Palace and met the future Queen Elizabeth.

Although doubts about the authenticity of the (half-)Indian identity he claimed had arisen in some quarters,[2] these never surfaced into public view until after his death. While the public furore generated by the exposure of Grey Owl's true identity eventually subsided, the controversy among literary critics and theorists over the significance of his imposture continues to this day.

On one side of the debate are those who see Grey Owl as a fraud and impersonator, dismissing him as a "fake Indian."[3] Literary critic Colin Ross strikes an even more contemptuous tone: "Once upon a time there was a pervert called Grey Owl, who lived in the Canadian woods. He is famous because he came to Canada and learned how to imitate the Indians – he wore a disguise and grew his hair long."[4] Stephanie McKenzie, in a review of the 1998 (re-)edition of Grey Owl's *Tales of an Empty Cabin*, makes no comment at all on the content of the book, merely questioning, seemingly disapprovingly, "why this text was reprinted at a time when contemporary Native literature is thriving and when debates about appropriation of voice have been challenging old publishing practises."[5] Native critics have been less judgmental. While at one point the Anishinaabe writer Drew Hayden Taylor condemns him as a "wanton cultural appropriator,"[6] in a later publication on Grey Owl he acknowledges that in some ways, "he did a lot more for Native culture than a lot of Natives did. Like I say, you can thank God and his sense of irony."[7] Anishinaabe writer Armand Garnet Ruffo's poetic biography is an insightful and highly sympathetic account of the life of Archie Belaney.[8] His representation of Grey Owl is further discussed towards the end of this chapter.

The views of some non-Aboriginal critics, too, can be situated on the positive side of the debate. Literary scholar Carmen Birkle acknowledges that Grey Owl's assuming a Native identity was an act of appropriation as the term is usually understood (in the sense of a member of the dominant culture speaking in the voice of a dominated culture that has no control over its representation).[9] Birkle points out, however, that Grey Owl "positioned himself within and 'mimicked' the so-called weaker culture to manipulate the dominant culture into environmentalist actions."[10] Grey Owl thus used "appropriation" not on behalf of, but against the dominant culture; his "passing" as an Indian subverted the norms and values of a culture and society that was both racist and classist.[11] Like Albert Braz in *Apostate Englishman*, Birkle argues that Grey Owl, as a white Englishman, in assuming a cultural identity considered to be inferior to the dominant one into which he was born, "disrupted another contract, namely the constructed unwritten rules of ethnic positioning. As far as his audience was concerned, his imposture undermined and thus threatened the conventional social orders of society."[12]

Literary scholar and theorist Susanna Egan does not see Grey Owl as an appropriator in the racial sense, but as someone who acculturated himself "into another ethnicity." "For me," Egan writes, "Grey Owl is the morally benign impostor 'who gets away with it;' not only did his charade cause no one harm, it actually created an imaginative or narrative future both for Canadian Indians and for Canada as a nation."[13] This idea that the myth of Grey Owl's identity also represented "a myth which allowed Canadians to invent a history and a place of belonging for themselves via the specifically Canadian landscape," as Caroline Rosenthal phrases it,[14] is shared by Margaret Atwood. In her essay "The Grey Owl Syndrome," she stresses Grey Owl's ecological contribution as one for Canadians to emulate: "Perhaps we should not become less like Grey Owl and Black Wolf but more like them."[15]

In the same essay, Atwood also searches beyond Grey Owl's assumed identity to ascertain its motivation: "Why did [he] do it? Imitation, after all, is the sincerest form of flattery. What was it that the Indians had – or were thought to have – that the imitators wanted?"[16] There is an implicit reductiveness in these questions: they suggest that Grey Owl's adoption of an Indian identity was undertaken merely for reasons of expediency – to obtain something "the Indians had" and that he "wanted." That Archie Belaney in reinventing himself and passing as an Indian was not driven by the "expediency" of passing (in the usual sense of seeking a more desirable status by posing as someone he wasn't)[17] but rather constituted a sort of reverse "passing" is pointedly implied by Jane Billinghurst, author of a book on Grey Owl: "In a time when the cowboys always won, Archie wanted to be an Indian."[18]

A plausible explanation for Archie Belaney's assumption of an Indian identity at a time when "the cowboys always won," and when in North America the very survival of the Indians and their way of life was threatened, was the vision, widely prevalent in Britain and throughout Europe in the late nineteenth and early twentieth centuries, of the North American wilderness as a primeval Eden, a place to escape from the constraints of a Western civilization that had exhausted itself in waging wars and maintaining empty conventions based on social hierarchies. Albert Braz, in *Apostate Englishman: Grey Owl the Writer and the Myths*, argues that it was Grey Owl's perceived rejection of his own privileged white European culture, which he abandoned to assume a "primitive" Native identity, that gave rise to the outrage expressed by a number of critics – most of them white – after his imposture had been exposed.[19] That Archie Belaney "forsook British culture – at a time when the British Empire was one of the most dominant powers in the world,"[20] to make a new life in a supposedly less advanced culture (and a disempowered one at that), Braz argues, lay at the heart of the condemnation of Grey Owl's fraud.

Braz suggests that Grey Owl was, in essence, a "transcultural," who felt deeply that he was a misfit in the Western European culture into which he had been born. He cites the novelist Francine Prose, who analogizes transcultured individuals to transgender ones: "since there are, as we know, transsexuals – men and women who grow up knowing instinctively and beyond persuasion that they have been doomed to inhabit a different gender from their brain and heart – surely there must be transculturals – people who have been born in the wrong society and for whom going native represents the equivalent of a surgical correction."[21]

Whether in "going Indian" Grey Owl was, consciously or not, rejecting, *in macro*, the proud imperial status of the culture into which he had been born may be a subject of speculation. What does seem clear, in the context of Grey Owl's own writings and what Anahareo wrote about him in *Devil in Deerskins*,[22] is that Archie was rejecting, *in micro*, the version of that culture as it manifested itself in the life of the prescriptive, emasculating Victorian household, dominated by females, in which he grew up. Archie Belaney may have felt, like Frederick Philip Grove, that the circumstances into which he had been born constituted an accident of birth: he did not belong in the stifling Victorian household epitomized by his aunts' starchy parlour, but in the freedom of the wilderness that was to be found in the New World. This freedom, like the New World itself, was distant and unattainable from his life in Hastings, and closely associated with his (equally distant and unattainable) father. In the writings he produced as Grey Owl, Archie Belaney would reinvent himself in autofictional accounts that more closely coincided with his "true self" as he had always envisioned it.

THE PHANTOM FATHER

There was one element of truth in the stories that Archie told his Hastings friends about his parents: his father had indeed spent time in the United States, and he had indeed married his mother there. But George Belaney (whose name Archie was later to give as George McNeil) had hardly lived the adventurous life of a frontier fighter. Although his exploits were to have a profound effect on the entire Belaney family, they were not of a heroic nature. As a spoilt only son of a widowed mother, he lacked all self-discipline, and his dissolute behaviour ended up depleting the financial resources of his once-affluent family.

All Archie had been told about his father was that he was "in America." But before his departure from England, when Archie was about four, George Belaney could be seen every day, walking up and down the seaside Parade of Hastings, "a tall, elegant figure, wearing a large sombrero-type hat."[23] This image was to remain indelibly etched in little Archie's memory, the only source to draw upon in imagining his father's life, elsewhere. This life away from Hastings was somewhere in America, in the Southwest, perhaps Mexico, in the exotic setting of an unfamiliar culture, and it was not only unconventional, like George Belaney's wearing a sombrero in Hastings, but also full of adventure, like Buffalo Bill fighting the Indians in the frontier country of the Wild West.

As a child, Archie had received a gift, a miniature Mexican ranch complete with toy animals and human figures, ostensibly sent him by his faraway father. Grey Owl biographer Donald Smith suggests that the ranch may actually have been purchased by Archie's grandmother or aunts, who said it was from his father.[24] But in the boy's eyes, this gift was an invitation to enter his father's world and become part of it. Smith observes that Archie would later tell an acquaintance in Canada "that he had 'spent the better part of three years on the trail with my father,' before travelling over the 'Canadian wilderness' from 1906 to 1932. He had, but only in his mind."[25]

Decades later, in telling his wife Anahareo about the toy ranch, he recalled his fantasies in some detail: "My father sent me a miniature ranch – I was about five at the time. I thought it the most wonderful thing in the world, and it was. It had little adobe houses, stables, and carved wooden horses – they had Navajo blankets instead of saddles on their backs, and little Mexican figures. Two of these figures I picked out as being my father and me, and I used to spend hour upon hour moving them about, imagining that he and I were working together on our ranch. Later, when I was able to read, I got hold of a book about Mexico and found that the hacienda, as they're called there, was absolutely authentic, right down to the little rawhide water buckets."[26]

Deprived of his parents, teased at school by his classmates about his origins, he re-invented parents who corresponded to the cherished fantasies he spun to escape the pain and humiliation he suffered as an abandoned child. In engendering his parents, so to speak, he was also recreating himself. Archie Belaney was not who he appeared to be, an abandoned child raised by his grandmother and elderly aunts in a dull, provincial, middle-class English household. He was really the son of a Western adventurer and an Apache Indian. His childhood fantasies were further nourished by the adventure stories he avidly read as a schoolboy, recounting tales of life in the North American wilderness and on the American frontier.

Archie's construction of what he saw as his true self in the stories which, as a young boy, he told his friends was thus an early form of the autofiction he would later create in his writings, signed Grey Owl. In stating his youthful claims that he was of mixed-race identity, he was doing what the life-writing theorist Paul John Eakin calls "living autobiographically." According to Eakin, the way we represent ourselves and the stories we tell others about ourselves are part of everyone's identity formation and constitute an evolving process in that our self-narratives are constantly shifting. For autobiographers, such self-creation of identity represents a phase that precedes the *written* autobiography, in which the self-reinvention becomes a fixed narrative identity.[27] In the case of Archie Belaney, the self-created identity had become firmly fixed long before he was producing the autobiographical writings that authenticated his identitary claims.

In the summer of 1903 – Archie was fifteen – Buffalo Bill and his Wild West Show came to Hastings. Archie, of course, attended. This event was significant not so much because it featured real-life "heroes" of the kind he had hitherto encountered only in books, but because its physical experience anchored the fantasies about his identity that he had been nurturing for years. These figures from the "Wild West," appearing before his eyes, in Hastings, represented a link with the absent father of his imagination, with the fictive reality of his father's life that to him had become reality itself.

Although Archie occasionally saw his mother while he was growing up in his aunts' household, there was no real bond between mother and child. And Archie was never again to see the father whose dashing image had so strongly imprinted itself on the mind of his small son, for George Belaney had been exiled by his family. It is unlikely that Archie was ever told about his father's true past, or even that it was his family who had sent him away.

To say that George Belaney had a chequered past would be an understatement. At the age of twenty-four, he had married the fifteen-year-old Rose Hines, an innkeeper's daughter, who gave birth to his child six months after the marriage. This child, a daughter, was abandoned by both parents and died at a year and a half. There is no record that George and Rose were ever divorced, and George kept this marriage secret from his family.

A few years later, having persuaded his mother to finance a real estate venture in the United States, he set off for Florida with Elizabeth Cox, his intended bride, and her sister Kittie. Elizabeth, whom George may or may not have married, died in 1886, and a few months later George married Kittie, then fifteen. When Kittie became pregnant, the couple returned to England, George's venture capital being exhausted. The couple left behind George and Elizabeth's daughter, Gertrude, to be raised by a family in Florida.

After the birth of their son Archibald Stansfeld Belaney, Kittie and George lived in rented lodgings in Hastings until 1890, when they moved to a small town in Kent. When George, always a heavy drinker, had to be hospitalized for alcoholism, George's older unmarried sisters, Ada and Carrie, took Archie to live with them and their mother in Hastings.

Shortly after Archie's removal from his parents, George was effectively exiled from England: he and his wife Kittie would receive living allowances from his family, but only if he lived abroad and never attempted to communicate with his family and his wife. If he breached this agreement, drawn up by lawyers and duly signed by him and Kittie, the allowances would cease to be paid out.[28]

Not much is known about George's life after his departure from England. Sometime between 1905 and 1910, he was in Canada visiting distant Belaney relatives in Manitoba, who soon threw him out due to his drunkenness and his attempt to steal money from them. He is said to have died somewhere in the United States shortly after this visit.[29]

THE FORMIDABLE AUNT ADA

Two of the three women in the household in which Archie grew up were fond mother surrogates: his beloved grandmother and his Aunt Carrie, who would stand up for the boy when his Aunt Ada, who took charge of raising the nephew and who was a stern disciplinarian, treated him with excessive severity. Twenty years after he had left Hastings, Archie's memories of his Aunt Ada's harshness and its mitigation by his grandmother and Aunt Carrie remained vivid.

He spoke of his upbringing in some detail to Anahareo (whose given name was Gertrude Bernard), the young Iroquois woman who would later become his wife: "Aunt Carrie was always kind and affectionate. She never went stomping about, breathing fire and all that crap like Aunt Ada. Still, for all her apparent timidity, she had guts, for she often came to my rescue when Aunt Ada was pulling her stuff."[30]

The always astute Anahareo soon decoded the subtext underlying Archie's accounts of the detested Aunt Ada: if the life in the Canadian wilderness that Archie had chosen had been largely motivated by fantasies of following in the footsteps of his supposedly daring, adventurous (and absent) father, thus achieving a sort of proximity to him,

Aunt Ada's oppressive regimen in raising her nephew played an equally significant role. He would choose a path that diametrically opposed what she was trying to make of him. Anahareo observes: "Paradoxically, when Archie was saying his worst about Miss Ada Belaney, he was at the same time revealing a most remarkable woman. But she made a mistake, and who doesn't, when she overindulged her vanity by attempting to turn her nephew into a super-being."[31]

The unreasonable demands Aunt Ada imposed on her young nephew with unrelenting severity, and her refusal to express the slightest approval even when he performed set tasks extraordinarily well, drove him to thoughts of suicide and at times of murder:

> Aunt Ada had me cowed. She had me scared to death for a while. I thought of suicide quite a few times. Once I tried to smother myself with a pillow – a nice soft way to go – but joking aside, she came close to making a lily-livered coward out of me. She'd have liked that – me as putty in her hands – to break my spirit. Luckily, I put up a fight, and she succeeded only in making a devil out of me. Then came the time when I dared to hate her. I was surprised that she didn't suspect this, because I'd been under the impression that she knew my innermost thoughts, and finding out otherwise, I enjoyed wallowing in my hate for her – glad that I was putting one over on her. But that stage didn't last long because I soon found myself planning ways to kill her.[32]

The effect of Aunt Ada's unreasonable expectations and withholding of any sign of approval would haunt Archie even after he had become the world-renowned writer and naturalist Grey Owl. On tour in England, he would insist that his hometown of Hastings should be put on his itinerary. He was prepared to risk exposure of his true identity to show Ada that he had made something of himself.

It is true that Ada's repertoire of tyranny was broad and varied. She insisted on calling her nephew by his full name, Archibald, a name he hated. (Years later, he was to write to a correspondent that "Archie is bearable but Archibald no."[33]) She demanded unconditional obedience in her attempts to make a conventional, well-bred upper-middle-class boy out of him. She watched over his piano lessons, sent him to an Anglican church school, and posted signs exhorting him to brush his teeth. Her determination to teach Archie self-discipline and diligence at all costs was no doubt motivated in part by Archie's striking

Figure 3.1 Archie Belaney in Hastings, 1901

physical resemblance to his father, who had disgraced the family for lack of precisely these qualities. Her resolve to avoid the overindulgent upbringing of her brother George, and the disastrous consequences thereof, were no doubt factors underlying Ada's severity.

But there were times when Ada's role as controlling superego gave way to nurturing maternal instincts. As a child, Archie was a loner and prone to illnesses, circumstances which caused her to indulge the boy's fondness for animals. She allowed him to keep a menagerie of mice, rabbits, and snakes on the top floor of the house. In fact, according to Lovat Dickson, who became Grey Owl's British publisher, it was Ada who gave him his first lessons in nature study: "She took him for all his early walks, and explained about trees and forest undergrowth, wild flowers, birds, insects, and creepy crawlers to him. The love of nature was born in him, and she first gave it form and names."[34]

Once at grammar school, Archie's favourite pastime was scouting wild animals in nearby St Helen's Woods. He also became more sociable, and although he eschewed the organized sports considered *de rigueur* for English lads of his age and social class, he had a group of friends known as the Belaney gang with whom he played at "Red Indians," Archie being the acknowledged leader. Grammar school friends later interviewed by Donald Smith suggest that Archie's knowledgeability about wild animals and Indians came from his reading of authors such as James Fenimore Cooper, Henry Longfellow, and Ernest Thompson Seton, as well as "penny dreadfuls" featuring cowboys and Indians, very popular at the time.

As he grew older, Archie began to live out the fantasy world that he had created around his parents' and hence his own identity as best he could, given the constraints of Hastings and his maiden aunts. He built a wigwam in the garden of his friend George McCormick, a re-enactment of Yan and Sam's adventures in Ernest Thompson Seton's *Two Little Savages*. The boys also built a "beaver dam" in St. Helen's Woods. Archie would signal his friend George by hooting like an owl. It was around this time, towards the end of his school years, that Archie first spoke of plans to go to Canada.

Smith suggests that Archie had become too rebellious for his Aunt Ada to be able to control him. When he turned sixteen, she finally let him leave school and seek employment, but he found the constraints of living with his aunts intolerable. After several exploits, one involving a plot to drop a heavy piece of statuary on his aunt, another involving setting off fireworks in his employers' office, almost burning down the building, his Aunt Ada gave in to Archie's wishes and sent him off to Canada. He embarked for Halifax at Liverpool on 29 March 1906.

"GOING INDIAN"

Archie spent a few months in Toronto, by then a burgeoning city, but his life there, working in a "large departmental store" as a clerk, was hardly the one he had sought. He went to Temiskaming, where a new silver field was being developed, hoping to find work. He found a temporary home with a woodsman and his family, the Guppys, and Bill Guppy taught him to snowshoe, to trap, and to canoe. Together Guppy and Archie set off for Lake Temagami, where Guppy was to work as a guide, passing through one of Ontario's last extensive pine forests never touched by loggers.

Archie frequently visited Bear Island, in the centre of the lake, a summer gathering-place for a band of Ojibwa, who were being displaced by the government's opening up the area to fishing, hunting, and tourism. Archie began to learn Ojibwa, and decided that rather than being a guide, he would become a trapper. Due to lack of experience and also no doubt lack of money, he failed to obtain a grubstake to go trapping. His only source for obtaining the necessary money was, of course, his family, and he returned to Hastings in late 1907, looking like an Indian, according to members of the McCormick family.[35]

While there does not seem to be a record of how much money his family gave him, or indeed if they gave him any at all, Smith observes that it was this visit to England that inaugurated the most dramatic change in Archie's life. On this visit he learned that his father was dead, and he found his mother, remarried and with two small children, more distant to him than ever. He was now determined to break with his past and, returning to Temagami, began in earnest to build an identity legend for himself.

When his erstwhile mentor Bill Guppy saw him in spring 1908, the transformation of Archie's physical appearance from middle-class Englishman to native Indian was complete:

> [Guppy] noticed how [Archie] had adapted to Indian ways. It was as though he had studied the Indian posture, a slight but perceptible forward inclination of the body, as though pressing against the headband that held the tumpline to which was attached the loaded toboggan, a way of walking as though wearing snowshoes, the knees lifting higher with each step. With his sunburnt and winter-wind-burnt face, with the high bridge to his nose, his long black hair untidy about his head, wearing moccasins instead of boots, and peppering his speech proudly with Ojibwa phrases, he looked as much Indian as white man. Only the blue-grey eyes, the voice with its English drawl and its educated accent, showed his exotic origin.[36]

Back in Temagami he met a young Native woman, Angele Egwuna, who introduced him to her family and Ojibwa elders. From this new "family" he learned woodcraft and bush survival as well as the spiritual values of the Indians, all the while advancing his knowledge of the Ojibwa language. One of Angele's uncles named him *ko-hom-see*, or little owl, "the young owl who takes everything in."[37] Over the next two years, Archie spent the summers guiding at a local camp and the winters trapping with Angele's family. He subsequently dated his "adoption" by the Indians to that time.[38] In summer of 1910 he married Angele, a union that produced a daughter, Agnes. While he was now systematically building his legend, explaining his long hair by reference to his "connection with a great race of fighters,"[39] the strain of maintaining his deception and assuming his responsibilities as husband and father weighed heavily upon him. By fall of 1911, Archie had abandoned his Ojibwa family and headed to an area north of Abitibi Lake.

The decision to abandon his family is one indication that Archie was hesitating to commit himself fully to the Indian way of life and to the Indian identity that he would later so proudly claim as his own. His conflictedness at this time, resulting from his marriage to an Indian and consequent stigmatization by the white men with whom he worked, on one hand, and his empathy for and identification with the Ojibwa family who had "adopted" him, on the other, was complicated by the thoroughly ingrained colonialist norms of the period. Archie had not broken ties with his English family and associates, and in accounts of his adventures in Canada (likely excerpts of letters submitted by his aunts) that appeared in the Hastings Grammar School's *Hastonian*, Archie's tone is that of the superior white man.

In spring 1912 he became a forest ranger at Biscotasing, familiarly referred to as Bisco, a rough railway village on a beautiful lake surrounded by forests, which were being aggressively logged. The culturally hybrid image he projected mystified the men with whom he worked. Although he looked like an Indian, performed "Indian stunts," and was an excellent canoeist, he was a haphazard trapper and unskilled at making and repairing tools and trapping perquisites, skills at which the Indians were adept. Further complicating the image of Archie Belaney was his ability to recite poetry. Dickson observes that "what won people over most of all was the contrast between his gentlemanly manners and cultured voice, and his ability in the bush in spite of his being a tenderfoot."[40] According to a fellow ranger, he "was considered a white man, with possibly a streak of Indian in him. He was an outstanding figure, imitating in dress and ways the Indians. He always wore moccasins. He wore his hair long, parted in the centre and down to his shoulders, but it did not look like Indian hair, being a dark brown … He was a great showman, showing off with all kinds of Indian stunts, and he was an adept at throwing knives. He was in his glory when reciting original poetry, and after giving one of these pieces he would say: 'That's by Bill Shakespeare, Tennyson, Browning,' etc., and laugh. He seemed a remarkable, likeable man, who, even in those days, wanted to hide his past."[41]

Archie's identitary and personal conflicts became even more wrenching in the years that followed. To his fellow forest rangers, he reiterated his original story from his childhood in Hastings, namely that he was the son of an Apache mother and Scots father and had been reared in Mexico. With his father safely dead and his mother out of the picture, he could now embellish his legend and also account for any elements in his story on which he was likely to be questioned. Thus he explained his English accent by saying that he had joined Buffalo Bill's Wild West Show on its British tour, and that in England he had "met his father's two sisters. These two ladies, who lived on the 'outskirts of London,' looked after his education in England."[42]

It was in the summer of 1914 that Archie began to show an interest in writing, an interest that coincided with increasingly heavy drinking. His excessive drinking may have been related to the fact that he was aware of the consequences of embarking on a career as a writer in which he would publicly claim an identity that he had himself invented. As Laura Browder points out, "In contrast to the ephemeral nature of other forms of performance, autobiography is fixed. The autobiographer presents a permanent self-definition to his or her readers."[43] In fact, Archie had actually begun to write, and showed his writing to his fellow rangers, some of whom were university students working for the summer. Thus far he had claimed his self-created identity by telling tall tales about his past, by changing his appearance, and by "performing," or "acting like an Indian." He knew that in claiming this self-constructed identity in the form of autobiographical writing, as he planned to do, he was taking a step that was irreversible.

But if his drinking was a way to escape the self-doubts he must have had about the project he was about to undertake, the project itself, namely his writing, was a way to escape his problematic personal circumstances. On paper, he could legitimize his Indian identity and inhabit a fictive persona whom, as its creator, he could free from the guilt and sense of doomed fatedness he may have felt at repeating the acts of infidelity and abandonment of his father. For not only had he abandoned Angele and their small daughter, he had also fathered a child, a son, by Marie Girard, a Métis woman who worked at the boarding house where he was staying, and whom he abandoned as well when he enlisted in the army in May 1915. At the time of his enlistment, in another act of deception, he gave his marital status as single.

Once in the army, Archie in no way backed off the legend he had been creating for himself. On the contrary: he kept his shoulder-length hair until he was forced to have it cut, and when asked about previous military experience, he said he had been in the "Mexican Scouts, 28th Dragoons."[44] He sailed for England soon after signing up, and went to visit his family in Hastings, dressed in his uniform. In the army, however, it was Archie-the-half-breed-Indian who made a huge impression on his fellow soldiers and also on officers. One officer recounted seeking out Archie, who had joined the Royal Highlanders of Canada, coming upon him in his tent: "Here was Belaney, with tears in his eyes, holding up a pair of kilts and telling me that an Indian could not wear women's skirts. I naturally did a little sniggering and patted him on the back. Away went Belaney to France as a Scotty."[45]

An excellent marksman, Archie was made a sniper. One of his fellow soldiers "was sure he was an Indian," and another "saw him squirm up muddy hills in a way no white man could. He had all the actions and features of an Indian."[46] In spring of 1916, Archie was wounded in the foot, and in the hospital in England, where he was being treated, he told his old story of being the son of a Scotsman and an Apache.

While Archie's Indian impersonations always had a playful side, as illustrated in the kilt episode, the "Indian" life he had left behind had allowed him to live out the fantasy by which he had defined himself ever since he was a child. But once again, back in England, Archie sought to escape from himself, this time by re-entering the world he had left behind to go to Canada. At the same time his abandonment of the new life he had found in Canada was a twofold betrayal: he could hardly have failed to recognize that his abandonment of his Ojibwa family was a re-enactment of the abandonment by his own father, which had caused him immeasurable suffering. But it was also a betrayal of his own desire to create a new life and a new persona for himself – indeed, of the person he felt, in his innermost being, he was. In England, he attempted to turn back the pages and reclaim his English life, apparently prepared to accept losing his Indian family. He pursued a relationship with Ivy Holmes, whom he had known before leaving for Canada. She had meanwhile become a professional dancer and had travelled widely. With her, he could resume his previous English identity, and while, to her, he never alluded to his Indian alter ego, he vividly described to her his Canadian adventures. To the now almost thirty-year-old Archie Belaney, Ivy, in every way a suitable partner, must have seemed like a lifeline tying him to his biographical identity, a possibility of affirming the identity of the Archie that was. In 1917, Archie, still legally married to Angele, married Ivy Holmes, with the understanding that he would return to Canada and that she would follow.

Discharged from the army, Archie returned to Canada as planned. The crossing was a difficult one for him physically, due to his painful foot injury, and above all emotionally. He had left behind his grieving aunts and his English bride, whose expectations he knew he would be unable to meet, and he was returning to an uncertain future in Canada, where he knew Angele and her people would confront him with expectations and accusations from which he saw no way of extricating himself. He was unfriendly to the comrades with whom he was making the crossing, in anticipation of the strain of re-assuming his Indian persona. Thus, to his associates on the ship, "he emphasized the Indian traits in his character; the actor making up his face for the part he was to play, his mind already assuming the disguise."[47] Upon arriving in Canada, he soon learned that Marie Girard had died after giving birth to Archie's son, now being raised by a Cree woman in Bisco. In his confusion, guilt, and general desperation at the grief he had caused, and seeing no way out of the labyrinth of deception he had himself created, Archie turned to Angele, to whom he seems to have confessed his bigamous marriage in England, and he finally also confessed the existence of his Canadian family to Ivy, who subsequently divorced him on grounds of bigamy. According to Dickson, Archie may have fathered another child with Angele. Robert Bernard Belaney, as his mother named him, was born 11 July 1918, making Archie's paternity plausible, given his autumn 1917 encounter with Angele.[48]

Unable to bring himself to face the consequences of the chain of events he had unleashed, unable even to bring himself to communicate with his orphaned son, Archie completely fell apart. The playful, spirited young man who had once charmed everyone he met became known in Bisco for his nasty temper and for provoking fights, behaving conspicuously and offensively everywhere he went. He re-assumed his Indian persona, but it was not a happy one. A young associate with whom he worked on a survey expedition described Archie "sitting around the fire, and tapping on a dish-pan in a dull, monotonous beat, singing ancient Indian songs – weird rhythmic melodies – that none of our Cree or Ojibway Indians had ever heard."[49]

According to Bill Draper, with whom Archie had worked as a ranger, Archie's assumption of his Indian persona had taken a perverse and destructive turn: "The wild streak in him ... was not inherited but got from a queer piece in him that said, Be a wild man, be an Indian. Disguise the fact that you have had a good education and can read music. Pretend you are playing by ear. If it is difficult to disguise that you are soft-spoken, lard your language with obscenities, and announce that you believe in neither God, devil, nor man."[50]

In Bisco, Archie was nevertheless not without friends. In the early 1920s, he lived with an Ojibwa family called Espaniel, and considered Alex Espaniel "a kind of adopted father."[51] Like Angele and her family, the Espaniels taught Archie "the Indian way of doing things," a primordial element of which involved conservation. Archie developed close ties with his new Indian "family" – he would later inscribe a copy of *Pilgrims of the Wild* for "Dad" (Alex Espaniel) – and once again affirmed his "Indian" identity, dyeing his hair black and using henna to darken his skin. These outward manifestations of his Indian persona, which also involved performing an Indian war dance of a variety unknown to the Cree and Ojibwa who attended it, coincided with an increasing seriousness about his writing, but also with increasingly serious drinking and aggressive behaviour. The locals, who had been sceptical of his tales about his origins, "began to believe what he had told them about his Indian birth in Mexico ... he began to be regarded as someone out of the ordinary, and like an actor who has had a thin scattering of applause he threw himself resolutely into the part he was creating."[52] After a run-in with the police for disorderly and drunken conduct, Archie left Bisco and returned to Temagami, where he frequently visited Angele.

The summer of 1925 was marked by an event that was pivotal for the future Grey Owl: he encountered an attractive, intelligent young Iroquois woman sixteen years his junior, whom he eventually persuaded to join him on his trapline in Abitibi for the winter. Her name was Gertrude Bernard, but Archie renamed her Anahareo. Archie introduced his young "bride" (he had sent his aunts a photo of her describing her as his wife) to the northern wilderness, teaching her trapping and survival skills. As a number of critics have remarked, Anahareo's background in some ways contradicts the image of her created in Grey Owl's writings and in her own memoir. Caroline Rosenthal observes that she was "completely alienated from her cultural roots," and that it is an "ironic back-to-front twist in the story of Archie Belaney that it is he who reminds [her] of her Native heritage," teaching her "how to survive in the woods as an Indian."[53] Braz, too, points out that Anahareo was "urban" and "formally educated."[54] These attributes (along with her Native identity) made her a more compatible partner for Grey Owl than any of the women he had previously been involved with.

The loneliness of their isolated camp on the trapline fostered emotional and psychological as well as physical intimacy. Anahareo soon recognized Archie's vulnerabilities, and he confided to her all the traumatizing secrets of his life: his unhappy childhood, the relationship with Angele, the marriage to Ivy, the child he had had with Marie Girard. What he never disclosed to her was that he had no Indian blood.

While the couple were living in the Abitibi, Archie had been asked by a local Indian band to advocate on their behalf: white trappers had used strychnine as bait. Not only was baiting with strychnine illegal, it had also killed the Indians' dogs, who had ingested it. In retribution the Indians had set fire to a trappers' shack, an offence for which they were to be tried in court. Archie's intercession on behalf of the Indians was successful, resulting in cordial relations between them. The local band chief, asked by Archie and Anahareo to marry them, complied, pronouncing them man and wife in an Indian ceremony.[55] Another result of the court case was to cause Anahareo to oppose trapping as an inhumane practice. Archie, who realized that the beaver were threatened with extinction in the area, gradually came around to her point of view. The strychnine incident thus marked the beginning of Archie's transformation from avid trapper to passionate conservationist.

Another event led to an equally significant turning point in Archie's life. His mother had contacted him to inform him of disastrous events in her family, mainly involving his half-brother Hugh, to which Archie replied sympathetically and eloquently, a letter by which his mother felt greatly moved: "The letter was so poetic that I sent it to *Country Life*."[56] On the basis of that letter, the magazine requested an article by Archie, subsequently commissioning a manuscript that would be published as *The Men of the Last Frontier*. His correspondence with his editor eloquently reveals not only the pains he was taking to disguise his true identity, but also his desire to impress upon his Aunt Ada, to whom he dedicated the book, the significance of his achievement. According to Dickson, he not only wanted to make Ada proud of him, he "even believed that she knew something about his parentage which she had not told him … At times he thought he had stumbled on the truth about himself, and out of some misconceived family pride she was unwilling to admit it to him."[57] It was as a published writer that Archie publicly and irrevocably adopted an Indian identity and the name by which he would henceforth be known: Wa-Sha-Quon-Asin, or Grey Owl.

GREY OWL, CONSERVATIONIST

Archie's first public appearance as a conservationist, which he had been invited to give by pure happenstance, was at a Quebec resort called Métis. His lecture on the beaver was so successful that a number of prominent people, including Charles Harvey of the Quebec newspaper *Le Soleil*, began to take an interest in him and published articles on him. In spite of his veteran's pension, Archie was always short of money, so to augment his income he wrote magazine articles for *Canadian Forest and Outdoors* (published by the Canadian Forestry Association). With a number of his own publications, and articles written about him, he was beginning to become quite well known. Meanwhile, he was working on his first book, *The Men of the Last Frontier*.

But while Archie alias Grey Owl was growing famous, his personal life was becoming increasingly lonely and unhappy. Anahareo, feeling lonely herself in their isolated cabin where Grey Owl was so engrossed in his writing that he was not much of a companion, left him and the foundling beaver they called Jelly Roll, whom they were raising in their cabin, for long periods of time. Archie's drinking was by now entirely out of control: in addition to beer and spirits, he also consumed copious quantities of vanilla extract and was rumoured to drink turpentine as well.[58] All these elements – the remoteness of his cabin, his beautiful Iroquois companion Anahareo, whom Charles

Harvey later described as Grey Owl's "*inspiration, sa passion et son tourment*,"[59] and his drinking binges – fed the legend of Grey Owl the passionate half-breed conservationist and writer who could communicate with the beaver.

In 1928 the National Parks Board made an appealing documentary film of Grey Owl's life with his two beaver (for Jelly Roll now had a foundling beaver companion called Rawhide), shot in his remote cabin,[60] and Grey Owl was asked to speak at a Canadian Forestry Association meeting in Montreal, where the film would be screened. His talk was a great success, and in the ensuing euphoria Grey Owl gave an interview to the *Montreal Star* that further anchored his Native identity, the journalist in question making him a full-blooded Indian ("Grey Owl is an Apache"), and evoking prevailing stereotypes about both races in the process: "On the floor beside him was an empty beer bottle, and on the bureau was a headache remedy, indicative of the fact that he knew the ways of the white man as well as of the redskin. But his outlook was that of an Indian, even though he is fluent in speech. He has a vocabulary that would put many of his paleface brethren to shame."[61]

When the Parks Board gave Grey Owl a job as conservationist at Clear Lake, Manitoba, in Riding Mountain National Park, the appointment turned out to be a stunning publicity coup that benefited both the national parks system and the conservation movement, for Grey Owl had by now become a beloved public figure whose image had grown indelibly linked with the living incarnation of Canada's national emblem, the beaver. In *The Men of the Last Frontier*, he would describe them as such: "This little worker of the wild has been much honoured. He ranks with the maple leaf as representative of the Dominion, and has won a place as one of Canada's national emblems, by the example he gives of industry, adaptability, and dogged perseverance; attributes well worthy of emulation by those who undertake to wrest a living from the untamed soil of a new country."[62] That Grey Owl's use of rhetoric in praising the beaver – the references to the virtues of the settlers, to Canada as a "new" country, the use of the term "Dominion" itself – echoed the values of "the Dominion," and in fact those of the imperial colonizing power to which it belonged, and replicated colonial discourse, seemed, for the time being, to raise no eyebrows.

In 1931, the year he took up his post at Riding Mountain, the Parks Board commissioned another film on Grey Owl and his beaver, shot at his cabin there. *Country Life* published *The Men of the Last Frontier* later that year, and the book was greeted with rave reviews both in England and in North America. Grey Owl was now famous on both sides of the Atlantic, and revelled in his fame. At the same time he now had good reason to fear the exposure of his true identity by people from his English past who might recognize him. Indeed, there is evidence that his ex-wife Ivy had seen one of his films and had recognized Archie Belaney in the "Indian" Grey Owl. Grey Owl memorabilia in family scrapbooks suggest that not only Archie's aunts in Hastings, but the wider Belaney clan, including the Manitoba branch that had once hosted his father, knew the true identity of the man who called himself Grey Owl. Archie Belaney alias Grey Owl's fear of exposure must have been heightened by the suggestion on the part of one critic reviewing his book that *The Men of the Last Frontier* had been written by a ghostwriter.[63] Grey Owl's insistence, in planning subsequent books, that his writings be published exactly as he had written them, complete with (deliberately introduced) spelling and grammar errors, and his declaration that his real name was not Belaney but McNeil, were both meant to create a *fausse piste*. His claim to his American publisher that he was himself an American was likely motivated by the same reasons, although another motive was surely that he thought his being an American would help sell the book in the United States.

THE MEN OF THE LAST FRONTIER

Grey Owl's first book, *The Men of the Last Frontier*, reads like a dramatization of the Englishman Archie Belaney's transformation into the Indian Grey Owl. While the book's prologue describes Archie Belaney's first impressions of the northern wilderness, it also seems to represent the first European penetration of the North American continent and the first contact with the Indians. The prologue opens with a panoramic description of a river running through a primordial forest, "dark, shadowy and mysterious." The narrator then narrows the focus to depict a bark canoe on the river, paddled by "brown, high-featured savages," with a lone white man, "bedizened with the remnants of the lace and ruffles of the courts of Europe," standing at its centre: "The white man's burning gaze is fixed ahead: Westward, Westward, from whence the river flows." The prologue's close coincides with the European narrator's entering a hitherto unknown world that promises to reveal the secrets of an alien civilization: "And so, unostentatiously, without pomp or ceremony, all unknown to the teeming millions of the Eastern Hemisphere, the long closed portals of the Western World swung open."[64]

Throughout most of the book, although the author offers highest admiration to the frontiersmen, his perspective – and the narrative voice – is consistent with that of the European, the white man, "bedizened with the remnants of the lace and ruffles of the courts of Europe," who sees the Indian as the alien Other who would be conquered and domesticated in the spirit of colonialism: "The trapper of today has no longer the menace of the hostile savage to contend with."[65] Or: "Men ... braved the horrors of Indian warfare."[66] Another passage even more clearly situates the narrator outside the Indian world: "We blame the United States for their short-sighted policy in permitting the slaughter of the buffalo as a means of solving the Indian problem of that time ... The white man's burden will soon be no idle dream, and will have to be assumed with what cheerful resignation you can muster."[67]

There are also pejorative references to "half-breeds," which, after all, Grey Owl claimed to be. Describing the plight of the beaver, whose near extinction in the Abitibi area he is writing about, the author says: "By common consent, of white hunter and Indian alike, [the two surviving beaver] were spared until a half-breed heard the story ... with the lack of sportsmanship which, unfortunately, characterizes so many of his type, [he] at the first opportunity killed both [the beaver]."[68]

At the same time, the narrator consistently expresses a reverence for the wilderness, imbuing it with an Indian spirituality, poetically evoking Keewaydin (the northwest wind), the Hunting Winds, or the Dance of the Deadmen (the Northern lights). His awed reaction to the forest, however, is expressed in a metaphor invoking the ultimate symbol of European civilization, the Gothic cathedral: "endless black forests of spruce, stately trees, cathedral-like with their tall spires above, and their gloomy aisles below."[69] "And a temple it is, raised to the god of silence, of a stillness that so dominates the consciousness that the wanderer who threads its deserted naves treads warily, lest he break unnecessarily a hush that has held sway since time began."[70] The European-Indian duality that characterizes Archie/Grey Owl at this point in his life manifests itself throughout the book. His paean to the unspoiled wilderness is subsumed in metaphors comparing it to sacred European places – temples and cathedrals. And while he describes the "Indian" as "savage" and "other," the author admiringly lists an inventory of Indian notables, mentioning the names of great war chiefs, World War I heroes, political figures, and writers, among them "Canada's foremost poetess ... Pauline Johnstone [sic] ... and writer Buffalo-Child Long-Lance [*sic*]." (Grey Owl was unaware that Long Lance was, in fact, like Grey Owl himself, an Indian impostor.[71])

The language and phrasing in *The Men of the Last Frontier*, written in the tradition of European nature writing, is poetic and elegant, further dramatizing the duality between the "Indian" spirituality that suffuses the content and the European perspective that prevails in the narrative voice. Small wonder that a reviewer thought the book had been written by a ghostwriter and not by a "half-breed" who claimed to have had little contact with the white man's ways.

It is only in the final chapter that Grey Owl describes his "becoming" a Canadian Indian, an identity which he depicts as having been chosen and not one into which he has been born: "Many years ago I cast in my lot with that nation known under the various appellations of Chippeways, Algonquins, Londucks, and Ojibways."[72] The ceremony in which he is "adopted" by the Ojibwa is an event that consecrates his acceptance into the tribe, part of the ritual involving Archie's stepping into the centre of the circle formed by the dancers. The fact that in his description of the Indian ceremony the author uses the cultural terms of reference of a cultured European indicates its true significance for the author: it marks the transcendence of the lonely, abandoned, stigmatized little English boy Archibald Belaney who, by virtue of an impressive Native rite of passage, is transformed into a Member of the Tribe, having been initiated into the secrets of the wilderness by the Ojibwa elder Neganikabo. As Dickson observes, Neganikabo "is both a repository of olden days in the forest and a teacher who imparts this wisdom to the young Grey Owl."[73] It is Neganikabo on whom Archie projects the patriarchal role he had so ardently desired of his lost father, but also the features of a soul companion and brother: "Neganikabo, my mentor, my companion in untold hardship and nameless tribulation, has pulled back little by little, the magic invisible veil of mystery from across the face of the forest, that I might learn its uttermost secrets, and has laid open before me the book of Nature for me to read."[74]

Fittingly, it is Neganikabo who leads the celebration of Archie's "adoption":

> A blood-brother proved and sworn, by moose-head feast, wordless chant, and ancient ritual was I named before a gaily decorated and attentive concourse, when Ne-ganik-abo, 'Man-that-stands-ahead,' whom none living remember as a young man, danced the conjurors' dance beneath the spruce trees, before an open fire; danced the ancient steps to the throb of drums, the wailing of reed pipes, and the rhythmical skirring of turtle shell rattles; danced alone before a sacred bear-skull set beneath a painted rawhide shield, whose bizarre device might have graced the tomb of some long-dead Pharaoh … The sensation of stepping into the motionless ring [of Indians] was that of suddenly entering a temple, devoted to the worship of some pagan deity, where the walls were lined with images cast in bronze; and there I proudly received the name they had devised, which the old man now bestowed upon me.[75]

Years later, searching for a hunting ground, Grey Owl finds himself at the site of his initiation, the Ojibwa village now deserted. His visit to the place is no coincidence: he is drawn to it out of "a feeling akin to homesickness for his early life, for "those waters [where] I had embarked on the restless wandering life of a trapper."[76] The "place" can be readily identified as Bear Island, where he had known Angele and her family and where he had abandoned her and their two children. In addition to the feeling of "homesickness," we can add the feeling of guilt at having inflicted on his family the irresponsible abandonment he had endured from his own father. As the author Grey Owl, he can compensate for this act of betrayal and disloyalty as a husband and father by redeeming himself (in his writing) as the faithful and worthy "son" of his Indian mentor, Neganikabo. Preparing his camp near the lake, he hears the persistent, unchanging beat of a drum, and late the next day Neganikabo, whom he has thought long dead, appears in a canoe. Grey Owl as narrator describes the incident as an instance of possible telepathy, the beat of the drum a call to assemble the lost tribe. Only Grey Owl has heard this call. Neganikabo says: "Washaquonasin, Grey Owl, I see you do not forget. I called, and, of them all, you came." He then addresses Grey Owl as his son, the only worthy survivor of the tribe: "Three days have I called and none came; this is the last day, the day of Two Sunsets; to-night I go away from here; to-morrow you would not have found me. My son, I have seen many snows come and go; to me you are a young man … yet of all my people, you are the only one who remembers the way of our race."[77] As Braz sees it, this episode marks the final stage of the metamorphosis Grey Owl undergoes in the course of the book, and completes his transformation from "the unabashedly pro-British Empire white trapper to … the depository of the collective memory of the Anishinaabe."[78]

As the two men sit by the lake at sunset, Neganikabo proceeds to sum up the history of the people who have inhabited the wilderness, Indian and white man, and prophesies that the sun will set on them all forever, as the wilderness and the life associated with it are destined to disappear. In the silence that follows his speech, Grey Owl touches him, and finds that he is dead.

With this story, Archie Belaney alias Grey Owl reveals himself not only as a faithful member of the tribe into which he has been adopted, a worthy son of his Ojibwa family: Archie, the unloved little boy who was abandoned by his parents, mocked and ostracized by his peers, and whose only close relatives considered him a failure, as Grey Owl the Ojibwa turns out to be the chosen one, privileged, loved, and above all acknowledged by the patriarch of the tribe. Of all the incidents related in *The Men of the Last Frontier*, it is this one, with which the book concludes, that marks Archie alias Grey Owl's triumph over circumstance, the attainment of his goal. More than any other of his stories, it is this one that will prove to his aunt that her errant nephew, of whom she had expected nothing, has made good. In citing Neganikabo's words of recognition and approval, and by dedicating the book in which they appear to his stern aunt, he is seeking to obtain the same acknowledgment from her, to erase the unhappy years in which he felt rejected, abandoned, and unworthy.

Whereas the prologue focused on a lone white man from Europe, standing erect in the canoe in his European finery, surrounded by "noble savages" bending their backs in harmony as they paddle the canoe, the epilogue evokes an equally powerful visual image. A white man and an Indian stand "at the brow of a high eminence." The white man stands "nearest the edge of the cliff … gazing out over the tilled fields, towards the city beyond, while the Indian "regarded not the city, but stood motionless, his gaze roaming over the sweep and swell of the wilderness." The Indian turns and touches the white man, and, pointing to the west, urges the white man to follow: "For a moment ... the frontiersman stood irresolute, and then with a gesture of finality, his face set in the stern lines of one who has made a sweeping and unalterable decision ... followed the Indian."[79]

Together, the opening and the closing scenes in the prologue and epilogue represent an autofictional dramatization of Archie Belaney's double identity, and of his conscious choice to "become" Grey Owl, to "follow the Indian" in him, to live out the identity he had begun to assume since early childhood. The metamorphosis is, without a doubt, a protean act: I can become what I desire to be. But the final image in the epilogue also suggests that the transformation is a redemptory one: the white man (Archie Belaney's European self?) stands precariously "nearest the edge of the cliff," and where he gazes over the "tilled fields" and "the city beyond," emblems of the white man's civilization, the Indian, in a few words, invokes the cost at which the wilderness has been domesticated: "The sun is setting, my ears are filled with the sound of falling trees; it is enough. See! the shadows lengthen; let us go."[80]

PILGRIMS OF THE WILD

By 1932, Grey Owl had taken up a post at Beaver Lodge in Prince Albert National Park, Saskatchewan, where he remained until his death, and where he wrote three more books: *Pilgrims of the Wild*, *The Adventures of Sajo and Her Beaver People*, and *Tales of an Empty Cabin*. While he basked in all the media attention he was getting – a new film was in the works – and in the admiration of his many adoring visitors, his personal life was disintegrating. Anahareo stayed with him for a time at Beaver Lodge, and gave birth to a daughter, Dawn, in summer of 1932. But the loneliness of living with a man increasingly preoccupied by his writing and his conservation mission as well as the intrusiveness of visitors, journalists, and film crews drove her away. She returned to Beaver Lodge only for brief visits, leaving Dawn in the care of an English woman in Prince Albert while she went off on various ventures, one of them a prospecting trip along the Churchill River.

With Anahareo gone, Archie devoted himself heart and soul to his writing. Between 1932 and 1934, he was working on *Pilgrims of the Wild* (which appeared in 1934) as well as on a children's book, which would become *The Adventures of Sajo and Her Beaver People*,

Figure 3.2 Grey Owl portrait by Yousuf Karsh, 1936

published in 1935. Both were enthusiastically received, in Britain as well as in Canada and the United States.

If *The Men of the Last Frontier*, first published in England, had been signed "Grey Owl," Archie's next book, *Pilgrims of the Wild*, included a preface signed "Wa-Sha-Quon-Asin," followed by "Grey Owl," between parentheses. The narrative perspective of *The Men of the Last Frontier* had been Eurocentric, and that book contained few if any references to the author's past. In *Pilgrims*, however, the perspective is Indian or "half-breed," and while there are references to the narrator's childhood past, these serve mainly to account for his abilities as an author: he had, he says, "received some pretty intensive home tuition from an ever-blessed aunt"[81] whose teaching of English, he implies, enabled him to write the present volume. Specific references as to the identity of this aunt, or where he had undergone "home tuition" in geography, history, and English, are absent, and he goes to some lengths to explain how "foreign" the use of English has become to him: "my precise and somewhat stilted English was, like a stiff and ceremonious suit of Sunday best, something to be taken out of the closet and worn on occasion, and its use ended, returned to the limbo of unneeded things."[82]

In fact, in *Pilgrims of the Wild* it is England that is portrayed as an "other" world incomprehensible to the Canadian half-breed Grey Owl. In *Pilgrims* he describes how, in their isolated cabin, he and Anahareo tell each other tales, Anahareo offering Indian legends, Grey Owl tales of his adventures in the northern forests, some of which he writes down, adding stories about the wildlife surrounding their home in the wilderness. Grey Owl recounts how he decides to mail some of his writings to England, which he depicts as if he didn't know it: "I mailed the parcel to a war-time address in England, which country, I had always understood, was the market for such material."[83] When his work is accepted for publication, the author's "feelings were not a little mixed." He attributes his ambivalent reaction to the fact that "[t]his correspondence was my first contact with a world that had been as far removed from my grasp as was the throne of Egypt."[84] On contemplating the cheque accompanying the acceptance letter, Grey Owl registers "an indescribable sense of freedom, of having stepped through some dark and long closed door into a new, unmapped territory that lay waiting with all its unknown and untried possibilities."[85]

This statement describes Archie Belaney alias Grey Owl feeling that he has stepped through the looking-glass: his sense of triumph is derived from the fact that he has successfully "passed," that his new identity has been accepted in England, disencumbering him of his old Self, allowing him, as Grey Owl, to transcend his traumatic English childhood and youth as an abandoned orphan, raised in a cheerless spinster household determined by the constraints of middle-class goals and values. Archie Belaney's public acknowledgment as Grey Owl by a distinguished English magazine marks a turning point that gives rise to euphoria in anticipating the freedom of the future: "And I inwardly rejoiced that the bloodless happy hunting ground of my imagination was now within the bounds of possibility."[86]

In *Pilgrims of the Wild*, the loss of the wilderness foreshadowed by the words of the Indian in the epilogue of *The Men of the Last Frontier* becomes manifest. On his way from Bisco to the Abitibi of northern Quebec, Grey Owl describes a once-pristine landscape made desolate by the encroachment of the railroad and peasant settlers, barely able to survive on their "stone farms." The bush having been burnt and the forests cut, what remains are "bare rocks and twisted rampikes, miles of staring desolation."[87] Like Will James mourning the loss of the Old West, Grey Owl laments not only that "the whole Wilderness [was] falling about our ears,"[88] but also the disappearance of the old fur trading days and his old companions. For Archie, who dwells in the wilderness, this loss represents an existential crisis that threatens his very survival: "Fire, railroads, power projects, the aeroplane, they were tearing the old life apart. The Frontier was rolling back like a receding tide. I must hurry."[89]

This sense of urgency to pursue the receding wilderness in an effort to prolong the "old life" leads to a fateful decision. Setting up his traps late in the season, after the beaver would have had their young, in an area almost depleted of wildlife, he snares a pair of adult beaver, orphaning two beaver kittens. Anahareo's pleas to save the kits, and his own remorse, transform Grey Owl from trapper to conservationist: he becomes so attached to the little creatures he has orphaned that he resolves to give up the beaver hunt for good.

This decision fundamentally transforms the way he perceives the wilderness and his own role in it, leading to an astonishingly modern eco-consciousness: "these persecuted creatures [the beaver] no longer appeared to me as lawful prey, but as co-dwellers in this wilderness that was being so despoiled, the wilderness that was so relentless yet so noble an antagonist. They too fought against its hardships and made their home in it; we all, man and beast, were comrades-in-arms."[90]

It also marks the beginning of a new role for Archie Belaney, one that had not been pre-scripted in the romantic dreams of his childhood. In the Canada of the 1930s, nature conservation was a nascent phenomenon, and it is clear that Grey Owl, left alone with his beaver in the remote cabin at Birch Lake in the Abitibi, was seeking to reconcile his self-constructed Indian identity and the freedom of his nomadic life with the new role he was about to assume. Again and again in *Pilgrims*, he expresses nostalgic yearning for the "old days": "To beings of our kind, cessation of travelling, the denial of that unappeasable urge to see what lays [*sic*] beyond the hills, meant stagnation, almost a cessation of living, and worse, long hours of idleness with their dark attendant introspection."[91]

In *The Men of the Last Frontier*, Grey Owl had described his "becoming" an Indian, a sort of consecration of the identity to which he had aspired all his life. But in documenting his self-constructed identity in writing, he had made this new identity irrevocable. There could be no turning back. Although in *Pilgrims* he repeatedly describes the writing of the book as cathartic ("I had got some stuff off my chest where it had been fermenting for a long time"[92]), the experience of writing *The Men of the Last Frontier* had in fact been a wrenching one, fraught with feelings of guilt and betrayal – betrayal of his well-intentioned aunts, and the English girl he had bigamously married, but above all the betrayal in his abandonment of Angele, his children from that union, and the Indian family who had "adopted" him: "And ever in my heart there was an aching loneliness for the simple kindly people, companions and mentors of my younger days, whose ways had become my ways."[93]

His conflictedness about the trajectory his life was about to follow must have been compounded by the fact that he was simultaneously writing about the "old days" and the "simple kindly people" who figured in them just as he was about to embark upon a new career in which the "old ways" would be abandoned. Archie at this point had recognized the power of his gift as a writer to validate his constructed identity, but the introspection and reflection that his writing demanded resulted in a self-examination that created anguish and self-doubt. The process of producing his first book, an "autobiographical" account which would prove so appealing to his readers, coincided with the deepest loneliness he had ever known as he watched his beaver in the cabin he had shared with Anahareo. The fact that the Grey Owl legend he had constructed was soon to be presented as fact to a broad readership in England and elsewhere would also lead to the increasing danger that his true identity would be exposed.

While a number of passages in *Pilgrims* echo the sombre introspection that went into the writing of *The Men of the Last Frontier*, there are also playful, light-hearted references to impostor figures that echo deceptions he himself had practised as he went about constructing his Indian identity. Grey Owl is here parodying his own autofiction. There is "Tommy Saville, the White Indian, adopted by the Ojibways when young."[94] Then there is a man he meets in Cabano, with whom

Archie alias Grey Owl shares numerous predilections: "In town I met one Indian … He had a broad Cockney accent, and a large repertoire of shanty songs which he rendered most entertainingly. He was more or less of a hobo and was well versed in his art … I had him stay with me a while … But he was afflicted with what he termed 'itchy feet,' a malady which could only be alleviated by the soothing contact of long stretches of railroad ties, applied at regular intervals. So one morning, with one of his small baskets filled with supplies, he set out, bound for no particular place, singing happily as he went, a piece of drift flung from the spinning flywheel of Modernity, a shred of waste material spewed from the Machine that would some day engulf us all."[95]

And there is also a Micmac Indian from New Brunswick, "an accomplished liar" and, like Archie Belaney/Grey Owl, a spell-binding storyteller. In describing him, Archie seems to be mocking the credulousness of his own readers as he weaves his tales of the Indians and the wilderness:

> His name was, we will say, Joe Isaac. He was actually called some other biblical appellation, but I refrain from using it here out of respect for his feelings, should he ever peruse this account. However, he read, he said, nothing but the best of literature, so that leaves me fairly safe. In my wanderings I have met numbers of pretty fair liars, artistic and otherwise, and of these he was by far the most accomplished. He was a natural and to the manner born; one of those men who holds you in a kind of trance, and whom you must believe as you hear him, even though after you escaped the spell gradually wore off, and you began to see the light … His experiences seemed a little crowded for his apparent years, but by careful calculation on that basis we were able to compute his age at about one hundred and eighteen. Altogether a man of parts.[96]

Underlying the light-hearted self-parody contained in the descriptions of these colourful characters, however, is the uneasiness at the possibility of exposure. In one passage, describing a highly successful lecture on conservation in a small Quebec community, one senses this fear even in the apparent harmlessness of Archie's statement: "On our last night, a missionary of the Canadian Bible Society, an old acquaintance whom [*sic*] I had not known was present, rose at the close of my farewell speech, and told how he had known us in the far North, and established without doubt our identity."[97] The passage that follows suggests this uneasiness, but also that there may be a certain complicity in Archie's deception on the part of some of his listeners:

> To these people, each and every one of them, who so accepted us without endorsement of any kind, mountebanks as we must at first have seemed to them, I owe a debt of gratitude that no words written or spoken, could convey. I had not known that people could be so kind. And when one courtly, gracious lady, high in the society of a large city, said to us in parting that we had taught the people something, I remembered the words of an Eastern prophet of whom I had once read and replied, tritely, perhaps, but none the less sincerely, "Have I taught? – then have I also learned."
>
> And there was more meaning in my answer than perhaps she ever guessed.[98]

THE ADVENTURES OF SAJO AND HER BEAVER PEOPLE

Grey Owl's enchanting children's book *The Adventures of Sajo and Her Beaver People* was written for his and Anahareo's daughter Dawn. It recounts the adventures of two Indian children, Sajo, the little girl, and Shapian, her older brother, who lose and then recover two beaver kits their father has rescued and given them as pets. The story ends with the children releasing the young beaver back into the wild where their father had found them, and where the beaver are reunited with their parents.

When read in the light of Grey Owl's biography, a number of elements in this children's tale that ends so happily evoke significant features of Grey Owl's own troubled past. While some of these elements resemble, or correspond to, people and events in Grey Owl's life, others may be seen as displacements of certain circumstances in the childhood and youth of Archie Belaney. Taken together, these quasi-biographical parallels create paradigmatic family configurations suggesting that with this story, Grey Owl was (whether consciously or not) re-writing the most traumatic events in his life. *Sajo*, it can be argued, reveals the same autofictional quality as Grey Owl's "autobiographical" writings. A number of elements in the story can be seen to represent both fulfilment of childhood desires denied – the presence of the parents who had abandoned him – and atonement for his own abandonment of the children he had fathered with Angele and Marie Girard.

The resemblances between key figures and circumstances in the *Sajo* tale and Grey Owl's biography are easy to establish. In the children's story, the mother is dead, a circumstance that parallels the absence of Archie Belaney's mother, who had abandoned her son. (Grey Owl repeatedly claimed to be an orphan.[99]) The description of the children's father, "a tall, gracefully built man with keen dark eyes, and long black hair that fell in two braids over his shoulders,"[100] is a faithful portrait of Grey Owl as he looked "in the old days." His characterization as a loving, caring father who absents himself from his children only in order to be able to provide for them can be seen as a re-engendering of the father as the kind of figure who can fulfil Archie Belaney's childhood desire for the approval, love, and above all presence of his father, but also as an idealized reincarnation of the wayward and irresponsible Grey Owl himself, who has abandoned his own children. Just as young Archie Belaney had recreated himself as the son of a frontier fighter and an Apache chieftain's daughter to compensate for his real parents' absence and abandonment, the aging Grey Owl "corrects" the deficiencies and lacks that had traumatized him as a child, and also his own inadequacies as a father.

The depiction of the beaver kits as almost-human "little brothers" in their suffering and bewilderment when they are separated from their parents, and then their sense of solitude and abandonment when they are separated from their playmates and each other, is an apt rendering of the anguish and loneliness little Archie endured as he was growing up parentless in the severe household of his aunts that to him had seemed a kind of prison. Chikanee, the beaver kit who has been sold to a zoo (and thus is literally imprisoned in a cage), never quite gives up hope that he will be reunited with his playmates (Sajo and Shapian, who symbolically can also be seen as parent figures to the two beaver) and his brother Chilawee: somehow, he thinks, they will come to rescue him, and "all these hard times would be forgotten."[101]

In reading *Sajo* as a projection of wish-fulfilment of the most ardent desires of the author, it is significant that the story does not end with the rescue of Chikanee and his reunion with his brother and his loving owners and surrogate parents, Sajo and Shapian, but with a return to his "true" home, the "home-pond of the Beaver people," where both young beaver are welcomed by their real parents. This joyful reunion does not occur spontaneously, but is brought about in response to the beaver call of Gitchie Meegwon (the children's father), which he is able to reproduce as convincingly as Archie Belaney had been able to imitate the hooting of an owl.

The story dramatizes the fulfilment of Archie Belaney/Grey Owl's ultimate fantasy: the loving acceptance and acknowledgment of his parents and the ensuing joyful family reunion. It is through the figure of Sajo that this fulfilment is expressed: "Sajo scarcely breathed; it was just what she had hoped for, but had not dared to believe – the beaver father and mother were really coming, at Gitchie Meegwon's call, to meet them! Everything was coming true, *everything* –"[102] While in his other works Grey Owl had created the Indian persona he had fantasized about being from early childhood, in *Sajo and Her Beaver People* he appears in the form of a number of alter egos that allow him to play a multiplicity of roles. There is, first of all, the noble and benevolent father figure who physically resembles his author, Grey Owl. Sajo and Shapian can both be seen as extensions of little Archie Belaney, whose efforts throughout the story are bent on being reunited with the (lost) beaver and also on pleasing their father. But it is the beaver kits who, in their helplessness and bewilderment when they are "lost," abandoned, given up, or separated, most poignantly incarnate alter egos of Archie Belaney as he experienced his childhood.

This children's book further enhanced Grey Owl's image as a dedicated conservationist and a gifted writer. In Britain alone, *The Adventures of Sajo and Her Beaver People*, also published by Lovat Dickson, was a huge commercial success, selling 1,000 copies a week.[103] *Pilgrims of the Wild* was also continuing to sell very well. Convinced that the author's charismatic persona would win over even more readers and further augment sales, Dickson invited the eminent conservationist to give a lecture tour overseas, proposing an itinerary that would cover much of Great Britain.

GREY OWL CONQUERS BRITAIN

By 1935, Grey Owl's fame was such that many of his British lecture-performances – of which he gave up to three a day – were sold out. The British public knew and loved his books, and welcomed their author as a star. The celebrated Canadian conservationist known as Grey Owl drew crowds that numbered in the thousands, most of whom had no doubt read his *Pilgrims of the Wild*, 35,000 copies of which had been sold in Britain within three months of publication.[104]

In London, Grey Owl stayed with Dickson, his British publisher, who was familiar with Canada, having worked in a mining camp near Jasper and then studied at the University of Alberta. Dickson acted as impresario for the Grey Owl tour. During his stay in Britain, Archie never once let his guard down, for after spending weeks in his company, Dickson remained convinced of the Grey Owl legend although in fact he knew little about the man's origins: "All he had let drop were a few principal details. He said that his father, a Scotsman named George MacNeill [sic], had been an Indian scout in the wars against the Indians in the south-western United States in the 1870s. His mother had been Katherine Cochise of the Jacarilla band of the Apache tribe."[105] In short, Grey Owl had reiterated his old story, including that his father had spent time in Britain with his friend Bill Cody and his Buffalo Bill Wild West Show, a possible alibi with which Grey Owl could explain his English connections. In May 1936, Dickson published a captivating profile of Grey Owl, consistent with what Grey Owl had told him, in *The Strand Magazine* under the title "Grey Owl, Man of the Wilderness."[106]

There can be little doubt that Grey Owl's phenomenal success as a speaker and media darling owed as much to his exotic and charismatic Indian persona as to his passionate advocacy of the wilderness, expressed, according to the Manchester *Guardian*, "with the nasal twang of the Canadian Indian." The *Sunday Express* observed that "[t]here never came a Redder Red Indian to Britain."[107]

Unbeknownst to the journalists who were so enthusiastically chronicling his speaking tour and documenting his spectacular public success, Grey Owl's visit to England was, above all, a personal triumph. His acclaim in England as the Indian Grey Owl marked the ultimate realization of the cherished fantasy of Archibald Belaney, born and raised in Hastings, England. The accolades of Grey Owl by the British press had legitimized the Indian identity he had claimed from childhood, before the very eyes of his former neighbours, the classmates who had once taunted him, and the two people whose approval mattered most to him: the aunts who had raised him.

His performance as Grey Owl-the-Indian-on-tour in Hastings, with his aunts and former associates watching in the audience, was consummate. Smith gives this account of the event: "The audience took their seats for the afternoon performance. The theatre darkened. A gramophone, unseen behind the platform, played classical music. Then a lone spotlight revealed a tall, dark, hawk-faced man, clad in moccasins and buckskins, with a single eagle feather in his hair. He walked across the stage as if it were forest moss under his feet. The opening bars of Beethoven's 'Moonlight Sonata' played until the spotlit figure raised his hand, saluting the audience of 1,400 people with the Indian greeting 'How Kola.'"[108]

On stage, his mask intact, the performance of Archie Belaney as Grey Owl proved irresistible. As Smith observes: "The 'red Indian' looked exactly as his audience in the English seaside resort of Hastings imagined he would. The British press had already commented on his poise and dignity. Shortly after his arrival in Britain, the London *Times* reported: 'A picturesque figure in Indian dress, with the thoughtful face of the philosopher, Grey Owl comes as the friend of nature.'"[109]

Nevertheless, the greeting "How Kola" and the use of Beethoven's "Moonlight Sonata" as a background for his performances did raise some eyebrows. An Oxford ethnologist attended one of Grey Owl's lecture-performances and observed that "How Kola" was a Sioux phrase, not used by the tribes Grey Owl associated himself with, the Ojibwa and the Apache. And when questioned by a journalist about his use of Beethoven in his lectures, Grey Owl claimed that listening to Beethoven was a kind of Indian tradition: "I love classical music. Wherever you find an Indian camp, you will find a gramophone and a pile of records, most of them of Beethoven."[110]

But in the face of Grey Owl's passionate performances and their seemingly irresistible appeal to huge, spell-bound audiences, any doubts as to his authenticity melted away. The tour was a triumph, as Grey Owl was well aware. On the passage back to Canada, he was already working on sections of *Tales of an Empty Cabin*, the book that was to be his last.

BACK IN CANADA

Before returning to Beaver Lodge after his British tour, Grey Owl made stops in Montreal, Ottawa, and Toronto. The brief Toronto sojourn almost undid him, for a newspaper there had published news of his hugely successful tour in Britain and his presence in Toronto, whereupon he found himself confronted with shadows from his past.

Arthur Stevens, the justice of the peace who had married Archie and Angele at Temagami and to whom Ivy Holmes, Archie's English wife, had written to help her obtain a divorce, turned up at the home of Grey Owl's Toronto hosts, as did former associates of Archie's from Bisco, who knew about Archie's liaison with Marie Girard. These visitors knew Archie's true identity, but they did not contradict the legend he had built, and he readily acknowledged his association with them in Temagami and Bisco, respectively, in fact calling on them to corroborate colourful adventures from his past in front of his Toronto hosts. Yet the question of whether these visitors would or would not expose his true identity put Archie on edge. His Canadian publisher Hugh Eayrs later wrote to Lovat Dickson: "He gives us the impression of being actually afraid of folk he meets in Toronto, and that has been plain on each occasion."[111]

But his agitation was due not only to the fear of exposure: the unbidden visitors would also have evoked memories of traumatic periods in his past – his relations with Angele and Marie Girard and the children he had fathered with them, his sense of guilt and failure at abandoning them, and also his bigamous marriage with Ivy Holmes, whom he had deceived and betrayed. What should have been a triumphant return to Canada was further marred by a newspaper interview he gave in which he claimed that Indian rites and beliefs were as valid as Christian ones. The piously Protestant journalist to whom he gave the interview was outraged, and he sensationalized and misquoted Grey Owl's statements. Although the article was toned down before publication and the journalist made to apologize to Grey Owl, it still drew angry reactions from a number of citizens of Toronto, a city where "Sunday-school attendance [led] the nation, possibly the world."[112]

In those few brief days in Toronto, Grey Owl had had to confront figures from his past, people who could challenge his legend. He had also been forced to confront his own demons. And he had made enemies.

Even back at Beaver Lodge, Grey Owl was beginning to show the strains resulting from constant public appearances as an Indian, from the fear of exposure, and from his isolated life. One of his notebooks of 1936 contains a draft of a letter to a Parks commissioner in which he complains of his life at Beaver Lodge as a kind of imprisonment: "Can't go on with this frustrated, dried out, saintly, unfulfilled, static vegetating life. I am an idol in a niche, & getting to be as full of ideas.

My mind is empty, my soul shrivelling in that hard, avaricious, narrow-minded, (European) farmers West. Jealousy & meanness. Beaver Lodge is truly a refuge, but is at times a cell!!"[113]

Nevertheless he continued to pursue his efforts to promote conservation of the Canadian wilderness. One of his projects was to find funding for a film on the Mississagi River area, in the Algoma and Sudbury districts of northern Ontario. To that end, he was lobbying the governor-general and Ottawa politicians. Whilst in Ottawa on this mission, he went on a drinking binge that came to the attention of the Parks Board, his employer, and almost got him fired. Hearing that his daughter Dawn was seriously ill in Prince Albert, he returned to Saskatchewan and to Beaver Lodge, but once there he continued his binge drinking. In his excited, inebriated state, he broke with Anahareo, who, in spite of her absences, had remained his partner and companion. Desperately lonely, Grey Owl now sought to re-establish links with his old aunts, writing to Hastings authorities to ask for their address,[114] all the while working on the manuscript of *Tales of an Empty Cabin*, the title of which evokes his loneliness, his "cabin" without Anahareo.

TALES OF AN EMPTY CABIN

Tales of an Empty Cabin consists of a series of essays and tales describing life in the wild and the threatening loss of the wilderness, including the disappearance of "the old ways" of the Native peoples and the trappers. In his preface, Grey Owl describes his conversion from those "old ways" to conservation in Biblical terms: "ultimately I laid aside my rifle and my traps and like Paul, worked for the betterment of those whom I had so assiduously persecuted."[115] It seems clear that Archie Belaney, in constructing an archetypal Indian persona, was not deliberately incorporating Christian values and Bible stories into his "autobiographical" narrative. In this account of his conversion from Native hunter and trapper to (Native) conservationist, the Biblical allusions create a sort of discursive dissonance. Like the cathedral metaphors in *The Men of the Last Frontier*, their effect is to undercut the Indian persona he had constructed in his public performances, interviews, and personal interactions with publishers, employers, and admirers.

Although some colloquialisms occur throughout the book, mainly in accounts of humorous anecdotes, all but one of the texts gathered in the collection are written in the voice of a well-educated narrator. Yet a number of passages in the preface disingenuously profess Grey Owl's inadequacy as a writer. Underlying these professions, however, is a sense of real vulnerability and of impending catastrophe that is determined as much by his imposture and the risk of exposure as by the threat of the loss of the wilderness and the animals that dwell in it: "I fear my kinsfolk, human and animal, are leaning on a reed that if not quite broken, at least bends at times quite dangerously ... Most aspiring authors get their punishment at the very outset; mine, no doubt, will come later when it will hit the hardest, and I am waiting for the crash any time now."[116] He continues in this vein: "my greenness as a writer may serve after all, as a protective colouring, and will mingle well with the foliage of the forest in which I may yet have reason to wish that I had stayed."[117]

It is as if the mature Grey Owl, sensing that his remaining days are numbered (in fact he would die two years after the publication of *Tales*), is taking stock of his life, tracing it through elegiac evocations of the now-empty cabin at Abitibi, where he had spent happy times with Anahareo, to the description of his present life surrounded by animals of the wilderness at Lake Ajawaan, the site of his beloved Beaver Lodge.

Yet he can not resist including in this collection a piece titled "The Letter," presumably a letter Archie Belaney wrote to a nurse in London who had cared for him for months after his war injury, and with whom he had corresponded after returning to Canada.[118] Riddled with spelling and grammatical errors, the letter contains a detailed description of the life of a semi-literate "half-breed" in the wilds of Canada. Grey Owl's brief introduction to "The Letter" in this volume of elegant and at times poetic prose indicates that its inclusion represents a nod to the irrepressible young Archie Belaney of old, passing himself off as an Indian: "This epistle was written by a North American Indian, an ex-sniper for the Canadian Expeditionary Force in France during 1915–17. It was addressed to a nurse in an English hospital, where the Indian had lain recovering from his wounds, previous to being sent back to Canada for discharge. It is interesting to note the contrast, amounting almost to a conflict, between his original style and spelling, and that resulting from his attempts at self-education. The newly acquired erudition stands out rather incongruously in spots and was, happily, beyond the power of the writer to maintain throughout."[119] The author's playful reference to his "acquired erudition" resulting from his "self-education" is ambiguous, as it could refer to Belaney/Grey Owl's "self-education" in the ways of the wilderness or to his (ostensible) "self-education" as a man of letters.

"The Letter" evokes the Archie Belaney of old in the process of claiming Indian identity. Its inclusion, accompanied by an ironic prefatory commentary, in *Tales*, like the protective forest camouflage evoked in the preface, suggests that Grey Owl was aware that his exposure might be imminent, and that he was now prepared to let the chips fall where they might.

In summer of 1936, Grey Owl was looking forward to a Great Plains Indian meeting to be held near Saskatoon. He attended the meeting, oblivious to the fact that his participation in the dance performance in honour of Governor-General Lord Tweedsmuir had given him away as a non-Indian. Years later, an Indian who had attended the entire meeting commented on the Indians' reaction to Grey Owl's dancing: "It was at this dance that people recognized Grey Owl as not having the genre and ethos of an Indian. He looked awkward and out of place as he danced with the rest."[120]

According to Smith, the Indians did not expose the fake Indian "because they knew that he was on their side."[121] Grey Owl, for his part, revelled in what he supposed to be Indian belief in his assumed identity: "that trip to Carlton where I was received and given recognition by my own kind of people, somehow rejuvenated me, rolled back the years of my younger days, gave me a lift; it was something I wanted for so long: the approval of my own king [kind]. I spoke in council before 43 Chiefs (as computed) and several hundred men, and was cheered and applauded all through. That meant a lot to me ... I have that to remember and I am wrapped up in my work here. I realize more perhaps than I ever did, that I have a place to maintain in the public eye, a trust to fulfil, not only to the public, *but to my own people who have at last, and in a big way, acknowledged me.*"[122]

In the fall of 1936, Grey Owl was scheduled to appear at the Toronto book fair, the first to be held in Canada. His address was a huge success, and his new book, *Tales of an Empty Cabin*, was selling very well. During his stay in Ottawa earlier that year, Archie alias Grey Owl had met an attractive young French-Canadian woman, Yvonne Perrier, with whom he reconnected during his visit to Ontario in the fall. At the end of November 1936, he married her in Montreal under the name of Archie McNeil. Like the marriage to Ivy Holmes, this was a bigamous marriage, as his union with Angele, from whom he never divorced, had been legal. Yvonne clearly had no idea of Archie's true identity. After his death, she recounted his version of his antecedents and important events in his life as he must have told it to her to the Regina *Leader-Post*.[123]

But by now, Grey Owl's identity was known. A reporter from the North Bay *Nugget* interviewing Grey Owl mentioned the name Archie Belaney in connection with Temagami, from which Archie alias Grey Owl correctly deduced that the reporter knew that he was a fraud. Although Grey Owl immediately ended the interview, he knew he was found out. The editor of the *Nugget* in fact had learned of Grey Owl's true identity two years earlier, when a reporter followed up a tip leading to Angele, who described Archie Belaney as an Englishman to whom she was still married. Although he knew the truth, the editor held the story. Like the Indians at the Great Plains meeting the year before, he was cheering for Grey Owl and did not expose him.

Two more Grey Owl films were planned, directed, and produced by Grey Owl himself.[124] One was shot in the winter of 1937 in the Abitibi region (*The Trail – Winter*), the other in the Mississauga Forest Reserve in the summer of the same year (*The Trail – Summer*). Once the filming was finished, Grey Owl and Yvonne spent time in Toronto while the film was being edited, with Grey Owl's drinking again out of control. Grey Owl and Yvonne stopped at Bisco both on the way to and from the film locations. Inevitably, they met members of the Espaniel family (Alex, whom Grey Owl had referred to as "Dad," had died), who knew his true background. After the filming, Grey Owl insisted on putting on a war dance in Bisco. According to the Espaniels, the Indians in the audience were "silently amused."[125]

While in Toronto to edit *The Trail – Summer*, Grey Owl was invited by the Indian Defense League of America to join their group in crossing the Canada-US border, a symbolic assertion of the Indians' right to freedom of movement between the two countries. On this occasion, Yvonne was adopted into the Iroquois Beaver clan and given the name "Silver Moon."

THE SECOND BRITISH TOUR

In September 1937 Grey Owl, with Yvonne alias Silver Moon, set off for Britain for another lecture tour. In London, where he stayed for a month, Grey Owl gave a total of fifty lectures to sell-out crowds. Yvonne was introduced as his secretary to avoid disclosure of Grey

Owl's separation from Anahareo, who was popular with his British readers and audiences – they knew her from Grey Owl's books, and some had seen her in the beaver films.

After a harrowing tour throughout England, with daily lectures, Grey Owl was invited to give a Royal Command Performance at Buckingham Palace. The performance was followed by conversation with the royal family and an invitation to stay for tea. Dickson wrote to Hugh Eayrs describing the event:

> We had the lecture in the Throne Room, which had been specially fitted up with two 35 mm. projectors. The King and Queen were there, the two Princesses, Queen Mary, and the Earl and Countess of Strathmore, the Queen's father and mother as well as a number of other people attached to the Court. I had instructed Grey Owl how to begin his address, and he started off in grand style with "Your Majesties, your Royal Highnesses," but when we left the King three hours later – for we were with him that long – Grey Owl said, putting out his hand, "Well, good-bye, Brother, and good luck to you," and the King's face broke into a really genuine smile as he thanked him.[126]

Inevitably, Grey Owl's appearances in England heightened the risk that people who had known him from childhood might come forward and that his true identity might thus be exposed. In Oxford, Grey Owl's mother visited him in his hotel. She approached him for money, and he gave her a ticket to his evening lecture performance. Yvonne, who knew nothing of this English mother, was nonplussed by her appearance, but Kittie did not expose her son, saying only that she was "closely related to Grey Owl."[127] In Hastings, where Grey Owl had specifically asked to give a lecture, his old friend George McCormick's sister was in the audience and recognized Grey Owl as Archie Belaney, but like Kittie, she did not expose him.

Grey Owl's motive in wishing to appear in Hastings was certainly to see his aunts, whom he introduced to Yvonne as "aunties" whom he knew from the time he had spent in England during the war. Both Ada and Carrie were too frail to attend Grey Owl's evening lecture, but he visited them at their home, with Yvonne, the next morning. The conversation must have been somewhat one-sided, Archie/Grey Owl basking in the glory of his successful performance at Buckingham Palace, ultimate proof that the wayward nephew his aunts had raised had made good. Realizing that Yvonne had no inkling of their nephew's true past, the aunts were unable to talk to him freely about old times, as they must have yearned to do. They, like Archie/Grey Owl himself, would have known that this would be the last time the relatives would meet.

THE LAST TOUR

On his return to North America at the beginning of 1938, Grey Owl embarked on a three-month tour of Canada and the United States. The tour ended in early April, with both Grey Owl and Yvonne in a state of total exhaustion. A few days after reaching Beaver Lodge, Grey Owl was hospitalized, and he succumbed to pneumonia a few days later.

Immediately after his death, the North Bay *Nugget* revealed his English identity, based mainly on Angele's statements. Shortly thereafter, a Hastings newspaper researched his biography locally, publishing further details about Archie Belaney alias Grey Owl and corroborating Angele's story.

Public reaction to the news that Grey Owl was a fraud ranged from disbelief on the part of his British publisher Lovat Dickson to venomous outrage. The Nova Scotia writer Thomas Raddall viciously parodied Grey Owl's imposture in a short story titled "Bald Eagle."[128] But there was also amusement. Many of the Canadian press articles and editorials about Grey Owl's exposure were written in a comical vein: "A great chuckle has gone right across Canada at the suggestion that the national leg has been well and truly pulled."[129] But the great impostor was unanimously praised for his extraordinary contribution as a writer and conservationist. Anahareo, however, summed up the tragic dimensions of his deception: "When, finally, I was convinced that Archie was English, I had the awful feeling for all those years I had been married to a ghost, that the man who now lay buried at Ajawaan was someone I had never known, and that Archie Belaney had never really existed."[130]

Almost sixty years after Grey Owl's death, Armand Garnet Ruffo, a descendant of Alex Espaniel, published a poetic biography titled *Grey Owl: The Mystery of Archie Belaney*.[131] Ruffo puts his finger on emotional and psychological elements in Archie Belaney's biography that led to his metamorphosis into Grey Owl. Ruffo's poems link the pain of Archie's abandonment by his parents, particularly his father, with his imaginary images of his father's life among the Apaches in Mexico and the southwestern United States, a people bloodied and humiliated by the Europeans. Ruffo suggests that Archie was much affected by Cochise's personal story, identifying passionately with the Apache chief's loneliness and loss of his parents.[132]

Alluding to the fact that Archie deliberately obscured his familial relationship with his aunts, at times explaining their role in his life as that of kindly elderly women whom he had met in England during the war, at times describing them as distant relatives who had come to hear of him and admired him, Ruffo points out that Archie nevertheless never denied them. As Ruffo succinctly observes, "Who he denies is Archibald Belaney."[133]

As Rosenthal points out, Ruffo's Grey Owl poems also reveal the degree to which the representation of Indian culture had come to consist of European projections: "Ruffo reminds us that with the first contact between white settlers and indigenous cultures authenticity had become impossible because from then on whites read into Indian cultures whatever they needed to see." Thus, Rosenthal argues, Ruffo's poem "Romantic" portrays Grey Owl's imposture as a "Trojan horse, showing how Belaney played on stereotypes and white reader expectations to transmit his message, which, however, is Native, regardless of the ethnic identity of its messenger."[134] The concluding lines of the poem read as follows:

I say if they want romance
                    give it to them.
If they expect beads and braids
                    Give it to them.
Butter the facts.
Spread it thick.
The point is
To get the message
Across,
Isn't it?[135]

Another of Ruffo's Grey Owl poems that astutely sums up how the people to whom Grey Owl claimed to belong viewed their friend and advocate may stand as a fitting epitaph to the great impostor:

We know Wa-Sha-Quon-Asin is not born of us, and we say nothing.

For us it is of no importance. We do not waste our words
but save them, because we know in this struggle of generations
they are our strongest medicine. This man flies for us true and
sharp, and we are thankful he has chosen our side. While
we cheer, and the elders nod in approval, we can see the light
shine in his face. This is good. This is how it should be,
to feel good about yourself and your duty in the honourable way
Wa-Sha-Quon-Asin, we say, dance with us, as you can.[136]

EPILOGUE

Archie Belaney's claim to be part Indian was initially a vehicle that allowed him to escape the humiliations and lacks of his biographical identity. The persona he created was inspired in part by fantasies of his absent father, whom he pictured living in the wild frontier West of America, and in part by the nature and adventure stories he read as a boy. How strongly he identified with the heroes of the tales he read is evident even in his last book, *Tales of an Empty Cabin*: in the piece titled "The Mission of Hiawatha," the narrator implicitly lays claim to the legacy of Longfellow's poetic hero and the historical figure who inspired him.[137]

Yet Grey Owl never claimed to be a full-blooded Indian, saying he was a half-breed. But in focusing on his "Indian" side, the Grey Owl persona he had himself created took on a life of its own, beyond his own claims and expectations, with press accounts describing him as a full-blooded Indian. Anahareo, recounting Grey Owl's dismissive reaction to one such report, writes: "Had Archie known how seriously people were going to take his ancestry, this would have been the time to have clamped down on that 'full-blooded Indian' stuff. But how was he to know that the more he wrote, the more Indian he became in the eyes of the public?"[138]

It is possible that Archie Belaney really thought, as Dickson contends, that there was a mystery surrounding his parentage – that Aunt Ada had withheld some crucial elements of his past from her nephew.[139] Archie's claims to be a "half-breed" may have been at least partially grounded in Aunt Ada's secretiveness concerning his father's whereabouts, both before and after his son's birth, leading Archie to speculate that he was not Kittie's child, but born of an Indian mother, whom his father might have encountered in his travels in the American West. What role Archie's suspicions about his origins played in his imposture cannot be ascertained – Dickson does not document his contentions.

It can certainly be argued that Grey Owl clung to the duality expressed in his self-created identity: he was a half-breed, part white man, part Indian. The role of the parents he had created for himself – a dare-devil adventurer for a father, an Apache princess for a mother – was eclipsed by a large extended family in the Ojibwa who had adopted him. Like Felix Paul Greve, he refused to accept the constraints of the circumstances into which he was born by creating a legend, and subsequently living it out.

He was determined to choose his identity, to control his destiny: "Don't let the circumstances make you – you make the circumstances. Be the captain of your own destiny" was one of his favourite sayings.[140]

Archie Belaney's transformation into Grey Owl can be seen, among other things, as an act of redemption of the romantic Other Self that was all but stifled by the little English gentleman his Aunt Ada was trying to make of him. In assuming the persona of his Indian alter ego, Grey Owl, Archie Belaney came not only to escape his hateful past, but also to live the life he desired and for which he felt he was destined. What he had not foreseen was that his imposture would make him not only the advocate and spokesman *par excellence* for "the Indian," but for the Canadian wilderness itself, and that Grey Owl's mission of conservation, which he promoted in his films, his lectures, and above all in his books, would resonate around the world.

4

Will James: A Lone Cowboy from Quebec

His race towards the sunset
Was the high and lonesome kind
Like coyote always looking back
He left no tracks behind

Ian Tyson, "The Ballad of Will James"

ERNEST DUFAULT / WILL JAMES

When the famous American Western writer and artist Will James died in a Hollywood hospital in 1942, of the effects of alcoholism, only a handful of friends and relatives were aware that the revered author of classic cowboy tales such as *Smoky the Cowhorse*, *Lone Cowboy*, and *Home Ranch* was in fact a French-Canadian from Quebec, whose real name was Ernest Dufault. The fifteen-year-old Ernest had boarded a train and left Quebec in 1907, carrying ten dollars and a bagful of cookies as his only assets, bound for an imprecise destination: the West. When he died at the age of fifty, he had realized his dream of becoming a frontier cowboy in the tradition of the Old West, and he had also developed the artistic gifts others had recognized in him early on – his talents for drawing and storytelling.[1]

His initially innocent tale-telling in the persona of Will James, born in Montana, took an irreversible and catastrophic turn when, against all odds, it made him famous. As the personification of the lone cowboy of Western legend he published and illustrated over twenty books, novels, and collections of short stories, including the "autobiographical" *Lone Cowboy*. A number of his books were filmed by major Hollywood studios, and as a sought-after speaker on the Old West he became the toast of New York and Hollywood and all points in between. Exposure of his true identity would have put a quick and scandalous end to his brilliant career. What he may have feared even more, however, is that it would have invalidated the legend of the Old West which he had come to personify and represent – indeed, which he had had a large part in creating. So terrified was he of exposure that when he wrote his will in 1940, two years before his death, he made a cardinal slip, bequeathing his residual estate not to his brother Auguste Dufault, as he had intended, but to "Ernest Dufault," that is, to himself.

Unlike the works of Felix Paul Greve/Frederick Philip Grove or Archie Belaney/Grey Owl, not a single one of Will James's books contains the slightest allusion, however oblique, to his true origins. Will James deliberately and systematically covered his tracks, both literally, in the geographic sense, and metaphorically, in the biographical one. Commenting on the absence of any geographical points of reference in James's "autobiography," *Lone Cowboy*, Ross Santee, a friend and associate of James's and a noted Western artist and author himself, criticizes this deliberate imprecision: "Goddam it, states have names, and when a cowboy works for an outfit the brand is known."[2] What is more, Ernest Dufault, who had both parents, three sisters, and two brothers as well as a large extended family living in Quebec, reiterates time and time again, in the "autobiographical" *Lone Cowboy*, that he is an orphan and has no living family.

To the last, Ernest Dufault alias Will James lived in fear that his true identity would be discovered. Astonishingly, given the problematic error in his will and the ensuing legal difficulties, and also given the fact that not only his heir and brother Auguste but also his mother outlived him, the Will James legend remained intact for over twenty years after his death. It was not until the 1960s that Anthony Amaral, in preparing a biographical study of the famous cowboy writer's later years, stumbled upon the flawed will, searched further, and published what he had found in a full biography: *Will James: The Gilt Edged Cowboy*. Amaral's biography of Will James, published by a relatively obscure western press, initially had little effect on the reception of either the author or his oeuvre. To the general public, and even in standard reference works, Will James remained the cowboy author, born and bred in the Old West, that he had made himself out to be.

Thus, almost forty years after his death, the 1981 edition of the *Encyclopedia Americana*, for example, contains no mention of his true origins and antecedents, giving his birthplace as being near Great Falls, Montana.

The discovery of his true identity did not, however, solve the enigma of Will James. Attempts to explain the young Québécois Ernest Dufault's metamorphosis into the Western American cowboy Will James range from the banal and simplistic to the ideological. Judith Dudar for instance maintains that Ernest Dufault was a boy who liked to play cowboy and who simply "did not outgrow [this] desire,"[3] while Jacques Cardinal argues that Dufault's new identity represents an attempt to re-write the Self as an Other in history, that it is "the enactment of a massive transfer to the other as the site of truth of the subject's desire," a transfer that reflects less a rupture of the subject with his original (Québécois) identity but rather an appropriation of the Other, in which nevertheless the (Québécois) Self as subsumed in his name is obliterated.[4]

Culture critic Taras Grescoe proposes a more pragmatic explanation, observing that there has always been a fascination with the West in Quebec, a fascination that continues to this day. In *Sacré Blues: An Unsentimental Journey through Quebec*, Grescoe describes the huge popularity of Western festivals in rural Quebec, including one which is the biggest such event to be held in Canada, apart from the Calgary Stampede. Nor is this Québécois predilection for the North American Far West restricted to the rural milieu: in Paris to interview Louis-Bertrand Robitaille, a long-time European correspondent for Montreal's *La Presse*, Robitaille greets Grescoe wearing a leather jacket and suede cowboy boots, and looking generally more like an outlaw American than the "bookish European" Grescoe had expected. In the same vein, in the 1987 National Film Board production *Alias Will James*, filmmaker Jacques Godbout frames the Will James story with documentary interviews with contemporary cowboys from Quebec who, like James – but with only a passing knowledge of their famous precursor – have gone west. However, Grescoe's suggestion that the Will James saga (and, by extension, the Québécois fascination with the West) is an illustration of cultural schizophrenia, dramatizing Quebec's position between two worlds, the European and the American, seems a stretch.[5]

Certainly by the late nineteenth and early twentieth centuries, tales of the Wild West and the cowboys and Indians who inhabited it were hugely popular, spawning a burgeoning genre of Western novels written by a host of North American Western writers, many of whom posed as Westerners.[6] Nor was the fascination with the West limited to North America. The French writer François-René de Chateaubriand (1768–1848) had published a travel account (*Voyage en Amérique*) as well as a number of works of fiction (*Atala*, *René*, *Les Natchez*) based on his extended stay in America, during which, he claimed, he had lived with Native American Indian tribes. Although Chateaubriand's romantic accounts of life among the "noble savages" in the remote forests of North America took the French public by storm, his popularity was eclipsed by another European writer who, a few decades later, was to write a series of adventure novels set in the Wild West that continue to enjoy a large and enthusiastic following to this day.

The Western stories of the German writer Karl May (1842–1912) feature a noble Apache chief called Winnetou and his "blood brother" Old Shatterhand, a German immigrant to the United States whose identity, his author claimed, was actually his own. May authenticated his self-created persona with portraits of himself dressed as "Old Shatterhand," taken against exotic backdrops, and by appearing in public with props such as the "Bear Killer" (a Henry Rifle, the fabrication of which he had commissioned from a Dresden rifle maker) that figured prominently in his Western stories. Although May had never set foot in America, and his accounts were pure fabrications, his Wild West adventure tales and his own purported role in them enchanted all who read them, from German school children to the Habsburg emperor (who received May at court in Vienna).

The appeal of May's stories was due, in no small measure, to the general perception that they were "authentic," and that their author had actually experienced the events described: it was indeed possible, it seemed, to escape the constraints of conventional European society (and the grinding, never-ending European wars) by entering the Utopian space of primeval forests and pristine rivers, where German immigrants could become "blood brothers" of noble Native chieftains. In fact, when Karl May finally made his first (and only) journey to America, a few years before he died, he visited only New York, Boston, and Niagara Falls. As one journalist writing to commemorate the centenary of May's death dryly observes, "The man who had called the Wild West his home dutifully completed the tourist circuit, bought souvenirs for himself and his wife, and wrote postcards to Germany."[7]

Whether or not Ernest Dufault had read Chateaubriand or Karl May as a schoolboy in Quebec is not known. However, as part of the French literary canon the works of Chateaubriand would have been available in Quebec's public libraries and may have figured in Quebec school curricula. French editions of Karl May's Winnetou stories were published as early as 1884,[8] and excerpts may have appeared in the popular press, whose images and accounts of life in the Wild West were enthusiastically received, as were the Western movies emerging from the big Hollywood studios.

While Ernest's dream of heading west was likely inspired by the proliferation of picturesque images and dramatic narrative accounts of the western frontier, one can only speculate as to the immediate circumstances or events that led to his assuming his new identity.

All three of his biographers attribute Ernest Dufault's self-reinvention as American cowboy Will James to the fact that he was likely a wanted man in Canada, following his arrest for allegedly killing a sheepherder in an Alberta bar. But this theory hardly explains James's single-minded determination to eradicate all links with his former identity, necessitating a break with his family, to whom he was, by all accounts, a devoted son and brother. Furthermore, the sheepherder incident ended with Ernest's being informed that his supposed murder victim had in fact been killed in another altercation with someone else later that night,[9] presumably clearing Dufault as the killer. Also, Ernest's family claimed that he visited them in Montreal later that same year (1910). It is unlikely that he would have undertaken such a trip if he were wanted for murder in Canada.

Nevertheless Ernest Dufault's recreation of himself as Will James may indeed have been precipitated by the barroom incident that resulted in a death, although the circumstances surrounding the event remain nebulous if not entirely obscure. Later in his life, Will James was, on two occasions and while inebriated, heard to mumble an incoherent story about a "murder in Canada" and "burning down a log cabin jail" to escape.[10] It seems clear that for some time he was on the run for reasons that had nothing to do with the cattle rustling for which he was arrested and served a prison term. In *Lone Cowboy* he describes himself fleeing to Mexico and living "on the dodge," saying that he "even got used to the wrong name [he'd] given" when he started to work for an American cow outfit there.[11] While in *Lone Cowboy* his flight to Mexico is motivated by the risk of capture after a bout of horse stealing, this incident may be one of the many displacements and recontextualizations that characterize so many of the events that he recounts in his "life story."

It is far more likely that Ernest Dufault's metamorphosis into Will James was a more gradual one, initially perhaps meant to be transitional, to help him overcome the obstacles he foresaw in realizing his dream of becoming a frontier cowboy. According to one biography, "His early silences and evasions were obviously attempts to conceal his poor circumstances rather than deliberate moves in a carefully conceived plan to restructure his life."[12] After first leaving home, he wrote harmless postcards to his family in French, inquiring about them and informing them that he was well. Not until 1911 did he send his parents a postcard in which "W.R. James" is written in block letters as a signature, with *Ern* added in script. His later letters to his parents were in English, despite the fact that they did not know the language and would have had to rely on his brother Auguste for translations. In this first "Will James" postcard he gave his location as "Cache County, Jackson, Idaho" whereas its actual name is Cassia County, a presumably inadvertent and intriguing slip, given the meaning of "cache(r)," to hide, in French.

Whatever the plausibility of the outer circumstances that gave rise to his identity change, both his biography and his published works, notably *Lone Cowboy*, indicate that his self-recreation had deeper-lying causes that were rooted in his unwavering desire to head west and experience the American frontier of legend, a frontier that by all accounts had ceased to exist before Ernest Dufault was even born.[13] The cowboy tales and illustrations (and later, films) of the Old West that were so popular around the turn of the century, even in the magazines read by east-coast urbanites, represented a new and other world, a Utopian space on which to project the archetypal yearning for freedom, for new beginnings, for escape from the circumscribed and conventional lives of most North Americans. It is this lost world, as much as his own part as a figure dwelling in it, that Will James seeks to recreate, to make an incontrovertible reality. In the process, he must create a personal past that, on the one hand, lends plausibility and integrity to his accounts of life on the western frontier, from his very birth, and that, on the other hand, allows him to accommodate – to fictionalize – in some way the factual circumstances linking him to his former life. Hence his status as an orphan and the absence of any living family; hence also the invention of the French-Canadian surrogate father figure he calls "Bopy" to explain his lack of

Figure 4.1 The Dufault family, with Ernest next to his father (two Dufault children are missing from the photo)

competence in English and the fact that he is never able to shed his lingering French accent.[14]

THE LEGEND AND THE LIFE

As recounted in his "autobiography," *Lone Cowboy*, Will James was born near the Judith Basin in Montana while his parents were en route from Texas to Canada, planning to establish a "cow outfit" in the "northern cow country" of Alberta.[15] He claims not to remember his mother, of whom he says only that she was a Californian of Spanish and Scottish-Irish descent and that she died shortly after his birth. His father, who James says was born and raised in western Texas and also of "the Scotch-Irish nation," was, according to James, killed – gored by a steer – when Will was only four years old, having entrusted the care of his small son to a French-Canadian trapper by the name of Jean Beaupré. With "Bopy," as his young charge calls him, Will travels throughout the western United States and Canada, spending the summers in "cow country" and the winters on traplines up north. After Bopy's death, Will, now about fourteen, drifts alone from ranch to ranch, eventually becoming a "cow puncher," "horse breaker," and "bronc rider."

At one point, he is imprisoned for cattle rustling. Throughout his young life, on his travels with Bopy and later on his own, he has sketched pictures of his surroundings, particularly of horses, a skill he hones while in prison. After serving his prison term, he resumes his nomadic life until he is severely injured by a "bronc" he is riding, an incident that also loosens all his teeth. While having dental work done in "a city on the west coast" (as has already been pointed out, Will James is careful never to mention place names), he finds a job riding as a stunt man for Western movies for a time, after which he goes "east," where he is hired as a "bronc" rider by a rodeo outfit. He is seriously injured in another riding accident, and no longer able to follow this line of work. When he returns to "the country where he is at home," he finds that he has been drafted, and he is inducted into the United States army. Meanwhile, having continued his drawing, he is able to sell some of his drawings and paintings to magazines. Eventually, he begins to write as well, and becomes an established author and illustrator in the Western genre. Thus ends the story of Will James as he tells it in *Lone Cowboy*.

The true story of the man who called himself Will James reads very differently. In fact, Joseph Ernest Nephtali Dufault was born in the small village of St Nazaire d'Acton in southern Quebec, a region where both sides of his family had been established for generations. His father, Jean-Baptiste Dufault, who had kept a general store in St Nazaire which provided a solid family income, was injured in an accident, necessitating a change of occupation. The family never recovered from this change of circumstance, Jean-Baptiste's attempts at re-establishing himself in various other lines of business in and around Montreal, including one as proprietor of a small hotel in St Hyacinthe, meeting with little success. Ernest thus attended various parochial schools, where he was an average student whose only outstanding ability was his talent for drawing. His pencil sketches of cowboys and horses that he produced from a young age were so lifelike that they astounded his family. Stories and pictures of life on the western frontier were very much in vogue in the periodicals of the time, which little Ernest would have been able to peruse in his father's hotel and elsewhere. Many of these stories would have featured the work of the cowboy artist Charles M. Russell, who was to play a key role in the metamorphosis of Ernest Dufault into Will James. As Ernest grew older, his growing passion for the Wild West manifested itself not only in his sketches but in other, more dramatic ways as well. One of his escapades involved taking a livery horse from a Montreal stable out to the countryside, where he remained in hiding, with the horse, for two days, until the two runaways were found by the authorities who had been searching for them. Later, he used some of the money he earned as a bellboy at a hotel to buy a revolver, with which he practised the fast draw of the frontier and target-shooting in an abandoned quarry, his little brother Auguste watching him in awe.

At the age of fifteen, the lure of the West and his passion to experience it had become so strong that his parents, realizing that he would do so in any case, reluctantly gave him permission to leave. In the summer of 1907, having bought a one-way ticket, he boarded a train for Regina, Saskatchewan, bound for a region where he knew no one, and where his lack of knowledge of English would put him at a serious disadvantage even under the best of circumstances. He spent three years in western Canada, much of it at Val Marie, a small francophone enclave in southern Saskatchewan, working on ranches and literally "learning the ropes" as well as learning English.

The little evidence that exists to document this period of his life indicates that he was, at this point, still "Ernest Dufault." One of his biographers suggests that his decision to move to the United States and to alter his identity may have been motivated by the barroom fight which resulted in Ernest's being arrested and charged with murder. Once he had arrived south of the border, which he likely crossed sometime in 1910 or 1911, Ernest used a series of aliases, including C.W. Jackson, W.R. James, William Roderick James, and Bill James,[16] as he drifted back and forth throughout western America, between Mexico and the Canadian border. In 1914, when he was arrested for cattle rustling, he gave his name as Will Roderick James, his birthplace as Montana. Ironically, it was thus his prison sentence that legally anchored his identity, his status as an American citizen. As of his release from the Carson City penitentiary, on 16 April 1916, his life developed in closer parallel to the events he describes in his "autobiography," including the "bronc" riding, the stint in Hollywood, and his service in the United States army, his army record serving to further underpin and authenticate his American identity. He was demobilized in 1919. Having continued his drawing and even taken some art classes at the California School of Fine Arts in San Francisco, he was able to sell some of his drawings and paintings to magazines, thus launching his artistic career.

In 1920, he married "Miss Nevada," the attractive Alice Conradt, twelve years his junior, of Reno. She was the sister of his friend and fellow cowboy Fred Conradt. The couple lived an unsettled life, with Will James working at various jobs while trying to establish himself as an artist. It was while working on a ranch in New Mexico that he met a distinguished visitor of his employer, who had come to the ranch for a traditional hunting and fishing expedition. Burton Twichell, a dean at Yale University, was intrigued with the artist-cowboy, and offered him a scholarship designed for students with unusual backgrounds. While James actually went to Yale, he did not last long there, being frustrated with the exigencies of formal training and missing the freedom of the west. But his friendship with Twichell lasted a lifetime, Twichell frequently smoothing the way for James through his connections with editors and publishers, notably Scribner's of New York, who became James's publishers.

With the proceeds of his early publications, the Jameses were able to acquire a five-acre property in Nevada, on which they built a cabin, barn, and corrals. When his first novel, *Smoky the Cowhorse*, was published in 1926, it met with instant success, not only winning the prestigious Newbery Medal but also being slated for translation into Danish, Russian, Japanese, Yugoslavian, Swedish, and Dutch. His subsequent publications also enjoyed phenomenal success. There were film offers from Hollywood, and speaking and other celebrity engagements all over the United States. Thus, in the mid-1920s, he was able, with a sizable advance from Scribner's, to buy a 12,000-acre property in Montana,[17] which by 1927 was an operational ranch, with Alice's brother Fred and his wife Dolly in charge of managing it.

In spite of his literary and economic success, the relationship between Will James and his wife Alice was growing increasingly problematic. Alice's desire to have a child was not shared by her husband, who was withdrawing more and more from her. Always a hard drinker, Will's drinking was by now out of control, and his alcohol problem is alluded to in correspondence with Scribner's. In late 1929 he went to New York without Alice, agreeing to meet her in San Francisco. He never showed up there, and Alice ended up having to track him down, finally finding him, in a dissolute condition, on a dude ranch near San Antonio. He urged her to leave him, but she refused, invoking their project of writing his life story, which they had planned to undertake together.

Lone Cowboy, Will James's "life story," was duly written and published, and in the early 1930s the Jameses were in Hollywood, where both *Lone Cowboy* and the earlier novel *Smoky* were to be filmed by major studios. Will was to narrate *Smoky*, but he was so intoxicated when he showed up at the studio that most of his narration could not be used in the film.

The couple began to spend long periods of time apart. While Alice was in Reno with her family, Will went to see his publishers in New York. He subsequently cancelled a scheduled lecture tour and went to Tucson, Arizona, without letting anyone know where he was. There he collapsed, finally wiring his brother-in-law Fred to come for him. By the time Fred arrived, Will had been hospitalized. Alice had him committed to a sanatorium near Los Angeles for treatment for alcoholism.

When he returned to his ranch in Montana, James sobered up enough to write *Home Ranch*, but he was sullen and morose, isolating himself more and more from Fred and Dolly, who were helpless to deal with him. Alice was spending more and more time in Reno with her family, and in 1935 she finally decided to leave him. When James brought a woman to the ranch, who interfered with Fred's management of it, Fred and Dolly and their son Clint, whom Will adored, decided to leave. They never saw Will James again.

Will was now almost entirely isolated. He had lost his wife and all contact with her family, with whom he had a close relationship. His behaviour was growing more and more bizarre. While intoxicated, he sold the huge ranch to a "friend" for one thousand dollars. Quick legal action nullified the sale, but Alice now sought a legal separation. Still, Will managed to work and publish, his books being received with favourable reviews. A review of *In the Saddle with Uncle Bill* (1935) concludes: "To read of Uncle Bill's horsemanship is almost as good as watching a rodeo, particularly when the account is enriched by Will James's picturesque style and illustrated with his remarkable pictures of horses and cowboys in action."[18] A reviewer of *The American Cowboy* (1942), alluding to the twenty-one books by James that had already appeared, adds: "from this reviewer's point of view, he can add as many more books as he likes, provided that he keeps on drawing the pictures for them."[19]

In spring of 1937 he was involved in a car accident, charged with driving while intoxicated, and committed to the Hospital for Inebriates at Warmsprings, Montana. In the nine months he spent there he managed to do some work, but on his release he was subdued, withdrawn, and sullen. He stayed for some time with friends in Billings, where he also owned a small property, the large ranch having been liquidated. He still had some Hollywood contacts, and spent time with film people in Hollywood and Palm Springs, working on *The American Cowboy*, which was to be both a book and a Hollywood film.

In summer of 1942 Alice, who was visiting Los Angeles, felt compelled to look in on her estranged husband. She was greeted by a woman who introduced herself as his secretary. When Will entered the room, she was shocked: he was "thin, decrepit, unkempt, withdrawn,"[20] and Alice was unable to engage him in conversation. Later that summer, Will James was once again hospitalized, and he died a few days later. According to his wishes, his ashes were scattered over his property in Billings.

THE FLAWED WILL

If most of the provisions of his will, including instructions as to the disposal of his remains, were clear and straightforward, there was one paragraph that dramatically illustrates to what point Ernest Dufault had, in his own mind, become his self-created alter ego Will James. For while the legitimacy of the testator's identity as Will James was implicitly reiterated by virtue of a legal document whose terms were consistent with the persona whose "life story" is described in the "autobiographical" *Lone Cowboy*, his inadvertent naming of "Ernest Dufault" (rather than his younger brother Auguste Dufault, as he must have intended) as beneficiary gave rise to a legal action that would unmask its author, revealing his true identity, a situation which James would have sought, at all costs, to avoid. The paragraph reads as follows: "All the rest and residue of said estate … I give, devise and bequeath unto Ernest Dufault, 45 St. Andrew Street, Ottawa, Ontario, Canada, he being the sole heir and survivor of my dear old friend Old Beaupre [*sic*], who raised me and acted as a father to me."[21]

All James biographies consider James's "flawed" will to be crucial in any attempt to determine whether James intended the ultimate exposure of his true identity or, on the contrary, sought to conceal it even in death. Jim Bramlett adheres to the latter theory, quoting from Auguste Dufault's deposition in claiming the estate of his brother:

> I understand how difficult it was for him to decide to write my name down on his will, as that would have aroused curiosity and while he was living to risk letting his true identity leak out, especially after he had written such a book as *Lone Cowboy*. By writing Ernest, instead of Auguste, he might have thought that while living I could easily say that nobody by that name lived here [at the address in Ottawa] and he most likely thought that it would be easy for me, after his death, to have the matter adjusted as common sense shows that the only sensible and reasonable solution to the problem is that in this case "Ernest Dufault" was for "Auguste Dufault."[22]

Anthony Amaral agrees with this position: "James entered his own name on his will. The court could not act upon this paragraph of James' will without first finding Ernest Dufault who, technically, no longer existed. By depositions from Canada, Auguste was forced to prove that Ernest and Will James were the same persons and that, obviously, James had meant to say, Auguste. One point is certain: even in death James wanted to hide his true identity."[23]

While Auguste Dufault and Anthony Amaral argue that Will James may have deliberately inserted the name "Ernest Dufault," William Gardner Bell suggests that James's naming of "Ernest Dufault" as the beneficiary of his will was an inadvertent slip: "In mentioning Jean Beaupré, James appears to have been determined to perpetuate the fictional life story he fashioned when he left Canada and which he later formalized in his autobiography *Lone Cowboy*. But he committed a cardinal error when he designated himself as residual legatee. It was obviously, for whatever reason, a slip: the Ottawa address was that of his brother, and undoubtedly he meant to name Auguste – lifelong confidant and family contact – as his residual heir."[24]

It is difficult to follow Bramlett's, Amaral's, and indeed Auguste's logic in arguing that James may have inserted Ernest's name in the will to avoid exposure. On the contrary: in the depositions necessary to claim his inheritance Auguste would be forced to explain how the name "Ernest" came to be in the will, and this explanation would inevitably lead to the unmasking of Will James as Ernest Dufault. Although Auguste was in the end successful in claiming his brother's estate,[25] the fact that Will James was in fact Ernest Dufault did not become public knowledge until Anthony Amaral published his first James biography in 1967.

Bell's theory of an "inadvertent slip" seems the likelier explanation. The provisions in this part of the will, drawn up in 1940, by which time the persona of Will James had become ever more solidly anchored in over twenty books with unmistakably "autobiographical" first-person narrator/heroes at their centre, seem rather to point to the obliteration of the Self who was Ernest Dufault by the self-created persona of Will James. Yet the latter could not (and perhaps did not seek to) erase entirely the bonds that tied him to his former Self. Will James's link to the Ernest/Auguste named in the will was indeed fraternal, but in the terms of the will it was a link which he himself had fashioned, derived not from the Dufault brothers' biological father, but from the father figure Ernest alias Will James had, in his "autobiography," himself created, namely the French-Canadian trapper Jean Beaupré (who, significantly, has the same initials as Ernest's biological father, Jean-Baptiste).[26]

FATHERS AND SONS

The mention of "Old Beaupre" in James's will was the link that joined the fictional world James had created with his true past, representing both as possessing the same validity. A deliberate move on James's part, to authenticate his legend, or an inadvertent "slip," like the naming of "Ernest" rather than "Auguste" Dufault as his heir? Had Will James, by the time he wrote the will in 1940, internalized his self-created "life story" to the point that he could no longer distinguish it from his true biography?

There can be no doubt that the (entirely fictional) French-Canadian trapper Jean Beaupré, Will's surrogate father in *Lone Cowboy*, met both Will James's pragmatic need for a childhood "legend" to explain his past and Ernest Dufault's psychological need for a heroic father figure, tough and resourceful as befitted a rugged outdoorsman of the Wild West.

In Bopy, James superimposes features of his biological father and his fictional surrogate father, the French-Canadian origins of the two representing an element they hold in common. On the other hand, Bopy's close friendship with Will James's "deceased" fictional father Bill James constitutes the link to the latter's heroic Western exploits, so proudly recounted by his "son." Above all, Bopy is the Chosen Father, resulting in a bond, a "kinship," that he has not experienced with his own "blood relations": "The Old-timer, Jean Beaupré's dad was of the Northwest, the same as him. He could talk many Indian languages and sign talk all mixed with French. French was his main language and he could talk very little *anglais*. I remember it used to be pretty hard for my dad to understand him sometimes, and as I'd hear Trapper Jean talk I'd got to natural like picking up many of his French words, specially when he spoke to me alone. ... There was no kin between him and my dad but the way he took care of me and watched over me, even before I could remember, showed a kinship that blood relations often fail at showing."[27]

What is more, Bopy is the embodiment not only of the frontiersman father figure who, on their wanderings, teaches him survival in the outdoor wilderness and gives him his first horse, but also of the indulgent, nurturing mother who teaches him to cook, read, and write, and provides him with pencils and drawing paper. There is a maternal aspect to Beaupré's nurturing of his "son": he is protective, loving, and understanding of young Will's passion for horses and the frontier life as well as indulgent of his artistic talent and interests.

One incident described in *Lone Cowboy* dramatizes the maternal, care-giving role attributed to Bopy in a striking superimposition of an event that actually took place in Ernest Dufault's childhood, involving his real mother, when the family had just settled in Montreal. In a letter to Anthony Amaral, Auguste describes how young Ernest had entered the kitchen and drunk a white liquid that he took to be milk, but that was pure lye. Ernest's mother, coming upon the scene, immediately forced him to drink large quantities of milk, while waiting for the doctor to arrive. Her intervention and the doctor's managing to induce vomiting saved Ernest's life.[28] As recounted in *Lone Cowboy*, Bopy and young Will are spending the winter in a cabin up north near Bopy's traplines. To clean the traps of blood, Bopy has concocted a lye solution, which young Will, left unattended for a moment, drinks. Bopy saves Will by forcing him to drink condensed milk to induce vomiting, and then tenderly nurses him back to health throughout that winter.

But Bopy is more than the incarnation of the ideal parent, incorporating both the masculine and the feminine principles, and engendered by the son to meet the fantasies of young Ernest and the later Will James. He is also an alter ego of the "son" himself, the young

French-Canadian Ernest Dufault, whom Will James "leaves behind," "drowning" him, in *Lone Cowboy*, in a fast-moving river by a lonely camp once the young lad is old enough to make his way alone. After Bopy's disappearance, young Will, grieving and desolate, continues to search for him for a time, but it is not until Bopy's death that he tastes the freedom – and the loneliness – resulting from his absence: "I was so free that I felt lonesome. I could go anywheres I pleased, do anything I pleased, and there wasn't a soul to answer to ... There was nobody to care what I done."[29] But like young Ernest, who recorded his outward transformation in a photo taken at a line camp at Sage Creek, Alberta, during his first winter on the frontier, showing him in full cowboy garb with his horse, every inch the Western "mustangeer,"[30] young Will "re-outfits" himself at a saddle shop and strikes out on his own, as young Ernest Dufault had done when he first went west. Though he feels for a time that Bopy will reappear "and we'd be together again," that feeling, too, disappears: "I'd left Bopy behind for good and there was nothing ahead for me but great scopes of country and a freedom to match it."[31]

But Bopy does resurface again, metaphorically speaking, in young Will James's homesickness, or, to use the French term, his *nostalgie de pays*, as the embodiment of the home and family that Ernest has left behind. Although the narrator of *Lone Cowboy*, in describing how he is retracing his footsteps in the direction of "the country in which he was born" and where he first knew Bopy, says he is heading "South," it is the emotionally charged tone of one passage as much as biographical evidence from that period that indicates that he is in fact going north, returning to his childhood home, in his narrative reversing the direction in which he is headed to avoid any possible risk of exposure:

> I've often wondered what power keeps drawing a human or animal back to the place where daylight was first blinked at. Many a time a man will go back to the country of his childhood when there's not near as much for him at that home spot as where he just left ... That same power must have drawed me ... as natural like and without thought, I drifted to where I first stood up and talked ... After I left the ranch and crossed the river, it wasn't but a few days that I begin to notice something mighty familiar about the country. The further South I went the more familiar it got and I begin to feel mighty contented, like as if I was at home and amongst my own folks.[32]

Figure 4.2 Will James, cowboy. Sage Creek, Alberta, ca. 1907

The familiarity of the landscape makes him feel "as if Bopy was near and just ahead of me a ways."[33]

Geographical *fausses pistes* such as the reversal of direction – "North" becoming "South" – occur throughout *Lone Cowboy*, and at times they have a playful touch. Thus at one point the author describes how strange he feels in "the northern country" winters that he spends on Bopy's traplines, winters that would have been so familiar to young Ernest Dufault: "Them short days and light nights was one of the things which made that winter sort of strange for me. The shimmering of the 'Northern Lights' or the reflections of what some called 'The Midnight Sun' always had me guessing, it was something I'd never seen in the country to the South. Then there was the 'Sundogs' which was on both sides of the sun in day-time, and with all them strange lights a shining on a frozen world of deep snow, it didn't make me feel like I was any too much at home."[34]

But it is in another passage, intriguingly self-allusive, that Will James comes closest to revealing that there is a complex mystery underlying the linear narrative of *Lone Cowboy*. Reflecting on his movements across western North America – and doubtless on his true "life story" – James uses the image of a geographic puzzle representing a life's path that cannot be traced to its beginnings:

> I often think, as I write this story, of what a time I'd have if I was to try and follow the same trails I made and which scattered from Canada to Mexico. If I was to mark them down on a map of the Western country it would look as if a centipede had dipped all its legs in ink and then just sort of paraded around on that map for a spell. Some states would be more marked up than others of course, and then there'd be many zigzagging lines going acrost here and there. All them zigzag lines and circles and doubling-backs would look like a puzzle that would be impossible to figger out as to where the start of that line could be.[35]

It is through the figure of his creation Bopy that Will James is able to mask not only "the start of that line," but a good stretch of its continuation, including Ernest Dufault's conflicts with the law. One summer Bopy decides, uncharacteristically and for reasons young Will claims not to understand, to head "north and east, but mostly north," rather than to stay in the "cow country" of the southwest. As they approach the Canadian border, it becomes clear that Bopy is a wanted man in Canada. In a long passage describing Bopy's run-in with the law and his consequent clandestine movements, which include the necessity of constant disguise, Bopy emerges as an alter ego of Ernest Dufault the fugitive, a clear extension of the start of the mysterious line leading to the metamorphosis into Will James. Bopy's story not only offers a number of clues as to Ernest Dufault's movements after the fatal barroom fight in Alberta, but also represents an attempt on the part of Ernest Dufault/Will James, through the medium of Bopy, to explain and justify himself as an honourable and principled man, following in the footsteps of a father figure whose judgment can be trusted and who can safely be emulated by his "son":

> One day, in our drifting, Bopy stops the outfit by an iron post standing all by itself on a ridge. He steps off the wagon and I steps off my horse and we gather by that post. It was the dividing mark between the U.S.A. and Canada. Bopy points to the south from that post and waves an arm and says, 'C'est ton pays, mon enfant' (that's your country, my child). Then he waved to the north and said as to how that was *his*. But as I understood him say then, he wasn't so free in that country and that I'd have to be careful not to mention the name of Jean Beaupré from now on.[36]

If the barroom fight in Alberta that had led to Ernest's arrest is thus ascribed to Bopy, James's alter ego, it is Bopy's upright character and independent-mindedness that is invoked to justify young Ernest's role in the turn of events implicating him in the barroom fight: "I know that whatever he done which might of been against the law, sure was something he couldn't help doing, or where he figured he was in the right. Bopy's laws was like his religion, they was of his own making. But, as Bopy used to tell me, whether you make your own laws, or follow them that's on the books, nobody can't tell when you get mixed up in the thick of trouble sometimes and have sudden happenings make you a hunted outlaw."[37]

The autofictional element is equally pronounced in James's self-allusive references to "Bopy's" disguises and name changes as a way to elude the authorities "in case a feller gets into trouble," his Achilles heel being his language: "He used to tell me that about the only thing he could be recognized by was his talk, his mixture of French and English. As for his looks, he'd disguised that … He'd tell me that it always pays to keep a good disguise in mind in case a feller gets into trouble, and another thing, to take on a new name with every new country while drifting around, whether you get in trouble or not, because then, if you do get in trouble more than once, it would be hard to trace you back and connect you with the other."[38]

Thus James attributes his disguises and name changes to Bopy's "advice," acknowledging the identitary confusion he experiences at times due to his multiple name changes:

> I was glad I changed my name a few times, but sometimes that got sort of confusing. I'd be riding for some strange outfit and somebody would holler at me by the new name I'd just given and I wouldn't even turn my head or answer. I wasn't used to the new name yet and I'd forget. Some thought I was deaf, others got

> suspicious, and then I'd often answer when somebody else's name was called which wasn't supposed to be mine at all. That didn't look right either. Quite a few times, when I'd be writing a bill of sale or something, I come near writing another name than the one I'd just given. That wouldn't of looked so good for me if I had, and it would of been hard to explain that mistake.[39]

The "Bopy" represented in James's lengthy account of his purported mentor's adventures is none other than Ernest Dufault/Will James himself, James's account encapsulating, in miniature, his own story, including his run-ins with the law. At the same time the representation of Bopy also embodies the parent and mentor figure of young Ernest Dufault's fantasies: the brave and daring Jean Beaupré who makes his own laws, whose only home is the western plains and mountains and the northern wilderness, could not be more different from his own father, Jean-Baptiste, the modest small-town merchant of St Nazaire, whose subsequent failures and bad luck sank the family into a poverty from which there seemed to be no escape. As French-Canadians *de souche*, embedded in a social culture the mainstays of which were, at the time, the Catholic faith, the French language, and the cultivated landscapes of the St Lawrence valley, the Dufault family could not envision a solution to its existential problems other than moving into one of the crowded working-class neighbourhoods of Montreal in search of employment. Small wonder that to young Ernest, in his impressionable and vulnerable young teens, avidly reading stories of the Wild West and studying their accompanying pictures, which vividly depicted untamed landscapes where everything was possible, the freedom of the western frontier was perceived to be a sort of promised land, an escape from the realities of his family's dismal existence determined by the constraints of poverty and the conservative ethos of a father who sought nothing more than to preserve life as he knew it.

But the family bond was strong, and the moral ethic of the close-knit French-Canadian society thoroughly ingrained, features that in *Lone Cowboy* Will James was able to reconcile with the adventuresome but principled French-Canadian trapper to create a "kinship" that the "blood relations failed at showing." In the figure of Bopy, Will James can venerate the strengths of his French-Canadian upbringing, all the while suppressing its stifling limitations. Bopy emerges as the persona through whom James can come to terms with Ernest Dufault's abandonment of his French-Canadian family and culture.

In living out the life for which the fictitious French-Canadian Jean Beaupré had prepared him, Will James had found a way to keep faith with Ernest Dufault's family, background, and upbringing, a past that blends the loving, nurturing ethical guidance – and even the language – of his conservative, strait-laced family in Quebec with the romantic life of the Western frontiersman, characterized by freedom and adventure. In all these aspects, Bopy is the parent-mentor of Ernest Dufault's dreams, but he remains so closely associated with young Ernest's past that he must be left behind, "drowned" in a fast-flowing western river only to re-emerge as Ernest/Will's alter ego when he becomes a wanted man seeking to hide, driven to a clandestine existence and multiple disguises.

"I AM CHARLIE RUSSELL"

While it is through Bopy that Will James expresses the values, views, and dreams of young Ernest Dufault, some of which can be associated with the strait-laced and principled upbringing of Jean-Baptiste Dufault, it is another alter ego figure, one who shares no common ground with Jean-Baptiste and who goes without mention in *Lone Cowboy*, that suffuses every element of the later developments in Will James's "life story." This figure is the cowboy artist and writer Charles M. Russell, whose name Ernest Dufault would have encountered and whose work he would have admired as he read Western stories and contemplated their accompanying illustrations in his father's small hotel near Montreal. When Ernest Dufault leaves home, he takes a stockpile of Charles Russell postcards with him. It is on an early postcard bearing the imprint "Chas. M. Russell" sent to his parents from Saskatchewan that he announces his imminent departure for Montana, Russell's home.[40]

In her study of *Doppelgänger* and alter egos, Aglaja Hildenbrock observes that "the *Doppelgänger* represents those qualities that are either painfully lacking in the subject's own image, or those that have been censored as 'taboo' and that have hence been repressed ... the *Doppelgänger* also represents a form of wish-fulfillment in that he can act in ways that the subject himself, for whatever reasons, is unable to do."[41] In the case of Will James, the deficiencies to be compensated, in the alter ego/father figures of both the fictional Jean

Beaupré and the non-fictional Charlie Russell, are those of James's biological father, Jean-Baptiste Dufault. But if the Bopy figure in *Lone Cowboy* incorporated a sort of ethical-moral superego function constituting a link to Dufault's biological father Jean-Baptiste as well as to "Bill James," Will James's fictive "biological" one, it is Charlie Russell, the man who made his own life, whom young Ernest Dufault sets out to become. It was not only Russell's drawings and stories but also his biography that represented the "site of desire of the Other" that young Ernest sought from the moment he decided to leave Quebec.

In 1911, around the time when Ernest Dufault crossed the border into the United States, Charlie Russell was approaching the height of his fame, having just had a one-man exhibition in New York. Like Ernest Dufault, he had left his home (in St Louis, Missouri) as a young teenager to go west, settling in Montana at the age of sixteen. And like the later Will James, he was a cowboy known for his sketches and ability to tell stories. Born in 1864, he would have been forty-seven when Will James first went to Montana, already established as an artist with a studio in Great Falls. Although James may have visited him there when he first arrived, there is no evidence to confirm this. However, the fact that James, bearing a collection of his own sketches, did visit Charlie Russell sometime between 1917 and 1918 is documented. According to William Gardner Bell's account, Russell's reception of Will James was less than cordial:

> Nancy Russell opened the door to greet James. She escorted him to the artist's detached studio at the rear of the house. Having seen many examples of Russell's work, and having been exposed to original paintings on living-room walls, James admitted to feeling "mighty insignificant" as he was introduced to the artist. He saw "the whole map of the cow country" on Charlie's face and knew instantly that "he was all cowboy as well as artist."
>
> Russell was working at his easel on a half-finished painting and was so absorbed that he spoke only in grunts. But he finally took the sheaf of sketches that James offered, shuffled through them, and handed them back without comment. When James asked what he thought of them, Russell replied "good;" when the tyro asked where he might sell them, the master told him to "spread 'em around in saloons ... somebody might buy 'em." The perfunctory attention offended James, who departed in a

huff despite an attempt by Joe De Yong, a Russell protégé and cowboy artist who was present during the visit, to explain Russell's complete concentration when he was "fighting" a difficult painting.[42]

Despite this inauspicious beginning to their relationship, Will James remained in contact with Charlie Russell, both directly and through the latter's protégés, and the two men maintained a correspondence, based mainly on the drawings and paintings they were working on at any given time. Russell subsequently praises James's work: "[Will James] sent off a sketch to Charlie Russell and received an illustrated reply salted with approval. From the sketch 'and other worke [*sic*] I have seen of yours in the Sunset [magazine],' wrote Charlie, 'I know you have felt a horse under you. Nobody can tell you how to draw a horse ore [*sic*] cow.'"[43]

That Charlie Russell's romantic vision of the Old West and his seduction by the freedom of the wide-open landscape closely resemble those of the young Ernest Dufault is hardly surprising, as Russell's drawings and stories were crucial in inspiring Ernest's passion for the western frontier. But by the time Ernest Dufault arrived in Montana, Charlie Russell was already mourning the fact that the Old West of his dreams had largely disappeared. As Bell points out, the Homestead Act of 1862 and the completion of the transcontinental railroad in 1869 marked the beginning of the end of the open range and hence the end of the cowboy era. Bell also invokes the introduction of barbed wire in the 1870s, the spread of the agricultural frontier in the 1880s, and the government's proclamation in 1890 that there was no longer a frontier on western lands.[44]

Through their art and their writing, both Charlie Russell and Will James strove to keep alive the legendary world of the frontier West, a world personified by the cowboy "riding high." The mission to keep the Old West alive was one that James would never abandon. But for James, for whom Russell was both a father figure and an alter ego, this mission took on a dynastic, almost metaphysical dimension, in which the sons were bound to honour and uphold the vision of the fathers. In his last book, *The American Cowboy*, James describes the history of the cowboy in America through three generations, from the Texans battling the Mexicans to the Wild West days of the frontier of the 1880s and 1890s, to the domestication of the frontier, which Russell so deplored. The final words of this, James's last book, written in capital letters, read: "THE COWBOY WILL NEVER DIE."[45]

For Ernest Dufault alias Will James, who had given up home and family to pursue his dream of himself becoming a cowboy and part of the old western frontier, that dream, once realized, grew to encompass the preservation or rather the resurrection of the Old West itself, through his drawings and writings. But he eclipsed even his mentor Charlie Russell in his attempts to re-create the lost West. In his otherwise comfortable ranch house in Montana there were no bathrooms, but privies; bathing was done in the nearby creek. A bumpy dirt road provided access to the ranch, and, aside from corrals and pole fences to protect the buildings, there were no fences. To evoke the ranch of the past, James even imported a small herd of Texas longhorn cattle, a breed that was all but extinct.[46] As Charlie Russell had been, Will James remained haunted by his youthful fantasies of frontier life, and he attempted to re-create that life in his everyday reality as well as in his drawings and stories.

In 1926, when Will James was savouring the success of the three books he had published and actively planning the purchase of his large property in Montana, he was notified of two deaths, first that of Charlie Russell, and then, ten days later, that of his father, Jean-Baptiste Dufault. News of Russell's death would have been catastrophic for Will James: it marked the end of a numinous relationship that had determined his own life, that had, in a way, become his life's purpose. One must assume that news of the death of his father, Jean-Baptiste, whom Will James had rejected, would have brought not only grief but also feelings of guilt. Since leaving Quebec in 1907, he had paid only two visits to his family, the purpose of one of which had been to ensure that they could be relied upon not to reveal his true identity. Unable to mourn his father's death openly, he spent his grief, publicly, over the death of Charlie Russell, the "father" figure who can be recognized as such in the middle generation of James's *American Cowboy*.

Ernest Dufault's departure from Quebec with a stack of Charles M. Russell postcards; the fact that Russell was likely the most important Western artist and writer Ernest encountered as he pored over magazines as a young boy in Montreal; the fact that Will James was subsequently to give his birthplace as being near Great Falls, Montana, where he knew Russell was based; and finally, his profound grief and sense of loss at his death – all these elements suggest that young Ernest

Dufault's Western odyssey was motivated by the single-minded desire to live the life of his idol. Charlie Russell was more than a role model to emulate, and more than a friendly fellow cowboy artist: he had become simultaneously a father figure and alter ego. One incident in particular suggests that it was the legendary life and career of Charlie Russell that, from the beginning, James sought to re-create as his own. Both emotionally and in their common cause, the resurrection of the Old West, with its wild country and open ranges, Will James had seen himself as an extension of a life that had now ended.

In 1934, on hotel stationery, Will James writes a strange letter. Its salutation is addressed to himself, and he signs it, inexplicably, with the name "Frank Farrington." Its dateline is Ocate, New Mexico, which is the general area where James had been working as a ranch-hand in 1921. Oddly, it contains a reference to the recipient's living in Streator, Illinois. Although Will James had corresponded with someone from there from his ranch in Montana, the connection of that party to the letter is not clear.

Its contents consist of inordinately enthusiastic praise for himself. But what is even more striking than the fact that Will James penned a letter to himself praising Will James is that the entire letter is written in the voice of Charlie Russell. His opening greeting, "Hello Will James," is used by Russell in a May 1920 letter, and the closing, too, is typical of the way Russell would sign his letters to James: "the latchkey is always out, and the robes spread and the pipe lit for you." One sentence is taken directly from Russell's 1920 letter: "nobody can tell you how to draw a horse or a cow." Both Russell and James were in the habit of including or incorporating drawings in their letters, and in this letter one of the drawings, dated 1934, is a copy by James of one of Russell's drawings. The two other drawings that accompany the letter are copies of James's own earlier sketches, originally published in 1927 and 1929 respectively. As intriguing as the letter itself is the fact that it somehow ended up in the hands of the Dufault family.[47]

It is unlikely that James wrote the letter while on one of his alcoholic binges. As Bell points out, the writing and the drawings are done with a steady hand. In writing a letter full of self-praise for his own achievements, in adopting the authoritative voice of his mentor and idol C.M. Russell in a letter that ultimately ended up with his family in Quebec, Will James seems to be signalling – to his family? – that he has done what he had set out to do, that he has made himself who he was destined to be in assuming an identity that he has himself created. In the letter, Will James and his mentor, his spiritual father and alter ego, have become as one.

There is another intriguing indication that young Ernest Dufault's quest when he set out for the West may have been to "become" his idol: in all his books and stories he uses the cowboy vernacular that charms most of his critics but exasperates a few as well, a vernacular that is typical of the speech and writing of Charles M. Russell. A few rare letters in which James slips out of this vernacular suggest that his "cowboy speech" was part of the carefully constructed uneducated-cowboy persona that so closely resembled that of his revered idol. In a letter he writes from New York to his friend Earl Snook in Montana, he expresses himself in sophisticated prose: "How I envy you … I am rather jealous of you, for while you are amidst all that is nature [we] easterners are confined to the walls and formalities of congested civilization."[48]

In the constellation of fictive and non-fictive alter egos who make up the fragmented persona of Will James, there is also a small boy. Clint Conradt, the son of Alice James's brother Fred and his wife Dolly, was named after the central character of James's brilliantly successful first novel, *Smoky*. James subsequently publishes another novel, *Big Enough*, that "tells the story of a boy born to a cowboy rancher and his wife. The parents' plan to prepare their son for a more cultivated life than their own is frustrated when the boy, abetted by the companionship of the little horse that shares his upbringing, takes on the coloration of his rangeland existence and leaves home and family to be a cowpuncher, simply because he was born to that life and couldn't be anything else."[49] James dedicated this children's novel to his young nephew. For Will James, childless by choice, little Clint Conradt was by all accounts a surrogate son, with whom he would play for hours on end, and whose future education he promised to secure financially.

In *Big Enough*, the story of a young lad for whom the cowboy life is not a choice but an existential necessity, the young hero's leaving home to become a cowhand, "because he was born to that life and couldn't be anything else," echoes Ernest Dufault's own departure from his family in Quebec, motivated by the same sense of destiny. At one point in *Lone Cowboy*, the narrator says: "I wonder, sometimes, when I think back, if I ever could of had any interest in anything if there hadn't been no horses, no boots and no spurs."[50]

THE END OF THE ROAD

There is but tenuous and highly circumstantial evidence of the inner conflicts Ernest Dufault must have suffered as he lived out his life as the phenomenally successful Will James. The supreme irony of that life, an irony of which James himself would have been constantly and keenly aware, lay in the fact that it was the very fame and success he had sought that forced him to cut the bonds with those he most wanted to witness his achievement, the reciprocal acknowledgment of which would have compromised that very fame and success. Nevertheless, James maintained surreptitious contact with his family in Quebec, at intervals sending them large sums of money, a fact attested to not only in Jacques Godbout's filmed interviews with James's nephews, the sons of his brother Auguste, but also by his wife Alice, who (knowing nothing of her husband's true past until the issue of the will emerged) attributed the disappearance of funds to James's poor management and dissipated habits.

The inner conflict resulting from his secret life manifested itself clearly in his behaviour. All the James biographies and the correspondence quoted in them portray him as an extraordinarily likeable, outgoing, generous personality, as a man with a quick wit and a sense of humour, and above all as a man who loved the company of other men. In tracing his biography, his bouts of depression and withdrawal as well as his more excessive drinking sprees can be linked to certain specific events, notably the death of his father, Jean-Baptiste, which almost coincided with that of his mentor Charlie Russell, and that of his father-in-law, Ed Conradt. His mourning of the deaths of Russell and Conradt, who both were father figures with whom he had had a close relationship, may have precipitated strong feelings of guilt at his abandonment of his own father, whose failed life had nevertheless been determined by the needs of caring, as best he could, for his family, including Ernest. James's rejection of his real father's narrow provincial ethos of decency and conformism is implicit in virtually all his books, in which the father figure, bold, adventuresome, heroic, the antithesis of Jean-Baptiste Dufault, looms large.

It was in the year 1934 that James entered the final stage of his gradual disintegration as Will James; this was also the year that marked the dissolution of Ernest Dufault. In 1934, Will James paid his last visit to his family in Quebec and obliterated any trace that would link him to Ernest Dufault, destroying all the letters and sketches that his family had so carefully and lovingly preserved over the years of his absence. The same year he wrote, in French, a long letter to his brother Auguste, expressing concern for his mother's health. In English, he added: "I often wish that I hadn't misrepresented myself as I did, but I couldn't dream of the success I've had and now it's too late to change."[51]

It was also in 1934 that he wrote the strange letter full of inordinate praise for Will James, adopting the voice of his mentor–father figure and alter ego, Charlie Russell.

The year 1934 thus seemed to be the final turning point for Will James, after which he could no longer escape the irrevocability of his assumed identity and the cost at which it had been lived out. The final dissolution of Ernest Dufault coincided with the disintegration of the figure he had himself created: Will James's marriage was failing, his drinking was out of control, his finances were in serious disarray.

The crisis of that terrible year initiated a process in which Will James would lose everything he held dear – his wife Alice, his cherished ranch, his closest friends, Fred and Dolly, and Clint, his adored godson – one from which, emotionally, he never recovered. Although he continued to publish, and in his writing continued to create the appealing cowboy figures and the romantic world of the Old West, in his personal life the once fun-loving and exuberant Will James had become a dark, brooding, and above all solitary figure.

If the loneliness and self-alienation of a life of existential concealment came to dominate James's later years, a sense of isolation, of otherness, of being the ultimate outsider is latent throughout his life as he recounts it in *Lone Cowboy*. According to Hildenbrock, such isolation plays a key role in figures who lead double lives. Their integration in family or other social contexts is inevitably superficial, further aggravating the problems of definition of self identity and ultimately traumatizing the *Doppelgänger*.[52]

This sense of loneliness and isolation inevitably surfaces when he is on the run: after Bopy's death, when he seeks to avoid being taken in hand due to his youth by well-intentioned ranchers, this solitude is accompanied by an exhilarating sense of freedom and promise, but later, as a fugitive cattle rustler, it excludes him from the comfort of a settled life and the company of his fellow man. In a poignant passage strangely reminiscent of Frederick Philip Grove's description of himself as a stranger passing outside the lamp-lit farmhouses on a dark, snowy prairie night, Will James experiences the full desolation as well as the vulnerability of his solitary and secret existence, from which the lighted ranch house and its conviviality offer protection and security:

> I'd hanker for a place of my own when some nights I'd be shoving my stolen stock by within a few miles of a ranch house. I'd be seeing the lights of it and I'd sort of picture the family there, the bunk house and the boys by the stove a joking with one another or leaning back on their bunks, reading by good lamplight while the old box stove hummed and throwed sparks from cedar wood. I'd be shivering about that time, shoving sore-footed cattle, riding tired horses and looking back often for riders that might come up on me. Sometimes I'd ride thru groves of joshuas and, at night, some of them would take the shape of a rider with a rifle.[53]

But the loneliness and vulnerability of his life as a fugitive was not only the consequence of Will James's wilder exploits as a frontier cowboy: it determined the very existence of the man he had willed himself to become. Although he lived out the fictive identity he had himself created, he could not re-create the old frontier West in quest of which he had left Quebec. Young Ernest Dufault had been in search of a way of life to which he was irresistably drawn and which he felt he was destined to live. His lonely death in Hollywood, that purveyor of dreams that come true only on the silver screen, was in a way a fitting close to a life that was built on fiction, not only in the biographical sense, but in the larger historical one as well.

5

The "Professional Indian": Chief Buffalo Child Long Lance

> Oh, look down upon Long Lance,
> Thou knowest Long Lance,
> The Sun, the Moon, the Day, the Night;
> Tell me if it is real,
> This life I have lived
>
> Chief Buffalo Child Long Lance

"PASSING"

Sylvester Clark Long's metamorphosis from "coloured" janitor to the legendary Indian Chief Buffalo Child Long Lance represents only one instance in a long history of such ethnic-racial self-transformations, through which Americans of colour escaped the constraints of living under the restrictions of government-decreed colour designations.[1] In assuming his self-created identity, Sylvester/Long Lance, unlike other American "voluntary Indians" who were categorized as Black or coloured, took the added precaution of immigrating to Canada. In both countries, partly owing to literary and even historical representations of Indians as heroic and picturesque, Native North Americans were viewed more positively by the dominant white culture than Blacks or "Coloureds," who were physically more "other," and often descendants of slaves. Although racial (and ethnic) discrimination was widely prevalent in Canada as well, the country had not enacted the rigid segregation laws in effect in the United States that targeted people of colour.

The New World, and in particular the United States, which defined itself as a society of unlimited possibilities and had cultivated the mythos of the "self-made man," lent itself to individual self-reinvention, and represented a way for Americans to escape the Black/white binary imposed by government legislation.[2] These national mythologies had been in large part created by published narratives, many of which were autobiographical or supposedly autobiographical. Laura Browder argues that in the US, it was Benjamin Franklin's motivational autobiography, with its emphasis on "performance" – not only in actually cultivating virtues such as diligence and frugality, but also in cultivating an outward *image* that let him be publicly perceived to possess these qualities – that created the paradigm for self-construction.[3] It is the "appearance," or the performance aspect of such self-construction, that authenticates the identity of the assumed persona, the effectiveness of the authentication depending on the degree to which the performance is accepted by the audience for which it is destined.

In ethnic and racial passing, such performances of authentication involve "erasing details or certain aspects of a given life in order to move past perceived, suspected or actual barriers to achieve desired ends." They also require "the complicity, safe distance, or death of those who know the passers in their other context."[4] The effective assumption of the self-constructed identity in such cases thus requires the creation of a biographical "legend" that obliterates all traces of the past to ensure that the integrity of the self-invented persona is not threatened or compromised.

In the case of Sylvester/Long Lance, immigration to Canada was not only a means to escape American segregationist policies and all they entailed; the "safe distance" between Canada and his North Carolina home provided some assurance that he could erase his biographical past with impunity. Still, the fact that most of his family outlived him (and, from faraway Winston-Salem, were admiringly following his meteoric career as a "professional Indian") was a constant source of anxiety. The emotional price Long Lance paid for cutting off all connections with his family, which had been close and loving, included a nagging sense of guilt and betrayal, expressed explicitly in a letter to his brother[5] and implicitly in his "autobiographical" *Long Lance*. He must have keenly felt the deprivation of the unconditional love and support of those who were closest to him.

It was his complicated biological background that helped him stage his assumed persona even while he was still in the United States. His parents, though classified as "coloured," claimed to be of Indian/white descent, and some members of the Long family were not dark-skinned.

Sylvester himself was dark-complexioned, but he had straight hair and, from his appearance, could (as he later did) pass as an Indian. It was the cultural components of the Indian identity he claimed – knowledge of language, history, and customs – that were entirely lacking in the genealogy of the Long family. Once Sylvester had assimilated this cultural repertoire – and broken all ties with his family – nothing, it seemed, stood in the way of his self-creation as a full-blooded Indian.

SYLVESTER CLARK LONG ALIAS CHIEF BUFFALO CHILD LONG LANCE

Sylvester Clark Long was born in 1890 in Winston-Salem, North Carolina. Although his parents claimed to be of Indian-European descent, they were considered to be part Afro-American. The Long family's "coloured" designation meant that they suffered all the indignities resulting from racial segregation, and that there were few opportunities for professional, economic, or social advancement open to them.

Mother Sallie and father Joe Long, devout Baptists, were respected members of their community. They accepted their status as "coloured," as did three of their four children. Sylvester, however, the third child and youngest son, resented the exhortations of his family and Baptist preachers to obey the stringent rules that applied to the Black and "coloured" population but not to whites. As an adolescent, he recognized that the family's racial designation would impose severe limitations on any plans he might have for the future, and determined early on to use his mixed-race background to break out of the "coloured" ghetto and to make a new life for himself elsewhere.

Sylvester was too dark-skinned to pass for white, but he had the straight, black hair of a North American Indian. He used his appearance and the fact that both his parents claimed Indian as well as European antecedents to assume, at first, the identity of a Cherokee, and later, that of a Canadian Plains Indian, declaring himself to be a member of an Alberta Blood band of the Blackfoot nation.

In the persona of Chief Buffalo Child Long Lance, he would become a "professional Indian" and a celebrity, famous throughout North America as a public speaker on Indian culture and history and for his writings about Indians, including an "autobiography" titled *Long Lance*, published by a major American publisher. With his starring role in a Hollywood film, *The Silent Enemy* (1930), in which he portrayed the "authentic," "archetypal" Indian, he reached the zenith of his career. However, the increasing publicity surrounding him was centred on his flamboyant Indian persona. In the end, it was his spectacular success that led to the exposure of his true background, ultimately driving him to commit suicide.

AMBIGUOUS ORIGINS

Sylvester/Long Lance's biographer, Donald B. Smith, suggests that one factor which may have contributed to Sylvester's rebellion against the racist rules that governed daily life in communities such as Winston-Salem was that the Long family did not "look" Black. Mother Sallie was fair-skinned; father Joe and the two older boys were Mediterranean-looking, while Sylvester had Indian features. The youngest child, Katie, was the darkest. In fact the ethnic/racial origins of the Long family, with their (unqualified) designation as "coloured," were ambiguous.[6]

Although Sylvester's parents claimed to be of Indian-white descent, both were born into slavery on white plantations. Sylvester's mother, Sallie, and his grandmother, Adeline, were fathered by white plantation owners, and his father Joe said he was the son of a Cherokee mother and a white man. The family lived out their officially decreed identity as "coloured" under increasingly restrictive segregationist policies, although Sylvester's lighter-skinned brothers, Abe and Walter, are listed as "white" in some issues of the Winston city directory.[7]

Smith never explicitly states that the Long family was partly Afro-American, although he says that they "lived as blacks."[8] However, other sources do describe the Long family as being part Black, including Hartmut Lutz, a scholar of Native literatures, who states that Long Lance was of "Catawba, Croatan-Lumbee, African-American and European descent."[9] Indeed, throughout his biography, Smith presents indications that there were Afro-Americans in the Long family's genealogy. Sylvester's brother Walter's obituary in the *Winston-Salem Journal* carries the heading: "Walter L. Long, Widely Known Negro is Dead." Mother Sallie's obituary contains the line: "The passing of Mrs. Long removes another member of the city's best-known Negro families."[10] Father Joe Long was the manager of the Negro-only balcony at a Winston theatre. Brother Walter had founded a detective agency that served the Black community. Abe's wife,

Aurelia, was dark-complexioned, and had a hair-straightening salon in Winston-Salem. In his research for the Long Lance biography, Smith found a diary entry of brother Abe that reads: "We the better thinking negroes ..."[11]

Sylvester's mother Sallie self-identified as a Croatan-Lumbee, which the *Handbook of American Indians* of 1907 describes as "a convenient label for a people who combine in themselves the blood of wasted native tribes, the early colonists or forest rovers, the runaway slaves or other negroes, and possibly also of stray seamen of the Latin races from coasting vessels in the West Indian or Brazilian trade."[12] In other words, Croatan-Lumbee represented a mixed-race identity, one that included Afro-American antecedents.

Although the Long family was identified as "coloured," their claims to white and Indian antecedents and the arbitrariness of their racial designation may have played a role in Sylvester/Long Lance's privileging the non-Black branches of his racially complicated ancestry, as it has been outlined above. It is possible that unlike most of his family, he himself never identified as Black or "coloured." As a student at Carlisle, an Indian school, and throughout his career as a journalist, film star, and Indian advocate, Sylvester/Long Lance took great pains to conceal his mixed-race origins and in particular to distance himself from any suggestion that he might be part Afro-American. Although in assuming his new identity he professed to embrace the Indian part of his ancestry, his adoption of a full-blooded Indian persona seems to have represented a way to gain a greater level of acceptance and acknowledgment from the dominant white society of which, given his dark complexion and Indian features, he knew he could never be a part.

There are several indications that had he been as fair-skinned as most of his family, he would have chosen to pass as white. Statements that suggest this can be found throughout his career, beginning with his student days at Carlisle. Although in his valedictory address on graduating from Carlisle he expresses pride in being "a descendant of the natives of this vast and glorious land," and praises their "glorious heritage," he exhorts his fellow graduates to "cooperate with the white brother in his efforts to raise to a higher social plane our once powerful but uncivilized race." As a step toward what he sees as the inevitable (and desirable) assimilation of Indians into white culture, he proposes to eliminate individual tribal designations, encouraging his classmates to present themselves only as "Carlisle Indians, belonging to that great universal tribe of North American Indians, speaking the same language and having the same chief – the great White Father at Washington. We realize that the sooner we permit tribe with its customs and prejudices to become tradition, the better it will be for our own race as well as for that race with which we are destined to unite."[13]

Later, in the "autobiographical" essay "My Trail Upward," published in 1926, when he had already become a well-known journalist in Canada and in fact had acquired celebrity status throughout North America due to his career as the Indian Long Lance, he expresses his pride at having entered the "white world." Claiming to have been first taught by "missionaries in southern Alberta" and then urged by a "Dutchman" to further his education, he writes: "I have succeeded in pulling myself up by the bootstraps, from a primitive and backward life to this great new world of white civilization."[14] Although he also professes to be proud of his Indian heritage, the dominating perspective of the piece is Euro-American: "I'm proud to be as much like a white man as I am – but I'm proud, too, of every drop of Indian blood that runs through my veins."[15]

Long Lance's rhetorical turns of phrase in his valedictory address and in "My Trail Upward" are disconcertingly similar to those used more than half a century earlier by James P. Beckwourth, who describes the Crow who had "adopted" him as "savages" and "wily Indians." Like Long Lance, Beckwourth came from a family designated as "coloured" but, in his "autobiography," "passes as a white man, who is himself passing as an Indian."[16] As Browder points out, Beckwourth's memoir, "far from being a tale of the solidarity of people of color in the face of the crushing powers of the government," is in fact "an apologia for white racism."[17]

In one passage in "My Trail Upward," in which he expresses similar sentiments, Long Lance, like Beckwourth, effectively erases his true complex racial background as well as his regional origins by representing his identity as dual and binary: "I'm proud of my Indian heritage and I'm proud, too, of the land and people of my adoption."[18] Here, the reference to his Indian heritage and the culture he has "adopted" – implying that what is meant is "this great new world of white civilization" – constitutes a strategy to conceal his true identity, as his identitary claim is restricted to two ethnicities, the Indian and the white, and hence precludes any association with the "coloured" milieu in which he was raised. The project, for "progressive" Indians, is to abandon the old Indian customs and traditions and to become a part of this great new "white civilization" with which the Indians are "destined to unite." Long Lance's statements on Indian assimilation in "My Trail Upward" affirmed declared government policies in both the US and Canada and were consistent with the objectives of Richard Henry Pratt, the founder of Carlisle, who had declared that the government must "kill the Indian ... to save the man."[19]

BREAKING AWAY

Chafing at the restrictions and humiliations to which the Long family was subjected due to their colour designation, Sylvester found life in Winston-Salem increasingly intolerable. Years later he would write in an article of "the eternal urge of youth to struggle upward and outward toward a bigger world than that in which he was born."[20] When as a teenager he learned from his mother that Kit Carson, the famous Indian fighter and adventurer, was a distant maternal relative, he began to fantasize about the freedom and adventure of the Wild West.

At the beginning of the twentieth century, the "frontier West," associated with freedom and unlimited possibilities, held huge appeal, especially to adventure-seeking young men. It was hearing about the family connection to Kit Carson that may have given Sylvester the impetus to follow in the footsteps of his famous kinsman. At the age of fourteen, when he was still a student at the Depot Street School for Negroes, he ran away to join a circus, which included a Wild West show featuring Indian riders.

Although most of the frontier battles between Indians and Europeans had been fought and decided long before Sylvester was even born, the Wild West shows were enormously popular in the late nineteenth and early twentieth centuries, a phenomenon Browder ascribes to their "display of Native Americans reenacting the battles they had lost [softening] the brutal history of conquest" and making it "palatable for audiences."[21] Browder observes that the Wild West show was "the embodiment of ethnicity as performance; with its stress on both authenticity and theatricality, it was the perfect proving ground for Long Lance's self-fashioning. In his travels through the segregated South with the circus, it would not be hard for Long Lance to see how the 'exoticism' of his Indian role could enable him to escape the black/white binaries of the world in which he had grown up."[22]

Although his work consisted of menial jobs such as feeding the animals, becoming a member of the travelling circus, which included performers of many different nationalities (only African-Americans were barred), was a life-changing experience for Sylvester, who passed as an Indian to join. The socially marginal micro-culture of the circus world fostered solidarity among the performers, regardless of their racial or national origins, a solidarity that was reinforced because the circus was always on the move. His extensive travel with the circus opened up another world to Sylvester, letting him experience a freedom that made the rigidly prescribed circumstances of "coloured" life in the southern United States seem stifling.

When he returned to Winston after his stint with the circus, Sylvester's perspectives concerning his future remained undefined, but they had considerably broadened. He found work as a janitor at the public library, and on his breaks, he read avidly. Seeking to advance himself through education, he decided to enroll at a private school for Negroes. However, he grew increasingly aware that even further education would still lead only to limited possibilities, and that he was doomed to a future determined by all the constraints and indignities of being "coloured," a future he refused to accept. In 1908, he again joined the circus, this time as a rider in the Wild West show, following in the tradition of his relative Kit Carson. The fact that some of the Indian performers taught him the basic elements of Cherokee turned out to be crucial in permitting him to "pass" as an Indian on the basis of more than his physical appearance.

A year later, back in Winston after his second tour with the circus, Sylvester sneaked into an office in the white school where his father worked as a janitor, and set out to teach himself to type at one of the typewriters. He was caught, but instead of denouncing him to the police, the principal of the school – recognizing Sylvester's motives of self-improvement and no doubt admiring his audacity – suggested Sylvester apply to the Carlisle Residential School in Carlisle, Pennsylvania.

Founded in 1879, the Carlisle Indian Industrial School's mandate was to "civilize" the Native pupils who attended by assimilating them, and to make them "useful members of society" by teaching them trades. It was the first Indian residential school in the United States, and became the model for both federally funded and privately sponsored Indian boarding schools throughout the country. On entering Carlisle, students were given new English names; their hair was cut short, and their traditional Indian attire was replaced by "white man's clothes" (uniforms for the boys). The regimen was paramilitary, and discipline was strict. Carlisle offered its students numerous extra-curricular activities, including sports, and its athletics program became a resounding success. Its football team regularly competed with Ivy League teams such as Harvard and Yale and those from the famous military academies West Point and Annapolis.[23]

To gain admission to Carlisle, students had to be at least one-fourth Indian, and at least fourteen years old. To increase his chances, Sylvester took a few liberties with his biography. First of all, he made himself a year younger, but he also took the first steps in inventing his Indian identity. He gave his parents' tribal affiliation as Lumbee-Croatan (his mother Sallie) and Cherokee (his father Joe), in spite of the fact that neither of his parents were listed on tribal rolls. A Black school principal and a white store owner in sympathy with Sylvester's desire to escape the "coloured" ghetto were complicit in the deceptions necessary to meet the requirements for access to Carlisle: they signed the vouchers certifying that the applicant was known as and lived as an Indian. Thanks to the few Cherokee phrases he had learned from Indian circus riders, he managed to pass the mandatory language test.

BECOMING LONG LANCE

Sylvester was accepted at Carlisle as a half-Cherokee. The school turned out to be instrumental in allowing him to take the first steps to discard his stigmatizing "coloured" identity. Carlisle was dedicated to giving "the Indian a white man's chance," and in addition to the trade school curriculum – Sylvester chose printing – it offered numerous extra-curricular activities. Sylvester took full advantage of them, participating in the debating society, the school band, and track and field, where the future star athlete Jim Thorpe selected him as his training partner in long-distance running. Thorpe and his Carlisle schoolmate were to remain life-long friends.

Nevertheless not everyone at Carlisle welcomed Sylvester, who now called himself Sylvester Chahuska Long Lance. Some students suspected that he was Black, and protested his presence to the superintendent, calling him a "Cherokee nigger." Aware that the Croatans were considered to be a mixed tribe, a component of which was Black, Sylvester tried to deflect these accusations by focusing on his Cherokee heritage, writing articles about Cherokee culture for the school newspaper. But the accusations rankled.

Notwithstanding the hostility of some of his schoolmates, Carlisle gave Sylvester the opportunity to learn about the various Indian peoples and about the important events in the history of the confrontations between the Indians and the white man. Some of the school's pupils were sons or grandsons of the great chiefs who had been involved in these conflicts. Sylvester would later use some of his classmates' family stories to reconstruct his Indian past, passing them off as his own.

An incident that occurred while he was at the school reveals both his audacity and a high degree of narcissism, qualities that would define the strategies he would later come to use in assuming the identity of a Plains Indian. A small child had gone missing in the town of Carlisle, and Sylvester, along with some of his fellow students, joined the search party. Interviewed by the press about his involvement, and questioned about his background, he told reporters that he had come "from the plains and forests of the West." Sylvester enjoyed the attention paid him by the press, and cut out those stories mentioning him. These he placed in a scrapbook, which served a twofold purpose: not only did the articles he saved in it pay him personal tribute, they also documented the identity he would later claim so emphatically.

Sylvester/Long Lance's declaring that he came "from the plains and forests of the West" reveals his awareness that the eastern tribes were largely assimilated. But it also reflects a prevailing mythos of the time, namely that the "frontier West" represented the most authentic expression of North American identity. Consistent with this notion was the Euro-American conception of "authentic" Indians, according to which "the only 'real' Indians were western ones."[24] Louis Owens, an American of part-Native descent, writes: "In order to be recognized, to claim authenticity in the world – in order to be seen at all – the Indian must conform to an identity imposed from the outside. Native American writers are unavoidably conscious of this predicament, knowing that in order to be readily recognized (and thus sold) as authentically 'Indian' their art must be figuratively dressed in braids, beads and buckskin."[25]

Browder, too, stresses the importance of using stereotypes to create authenticity in identitary self-definition and self-presentation: "Both the reader and the writer of an ethnic autobiography understand the implied contract: the memoirist is not telling his or her own story as much as the story of a people. In order to be heard, the ethnic autobiographer must often conform to his or her audience's stereotypes about that ethnicity."[26]

Sylvester/Long Lance, with his vague assertion that he came from "the plains and forests of the West," was quite consciously playing to the white man's conception of the "authentic" Indian. Melinda Micco remarks that "Long Lance's form of ethnic transvestism was structured within a country's fantasized notion of what constituted a 'real' Indian."[27] Julie Rak points out that Sylvester/Long Lance's imposture involved the performance of an identity in which the public wanted to believe. Both Nancy Cook and Julie Rak argue that the Canadian "frontier West" was perceived to be more "authentic" than the American "West," and that the story as Long Lance later spun it, of being a Blood Indian from Alberta, was an example of "the construction of authenticity in the Canadian West."[28] That in his bid to perform an ever more "authentic" version of the Euro-American image of an Indian Long Lance would later authoritatively assume the identity of a Canadian Plains Indian constitutes, as Nancy Cook has remarked, an instance of "regional" as well as "racial" passing, one that lent his new identity an authenticity that the status of an American Cherokee, which he could more legitimately claim, could not bestow.[29]

The missing child incident thus represented a turning point in Sylvester's biography. Not only had he initiated his identitary transformation into a Plains Indian, he had also laid the groundwork for a verifiable documentation of this new identity by gathering published articles in which this identity was presented as fact.

Armed with the confidence in his abilities that he had gained at Carlisle – he had been a top student and was chosen valedictorian of his graduating class – he applied for a band scholarship at St John's Military Academy in Manlius, New York, where he was admitted as the only Indian in the school. Discipline was strict, and daily activities highly regimented, but the school placed a high value on socially valuable skills such as proper enunciation and dining etiquette, which were to stand him in good stead.

Long Lance, who by now had left off the "Sylvester" from his name, was as successful academically at the more challenging St John's as he had been at Carlisle. Being the only Indian at the school, he acquired the nickname "Chief."

By fortuitous coincidence, St John's offered the young Long Lance an extraordinary opportunity to publicly perform the identity he was in the process of inventing for himself. The school held an annual circus day, and on that occasion, Long Lance, drawing on his Wild West show circus experience, acted the part of the "Indian" to general acclaim: "Long Lance, the 'Chief,' stole the show, wearing flaming red blankets and a headdress, leading a party of Indians through a war dance, then running into the bushes to lie in wait for the unsuspecting palefaces. At exactly the right moment, out he leaped with his whooping followers, surprising a wagon train – according to a report in the *Syracuse Journal* – 'in true professional style.'"[30]

At St John's, Long Lance had learned to conform to strict military discipline, had gained valuable academic credentials, and had developed skills that enabled him to feel at ease in sophisticated social environments. He had enjoyed the military school, and in casting about for what he might do next, he decided to seek admission to the United States military academy at West Point.

Long Lance did not go about putting this plan into effect in the usual way: rather, he wrote to President Woodrow Wilson requesting to be appointed to the prestigious academy. Conditions of admission there, notably those of age, required further adjustments to his biography, and he composed his letter accordingly, claiming that he would be turning twenty-one on his next birthday (in fact, he would be twenty-four), and that he was a member of the Eastern Cherokee tribe. In response to the inquiries that ensued, Long Lance received warm recommendations from both Carlisle and St John's that included confirmation of his Indian identity. Long Lance was accepted at West Point, but his acceptance was conditional to his passing the admissions examinations.

In part because of his audacity in appealing directly to the president, and the fact that his acceptance there coincided with a wave of fervent patriotism following the outbreak of World War I, the press carried stories about Long Lance that served to further validate his claim to be a full-blooded Indian, and in doing so, helped to erase his true origins. The *Washington Post* wrote: "The appointment by the president of a full-blooded Cherokee to a West Point cadetship comes as a recognition of educational qualifications on the part of the appointee that promise to do further honor not only to his own race, but to the country as well."[31] In spite of the fact that the Winston-Salem newspaper, too, carried the story, with a photograph of "Sylvester C. Long-Lance" on the front page and a headline that read: "Full-Blooded

Cherokee to Enter West Point,"[32] no one contested the authenticity of the stories presented in the media.

However, the War Department, perhaps in response to queries from West Point, did seek further information from Carlisle about Long Lance, notably about his "alleged Indian ancestry." A former Carlisle official was asked to verify Long Lance's Cherokee background by searching for his family among the Eastern Cherokees. That search was, of course, fruitless.[33]

Meanwhile, Long Lance, after intense preparation, took the West Point admission examinations, which he failed. Smith calls his failure inexplicable, pointing out that he had done well at the academically demanding St John's and had been well-prepared for the exams. Long Lance himself later said in an interview that he had "purposely flunked" in order join the Canadian war effort. (The United States had not yet entered the war.) Smith suggests that he did deliberately fail, but for another reason, namely the possibility of being outed as "coloured" if West Point persevered in its investigation of his origins. The same investigation also threatened to reveal that he had lied about his age.

Although he never attended the institution, West Point was important to Long Lance. After the war, in subsequent embellishments of his biography, Long Lance repeatedly stated that he had actually attended West Point. He even claimed so in an article he published a decade and a half later, when he was at the height of his fame. His decision to write and publish this article, titled "West Point's Predicament: Why There Are Two Hundred Vacancies,"[34] is in itself odd, as his claim to have attended the elite institution increased the risk of exposure concerning this part of his biography, and also because his journalistic writing had otherwise focused strictly on Indians.

"LIEUTENANT LONG-LANCE," CANADIAN ARMY

After the West Point debacle, Long Lance did indeed enter the Canadian army, travelling to Montreal in August 1916 and signing up there. In filling out the necessary forms, he again adapted his biography to fit what seemed appropriate to the situation: he gave the name of his father, whom he had indicated as his next-of-kin, as Joseph Long-Lance, and lied again about his birth date, making himself a year younger. The form had a window heading that read "previous military experience," in which he wrote "West Point."[35] Long Lance was accepted and sent overseas, training in England, where he performed so well that he was soon promoted to acting corporal and then to acting sergeant.

Due to a sprained ankle, he remained in England for a time. This, however, did not prevent him from embroidering his successes by relating totally fictional battlefield exploits to his friends back home. He did this in the form of a poem:

I've just come out of the trenches
Where we made the Germans dance,
And I'm sending this Greeting to let you know
That he is still alive, Yours Truly, Lieut. Long-Lance;
Alive and fit as fit can be,
Though fighting's not all sport,
And manners "made in Germany"
Aren't quite what you and I were taught.[36]

Some of the people on his Christmas mailing list were Carlisle school teachers and officials. One of them, proud of the achievements of the school's alumnus, sent the poem to the press, who were glad to make use of it in patriotic articles. One story's headline read: "American Indian Is Fighting for Allies," another: "Lieut. Long Lance of Carlisle Surprises Teacher with Note from Trenches."[37]

Ironically, the day the story appeared was the day Long Lance was actually dispatched to France, where he immediately reverted to the rank of private. He fought at Vimy Ridge, and although he was not wounded in that battle, the brutality of the fight and the horrific conditions made an indelible impression on him. After the battle at Vimy Ridge, he was wounded twice within a few weeks, near Lens, and the shrapnel injuries he sustained in the second attack put him out of the war.

While he was at the front, Long Lance was interviewed and photographed by an American reporter. When the American press ran the story in July 1917, the Long Lance legend was further enhanced in a process of extraordinarily efficient myth-making. The story presented a seductive blend of fact and fiction, elements of the latter variety making him a "full-blooded Indian," a West Point alumnus, and a Canadian lieutenant, all of which he would later claim as factual as he went about establishing himself in Canada. *New York World* headlined the story "The American Full-Blooded Indian Who Fought at Vimy Ridge." The captions ran as follows: "Fenimore Cooper's Romances Have Nothing on the Real-Life Story of This Full-Blooded Cherokee from Kit Carson's Country – Trick Rider, Fistic 'Meeter of all Comers,' All-Round College Athlete, Prize Debater and Literary Essayist, Musician ... Carlisle and St. John's Graduate, President Wilson's Appointee to West Point Cadetship. He Now Turns Up as First Lieutenant of Princess Pat's Crack Canadian Regiment."[38]

When Long Lance returned to Canada in 1919 to be discharged, he gave Alberta as his destination, ensuring the greatest possible distance from his own true origins and the lynchings and hangings of Blacks that were taking place in the increasingly segregated United States.

Thanks in part to his real experiences at Carlisle, at St John's, and as a participant in the war, but above all to the largely contrafactual press stories written about him, Long Lance arrived in Calgary endowed with an impressive and comprehensive biography, the salient items of which were all documented in the increasingly voluminous scrapbook. This new biography successfully effaced all traces of Sylvester Clark Long and his "coloured" past in Winston-Salem, North Carolina. As Smith puts it, Long Lance had made his past "a child's slate board, and anytime he felt like it, he could erase it and start clean again, becoming anything he wanted to be."[39]

CHIEF BUFFALO CHILD LONG LANCE, CANADIAN JOURNALIST

After landing a job as a reporter for the *Calgary Herald*, Long Lance soon got his first by-line, complete with an unusually long editorial introduction: "Although an American citizen, born in Oklahoma and educated at St. John's Military Institute, Carlisle University and West Point, the famous military academy of the United States, he came to Canada during the war and signed on for overseas service. He served on the field as a private and NCO, receiving the *Croix de Guerre* for bravery when a sergeant, and afterwards being promoted to the rank of lieutenant. He also served in France as an officer before being elevated to a staff appointment in Italy. Captain Long Lance was wounded twice in the course of his war service. When the Canadian forces were demobilized, he returned to the United States, and after a brief stay there came to Western Canada and joined the staff of the *Calgary Herald*. In both his college and army careers, Captain Long Lance has been noted as an athlete and is well-known as a boxer, wrestler, footballer and all-round track man."[40]

As Smith points out, this was "an astounding example of reckless lying," and all the untruths – he had not attended West Point, Carlisle was not a university, he had not been either a lieutenant or a captain, he had not received the *Croix de Guerre*, he had never served in Italy, and he was not born in Oklahoma – could easily have been investigated and exposed.[41]

Why no one questioned Long Lance's biography likely had less to do with the authority of its editorial presentation than with the fact that the reading public found his story so attractive. In the climate of triumphant post-war patriotism that was sweeping the country, Long Lance was seen as an emblematic figure representing the gallant bravery of the Canadian troops, whose role was hailed as heroic both at home and abroad. As would be the case later, with the "authentic" Plains Indian persona he created, no one questioned Long Lance-the-war-hero's record for the simple reason that people wanted to believe it. The acts of bravery for which he was praised were also seen to be related to his Indian identity, carried out because "there was war in Europe, and it called to the warrior blood in Long Lance."[42]

Long Lance exulted in his status in Calgary: he was successful as a journalist, popular with his colleagues, and always aware of all the freedoms he could enjoy that were unavailable to the "coloured" people at home. Among the photographs he sent to his family, one shows him sitting in a park with a white woman, and in another he is sitting in a train or street car, surrounded by white fellow passengers. It was important to him to ensure that the "folks at home" knew.

Basking in his successes, professional and social, Long Lance found ways to heighten his profile. He dated wealthy white women, learned to fly airplanes, coached the Calgary Canucks Football Club, also becoming a member of their board, and generally presented a dashing, youthful image (in an interview he changed his birth date yet again, making himself three years younger than he was).[43]

Notwithstanding the freedoms that the absence of legislated racism allowed in Canada, racist prejudices did exist, particularly against Blacks, of whom there were not many in the Calgary of the 1920s. Long Lance's greatest fear was that he could be taken for Black, and several incidents point to the lengths to which he went to affirm his claimed Indian identity. One involved a visit to the city by Jack Dempsey, who had been quoted in the *Albertan* as saying he would never fight a coloured man, and that he absolutely drew "the colored line."[44] The next day Long Lance appeared at Dempsey's dressing room with his press card, interviewed him, and the day after took him to the YMCA, where the two boxed, wrestled, and went for a swim together. Long Lance had, once again, successfully passed as an Indian.

When he was taken for Black, as happened occasionally, Long Lance became outraged. He was sitting at the bar at the Palliser Hotel with a colleague one night when another guest, who had been shown to the stool next to him, refused to take the indicated seat, saying he wasn't sitting "alongside any nigger." Long Lance immediately punched him unconscious.

Such confrontations would have reminded him of the indignities of his life as a "coloured boy" in Winston-Salem, which he thought he had left behind. But they were also constant reminders that any suspicions about his real origins could ultimately lead to exposure of his true identity. He was a successful journalist for a Canadian newspaper, beginning to make a niche for himself as an Indian writer writing about Indians. Constructing this new public identity was not only a matter of denying any allegations that he might be Afro-American, but also of marshalling convincing evidence to shore up and document it. Thus for example Long Lance attached such significance to a casual remark by a fellow *Herald* employee – that he had never seen Long Lance "try to be anything but an Indian" – that Long Lance quoted it in an article written years later.

Long Lance went to his first out-of-town assignment for the *Herald* to write a story on the Blackfoot Indian Reserve near Gleichen, Alberta, sixty miles east of Calgary. His contact there was the Indian Agent George Gooderhan, who showed him around, explaining the consequences that relocation to the reserve had had for the Blackfoot. These explanations made it clear to Long Lance that Gooderhan had not accepted his claim that he was a Plains Indian, or indeed that he had any Indian background at all. Long Lance resented it, explaining to the agent that he was a Cherokee from Oklahoma, holding forth on his Indian past, the years at Carlisle, and his friend Jim Thorpe. His attempts to authenticate his Indian identity to Gooderhan culminated in his addressing baffled Blackfoot women in Cherokee, of which they could not understand a word (Blackfoot, an Algonquian language, is linguistically unrelated to Cherokee, which belongs to the Iroquioan language family). Nevertheless, the two men parted on friendly terms.

Long Lance made his experiences on this reserve into an edifying article for the *Herald*, expressing extravagant praise for Gooderhan and for Canon Stocken, an Anglican missionary among the Blackfoot, generalized to describe "the paleface missionaries" and Indian agents as "self-sacrificing."[45] Pleased with the article, the editor assigned Long Lance to write about the Sarcee Reserve, just south of the city. The result was an article focusing on the plight of the Sarcee (now known as the Tsuu T'ina) as a humanitarian tragedy, notably drawing attention to the high mortality rate due to tuberculosis.

Long Lance's Indian stories were well received, and his editor subsequently assigned him to write on the Blood Indians at a reserve more than a hundred miles south of Calgary. Here Long Lance met Samuel Henry Middleton, Anglican missionary on the reserve, an encounter that would lead to a life-long friendship between the two men. This visit to the Blood reserve turned out to be a fateful one, for it initiated the final phase in Long Lance's metamorphosis into a Canadian Plains Indian. A year later, he would claim tribal affiliation with the Alberta Bloods.

His assumption of the identity of a Canadian Plains Indian marked another step towards achieving the "authenticity" of what his white public saw as a "real" Indian. From his Carlisle days onward, he had iterated his Indian identity in such a way as to situate his origins further and further west. On his application for admission to Carlisle, he had written that he was a "half-Indian of the Cherokee Tribe located at Cherokee County, NC."[46] At St John's, he had claimed somewhat vaguely that he came from the "plains and forests of the West." To George Gooderhan, on the Blackfoot Reserve near Gleichen, he had said he was a "Cherokee from Oklahoma." In claiming to be an Alberta Blood, he was now striving to attain the ultimate status of Indian authenticity, one that would only be eclipsed by his subsequent claim to be a chief of that tribe. That he sought to achieve an ever more "western," "authentic" identity, however, was less motivated by a desire to inhabit an authentic Indian persona than by the desire to escape his "coloured" past by leaving it far behind him. With each new iteration of his Indian identity, he was increasing the distance – both geographic and identitary – from his true origins.

Middleton, when he encountered Long Lance on the Blood Reserve at Cardston, saw Long Lance as the "ideal Indian," one who "could measure up to any white man." Born and raised in England, Middleton had fantasies about the Indians similar to the "noble savage" conceptions of Grey Owl. His goal was "to bring the Indians into the twentieth century," and he tried to gain their trust by learning Blackfoot and preaching his sermons in that language (the Bloods, part of the Blackfoot Confederacy, spoke a Blackfoot dialect). As leader of St Paul's Indian School, he sought to model the institution after Carlisle, but underfunding was a constant problem, a grievance he communicated to Long Lance. In the story writing up his visit, Long Lance emphasized the Bloods' resourcefulness, but betrayed his ignorance by contrasting them with the Blackfoot (of which the Bloods are a part) and the Sarcee, a totally different people, implying that the latter two were equally foreign to the Bloods. When Middleton read the article, he was struck by certain of Long Lance's formulations that suggested a non-Indian perspective, and during the reporter's visit he had taken notice of his urban clothes and his direct, distinctly un-Indian manner in communicating with the residents of the reserve. At the time, he put all of this down to Long Lance's Cherokee origins and the fact that the Cherokee had been exposed to European culture for generations. Nevertheless years later he was to write: "He [Long Lance] was an interesting personality, sometimes Indian, oftentimes white, but the two together – never. They did not blend. He was inwardly torn by strange conflicting emotions."[47]

Middleton was taken with Long Lance, clearly appreciated his *Herald* story, and saw him as a role model for the students at St Paul's School. A few months after Long Lance's article had appeared, Middleton invited him to speak at a St Paul's reunion. Middleton introduced the guest speaker, invoking his brilliant school career, his athletic feats, and his distinguished military service – in short, Long Lance's past as he had heard it from Long Lance himself. Long Lance's speech exhorted his young Indian listeners to "realize themselves" by adopting the "pleasures and advantages" of the white man.

At Middleton's request, Mountain Horse, the father of one of the graduates, agreed to give Long Lance a Blackfoot name. In an Indian adoption ceremony, Mountain Horse gave Long Lance the name of a Blood warrior famous for his bravery, Buffalo Child. For Long Lance – as had been the case with a similar initiation ceremony for Grey Owl – this bestowal of an Indian name represented a rebirth into the identity he so ardently desired. The day after the ceremony, Long Lance asked to be photographed wearing a Blood war bonnet and a Hudson's Bay Company blanket. This photograph would later accompany articles about Chief Buffalo Child Long Lance in various publications.

Among his colleagues at the *Calgary Herald*, Long Lance was known as a lively man about town who enjoyed extended pub crawls and a bit of mischief. After a prank he played at city hall, which involved bursting into a council chamber wearing a gas mask and carrying a fake bomb, he was fired from his job at the *Herald*. As a result, Long Lance decided to pursue his career elsewhere, and in April 1923 he moved to Vancouver, where, having introduced himself as Chief Buffalo Child Long Lance, he soon found employment at the *Vancouver Sun*. For the *Sun*, he was to write a series of articles on the Indians of British Columbia. When the first one appeared, the editor introduced Long Lance as "a regular Indian," enumerating the fictitious distinctions Long Lance had by now claimed.

In spite of the blatant racism – not only against Indians but also against people of Japanese and Chinese descent – manifested notably in the *Sun* but also in the white population at large, Long Lance, with all his "distinctions," particularly his war record, was, for the *Sun*'s editor, a "presentable" Indian journalist who easily gained the trust of the Indians he was writing on due to the impeccably Native identity he claimed.

Throughout his journalism career in Canada, Long Lance's writing had about it the *cachet* of a "real" Indian writing about the Indians "from the inside." In his articles, Long Lance, the presentable and therefore trustworthy Indian, played the role of cultural mediator, professing to relay the culture as transmitted by a dying breed of respected old chiefs he was privileged to know, to white readers who were receptive to such representations. As Melinda Micco observes, "Following evolutions in American culture and literature whereby myths of Indians became entrenched as truths ... Long Lance created a non-threatening New Age-style remembrance."[48]

Long Lance's first story was on the Squamish Reserve at Mission. Briefed by the educated young Squamish Andy Paull, Long Lance now took a more critical view of the Department of Indian Affairs, and especially the Indian Agents, whose policies and practices he had praised in his Alberta stories. The disapproval on the part of government officials as well as missionaries of Native traditions had culminated in some ceremonies being outlawed. One of Long Lance's criticisms was directed at the prohibition of the potlatch, a ceremonial event involving the wealthy host's distributing food and gifts to those who attended. In fact, it also sometimes involved the giving away of wives and daughters.[49] The potlatch, which also had a regulatory function, to formalize the transfer of property and record marriage arrangements, for example, was made a criminal offence in 1921 on the grounds that it was a "wasteful, heathen" custom.[50] In his piece on the Squamish, Long Lance defended it: "The potlatch does not entail the giving away of anything. The Indian who holds it is either paying a debt to his guests for some material kindness which they have rendered him or for a similar potlatch rendered to him in the past, or is simply giving away what he knows he will get back."[51] In British Columbia, he became a more and more vocal advocate of the Indians, and wrote his stories for the *Sun* from an authoritative Indian perspective.

CHIEF BUFFALO CHILD LONG LANCE, PLAINS INDIAN

Even as he was in Vancouver working on his articles, Long Lance began to plan another move, this time to Saskatchewan, where he wanted to write about the Indians of that province before moving on eastward, eventually making a book out of the stories he would be writing.

Ever since leaving Winston-Salem, he had been systematically building a legend to legitimate his assumed identity. The published articles about him, which he carefully curated, were complemented by various forms of supporting documentation: school admission applications, letters of confirmation and recommendations, personal letters (both sent and received) referencing his new identity as being factual. Snapshot photos and portraits as well as public performances, which included participating in Indian dances and other ceremonies, constituted a visual documentation that contributed to the Long Lance legend.

To further enhance his authenticity as an Indian, he now *publicly* adopted the identity of a Plains Indian, whose traditional dress of beaded buckskins and feather headdress corresponded more closely with the public's image of an Indian than did the Cherokee, largely assimilated, the identity he had hitherto claimed publicly and in official documents.

On the basis of the Blackfoot naming ceremony among the Alberta Bloods – for whom the "adoption" had been purely symbolic – Long Lance, in his last article for the *Vancouver Sun*, alluded to his "fellow-tribesmen, the Blood Indians of Alberta."[52] In the scrapbook in which he had been documenting his journalistic (and personal) successes, he erased all references to "Cherokee," filling in the empty spaces with "Blackfoot" or "Blood."[53]

Figure 5.1 Long Lance in Plains Indian regalia, ca. 1929

Long Lance moved to Saskatchewan in the late summer of 1922 and approached the editor of the *Regina Leader* for a job, scrapbook in hand. He was duly hired, and commissioned to write feature articles on Saskatchewan Indians for the paper's weekend edition. By now, he could legitimately claim a substantial knowledge and understanding of Western Indians, both their culture and the issues confronting them. He now became an increasingly outspoken advocate of the Indians, encouraging them to resist the erosion of their rights by the Department of Indian Affairs. On his travels to various plains reserves, Long Lance talked to the elders, including ancient Chief Carry-the-Kettle, who told him their stories of the "buffalo boys," which Long Lance was later to use to good effect in his "autobiography," *Long Lance*.

In the articles he wrote after his visits to the Saskatchewan reserves, Long Lance proved himself to be a perceptive, astute observer, prompting leading Western Canadian historian Hugh A. Dempsey to comment that he was "carrying out valuable field work at a time when few ethnologists, and even fewer journalists, were concerned about the history of the Indian."[54]

His knowledge of the Plains Indians still had considerable gaps, however, and they revealed themselves even as Long Lance was working to authenticate his identity as one of their own. For example, he had himself photographed in Plains Indian regalia, including a wig with two long braids. However, the various components of his costume were mismatched. The vest was Blackfoot, the tobacco pouch Blood, the pants Crow (worn backwards, as Smith points out), and the headdress traditionally worn only at the Chicken Dance.[55]

While this combination would have seemed odd to the Indians, the portraits were no doubt destined to convince white persons of influence of the authenticity of his Indian identity. He actually justified his metamorphosis from Cherokee to Plains Indian to his friend Middleton, saying that he was now more familiar and more at home with the Plains Indians of Western Canada than with his own Cherokee, and that he believed that "as a Canadian Indian, which I have become in toto, I can do more for Indians who need something done for them."[56] Middleton ultimately accepted Long Lance's stance and did not expose him.

Following his plan, Long Lance moved eastward from Saskatchewan, arriving in Winnipeg in 1923. He used one of the portraits of himself in Indian regalia to accompany his first article for the *Winnipeg Tribune*. It was in Winnipeg, too, that he invented further credentials to embellish his already impressive biography, adding that he held two university degrees as well as the Italian War Cross.

His wildly exaggerated claims regarding his distinctions – his appointment to West Point and attendance there, his heroic war record, his athletic prowess, his status as an Indian chief – reveal a high degree of narcissism that seems to have been accompanied by a sense of invulnerability. No one had challenged his distinguished record, or confronted him with inconsistencies in his biographical accounts. He must have felt something akin to invincibility.

Long Lance's "performance" of his Indian identity became increasingly theatrical and flamboyant. Smith recounts how he once spontaneously executed an "Indian war dance" at a New Year's party given by the *Winnipeg Tribune*'s editor: "'the chief' was wearing a headband and two towels as a breechcloth. He began slowly, and, with sweat gleaming on his powerful torso, his feet made intricate patterns on the polished floor. He danced faster and faster, and for a moment his frenzy convinced even the most skeptical onlookers that he had indeed reverted to some wild, distant state of mind. He had 'gone Indian' some remembered years later. The dance became so frenetic that Long Lance had to be forcibly stopped."[57]

On a trip to Saskatchewan to research a story, Long Lance also travelled to Calgary, where he was still known, and where he was recruited to participate in a publicity stunt during the Stampede. Long Lance was to organize the "kidnapping" of the mayor. His involvement may have been sought in part to subvert the Department of Indian Affairs, which had attempted to prohibit Indians from taking part in the Stampede ever since its inception, as their participation was seen to counteract the measures the government was taking to eradicate their customs and traditions. Influential Alberta politicians and businessmen, realizing that the Indians' participation was an enhancement and in fact an attraction for the Stampede, saw to it that the edicts issued by Indian Affairs were overruled.[58] Various Alberta Indian tribes had been given permission to set up a tepee village on the Stampede grounds, and Long Lance, when he went to the mayor's office to "kidnap" him, was accompanied by a number of Indians, including Chief Running Rabbit, who was then "installed" as mayor. Running Rabbit then "adopted" the captive mayor as a Blackfoot before relinquishing governance of the city back to him.[59]

The carrying out of this hugely successful stunt – it was enthusiastically reported on across Canada – showed that Long Lance was well-known and trusted enough that Stampede officials decided to recruit him for it, and the fact that he executed it with Indian "accomplices" speaks volumes as to his acceptance and popularity among the Alberta tribes. The event also gave him a chance to act as a cultural mediator, to showcase Indian traditions to the white populace. Long Lance received not only a medal but also an invitation from the Stampede Board to participate in the 1924 Stampede.

Long Lance used his trip to Alberta to visit first the Stony Reserve, and then the Blackfoot Reserve, about which he wrote in the *Calgary Herald*, before travelling to the Sun Dance flats near Gleichen to take part in the Sun Dance ceremonies, which had been outlawed in the late nineteenth century and were no less reviled by missionaries and government agents than the potlatch.[60] He stayed in one of the tepees for about ten days, arriving a week prior to the actual festivities. It was the first time he had stayed among the Indians for such a long time period, and he was for the first time unaccompanied by any government or church representatives, such as missionaries or Indian agents. He was on his own, and his lack of knowledge of Indian customs and tribal protocol soon manifested itself to his hosts, including the elders. He was not allowed into the areas considered sacred, such as the Sun Dance lodge or the tepee of the Sun Dance Woman. It was clear to the Blackfoot that he was not one of them, and given the censure of such events by missionaries and government officials, it is hardly surprising that he was denied access to some parts of the ceremony. This did not keep him from writing, in a later article published in *Good Housekeeping*, an "eyewitness" account of "our Blackfoot Sundance."

Thanks to his astute questioning of his reluctant hosts, Long Lance's articles on the Sun Dance sounded authentic to his white editors and readers, by whom he was now regarded as a recognized expert on the Indians, especially the Blackfoot, his authority on the subject made all the more convincing by his claim to be one of them. As a result of his Sun Dance articles, the Canadian Pacific Railway commissioned him to write brief stories about the Blackfoot for its menu cards. They were signed, of course, "Chief Buffalo Child Long Lance."

Long Lance's expertise on things Indian was more and more received as being authentic, although many of his stories were full of inaccuracies, which remained unchallenged, even among those who should have been in a position to recognize them. Thus the librarian of the Saskatchewan Legislative Library wrote, in a publication titled *Saskatchewan and Its People*, that "the Chief is a highly educated man who ... has had considerable press experience, and his bright literary contributions to the lore and history of the tribes are not only interesting and well written but are valuable because of their authenticity."[61]

From his Winnipeg base, Long Lance paid further visits to Saskatchewan and Alberta, on one of them visiting Spotted Calf and Sounding Sky, the parents of Almighty Voice, the young Cree killed in a standoff for killing a Mountie who had been pursuing him for mistakenly killing a steer that belonged to someone else. Long Lance was fascinated by the story of Almighty Voice, which he wrote up and sold to several newspapers and magazines across Canada, and which he would later make into an account of the last stand of the "Blackfeet" [*sic*] in the penultimate chapter of his "autobiography," *Long Lance*.

The story of the Cree hero Almighty Voice (1875–1897) was one that Long Lance clearly found deeply moving. From a bluff near his parents' home at Batoche, Saskatchewan, Almighty Voice, together with his cousin and his brother-in-law, held off a force of almost a hundred Mounties and civilian volunteers for two days, killing three of its members before being themselves killed by cannon fire. According to the Long Lance story, Almighty Voice's mother Spotted Calf chanted to him during this entire siege from a hiding place nearby, exhorting him to fight and face death with courage. In Long Lance's description of the end of the battle, the night before Almighty Voice was killed, his mother's chant became a death song.[62]

What is striking in Long Lance's account is his empathy with Spotted Calf, especially his focus on her loyalty and love for her son. At considerable risk to herself, she ensures that he can hear her voice and words of encouragement even as he is hiding, at some distance from her, from the massive police and civilian force that is hunting him.

Long Lance's identification with the heroic Almighty Voice, including the injustice of his treatment by the white man, is clear. His delight at the reception he receives from Almighty Voice's parents, whom he is interviewing for a story on their son, is palpable: "I was pleased to learn that the old people knew me through their son, Prosper … I had not been here two days when the old mother asked me to exchange names with her and become her adopted son. Under these friendly relations, the old people, without my asking, volunteered to tell me the whole story of their son's career."[63]

His pride in being "adopted" by the hero's mother is reiterated in his "autobiographical" account of the incident in *Long Lance*, published four years after the press story. A number of elements in the story, when seen in conjunction with Long Lance's actual past, mark it as autofictional. Julie Rak describes Long Lance's attachment to his "adopted" parents Spotted Calf and Sounding Sky as an attempt to compensate for his neglect and denial of his own family, as an "affirmation of family connections": "in *Long Lance*, he attempts to 'borrow' a Native family to replace the family he lost."[64] The story of being adopted by Spotted Calf, although, according to Smith, almost certainly a fabrication, suggests an emotional transference to Spotted Calf of his feelings for his own mother, with whom he had had a close relationship. His mother Sallie had not only cared for him, she had also ensured that he assimilated elements of his own culture by taking him to church and community events. From her he had learned about her family and difficult past – that she was the unacknowledged daughter of a white plantation owner.

However, there is an element of narcissism in Long Lance's pride in the "adoption": it makes him the "brother" of Almighty Voice, vicariously lending him Almighty Voice's heroic stature. It is significant that Long Lance's identification with Almighty Voice is also based on the motivation of the latter's years of concealment: "Why did Almighty Voice choose to become a man-killing outlaw, rather than serve one month's imprisonment? Where was he during those two mysterious years in which the Mounted Police searched for him in every corner of the northern wilderness? ... Why did he suddenly appear, purposely to show himself to the Mounted Police?"[65] His questions about Almighty Voice's motives to reveal himself suggest that Long Lance may have been reflecting on his own disguise and concealment, and perhaps wondering what would lead him to uncover his true identity. His conclusion, that Almighty Voice was in the end caught "because he wanted to be found," reads like a foreshadowing of his own exposure and tragic end.

CHIEF BUFFALO CHILD LONG LANCE, RAILWAY PR MAN AND CELEBRITY

In summer of 1924, Long Lance, who still lived in Winnipeg, went back to Calgary to officiate at events at the Calgary Stampede, but he was also made the CPR public relations representative at the company's posh Banff Springs Hotel. Prior to beginning his engagement there, he attended the "Jubilee" at Fort Macleod, which was to commemorate the fiftieth anniversary of the founding of the town, a former North-West Mounted Police post. The number of Indians – Blackfoot, Bloods, and Piegans – who participated in this event by far outnumbered the townspeople. There were also thousands of tourists.

It was during the "Jubilee" that Long Lance acquired another adopted family. He approached the venerable Eagle Speaker, whose son had become the first Blood to study at an agricultural college, and whom Long Lance had met and with whom he had corresponded. Now, at Fort Macleod, Long Lance asked Eagle Speaker "if he and his son could adopt each other." Eagle Speaker acquiesced, but in spite of the impressive ceremony making the two younger men blood brothers, Smith claims Long Lance was never really accepted by the Bloods, some of whom felt that they were being exploited by him to help him advance his career.

In fact Long Lance, having tasted VIP status, living in luxury hotels such as the Banff Springs and Chateau Lake Louise, grew more and more accustomed to being solicited by and socializing with influential people. He was growing more and more ambitious. His status, however, was based on the Indian identity he claimed, and at this time, when he felt that he was on the verge of attaining true fame, his relationship with "his people" was souring. Many Indians felt exploited by him, while he felt that they were not appreciative of his efforts on their behalf.

Nevertheless, Long Lance's fame was growing, and in the fall of 1924 he was invited, in his role as an Indian chief, to address the Fourth Annual Ohio History Day in Columbus, Ohio. His speech, held at a historic site, was passionate on behalf of the Indians, and turned out to be a triumph. A month later, he was invited to speak, as a Blackfoot, to the Canadian Club in Montreal. In the same capacity he gave speeches to Canadian Clubs in Toronto and Hamilton. The Toronto *Star Weekly* ran a headline that read: "Extraordinary Is This Indian Chief." Long Lance had arrived and, like Grey Owl, assumed the role of professional Indian to which he owed his increasing fame and luxurious lifestyle. In doing so, he grew increasingly bold: to accompany the *Star Weekly* article on him, he gave the author a photograph of an old Plains Indian in full regalia, including the feathered war bonnet, saying it was a picture of his father.

Long Lance's responsibilities as public relations representative in Banff included acting as host to important guests. He was knowledgeable, socially skilled, elegant, and sophisticated, and he enjoyed the reaction of important personalities when he divulged his Indian identity. An elderly British journalist, Eldred Walker, was staying at the Banff Springs when Long Lance, in the line of duty, joined him on the verandah and engaged him in a conversation that showed off his knowledgeability and sophistication to best advantage. In his book *Canadian Trails Revisited*, Walker recalls his conversation partner as saying, "You are looking hard at me. Can you tell to what nationality I belong?" When Walker confessed that he had no idea, Long Lance pronounced: "I am a full-blooded Blood Indian. I am Chief Buffalo Child Long Lance of the Blood Tribe."[66]

One of Long Lance's tasks in connection with the Calgary Stampede had been to make one of the official guests, Field Marshal Earl Haig (who had been Long Lance's commander-in-chief during the war), an honorary member of the Sarcees. Long Lance officiated at the ceremony, acting as interpreter for the Sarcee chief Joe Big Plume. Although Long Lance knew no Sarcee, and made a huge historical gaffe in his presentation,[67] he accomplished his task with such fluency and aplomb that the event was a great success and resulted in Long Lance's being invited back by organizers of the Stampede the following year. Long Lance had now become so famous that the *New York Evening Post* ran a comic strip depicting him as the sophisticated, polished, impeccably dressed Indian hosting VIPs at the Banff Springs Hotel. He was what the white population came to see as a "model Indian," undeniably "authentic," yet one who was as comfortable in an elegant hotel wearing a tuxedo as participating in a pow wow dressed in full Indian regalia.

Another coup for Long Lance was his invitation to speak at the British Empire Club in Providence, Rhode Island, and also at the Dutch Treat Club in New York, where the editors of many important American newspapers were members. The Dutch Treat speech led to his being asked to write an article for *Cosmopolitan* magazine. He was invited to the home of its editor, Ray Long, who was also vice-president of Randolph Hearst's chain of publications. Long Lance stayed in New York for a month, and while there he had occasion to meet famous writers such as Sinclair Lewis, Kathleen Norris, and Peter B. Kyne, a writer of Westerns.

Long Lance was now extremely well connected, and he was invited to go on a lecture tour of the American Midwest. He was given free railway passes and could easily have arranged to visit his family in Winston-Salem while on his tour, but he did not. The fear of exposure, and the desire to separate himself from his former life, prevented him from giving in to the desire to visit his family, whom he had not seen in years.

"MY TRAIL UPWARD"

While Long Lance had been inventing distinctions for himself throughout his career and, when interviewed, had used half-truths (his "membership" in the Bloods, which was entirely symbolic) to suggest that he was a full-blooded Indian, he now took an irreversible and dangerous step in claiming his Indian identity, asserting unambiguously that he was a Blackfoot Indian and describing his childhood as a Blackfoot in a lengthy autobiographical article titled "My Trail Upward," published in *Cosmopolitan* magazine.[68] While some elements of his "autobiographical" essay were factual (his years at Carlisle, his service in the Canadian army, and his journalistic work with western Canadian newspapers), the Indian life he describes in "My Trail Upward" is pure fiction. Given his real childhood growing up in a coloured ghetto in North Carolina, there is a poignant irony in his statement: "I took [the trail] because I, a Blackfoot Indian, wanted to live like a white man."[69]

Long Lance wrote to Middleton, to whom he had told a different version from what was in the article, to let him know that the article had been published. Certainly he was appealing to Middleton for an alibi. At the same time the fact that he wanted Middleton to read the piece illustrates the conflict he must have endured all his adult life. On the one hand, he was proud of his achievements and the persona he had created. On the other, he must have dreaded exposure, the collapse of the life he was now leading. Notwithstanding the hubris he revealed in his audacious living-out of his self-invented identity, Long Lance realized that the divergence between the account of his life he had given Middleton and the account he presented in "My Trail Upward" made him vulnerable. Smith astutely points out the loneliness created by Long Lance's situation, demonstrated in the fact that there was no one, not even his "good friend" Middleton, in whom he could confide. A letter to Middleton written some time after the *Cosmopolitan* article had been published is as poignantly ironic as his statement in the article that as a Blackfoot, he had wanted to live as a white man. For to Middleton he wrote: "it is good for a globe-wanderer like me to have one good confidante like you; one whom I can be myself to, always, and speak what is in my mind."[70]

Long Lance's "autobiography" as he presented it in "My Trail Upward" is worth quoting at some length. Here is how it opens:

> Missionaries on a Blackfoot Indian Reservation in southern Alberta taught me my ABC's – but an old-fashioned bartender out in Laramie, Wyoming, first thrilled me with the idea that I might become educated and really make something out of my life.
>
> This man was a Pennsylvania Dutchman and so he happened to know about Carlisle Indian School. He asked me one day

> when I was in the old Central Bar with a crowd of cowboys why I did not go there and become educated. He explained that it was free for Indians.
>
> "But I can't even speak good English," I told him.
>
> "Well," he said, "you can educate yourself for entrance to Carlisle by reading. Read, read all the time – anything and everything you come across."
>
> I think that bit of advice changed the trend of my whole life. I was at that time sixteen years old and a full-fledged cow-hand. I could break and ride bucking horses. I could barely sign my own name and spell out words; but I could ride almost anything that stood on four feet. I was proud to be a cowpuncher; that was doing pretty well at that for an ignorant, half savage young Indian buck.
>
> A few days before I met this old bartender – I'm ashamed that I've forgotten his name – I had been fired from a ranch fifteen miles west of Laramie. At that time my temper was as wild and unbridled as a wolf's, and this was the cause of the trouble.
>
> This all happened in 1907, and I'd come down from the reservation to follow the round-ups. I had made this step on my own initiative, because I was curious to know about this Pale Face who had conquered my people and compelled us to live on comparatively small reservations. Up to this time I had never done anything but follow the Indians' line of least resistance – hunt and fool around with horses. I always went on the trail alone and I thought a lot. Finally one day I made a resolution; I was going out to meet the white man on his own grounds, study him and find out just what sort of fellow he was.[71]

The ending of the article shows to what degree Long Lance was prepared to disown his own true past and his own identity. The final paragraphs are fraught with irony as well as with a narcissism and hubris that might well be called tragic:

> Two or three times a year I go back to my Indian reservation, where I spent my boyhood and where my people still live. I was proud when they elected me a Chief. I had won my spurs fighting side by side with the white men – and my tribe had recognized this.

> I'm proud to be as much like a white man as I am – but I'm proud, too, of every drop of Indian blood that runs through my veins.
>
> I'm proud of my Indian heritage – and I'm proud, too, of the land and people of my adoption.
>
> I have reached to dizzy heights of material success, but I have succeeded in pulling myself up by my bootstraps, from a primitive and backward life into this great new world of white civilization.[72]

Long Lance's disavowal of his true past was a gesture of betrayal not only of his own family, but also of the entire community into which he had been born. The guilt and the dissolving centre of anything remaining of his true identity took an emotional toll. Long Lance was losing control, behaving bizarrely, using his Indian status to live the life of a privileged white man. With the distinguished clientele of the Banff Springs Hotel as his audience, he would, for example, perform wild "Indian" dances that did not remotely resemble authentic Blackfoot ceremonial dances, with the sole purpose of impressing white women.[73]

Long Lance's amazing streak of luck finally broke. An affair with a married American woman he had met in Banff represented the first time that his reckless risk-taking had serious consequences. The American had brought her Black butler with her to Banff, and during one of her trysts with Long Lance, the butler, who was drunk, went after Long Lance with a razor, wounding him in the leg, whereupon Long Lance attacked him with a poker, resulting in life-threatening injuries. Due to the resulting scandal, Long Lance was fired from his job with the CPR at the Banff Springs Hotel. Predictably, however, public sympathy was on the side of Long Lance: the *Fort Macleod Gazette* editorialized that Long Lance had been fired because he had taken "a lady's part against a 'nigger.'"

After leaving Banff, he went to New York to see Ray Long, for whom he was writing a commissioned article on General Custer.

In his article, Long Lance concocts a fantastic version of the events leading up to the "last stand," culminating in the contention that Sitting Bull had spared Custer because he considered him a blood brother, and that Custer had in fact committed suicide, faced as he was with thousands of Sioux. Long Lance's outlandish claims as to the circumstances of Custer's last stand were based on the description of two events involving Custer and Sitting Bull that were pure inventions, but that thematized traumatic events in Long Lance's own biography. One of them was the meeting of Custer and Sitting Bull at West Point, the elite institution that had rejected Long Lance, a rejection with which Long Lance was so obsessed that he contrafactually reiterated his acceptance and attendance there at every conceivable opportunity.

The other event was the story of Sitting Bull's adoption of Custer as a blood brother, paralleling Long Lance's "adoption" by Mountain Horse as a Blood at Cardston, Alberta, and also his "adoption" as a blood brother by Mike Eagle Speaker at Fort McLeod. Both of the "adoptions" had occurred at Long Lance's own request. They were purely symbolic ceremonies, and conferred no tribal status. But to Long Lance they meant everything. Not only did they serve to legitimize and authenticate his claims to a Plains Indian identity vis-à-vis the white reading public who adulated him, they represented biographical elements with which to fill the painful existential – psychological and emotional – gaps left by the erasure of his true identity, which he had deliberately discarded. Hence Long Lance's insistence on the deep significance of the Indian adoption ceremony that conferred the status of "blood brotherhood": "When an Indian declares another man his *Weh-hunka-wanzi*, it brings that man closer to him than his own consanguineous brother. On reaching manhood every Indian forms a 'blood brother' relationship with some particular member of his tribe whom he likes more than anyone else, and there can be no secrets between him and this person. In battle and in peace they are Damon and Pythias for the rest of their mortal lives, and no one can come between them."[74]

If Long Lance had approached celebrity status before, he certainly had it now. The editor of the Hearst newspaper group invited him to write a "boy's adventure story" on the Indians. At Long Lance's suggestion, the editor agreed that the book would be Long Lance's own life story (based, of course, on the identity he had claimed as a Plains Indian who had grown up as a Blood).

To ensure that his family would not expose him, Long Lance arranged to meet his oldest brother, Abe, in Philadelphia. Long Lance had not seen any of his family for almost twenty years, and the reunion must have been emotional, and above all difficult, for the two brothers, Abe recounting the family's fortunes since Long Lance/Sylvester's departure (nothing much had changed for the Long family, still living as "coloured" in Winston-Salem), Long Lance producing the scrapbooks not only chronicling his fantastic success, but also demonstrating the metamorphosis of Sylvester Long into Chief Buffalo Child Long Lance. There seem to be no sources documenting this reunion of the two brothers, but it is clear that Long Lance had attained his purpose in arranging it: neither Abe nor anyone from the Long family ever came forward to expose the true identity of their son and brother.

For his book, Long Lance drew on his earlier interviews with Indians, relying heavily on Chief Carry-the-Kettle, Almighty Voice, and above all his "blood brother" Mike Eagle Speaker. But many of the stories Long Lance had been told – and wished to use – were situated well in the past, resulting in numerous glaring anachronisms. An acquaintance, Maurice Fidler, whom he had asked to read the manuscript, pointed out that an area that Long Lance had described as Indian country and site of the buffalo hunt had, at the time Long Lance set his story (in the 1890s), long been ranching country: Fidler's grandfather had owned a large ranch in that very area. Long Lance himself, in an article published in 1924, situates the "passing of the final buffalo herd" in 1883.[75] Yet the "autobiography" was published as written, anachronisms and all.

LONG LANCE: THE STORY OF A BLACKFOOT BOYHOOD

Long Lance's "autobiography" in essence recounts the salient elements of Plains Indian life as he would have heard them from his Indian contacts, mainly from the elders and from Mike Eagle Speaker, whose own knowledge of Indian customs and historical events was derived from stories told to him by his grandmother. "His" story – that much is clear – is essentially that of Mike Eagle Speaker, but he sets it much earlier than the late nineteenth century.

While in *Long Lance* the buffalo are "vanishing," buffalo hunts are nevertheless still taking place. It is astonishing that this glaring anachronism – the buffalo hunt was a thing of the past by the time Long Lance was born – was ignored by the book's enthusiastic readers and critics, the latter consistently praising the "authenticity" of this "autobiographical" account.

The tales told in *Long Lance* are composed of the information its author had gathered over the years when he had been writing his newspaper and magazine articles. They consist mainly of accounts of day-to-day life among the Plains Indians and include descriptions of their norms, values, customs, and taboos. There are also colourful depictions of their conflicts and battles and of their legends, including stories of their heroic figures. For the most part, *Long Lance* reads like an ethnographic account of the life of Plains Indians before they came into contact with Europeans, and before the disappearance of the buffalo. As Browder remarks, Long Lance "was drawing from two distinct traditions of American autobiography: that of ethnic autobiography, understood by both teller and audience to be the story of a group as much as of an individual, and that of self-constructing the triumphant struggle upward of Benjamin Franklin or Booker T. Washington."[76]

When read against the background of Long Lance's true biography, however, a number of elements in the book stand out as being coded (and perhaps unconscious) allusions to his true childhood past, and to the deceptions he had brought into play in his self-engenderment as a Blackfoot chief. The incident with which *Long Lance* opens may be read as an instance of displacement of the trauma of his separating from his mother. It describes Long Lance's "first memory," when he was barely a year old, in which his mother is crying. Her hand is bleeding, and she hands Long Lance to his aunt before she rides away. His aunt later confirms this "memory," explaining that his mother's hand was bleeding because she had cut off her finger in mourning for the loss of her brother, who had been killed by the Crows, an enemy tribe. Long Lance's account of his grief, ostensibly as a baby, is one of the few instances in the book of raw personal emotion. He describes how he cries for his mother, feeling he will never see her again. While in the author's real life it was Sylvester who "rode away," the narrator's sense of grief, separation, and loss are palpable, possibly intensified by his own guilt at abandoning his family.

Apart from this traumatic incident, Long Lance says he has no more memories of his childhood until he has reached the age of four, explaining this mnemonic gap as being due to "the mystic sleep of infancy."[77] His next clear memory is of falling off a horse and of his brother putting him back on again. The anecdote evokes the affectionate brotherly relationship expressed in the letter Long Lance wrote to his brother Walter after meeting him in New York decades after he had left Winston-Salem: "my own darling brother, whom I used to romp and play with …"[78]

It is significant that *Long Lance* contains a number of transformative and adoption tales, some of which can be seen as displaced versions of his own self-invention. As such, they represent the inscription of elements of his own life in the form of autofiction. Such stories often reveal a narcissistic element in that their heroes are somehow "chosen," rewarded, or otherwise recognized for some outstanding characteristic or deed by leaders in their respective communities, usually a father figure. One wonders whether these adoption tales might have been to some extent inspired by James Beckwourth's "autobiography," *The Life and Adventures of James P. Beckwourth, Mountaineer, Scout and Pioneer, and Chief of the Crow Nation*. Beckwourth, who claimed to be white but was in fact part Black and born a slave, spun a tale of having been "adopted" by the Crow Nation, among whom he lived for years, adopting their dress and customs.[79]

One of Long Lance's adoption tales involves the ritual of initiation by a medicine man, who "picks out some youth in the tribe who has shown extraordinary qualities." He takes this boy away and remains away for about six months, initiating him into the secrets of the medicine man and making him endure various physical hardships. When the boy returns to his tribe, "he looks and acts differently, and he is never the same again to his playmates … such a boy seemed to have learned some great secret which he would not tell anybody, not even his own parents."[80] The boy's concealment from his parents of what he has learned and what he has become – he "looks and acts differently," and "is never the same again" – mirrors Long Lance's own "transformation" and "concealment" of his past, but also the sense of estrangement from his family. "Concealment" of what he has learned and what he has become through the initiation ritual may be a consequence of being "extraordinary" and being chosen, but the effect is inevitably a loss of the former self, and the rupturing of the once-existing familiarity and intimacy characterizing kinship. While being "chosen" may be an honour, there is a price to be paid for it.

In *Long Lance*, "transformations" can also be triggered by mere coincidence. Like the account of the initiation ritual, such tales are life-changing, and associated with a sense of fatedness. The book contains a number of such "life-changing" stories, most of which represent variants of "foundling" and adoption motifs, in which the element of fateful coincidence plays a role. One is the story of Eagle

Feather, whose wife does not bear children. Whilst out hunting, a wolf he is tracking leads him to a dead Indian woman and to her crying baby, hanging in its cradle from a nearby tree. Eagle Feather brings the child home, and he and his wife raise it as their own.

Another tale involves two white boys in a camp of "friendly Crows" and "half-breed buffalo hunters" in northern Montana. One of these white boys had been captured by the Sioux as a baby, but escaped, and has been raised by the half-breeds. The other boy remembers that he had come from England ("across the big water"), but was orphaned at age ten and adopted by the Crows. These foundling and adoption narratives evoke Long Lance's own successive "adoptions" – the first by Mountain Horse of the Alberta Bloods, the second by the Blood/Blackfoot Mike Eagle Speaker, the third by the Cree Spotted Calf and Sounding Sky (not to mention the mock adoption by Chief Running Rabbit during the Calgary Stampede). The profusion of adoption stories in his "autobiography" may reflect a fantasy dating back to young Sylvester Long's boyhood, that his birth into a "coloured" family in Winston-Salem, North Carolina, was somehow a "mistake." Two of Long Lance's "adoptions" took place at his own request, and were considered symbolic by the families involved, whereas the third, by the parents of Almighty Voice, was likely a fabrication. For Long Lance, however, they represented more than legitimation of his claims to an Indian identity: they were also rituals confirming his acceptance and belonging.

A significant feature of these adoption tales in his "autobiography" is that the adopted children long for their true families, echoing Long Lance's sense of loss at his alienation from his own family. Long Lance has one child who was captured by the Sioux say: "when I grew up and found I was different from the Indians, I ran away,"[81] a statement that evokes Long Lance's own running away from his family, his sense of being "different"' from his "coloured" community. A similar kind of displacement, this one emotional, is implied in the boy's longing to reunite with his real family. His rescue by an Indian woman is reminiscent of a rebirth myth: "They say that my parents were killed in the massacre, and that one of the Indian women snatched me up out of the mud and saved me."[82] Yet in *Long Lance*, in the story of the adopted white boy, an alter ego of the author and narrator, the longing for his true family persists: "But I wish I knew who my relatives are," the white boy says.

The weaving of his own contemporary role as a writer and journalist into these adoption stories is vintage Long Lance. He would have learned the story of the two white boys when he was researching an article for the *Winnipeg Tribune*, published 24 February 1923.[83] One of the boys, now an adult, finds a relative due to the relative's having read an article of Long Lance's published in *The Mentor*.[84] Long Lance claims that as a child he had met these boys in a Montana camp, and that as a journalist researching Indian stories he had come across family members of the two boys, enabling him to reunite them as adults and also to help one of them find a blood relative. Later, as an adult, having been "found" by Long Lance, the lost child reiterates the same desire he had expressed in the camp: "I would like to find out who my folks are." Long Lance no doubt enjoyed giving himself a quasi–*deus ex machina* role in reuniting the white boys and then "finding" a long-lost relative of one of them, and in the process putting himself at the centre of the narrative.

Long Lance's fun-loving streak also manifests itself in many of his stories, some no doubt directly transcribed from authentic Indian accounts of boyish pranks and tricking the enemy. He professes to be mystified by stories about White People, describing them as legends told by members of "other tribes." One such tale speaks of the existence of Black men, who "lived under the sun, where it rested when it went under the horizon, and who were 'scorched' until they were black."[85] While his citing of this "legend" may be read as an example of his love of playful deception and mischief (a sort of inside joke in that it references his own racial origins), Karina Vernon reads the passage as an expression of Long Lance's alienation from his Black origins: "Long Lance writes as though Black people were a race of aliens to him, one beyond imagining. They not only live in the unimaginable land beneath the sun, but they are also monstrous with their 'scorched' skins. Long Lance emphasizes the outlandish nature of these legends syntactically, by writing that not only was his tribe hearing about White People, but 'they *even* told us of "black white men."'"[86]

Although Vernon concedes that he may have heard the story from Mike Eagle Speaker, and that in his portrayal of Black people he has only reflected what he thought the Blackfoot thought (or would think) of them, she reads Long Lance's description as an "utter rejection of Blackness." Vernon further observes that this story about Blackness is not motivated by the narrative, and that its inclusion suggests a sort of acknowledgment of Long Lance's own racial origins: "It is as though in repressing his personal identification with Blackness, the Blackness he wishes he could admit nevertheless returns, and finds brief acknowledgement in his 'autobiography.'"[87] This reading is not inconsistent with Long Lance's genuine identification with the Blackfoot, and with First Nations people as a whole: "If, as Diana Fuss argues, identification is a 'psychical mechanism that produces self-recognition' via 'the detour through the other that defines self,' ... perhaps in identifying with First Nations and their histories Long Lance found a circuitous way of recognizing himself and identifying with his own Black history."[88]

One Blackfoot ritual described in considerable detail in *Long Lance* involves the consequences of lying, a taboo repeatedly referred to as "the great shame." Long Lance explains how Blackfoot suspected of lying are called before a council and made to "swear before the Horn" that they are telling the truth.[89]

As with the detailed account of Almighty Voice's standoff, during which the Cree hero is exhorted by his mother to fight and to die with honour, Long Lance's description of the Horn ceremony may have been partly inspired by the moral teachings imparted to him by his own pious Baptist mother. If according to the Bible "the wages of sin are death " (Romans 6:23), the consequences of committing the "great shame" of lying are equally dire in the Blackfoot culture. If, before the Horn Society, composed of "the most upstanding men and outstanding warriors in the tribe," the accused individual should "speak with a crooked tongue," death would inexorably follow: "It is said that if anyone lies before the Horn he will die within a half-year. And it is claimed with authority that instances of death from this cause have been known."[90]

In penning an account of his life that is entirely contrafactual, Long Lance makes himself guilty of committing what is considered a "great shame" both in his adopted culture and according to the precepts of the culture into which he was born. The earnestness with which he describes the "swearing before the Horn" ceremony and the consequences of not acknowledging "the great shame" of having lied suggests that Long Lance recognizes the enormity of the deception he is perpetrating. In the very act of writing about it, Long Lance was committing what amounted to a sacrilege, and one may assume that this act was likely accompanied by feelings of guilt and betrayal. He may also have felt a premonition that his "lie," too, would be exposed, and that he might suffer the ultimate penalty for his deception.

Thanks in no small part to the authenticity of its true sources – the tales of Mike Eagle Speaker as told him by his grandmother – as well as to its engagingly told stories and the fame of its author, *Long Lance* was published in August 1928 despite the numerous anachronisms and inconsistencies it contained. Its author cannily dedicated the book to the very men who would have been in a position to call into question every aspect of his account of his "Indian boyhood," namely Canon Middleton of Cardston, and Indian Commissioner Bill Graham, whom he knew from his time in Saskatchewan. The dedication is phrased as an acknowledgment, which would have made it even more awkward for either of the two to challenge Long Lance's version of events: "Dedicated to the two White Men who have guided and encouraged me most since I have taken a place in civilization." For good measure, he added Duncan Campbell Scott, deputy superintendent-general of Indian Affairs, to the list of dedicatees, apostrophizing the man who had strictly enforced the laws outlawing traditional ceremonies such as the potlatch and the sun dance, who had tried to ban Indians from taking part in the Calgary Stampede, and who for decades had overseen and expanded Canada's residential schools, as "a friend of the Indian."[91] He signed his introduction as follows:

BUFFALO CHILD LONG LANCE
Blood Indian Reservation
Cardston, Alberta
July 1, 1928

CHIEF BUFFALO CHILD LONG LANCE, CELEBRATED AUTHOR

It was a stroke of luck that *Long Lance* came to be prefaced by the distinguished American writer Irvin S. Cobb, whom Long Lance had met in New York at a cocktail party given by Hearst editor Ray Long. There is no small irony in the fact that it was the humourist Cobb, a rabid racist known for his "darkie" jokes, who was asked to write an introduction to the book. Cobb's brief foreword focused on the book's "veracity" and "authenticity," for which, he concludes, "the white man will owe [Long Lance] a debt for this work of his and … his people the Indians already owe him a debt for having performed it."[92]

As had been the case with the reception of Grey Owl's first book, the press was extravagant in its praise, emphasizing the authenticity of Long Lance's story. Not only did the first edition of *Long Lance* quickly sell out in North America, translation rights were sold to Dutch and German publishers, and soon a British edition appeared as well.

During his stay in New York, Long Lance was invited to Cobb's apartment on Park Avenue as well as to his Long Island house, and there and at other elegant society events he was the centre of attention, no doubt partly for his good looks (further enhanced by how well he wore his tailored tuxedo), but mainly for the entertaining Indian stories he told. While there was blatant racism against Blacks in New York, the Indians were a different matter altogether, in part due to a spate of literary works that had been published in the nineteenth century, the best-known of which was Longfellow's elegiac poem "Hiawatha." Unlike Afro-Americans, Indians were romanticized as "noble savages" who had lost their land before the inevitable advance of white civilization, and Long Lance was extraordinarily well-equipped to reinforce these conceptions, which he did to great effect at the many dinners and cocktail parties to which he was invited. Long Lance had become the toast of the town, and counted many glamorous women among his friends, including Natacha Rambova, widow of Rudolph Valentino, and the German Princess Alexandra, former wife of a son of Kaiser Wilhelm. He dated the likes of the actress Mildred McCoy and the singer Vivian Hart, and featured prominently in New York's society pages.[93] As Browder remarks, "As an articulate, handsome international spokesman for the Native Americans, he proved appealing to Europeans and Americans alike, furnishing them with a focus for their primitivist fantasies. Long Lance took characteristics that could have been disabilities, like dark skin, and used them to transform himself into a consumable icon."[94]

Not surprisingly, given that he was sought after as an escort by the famous and beautiful women he met at New York parties, he was sometimes asked for his views on mixed marriages and the offspring of such unions. Long Lance answered such questions with professed authority, on one occasion remarking that while white couples might have a Black child because of a "Negro element" in their family past, that did not happen with Indians: "After the fourth generation of intermarriage between white and Indian, all Indian features disappear ... There are no throwbacks."[95] One cannot help wondering whether the fear of having a Black or coloured child was the reason – or at least one of the reasons – Long Lance never married.

It is hardly surprising that Long Lance's celebrity status would come to be exploited commercially. He was now not only famous, he was also extremely popular, his image so "Indian" that the B.F. Goodrich Company recruited him to endorse a new line of canvas running shoes. These were subsequently called "Long Lance Sport Shoes," the name on the tag that came with the shoes showing an image of a bare-chested, black-braided, severe-looking Long Lance, arms crossed, wearing two feathers in his headband.

Ironically, it was not his "Indian" public image but his strong identification with the Indians and their plight that led to an investigation of Long Lance's origins by an official who was in sympathy with Long Lance's views. In a manuscript that appears never to have been published, Long Lance called himself a spokesman for the "Indians of America" for the first time. In this manuscript, he showed real anger in the accusations of exploitation and mistreatment he levelled at the Office of Indian Affairs, abandoning the role of the docile and amusing Indian who was eager to please. The fact that Charles Burke, commissioner of the Office of Indian Affairs, himself criticized his bureau's policies and acknowledged abuses was probably a factor in the Cosmopolitan Book Corporation's sending him an advance copy of Long Lance's book, asking for his comments. Before replying, Burke decided to investigate Long Lance's biographical claims, particularly those concerning his record at West Point and his status as a Blackfoot chief. Long Lance was almost certainly aware of Burke's inquiries due to letters he had received from some of Burke's respondents.[96]

Burke discovered that Long Lance had never attended West Point, having failed the admission exams, and this discovery led to further investigation and further exposure, including a statement from Bill Graham, the Indian commissioner for western Canada, that Long Lance's status with the Blackfoot Indians was purely honorary. The Blood Indians replied to Burke's inquiries as well, saying that Long Lance was not a Blood and had no tribal rights; furthermore, they had heard he was a Cherokee but did not know "definitely who he is and where he comes from."[97]

When Burke finally sent the solicited comments on *Long Lance* to Cosmopolitan, he said: "Gentlemen: Through your courtesy receipt is acknowledged of a publication of fiction entitled 'Long Lance,' for which please accept thanks. This book is very interesting and quite readable."[98]

Burke did not expose Long Lance in so many words, but in referring to the manuscript as "fiction" he sent a message that was unambiguous. Long Lance's career with the Cosmopolitan Book Corporation was over.

LONG LANCE, HOLLYWOOD FILM STAR

Long Lance, aware of Burke's investigation, soon left New York. It was due to the possibility of Burke's further exposure that he never published the untitled manuscript about the Indian Bureau. Although the general public was unaware that there were any doubts about his identity, he was now very much on the defensive. Nevertheless he had agreed to play a major part in a Hollywood film to be titled *The Silent Enemy*. It was to be shot in Canada, and its producer, Douglas Burden, was determined to avoid the clichés about Indians that had so far pervaded Hollywood films, and to offer an authentic account of Indian life in the wilderness before the arrival of the white man. It was for reasons of authenticity that he had chosen Long Lance for one of the principal parts.

Long Lance himself proudly wrote to his former Carlisle classmate Emma Newashe McAllister about his starring role in the film, alongside the famous Sioux chief Chauncey Yellow Robe: "As you may know, Yellow Robe is the nephew of Sitting Bull … We are the only two western Indians in the outfit. There are 17 characters in the picture, all Indians … We have a great time kidding one another … about the battles the Blackfeet and Sioux used to have."[99]

The film was to be shot in northern Ontario, around Temagami, with the local Ojibwa. The "silent enemy" of the title is hunger, caused by the diminishing caribou herds. Long Lance was to play Baluk, "the mighty Ojibwa hunter" who finds the caribou, thus saving the Indians, who are on the verge of starvation.

The nonchalant tone Long Lance adopts in the letter to his Carlisle friend belies the uneasiness he must have felt during the filming. In the United States, Charles Burke was pursuing his investigations. The presence of the famous Yellow Robe must have made Long Lance even more nervous. His anxieties were well founded: a photograph of Chauncey Yellow Robe had appeared in the previous year in *The American Indian* (a quarterly published by the Smithsonian National

Museum of the American Indian). Just below it was an article titled "Sylvester Long Lance, Cherokee," whose "pen name is Chief Buffalo Child Long Lance."[100] It was likely that Chauncey Yellow Robe would remember his coincidental co-occurrence in a journal with his now fellow actor Long Lance. By a strange coincidence, it was while filming near Temagami that Long Lance met a young waitress called Agnes Belaney, daughter of an Ojibwa mother and the Englishman Archie Belaney, who called himself Grey Owl. Agnes Belaney further contributed to Long Lance's unease. She told him "she had never seen an Indian with such dark skin," and she also said, "You must be a different kind of Indian."[101] Long Lance's angry response to Agnes Belaney's observations is charged with inadvertent irony: he told her that he was a full-blooded Indian, whereas all the Indians around Temagami were half-breeds. The latter was, of course, true of Agnes Belaney. (A further irony lies in the fact that Agnes's father, Archie Belaney, aka Grey Owl, had read *Long Lance* and, in *Men of the Last Frontier*, calls him "a splendid savage.")

Long Lance now was terrified of exposure, and to pre-empt the fallout if that should happen, he wrote a letter to his friend Canon Middleton to create an alibi. The pretext for these fictitious revelations was that Long Lance said he wanted to make Middleton the trustee of his estate:

> Now, here is the thing I want to talk to you about: I have several dangerous scenes to do in this picture – Well, to be exact, I have done all of them but one, but that one will be by far the most dangerous of them all; and for that reason they are leaving it to the very last shot of the picture, in case anything should happen to me. When I was down in Wyoming, I learned that my foster-parents, the only parents I have had since I was a child – Cherokee Indians who took me out of a Wild West Show when I was run over by a horse and had my hip knocked out of place, and kept me for several years – I learned that these foster-parents had died since I lost touch with them during the war.[102]

The letter was clearly an attempt to co-opt Middleton into not exposing him. Long Lance wrote his will in March 1929. It was witnessed by the film's producer, Douglas Burden, Ilia Tolstoy (the film's assistant director and a grandson of the famous Russian novelist), and Charlie Bonn, one of the film's technicians. Beneficiary of his personal property was Michael Eagle Speaker, Blood Indian Reserve, Cardston, Alberta. However, his estate was to go to "the St. Paul's Blood Indian School to be used 'to send promising Blood youth through higher schools on being graduated,'"[103] with Canon Middleton acting as sole executor and trustee.

The will fulfilled several purposes. First of all, the terms of the will authenticated the Plains Indian identity Long Lance had claimed vis-à-vis the people working on the film, thus pre-empting the possible expression of doubt by Indians working on the film and also locals he came into contact with, such as Agnes Belaney. Secondly, it also softened up Canon Middleton, named executor and trustee for the celebrity Long Lance, and whose school would be the sole beneficiary. Finally, as Smith points out, in it Long Lance "made provision to repay the tribe and the Indians who had adopted him."[104]

People working on the film expressed amazement at the intensity of Long Lance's acting performance in the scene where he is to be burnt to death due to his failure to find the caribou (although at the last moment, caribou are sighted, saving Baluk, Long Lance's character, and the Indians survive). Smith offers this description of the scene in question: "Naked from the waist up, at forty degrees below zero, Baluk climbs the funeral pyre. Tension rises as the flames crackle and Baluk sings his death chant … As the flames lick at his ankles, he beats the tom-tom, slowly at first, then faster and faster until – as one observer later wrote – 'it seemed as though forty devils were contriving to make one mad.' Long Lance changes the rhythm, slower again, then faster, then a steady, monotonous *tom-tom-tom-tom-tom-tom-tom*, and with this an eerie, chilling chant – his death song."[105]

In an article titled "How *The Silent Enemy* Was Made," William D. Laurence comments on Long Lance's performance of the death chant:

> On approaching the Sacrifice Scene of the Great Hunter, a highlight of the picture, the producers knew that authenticity demanded the singing of the Great Hunter of his Death Chant, the chant every Indian makes up for himself, when still young, for chanting at the hour of his death. They never even suspected that the young chief who played Baluk had his own Death Chant, and would under no circumstances have asked him to sing it anyway, since it is one of the most sacred of Indian rituals … It was not until several days after that Long Lance told [*sic*] he had sung his own Death Chant. He had not planned to do it,

he explained, but had been so carried away by the scene that he had found himself singing, much to his own surprise.[106]

Another piece on the making of the film credits Long Lance with teaching other members of the cast "The Dance of the Dead Men": "We tried very hard to teach a small group of young bucks some of the old steps. Under the patient tuition of Long Lance, who is one of the finest Indian dancers I have ever seen, we succeeded in staging the Dance of the Dead Men ... Not until Long Lance appeared with nothing but a breech cloth and war bonnet and executed a wonderful war dance did they really get interested."[107]

In April 1929, when the filming was finished, Long Lance returned to New York. The film was praised to the skies by critics, and publicity for it was based on its "authenticity": "Amazing! – because it's REAL!" read the heading above one publicity poster. Reviews emphasized the authenticity of the film as well, and in doing so focused on Long Lance. The *New York American* said: "The hero role is taken by Chief Long Lance, a superb figure, agile as a catamount and utterly fearless." *Variety* said: "Chief Long Lance is an ideal picture Indian, because he is a full-blooded one ... an author of note in Indian lore, and now an actor in fact."[108]

In short, the film was a triumph, and was expected to be released internationally. The studio had it dubbed into eight languages. Meanwhile, the B.F. Goodrich advertisements for the Long Lance running shoe were hugely successful. Many of them were published complete with a first-person story attributed to Long Lance, and the company asked Long Lance to write a thirty-four-page booklet titled *How to Talk in Indian Sign Language* as part of the publicity campaign. The booklet features Long Lance with a bare torso, but otherwise in Indian regalia, demonstrating the signs. Jim Thorpe, the Native football star and Olympic gold medalist, was recruited to write a testimonial endorsing both Long Lance and the shoe. Thorpe's story was captioned "The Greatest All-round Athlete in Modern History Adds a Word."

In New York, Long Lance had rented a room at the exclusive Explorers Club, whose members included distinguished explorers such as Roald Amundson and Fritjof Nansen as well as President Theodore Roosevelt and naturalist writer Ernest Thompson Seton. Long Lance, too, became a member, and the only non-white living at the club. His admission had been supported by warm letters of recommendation from Explorer Club director Dr Clyde Fisher and anthropologist Clark Wissler, whose area of specialization was North American Indians, in particular the Sioux and the Piegans. Long Lance made a point of cultivating friendly relationships with his distinguished fellow club members, no doubt hoping that the august company he kept would shield him against further investigation. Clark Wissler, author of *The American Indian: An Introduction to the Anthropology of the New World*, had read *Long Lance*, and although he must have known that its author was a fraud, he did not expose him, likely because of the positive impact of Long Lance's advocacy on behalf of the Indians.[109]

Long Lance lived a high-society life in New York, giving lectures on Indian culture. Notwithstanding the fame and social success he had achieved, he continued to invent increasingly outlandish details to further embellish his legend, telling an interviewer that he had played tackle for the teams on which the famous Jim Thorpe had played, that he had attended the Olympic Games in Stockholm in 1912, that he had been wounded eight times in France and been "decorated by three governments for gallantry in action."[110] Given these brazen lies, all of which could easily have been proven untrue, one cannot help thinking that, like Almighty Voice, Long Lance wanted to be caught.

"I SHALL WALK ON A TRAIL OF STARS"

Long Lance's fabulous career reached its zenith when, at the annual dinner of the Poetry Society of America held at the Biltmore Hotel 28 January 1930, before four hundred distinguished guests, he stepped to the podium to demonstrate the Indian sign language he had recently been lecturing on, and then launched into a recitation of "the heroic death song of his Blackfoot tribe which he had translated from their language."[111] The song went thus:

Oh, look down upon Long Lance,
Thou knowest Long Lance,
The Sun, the Moon, the Day, the Night;
Tell me if it is real,
This life I have lived,
This death I am dying.
Ah, the clouds are leaving my door,

The Outward Trail is no longer dark,
I see – I understand:
There is no life, there is no death;
I shall walk on a trail of stars.[112]

Thus Long Lance chanted his death song for the second time, publicly performing "the most sacred of Indian rituals" at a ballroom dinner – an act of blasphemy. In connection with his intoning of the chant in *The Silent Enemy*, Long Lance himself had explained and interpreted it: "Every Indian has his individual Death Song which he chants as he is passing out. Before this, he goes out alone and fasts until the last words of the song and the melody of the chant come to him, sometimes in a dream, sometimes in wakefulness. The 'trail of stars' is the Milky Way, also called the Ghost Trail and the Dance of the Dead Men. The Indians believe that this milky brightness is composed of millions of ghosts on their way to the Happy Hunting Grounds."[113]

It was as if Long Lance, in publicly performing his death chant, had acted on a premonition. Shortly after the evening of the poetry event, he was confronted by William Chanler, lawyer of Douglas Burden, producer of *The Silent Enemy*: when Long Lance walked into Chanler's office, having been summoned there, Chanler greeted him with "Hello, Sylvester."[114] In addition to the investigation initiated by Commissioner Burke, already in process at the Indian Affairs Bureau, there had been further allegations, this time from Chauncey Yellow Robe, who was also in New York to lecture on the American Indian.

Facing Chanler's accusations, Long Lance at first stood his ground, but then made an "admission," saying he was not a Blood Indian but was a Blackfoot, fabricating yet another story of having been raised by a Cherokee family whose name he thought might have been Long.

Charles Rhoads, Burke's successor at the Bureau of Indian Affairs, had, in response to the various allegations about Long Lance, determined that Long Lance was in fact a Croatan, people of mixed blood who had previously been known as "free negroes." He shared this information with Burden and Chanler, who were angry and dismayed: the fact that Long Lance was a "fake" threatened to compromise what seemed to be a bright future for *The Silent Enemy*, which had already been praised mainly for its authenticity, particularly in the figure that Long Lance played. In all the advertising, Long Lance had been billed as a full-blooded Indian, and his exposure would threaten the success of the studio's planned publicity tour.

Before being hired for the film, Long Lance had given Chanler the name of James Henderson as a reference. Henderson had been superintendent of Carlisle and then an agent for the Eastern Band of Cherokees. Chanler decided to write to Henderson, who replied saying that Long Lance "was never recognized at Carlisle by the Cherokees as a Cherokee Indian," and that "it was alleged that he was more of negro blood than Indian." Various circumstances conspired to identify not only Sylvester Long, but also members of his family in Winston-Salem. As Smith puts it, "All indications were that Long Lance, far from being a Plains Indian chief, was, by southern racial standards, a Negro."[115]

A letter from Canon Middleton, however, provided an alibi for Long Lance. Middleton essentially said that while Long Lance was not a Plains Indian, as he had claimed, he was indeed a Cherokee. Having received these conflicting reports, Chanler dispatched Ilia Tolstoy, who had worked on the film, to Winston-Salem to find out the truth about Sylvester Long alias Long Lance. Rumours were by now spreading in New York that Long Lance was part negro. Some people, such as Irvin S. Cobb, who had written the foreword to *Long Lance*, were furious: "To think that we had him here in the house. We're so ashamed! We entertained a nigger."[116] Many friends simply dropped him.

Others, however, stood by him, including a Scotsman named Seumas Clannfhearghuis (Chief of Clann Fhearghuis of Stra-Chur and Clann Ailpein), from the Explorers Club, to whom Long Lance had disclosed his mixed ancestry. Long Lance himself had told Chauncey Yellow Robe of his background, explaining how in the southern United States he had been segregated as coloured. According to Smith, "Yellow Robe must have respected the courage it took to challenge the color barrier, for he apparently forgave and accepted Long Lance."[117] Browder suggests that the reason Chauncy Yellow Robe did not expose his co-star was because he was "reluctant to unmask an Indian spokesman who had achieved so much."[118] When Yellow Robe fell ill before *The Silent Enemy* publicity tour to Hollywood, he agreed that Long Lance should go in his place. The film studio and its producer had no choice but to send their other star, dubious though they were about what might come of it.

Meanwhile, Ilia Tolstoy was investigating Long Lance's background in Winston-Salem, on behalf of Chanler and Burden. He went to see

Joe and Sallie Long, who told him they were Cherokee and referred him to their oldest son, Abe. Abe was at first reluctant to identify Sylvester, but finally admitted that he had a brother whom he hadn't seen in twenty years. Ilia interviewed numerous informants in the community, who explained the complicated history of the Croatans and also the fact that in Winston-Salem they were labelled as coloured, no matter that some of them were of Indian-white descent. Tolstoy decided to take a stand in support of Long Lance and, in his report to Chanler, stated that Long Lance's origins were Indian and white.

Under the pressures of growing doubts about his identity, Long Lance began to smoke and drink heavily. He reacted to the mounting skepticism by asserting more and more outrageous claims regarding his illustrious past. As Smith remarks, "He had lost his balance. He felt something closing in on him. It was as if he wanted to be caught, wanted to lose the hand he had dealt for himself so many years before, when he had first resolved to pass himself [*sic*] as the Indian he believed he really was."[119]

Except for a few friends who stood by him, Long Lance was now stigmatized at the Explorers Club, where he had once been a sought-after companion. It was clear that he was no longer welcome at the club, and when he was offered free flying lessons at Roosevelt Field on Long Island, he gratefully accepted, staying at a local hotel. After just a few lessons, he performed daring stunts on his first solo flights, and volunteered to demonstrate a new kind of parachute at an air show, although he had never used a parachute before. Predictably, his air exploits were written up in the press against the backdrop of his fabricated biography. The *New York Sun* wrote: "Chief Long Lance says there is something about the air that agrees particularly well with the temperament of the Indian. The ranginess and freedom akin to this continent before the advent of the white man appeals to the redskin ... Chief Long Lance has always proved himself to be the master of the unexpected. Up until he was in his teens, he could talk little English, could not read it at all and had never been inside a white man's house. He has since been an honor student at Carlisle, a West Point cadet, a winner of the *Croix de Guerre*."[120]

Letters he wrote to friends while he was taking flying lessons express the freedom he felt while he was up in the air. Given the situation in which Long Lance now found himself, it is easy to see how flying represented an escape from the pressures, the anxieties, and, more recently, the humiliations that had ensued after the revelations of Chanler and Burden's investigations into his origins.

It was at this time of crisis that he was also brought face to face with his abandonment of his family, creating almost unbearable emotional turmoil as he confronted what he had done. Early in the new year of 1931, his brother Walter arrived in New York to see him. With no contact information for his brother, Walter had been forced to ask around in New York as to Long Lance's whereabouts. The purpose of Walter's visit was to solicit help to pay for medical expenses for their ailing and elderly parents, which Walter and brother Abe were unable to manage on their own.

When the brothers finally met, after not seeing each other for twenty-two years, the reunion was emotionally charged for both.

After the meeting with Walter, Long Lance was tormented by guilt and also nostalgia. The morning after seeing his brother, he wrote him a long letter:

> I must have been in a sort of daze. I don't remember how I said goodbye. And it was only when I had gotten on the train and my brain had cooled a little that I remembered seeing you reaching for the taxi fare, and then realized that you, too, must have gotten out at Penn Station. I had been under the impression that you were going to take the taxi on to some other destination. And when I got out my mind was so fixed on not making a fool of myself saying goodbye to you, that my eyes actually saw things that did not register in my mind until I got home.
>
> I lay awake most of the night, wishing that I could phone you ... kicking myself because I had not stayed at the apartment all night with you, and a thousand other things that came to my mind when it was too late. I would have given anything to have seen you again. I don't think that I have ever felt the emotions that my visit with you brought into being.
>
> I have not yet fully untangled these emotions: my own darling brother whom I used to romp and play with, coming to me after twenty-two years, wondering if I were going to be ashamed of him.[121]

Long Lance did send money home to his family, but he did not go to see them. The letters that accompanied his cheques were loving and tender, but also cautioned his family not to expose him: "If there is anything in the papers, Abe, you will be careful about names, won't you."[122]

THE LAST CHAPTER

While he was in Hollywood promoting *The Silent Enemy*, Long Lance had been introduced to the who's who of Hollywood, including Anita Baldwin, one of the richest women in the United States and a divorcee. In spring of 1931, at loose ends after his promotional stint was over – he had also appeared as a special guest at film screenings to promote the film in New York – he gladly accepted an offer of employment from her. Officially hired as Anita's secretary and bodyguard, Long Lance was to spend several months in Europe with her and her entourage. In his passport application, Long Lance gave his year of birth as 1896, said he had been born in Sweetgrass, Montana, and that his father, Pitah, had died when he was just a few years old. He indicated the purpose of the trip as "pleasure." To witness his statements, he appealed to an old friend from Carlisle, Emma Newashe, who duly confirmed them in an affidavit. Long Lance's passport forms were clearly not verified by the State Department, and the passport was issued.

Although Long Lance left notes on the Europe trip about his impressions, he never mentioned anything untoward. However, Anita's letters reveal that Long Lance had experienced a depression and made several suicide attempts on the trip, the first on the first night aboard the *Ile de France*, en route to Europe. In Berlin, he had arrived drunk at dinner in the elegant Hotel Adlon and threatened one of his and Anita's entourage with a carving knife.

After Anita and her group returned to the United States, Long Lance stayed in New York, as he had been "given up as too much of a responsibility" by Anita.[123] Long Lance moved back into the Explorers Club, where he was still a member.

Soon after returning to New York, he made the acquaintance of Elizabeth Randolph Clapp, daughter of a wealthy family, who had become a dancer. "Bessie," as she was known to her friends, was only eighteen, and believed she was part Indian. She was irresistibly drawn to the much older Long Lance, fell deeply in love with him, and wanted to marry him. While there are indications that Long Lance reciprocated her affections, he never proposed marriage, explaining that he was "engaged to someone else." When the relationship ended, Long Lance found himself cut off from all the friends he had in the past drawn into his confidence. The only person he had left to turn to was Anita, with whom he pleaded for help and who eventually agreed to pay for further air school training and to help him buy an airplane.

In December 1931 Long Lance returned to California. His background was being further investigated, this time by the Explorers Club, where he had been living in New York. His invented identity as a Plains Indian chief, his stories of his glorious war record, his reckless lying about virtually his entire past, now seemed to have caught up with him. The search for his true identity would be thorough and relentless. He was now to pay the price for his self-reinvention. He had fraudulently claimed a Plains Indian identity, but in assuming that role, he had displayed a remarkable range of talents. These had let him accomplish extraordinary feats that, in addition to benefiting him personally, also constituted a genuine contribution in disseminating knowledge about the Indians and in drawing attention to their plight. As a "professional Indian" who seemed as much at home in the society salons of New York as in the forests and plains of Western Canada, he defied stereotypes, becoming an Indian role model *extraordinaire.*[124] It would be the brilliant success of his real achievements as a journalist, a friend and advocate of the Indian people, an engaging author and public speaker, and a film actor that would lead to his ultimate downfall.

Long Lance now felt the full impact of the consequences of his imposture. In going to California, he was literally escaping, seeking a refuge from the shame and humiliation that he knew were imminent. Anita was his last hope. When the two had first met, Long Lance had been at the height of his career – a celebrated writer, speaker, and film star. Anita had been romantically attracted to the handsome, dashing, engaging, and most unusual society darling. Although she had acquiesced with some reluctance to his pleas for help, she may have held out hope that their relationship would turn into a more romantic one.

When Long Lance arrived in California, his first encounter with Anita was cordial. He had told her that his plan was to take more flying lessons to obtain a commercial pilot's licence and to acquire a plane, presumably to operate a commercial flying service. Long Lance regularly visited Anita, who invited him to use her home as a base and also paid for his advanced flying lessons.

Overt conflict developed with Anita when it became clear that she would not be buying Long Lance the airplane he wished to acquire, which he had counted on. He took this as reneging on an earlier promise he had understood her to have made to him. Long Lance now had no prospects for the future. His desperation at the situation he found himself in was heightened when he received a telephone call from Bessie Clapp, informing him that she had just married.

On 19 March 1932, Long Lance, who had been drinking, hired a taxi to take him to Anita's. He was carrying a gun. He arrived at about midnight, and Anita soon retired, leaving Long Lance in the library. From her bedroom, she heard a shot. Long Lance was found dead, killed by a self-inflicted gunshot.

It is not difficult to identify motives for his suicide. According to Anita, Long Lance had made several suicide attempts on the trip to Europe. His battle with depression may have been an ongoing one. In California and towards the end of his sojourn in New York, he had been severely depressed, and was drinking heavily. His situation seemed hopeless and desperate: he was the somewhat reluctantly tolerated protégé of Anita; he was at the point of suffering the shame and humiliation of exposure as a fraud; he had become estranged from his family, whom he loved and by whom he was loved; a woman he loved and might have married had just married someone else; and finally, his hopes of starting a new life as a pilot, which he had clearly envisaged, had been dashed due to Anita's refusal to buy him a plane.

When Long Lance took his own life, he must have felt he had exhausted even the limited possibilities remaining to him. His financial resources were depleted. He had felt fully and keenly the public humiliation of exposure, and the personal loss of final, irreparable estrangement from his family. Left now with no prospects for a future that might have let him escape into yet another existence – that of becoming a pilot – Long Lance felt he had no choice but to end it all.

After Long Lance's death, Anita hired a detective to look into his origins. The report read: "Subject's father full-blood negro. Joe S. Long, 95, Brookstown Avenue, Winston-Salem, North Carolina. Mother half Indian. Two brothers, one sister respected negros [*sic*]. One brother negro detective. Sister divorced from negro preacher. Father was a janitor at high school for 25 years; now retired. Owns property. Subject's name Sylvester."[125]

The tenor of the terse investigative report, which contained truths, untruths, and half-truths concerning Long Lance's complicated real antecedents, represented the kind of verdict as to his identity that he had probably always feared. It was fearful anticipation of just such a "verdict" that contributed to his decision to commit suicide. The report attributed to him the "coloured" identity that had been imposed upon him from childhood, one he had worked hard to effectively erase and had deliberately discarded. Having systematically attempted to obliterate his old identity, the persona that Long Lance had created to replace it was now itself destroyed.

Long Lance's family, when they heard of his death, wanted his body to be brought to Winston-Salem for burial, but could not raise the money. Long Lance, dead at age forty-two, was buried 30 March 1932 in the Inglewood Cemetery in Los Angeles.

THE LONG LANCE LEGEND

Some of Long Lance's old friends from Carlisle ensured that his legend as he had created it would survive: *Redman Echoes: Comprising the Writings of Chief Buffalo Child Long Lance and Biographical Sketches by His Friends* is a compendium consisting of miscellaneous writings about Long Lance, a number of his own texts, and several documents supporting the identity he had claimed. It was compiled by a young admirer of Long Lance, Roberta Forsberg, but the project was likely initiated by Carlisle classmate Emma Newashe McAllister, who wrote the preface. It was published in 1933, a year after Long Lance's death, and the overall tone of the collection is that of a eulogy.

In addition to honouring their friend with a lasting tribute, the intention of those responsible for the volume seems to have been, at least partially, to counteract the accusations of imposture following the exposure of Long Lance's true identity, and to ensure that his legend remained intact. Although the contributors associated with Carlisle would have known that Long Lance was not a Plains Indian from Canada, he is depicted as such by "R.J.F." (presumably Roberta Forsberg) and Emma Newashe McAllister in poems dedicated to him.[126]

Long Lance's Carlisle English teacher, in testifying to the veracity of the Long Lance legend in "An Appreciation," goes so far as to misrepresent the circumstances of his name change from Sylvester Long to Long Lance: "One auspicious day in early summer there arrived a handsome boy who announced himself as Sylvester Long Lance. A romantic sounding name, suggestive of knightly deeds in tilts of skill and valor ... The authorities pondered the name and finally decided that it did not accord with the democratic and practical ideals of the school, therefore Lance was eliminated and the boy was listed simply as Sylvester Long. Not until he became famous did he assume his rightful name and title of Chief Buffalo Child Long Lance."[127]

Emma Newashe McAllister is more circumspect, not to say evasive, in testifying to the veracity of the Long Lance legend: "Not being a biographer of Long Lance, I refrain from referring to his native environment and early training. Those are all covered in his own works: they need no comment from me. That he lived the life he loved and wrote about there can be no dispute."[128]

A contribution to the volume had also been solicited from Long Lance's old friend Canon Middleton, of Cardston, Alberta. It is Middleton who, in his obliquely phrased tribute, comes closest to reconciling the "imposture" with the truth about Long Lance: "I knew Long Lance and knew him well. I knew him shorn of paint and feathers, bared of the uniform of a soldier, and divested of the equipment of a modern journalist. I knew the Indian, the man, which he truly was, groping for higher things through a very complex transition, hindered withal by many apparent contradictions, yet holding fast to an indefinable something which gained for him a place amongst the immortals of the noble 'Red Man.'"[129]

If the Long Lance legend, although less well known than that of that other "glorious Indian impostor" Grey Owl, has survived, it is likely due to the impressive record of its hero's actual accomplishments and exploits. In so flamboyantly living out the life of the persona he had himself created, in inscribing this self-created identity into an autofictional "autobiography," and in offering it up as the subject of innumerable articles perpetuating the myth of the Plains Indian chief, Long Lance had also inadvertently played a considerable role in reinforcing a larger mythical entity, namely the romance of the Canadian West, in which the factual and the fictional/legendary remain inextricably interwoven to this day.

6

Hybrid Identities: The Eaton Sisters

"You are you and I am I," says Confucius. I give my right hand to the Occidentals and my left to the Orientals, hoping that between them they will not utterly destroy the insignificant "connecting link." And that's all.
Sui Sin Far

THE EATON SISTERS

Among the Canadian autofiction writers of the early 1900s were two sisters, born into an unusually large, gifted, mixed-race family. Edith and Winnifred Eaton were the children of an English father and a Chinese mother who had met and married in China in the 1860s. Both sisters were journalists and fiction writers who began their writing careers in Montreal, and both were pioneers of Asian North American literature. Winnifred, the first Asian North American novelist, concealed her Chinese identity behind a Japanese pen name, Onoto Watanna, assuming a Japanese persona in her writing and publicly presenting herself as being Japanese. Edith, who assumed the *nom de plume* Sui Sin Far, wrote mainly in the voice of a Chinese persona, and her short stories are considered to be the first Asian North American works of fiction.

Their father, Edward Eaton, a silk merchant, had gone to China to further the interests of his family's business, which was based in Macclesfield, England, at the time a major silk manufacturing centre. In her recent book on Edith Eaton, Mary Chapman suggests that their mother, Grace Trefusis (whose Chinese name translates as Lotus Blossom), may herself have been of mixed race. Chapman gives Grace's full name as Achuen "Grace" Amoy. She also provides further particulars about Grace's early life that explain some of the references to travelling actors and acrobats in Edith's and Winnifred's writings. According to Chapman, as a young child Grace had been sold to the leader of a Chinese acrobatic troupe with whom she went on tour in the United States, Europe, and Britain. In London, she escaped from the troupe thanks to missionaries who believed she was being abused, and who began training her there as a missionary.[1] There is general agreement among biographical sources that Grace subsequently returned to China, and that she met and married Edward Eaton in Shanghai.

By the mid-1860s the couple had moved to England, where they lived with the extended Eaton family in Macclesfield and where Edith, the second child and oldest daughter, was born in 1865. In the early 1870s, the family migrated to North America, settling in New York, where Edward established a business that subsequently failed. The family then briefly returned to Macclesfield before moving to Montreal with six children in tow. In Montreal, ten more Eaton children, including Winnifred, were born.

Why the family emigrated is not clear, but racist attitudes towards the Chinese in Britain and particularly in small centres such as Macclesfield likely played a role. Amy Ling, who wrote about both Edith and Winnifred Eaton, maintains that Edward's family disapproved of their son's marriage,[2] and Annette White-Parks, Edith's biographer, suggests that Edward and his family may have been asked to leave Macclesfield. Various sources indicate that Edward was seen as the proverbial "black sheep" by the family and sent off to America, perhaps receiving a remittance from them.[3]

In spite of her mother's adaptation to English ways, including manners and dress, and in spite of her privileged life as the child of a genteel English family on her father's side, Edith, born in England, met racism early on. In an autobiographical essay titled "Leaves from the Mental Portfolio of an Eurasian" published in 1909,[4] she recalls that in Macclesfield, at the age of four, "in a green English lane," she overheard her nurse telling "another of her kind that my mother is Chinese," upon which the other nurse exclaimed "Oh, Lord!" and proceeded to examine her "curiously from head to foot." She was taunted for being Chinese by other children, and summoned into the drawing room for curious inspection by the adults in English houses into which she was invited by playmates. At her private school, she was taught that "China is a heathen country being civilized by England."[5]

Edith remembered reacting to the taunts and colonialist attitudes with fierce defiance, but also that they caused her to develop, at a very early age, a sense of her "difference." Stigmatized as she was as a "half-caste," she nevertheless felt that her mixed racial background gave her a kind of special status, an added dimension that would prove to be an asset in realizing her literary aspirations. She would later write in her autobiographical essay "Leaves": "At eighteen years of age what troubles me is not that I am who I am, but that others are ignorant of my superiority. I am small, but my feelings are big – and great is my vanity."[6]

Edith's early memories of racism in Macclesfield appear harmless compared with what the Eaton children encountered growing up in Montreal. She describes the intrusive curiosity with which she and her siblings were examined: "Now and then we are stopt [*sic*] and plied with questions as to what we eat and drink, how we go to sleep, if my mother understands what my father says to her, if we sit on chairs or squat on floors, etc., etc., etc."[7] Not only were the Eaton children taunted verbally by other children, they were also physically attacked: "They pull my hair, they tear my clothes, they scratch my face, and all but lame my brother; but the white blood in our veins fights valiantly for the Chinese half of us. When it is all over, exhausted and bedraggled, we crawl home, and report to our mother that we have 'won the battle.'"[8]

In Montreal, the Eaton family took up residence in the working-class neighbourhood of Hochelaga, an area then dominated by mills and factories. White-Parks suggests that Edward Eaton may have been employed in one of them as a clerk.[9] Nonetheless, as part of a genteel English merchant-class family, the Eatons clearly felt that their social status was well above that of the working-class community in which they lived. Their self-perceived social superiority was derived as much from colonial attitudes as from an entrenched sense of class distinctions. In Winnifred's (auto)biographical novel *Marion*, the narrator mentions her father's paintings being taken "back to England … as representatives of Canadian art," adding "which it was not – papa had studied in France, and was an Englishman, not a Canadian."[10] Notwithstanding the family's poverty, the children were initially sent to private schools, as they would have been in England. Once they were withdrawn, they were home-schooled, taught by mother Grace.

On the basis of other passages in *Marion*, but also some references in Edith Eaton/Sui Sin Far's autobiographical essay, it is clear that in

Hochelaga the Eatons continued to follow the genteel pursuits of a privileged English family. The children were encouraged to read, to write poetry, and even to write and stage plays. These same references reveal that Edward was something of an artist, and Edith mentions that she was sent out to sell her father's pictures as well as "some lace which I made myself."[11] Thus the Eaton family, living in rented company housing where they kept a few domestic animals in their small, unkempt back garden, lived a somewhat bohemian life that was at odds with their working-class surroundings.

Conditions in the Eaton household, consisting of fourteen children (two Eaton children died) and two adults living in cramped lodgings, were chaotic, and it was the older children who were the most affected. As the eldest daughter, Edith was made to take on adult responsibilities from the age of ten, not only selling her father's pictures and lace she had designed and made herself, but also looking after her growing brood of younger siblings. She expresses her traumatization by the succession of births – which took place at home – in "Leaves": "My mother's screams of agony when a baby is born almost drives me wild, and long after her pangs have subsided I feel them in my own body." She also felt keenly the tensions in the household: "If there is any trouble in the home – between my mother and father, or if any child is punished, how I suffer!"[12] The family was constantly moving to new lodgings, either to economize, or to accommodate the incessantly growing family, or because someone who "lives near us ... has seen my mother."[13]

WINNIFRED EATON ALIAS ONOTO WATANNA

Although Winnifred was ten years younger than Edith and had been born in Montreal, she grew up in circumstances similar to her sister's. Racism against the Chinese was still rampant, and, even with the older children contributing to the household, the Eaton family was still poor. With her older sisters gone, Winnifred was now put in charge of her younger siblings and helped maintain the chaotic household, both of which tasks she loathed.

Winnifred felt early on that she had special gifts: "I had always secretly believed there were strains of genius hidden in me; I had always lived in a little dream world of my own, wherein, beautiful and courted I moved among the elect of the earth," she writes in *Me*.[14] Both sisters tweaked their biographies, Edith making herself three years younger than she actually was, Winnifred altering her birth date, 1875, by four years, stating that she had been born in 1879. (After her death, Winnifred's children were startled to learn that she had changed their birth dates, too, making them all two years younger than they were.) Winnifred, who had been christened Lillie Winifred, also modified her name, dropping the "Lillie" and doubling the *n* in "Winifred." Although it is not clear exactly when Winnifred made these alterations to her personal particulars, one wonders whether her suppression of the name "Lillie" may have coincided with Edith's adopting the pseudonym Sui Sin Far, which translates as "Chinese lily."

Two books published late in Winnifred's writing career – in 1915 and 1916 respectively – offer a great deal of insight and information about the Eaton siblings and the dynamics of life in the Eaton household, although the recounting of events is no doubt at times factually unreliable. *Me: A Book of Remembrance* is a sort of memoir, presented as an account of the author's life. *Marion: The Story of an Artist's Model* is a biographical novel based on the life of a younger Eaton sister, Sara. Both are works of autofiction insofar as they construct a narrative reality centred on the author (notwithstanding the fact that in *Marion* Winnifred is supposedly telling her sister's story). Nevertheless, the characterization of many of the family figures who appear, only thinly disguised, in these autofictional works is consistent with factual information presented by the biographers of both Winnifred and Edith, and also in Edith's autobiographical "Leaves." Winnifred's and Edith's biographers both frequently draw on *Me* and *Marion* to establish points of reference in recounting the lives of their respective subjects.[15]

Based on indications in the sisters' biographies and in Winnifred's biographical novels, it is clear that temperamentally Edith and Winnifred could not have been more different. Winnifred was a fun-loving extrovert who grew up to be an incorrigible flirt, at times being engaged to three men at once. "I had the most decided and instinctive liking for the opposite sex," her alter ego Nora declares in *Me*.[16] Her sister Edith, on the other hand, is portrayed as an ever-dutiful daughter and sister with a strong sense of propriety. In *Marion*, Winnifred sums up Edith's views on the male sex by having Ada, who stands in for Edith in the novel, state: "There is no need to get married if you can earn your own living ... I think most men are hateful."[17]

In spite of their different temperaments, there can be no doubt that Edith's career, first as a stenographer and journalist and then as a fiction writer, influenced Winnifred's, which followed the same trajectory. Her first story signed Onoto Watanna appeared in 1897, less than a year after Edith's first story was published under the name Sui Sin Far. The careers of both sisters were to some extent facilitated by the husband of their sister Grace: Walter Blackburn Harte was an English-born essayist who founded a literary journal called the *Fly Leaf*, which published some of Edith's earlier work. He was also known for his articles on Canadian intellectual life and letters that appeared in major magazines in the United States.[18] The fact that Harte himself was interested in Orientalism and wrote articles about Japanese art likely played a role in Winnifred's assuming a Japanese persona when she began her career as a writer.

In 1896, probably through her own or Edith's Montreal contacts in journalism, Winnifred offered to take a position as a reporter for a newspaper in Jamaica. About her departure from Montreal she writes in *Me*: "my heart was light, and I had not been happy at home."[19] This passing remark speaks volumes as to how intolerable conditions in the crowded Eaton home had become for Winnifred, now almost twenty-one (in *Me* she says she was seventeen). No doubt she saw a stint in Jamaica, living on her own, as an adventure and an opportunity to further her career as a writer. It also represented the possibility to cast off her problematic half-caste identity.

She remained in Jamaica for about six months, her departure occasioned, she writes in *Me*, by the trauma of being assaulted by a wealthy, influential government official, an older Black man, who subsequently proposed to her. She got Edith to take over her post with *Gall's News Letter*. (Edith, too, remained in Jamaica for about six months, her return to Montreal occasioned by a bout of malaria.)

The Jamaica experience was a crucial one for both sisters. Racial tensions between the dominant white minority population and Black Jamaicans manifested themselves everywhere, including at the exclusive Myrtle Bank Hotel (owned by their employer) where the sisters were lodged. Winnifred passed as white, never mentioning her mixed ancestry. It is clear that throughout her stay, she identified herself with the small, exclusive, white minority that ruled the island. Whereas Edith identified with the Black and coloured Jamaicans, Winnifred saw them as "other" and vaguely threatening. In a description of her arrival in Jamaica in *Me*, she tells of being overwhelmed by the crowds of "negroes" meeting the ship on her arrival: "It was ... with a genuine thrill of excitement and fear that I looked down upon that vast sea of upturned black and brown faces. Never will I forget that first impression of Jamaica. Everywhere I looked were negroes."[20]

For contemporary readers aware of Winnifred's true origins, what is more shocking than the latent racism expressed in this passage is that she professes that she had known nothing of racial prejudice before coming to Jamaica: "I had never even heard the expression 'race prejudice' before, and I was as far from feeling it as any person in the world. It must be remembered that in Canada we do not encounter the problem of race. One color there is as good as another. Certainly people of Indian extraction are well thought of and esteemed, and my own mother was a foreigner. What should I, a girl who had never before been outside Quebec, and whose experience had been within the narrow confines of home and a small circle, know of race prejudice?"[21]

Her categorical declaration that she knows nothing about race prejudice, as "such did not exist in Montreal," is a blatant denial of the racism she and her family had encountered in Montreal. She could hardly have forgotten the racial discrimination that she, like the other Eaton children, had experienced. In recounting her Jamaican experience, she is recounting more than a foreign "adventure": going to Jamaica was an opportunity to leave the dysphoric circumstances of her previous life behind her. Having left Montreal, where she and her family were known, she was now free to pass as a white Canadian whose only "exotic" feature was that she came from a predominantly French-speaking province. With her comments on race prejudice, she was deliberately avoiding and explicitly denying her own half-caste identity. As telling as her professed innocence regarding racism is her reference to her mother as a "foreigner," thus replacing the traumatizing racial identity with a less compromising national one.

The trauma of race shame that Winnifred is so intent on escaping in Jamaica explains her excessive reaction to the proposal of the Jamaican government official Mr Burbank, who is both Jewish and Black, and whom she describes in *Me* as "a great black man, the 'bogy man' of my childhood days."[22] Shirley Geok-lin Lim explains Winnifred/Nora's reaction to Burbank's advances as race panic: "Her hysteria when Burbank kisses her is understandable only in light of race panic. Burbank's sexual claim on her, a black Jewish man acting on the unspoken assumption that his mixed-race status is equal to hers so as to permit this physical intimacy 'robbed me of all my physical and mental powers' [*Me*, 55], because it has made overt and visible her own non-white status."[23]

Winnifred's whereabouts after her stay in Jamaica are somewhat uncertain, as they can be traced only through her novels *Me* and *Marion*. According to these sources, she goes first to Boston, where she meets a man she calls Dr Manning, who offers her a job in Richmond, Virginia. On the train to Richmond, she meets an older man whom she calls Mr Hamilton, with whom she falls in love. When Dr Manning "slips into [her] bedroom at night" shortly after her arrival in Richmond, she flees, and with money sent to her by Mr Hamilton, she seeks to establish herself in Chicago.[24] Her tumultuous love affair with Mr Hamilton, who helps her financially and seeks to "keep" her but will not commit to legitimizing the relationship, stands at the centre of *Me*, and the book ends with Nora leaving Chicago and boarding a train to New York, having learned that Hamilton is not only married but in an adulterous relationship with another woman.

It was in Chicago that Winnifred began to write and publish "Japanese" stories signed Onoto Watanna. A number of factors would have played a role in her choice of literary disguise, which she soon extended to encompass her personal identity as well. One of these was certainly the fact that (Japanese) Orientalism had become fashionable around the turn of the twentieth century. Whereas in Montreal, like everywhere else in North America, the Chinese were maligned and stigmatized, Japanese styles, summed up in a trend called *Japonisme*, were much in vogue. Diana Birchall, Winnifred's biographer, remarks that the Gilbert and Sullivan operetta *The Mikado* was presented in Montreal in 1886, and describes a family photograph of three Eaton sisters taken about that time, "waving fans and wearing kimonos."[25]

Another factor was that Winnifred could draw on a great deal of literature about Japan to authenticate her stories. By the late nineteenth century, fuelled by travel accounts of the Far East that focused on the mystery and romance of Japanese culture, a spate of literature about Japan had appeared, some works of which were wildly popular. Pierre Loti's *Madame Chrysanthemum* was available in English translation as of 1888, and John Luther Long's story collection *Miss Cherry-Blossom of Tokyo* had been published in 1895. *Miss Cherry-Blossom* was followed by his novel *Madame Butterfly* in 1898, which a few years later gave rise to Puccini's opera. Another source would have been Lafcadio Hearn, who had gone to Japan in 1890, where he published his collection of Japanese legends, fairy tales, and essays about Japan. There would have been a wealth of literature about Japan readily available in libraries for Winnifred to consult, both fiction and travel writing, with the help of which she could create a sense of authenticity in her stories. As for authenticating her "Japanese" identity, her physical appearance was an asset. Although she was fair-skinned, she was small, dark-haired, and "foreign-looking," sufficiently "exotic" to assume the Japanese persona of Onoto Watanna, particularly when she wore her trademark Japanese kimonos and other Japanese accessories.

BECOMING ONOTO WATANNA

While there can be no doubt that Winnifred as a Eurasian cannily exploited the fact that *Japonisme* was all the rage, becoming "Onoto Watanna" and passing as a Japanese was a strategy of concealment, a way to divest herself of her stigmatizing Chinese half-caste identity. Literary scholar Dominika Ferens cites Erving Goffman's *Stigma: Notes on the Management of a Spoiled Identity* to describe this phenomenon: "passing is a strategy available to people who possess what is designated within their society as a stigma yet whose stigma is not immediately apparent. Stigmatized individuals may partition their world into what [Goffman] called 'forbidden, civil, and back places' (81) and manage information about their stigma accordingly. In some spaces, the stigma remains concealed; in others, it may be revealed to a circle of the 'wise.'"[26]

As Ferens points out, Winnifred negotiated a sort of compromise between these two alternatives: "Winnifred certainly engaged in various levels and strategies of passing – passing of a particular kind, for she embraced a stigma and turned it into an asset. Besides her parents and siblings, it is likely that her husband, Bertrand Babcock [whom Winnifred married shortly after arriving in New York], and close friends ... were among the 'wise'; to her New York neighbours, publishers, and readers, she was simply Onoto Watanna or Mrs. Babcock; in public places where she was unknown, she probably passed for white."[27]

While Edith, as Sui Sin Far, asserted her Chinese identity by adopting a Chinese name and writing "Chinese" stories that were intended to "humanize" the Chinese in the eyes of white readers, Winnifred, in choosing to adopt the socially more acceptable Japanese persona, implicitly acknowledged that her choice was opportunistic. "Ideals," wrote the writer who called herself Onoto Watanna, "are luxuries that few of us could afford to have."[28]

Winnifred's "Japanese" stories were well received, and articles began to appear about their exotic author. Although she acknowledged that Onoto Watanna was a *nom de plume*, the biographical information she gave out is of breathtaking contrafactuality. A profile that appeared in *Current Literature* read:

> Kitishima Kata Hasche is the real or family name of the clever Japanese girl who is living in Chicago at present and winning fame by writing for the magazines and newspapers of Chicago and the East under the pen name of Onoto Watanna, while more dollars come from her work as stenographer. Miss Hasche, or, as she prefers to be called, Miss Watanna – the two names meaning the same thing, but belonging to different Japanese dialects – though scarcely past her twenty-first birthday, has seen more of life and experience than the average woman of twice her age … Born in Yokohama, Japan, she was taken by her parents, and in company with the three brothers and nine sisters who shared with her their care and supervision, to Liverpool, England, and from thence to Manchester, before she was eight years of age. The journey from Japan to England was made by sailing vessels, and occupied an entire year.[29]

Winnifred's biographer points out that virtually all the information about the "Japanese" author is untrue. She had probably heard about sailing voyages between England and the Orient from her father, who, in addition to his sojourn in China, had indeed visited Japan.

As for the significance of the meaning of the two names, "Hasche" and "Watanna," Birchall observes that both names used in the article cited above do indeed "mean the same thing" in Japanese as neither name means anything. But there are indications that Winnifred may have deliberately chosen these names to encode a key to her imposture in her Japanese name in the form of her author's signature. Yuko Matsukawa reads this signature, an "illegible scrawl," as a deliberate pun composed of Chinese ideograms and one of the Japanese phonetic alphabets, pointing out that the last name "Watanna" is "composed of the Chinese ideograms (Japanese pronunciation) for 'to cross' but also 'to cross a body of water and reach the other side,' 'to convey,' 'to pass,' 'to go abroad.' 'Watanna' is a contrived name in that the ideograms were probably chosen for their meaning and then someone determined how to pronounce them. In any event, the characters that represent her last name suggest that she is indeed deliberately crossing boundaries and that her name allows her to cross over or pass."[30]

It was John Long's *Miss Cherry-Blossom of Tokyo* that inspired Winnifred's first novel, as evidenced in its very title, *Miss Numè of Japan* (*Numè* means "plum-blossom"). Her early "Japanese" stories are characterized by the same formula as Long's, which Birchall sums up as "the coupling of a big blond barbarian and a charming little Japanese maiden."[31] Most of her Japanese novels were variations on this theme.[32]

Notable among the "Japanese" writings Winnifred published before her first novel appeared are an essay and a short story, both titled "The Half Caste." The essay presents a typology of the Japanese-Caucasian half-caste that, on the one hand, describes the stigmatization of children of such mixed marriages by the dominant white society, where they occupy a "pitiful and undesirable position," a tacit allusion to the treatment of the half-Chinese Eaton children in Montreal.[33] On the other hand, the essay characterizes the half-caste as "exceptional," accurately describing Winnifred's own self-image: "They are seldom ordinary – seldom normal." And she goes on: "They generally have fine physical constitutions, though they are nervous, highly strung, jealous, conceited, yet humble and self-deprecating and overly modest at times, sarcastic, skeptical, generous and impulsive. It is hard to analyze their natures, because they are so changeable. They are born artists ... extremely ambitious, but generally meet with so many disappointments and hamperments that it is not a common thing for any of them to be more than ordinarily successful in life. Often the greatest impediment to their success is their own erratic, proud natures."[34]

The short story "The Half Caste" (first published in *Frank Lesley's Popular Monthly* in September 1899) tells of a transracial relationship between an American who goes to Japan and becomes involved with a Japanese woman whom he abandons, but who bears his child. Years later, in search of the child (whose mother has died), he courts a "dancing girl," whom he wants to marry but who turns out to be his daughter, the child he has been looking for. In spite of the pidgin

English rendering of the dialogue (à la John Luther Long), this story is troubling in its thematization of an incestuous as well as transracial relationship, and suggests that Winnifred was capable of handling themes that were much more complex than those she developed in her romance novels.

When Winnifred moved to New York City in 1901, she was already well established as a writer, having published numerous short stories in important journals and *Miss Numè of Japan* with a major Chicago publisher. She continued to work in journalism, however, and became involved with a fellow journalist, Bertrand Babcock, whom she married in the summer of 1901. Her second novel, *A Japanese Nightingale*, appeared with Harper Brothers the same year. Beautifully produced and richly illustrated with Japanese motifs, the visual elements executed by a gifted Japanese artist living in New York, the novel did much to authenticate the author's "Japanese" identity. One critic astutely observed that it was "Yeto's [the illustrator's] name [that] lent authenticity to novels such as *A Japanese Nightingale*."[35]

Winnifred, determined to make her mark on New York's literary establishment, used the public and critical interest generated by *Miss Numè* and her latest novel to further enhance her Japanese image, the main purpose of which was the authentication of the identity she claimed. As Caroline Rosenthal has remarked, an assumed identity "is constituted in performative acts and becomes real or true when others take the masquerade at face value ... Authenticity thus functions as the 'currency' of identity formation."[36] One of Winnifred's main strategies of authentication was the use of portrait photographs in which she appeared in Japanese dress, and striking a "Japanese" pose, which were given to the press to accompany articles about her. Domenika Ferens describes a profile of Winnifred that appeared in an article titled "General Gossip of Authors and Writers"[37] in the magazine *Current Literature*: "Her image featured on the first page of the magazine is very different from the smiling passport-style snapshots hitherto reproduced by syndicated newspapers across the country. The new Onoto Watanna is photographed almost full length, in a kimono against a Japanese screen. She stands turned away from the camera, looking down into a book, her face shaded by an upswept hairdo. The individual features are muted; all the elements of the photograph project her as a type: a subdued, genteel Japanese woman."[38]

At the same time Winnifred was basking in her literary and public success as the Japanese writer Onoto Watanna, she was also basking

Figure 6.1 Onoto Watanna, pictured in the frontispiece from *The Wooing of Wistaria* published in 1902, with a facsimile of Winnifred's autograph in Japanese.

in her new status as the wife of Bertrand Whitcomb Babcock, son of an old and distinguished American family. The *Current Literature* article makes clear that the combination of the fetching and successful

Japanese writer Onoto Watanna and the "private" Mrs B.W. Babcock successfully obliterated all traces of her half-Chinese heritage. As Ferens remarks, her marriage played a more significant role than her public success as Onoto Watanna in the erasure of her true background: "Establishing a respectable middle-class background takes precedence here over the 'self-made woman' image. For this reason, her parents' identity is foregrounded, 'her father being an Englishman in the consular service, and her mother a full-blooded Japanese.'" Ferens also points out that Winnifred's literary fame was determined by her "Japanese" origins: "it was her liminal racial status, particularly the association with Japan, that sold books."[39]

It was in reviews of *A Japanese Nightingale* and in profiles published about its author that the myth of Onoto Watanna became firmly entrenched in literary circles. According to the *New York Times*, the book was written "by a young Anglo-Japanese girl whose opportunities for observing her countrymen have been exceptional and whose mind has been trained to the European point of view."[40] The review compared the heroine to Chrysanthemum and Butterfly, "the same delicate melancholy charm, the same emotional force, they alike illustrate the element of childishness allied to the elaboration of their complex civilization."[41] The *New York Herald Tribune* wrote that "the young Americo-Japanese woman ... was born at Nagasaki."[42] Remarkably successful as a novel, *A Japanese Nightingale* was made into a Broadway play, and also filmed as a silent movie.

While she was producing her "Japanese" novels at an astonishing pace – between 1899 and 1912 she had published nine of them, plus the "Irish" novel *The Diary of Delia* – over a period of ten years Winnifred gave birth to all four of her children, despite being trapped in an unhappy marriage. Babcock had turned out to be an abusive alcoholic. She would later joke that during this period she turned out "a book and a baby a year."[43]

Although some reviews still praised the delicacy and exoticism of her writings, an increasing number were expressing doubts about her Japanese identity. Such doubts had begun to emerge early on in Winnifred's career. A review of *Miss Numè of Japan* published in the *Chicago Tribune* said about the author: "She is said by those who ought to know – namely the publishers of the story – to be herself a Japanese ... but the reader cannot escape the conviction that some bright American girl who has traveled in Japan is coquetting with him under the guise of Onoto Watanna."[44] One of Winnifred's editors flatly stated that she "has claimed to be half Japanese and half English, but of course she is not," and dismissed her as being less talented than her sister Edith.[45]

Subsequent accusations of inauthenticity were even more damning. In *Out West* magazine, where Edith had published many of her Chinese stories and articles, a reviewer openly questioned Winnifred's authenticity as a Japanese writer: "*Daughters of Nijo*, by Onoto Watanna, is a sufficiently ingenious and readable story; but its name, its illustrations, and all its elaborate stage setting no more make it a Japanese story than the author's name makes her a Japanese woman."[46] A statement from the Japanese poet Yone Naguchi, who had lived in New York and with whom Winnifred had been friends, culminated in this indictment: "The saddest part about Miss Watanna is that she is still posing as a Japanese, a half caste at least."[47]

Winnifred's strategy in countering such reviews – and rumours circulating in New York that she was not who she said she was – was to use the Russo-Japanese War as a pretext to make passionately patriotic statements expressing her devotion to Japan. In a 1904 interview she said: "If I were not married and did not have a baby nothing could keep me away from Japan." She went on: "I probably know less about the war than you do, but I know Japan and the Japanese, of course, and in their time of trial all my sympathy goes out to them. I certainly hope the Japanese – No, I mean I know the Japanese will win. If you knew them as I do, knew their courage and skill in arms, you would not have any doubt either."[48]

Oddly, she used the same interview to speak positively about her true origins, going so far as to acknowledge that she had Chinese relatives: "The Mikado has no desire to seize China. Japan had to whip China, as a father whips his bad son, but it was only to make her better. The Chinese, you know, are really our brothers, for we all come from China in the beginning. I myself have great love for the Chinese. I ought to have, for some of them are my relatives."[49]

In spite of the growing chorus of voices questioning her Japanese identity, Winnifred continued to enjoy the friendship of some of the leading literary figures in New York. She was invited to Mark Twain's seventieth birthday celebrations, and also to Dean Howells's seventy-fifth, the latter attended by President Taft. She had made friends with Mark Twain's great-niece, Jean Webster, author of *Daddy-Long-Legs* and the daughter of Charles Webster, a descendant of the famous lexicographer Noah Webster. Jean Webster later wrote the introduction to Winnifred's autobiographical novel *Me*, and remained her loyal friend until Webster's death in 1916.

Winnifred, aware that her "Japanese" identity was being openly challenged and also that *Japonisme* was falling from public favour, had been making attempts to diversify her writing. She was moving away from the romantic themes that had dominated her earlier novels and introducing non-Japanese ethnic elements. *A Japanese Blossom*, published in 1906, had children as its main characters, and, although the children belonged to a Japanese family, their Irish maid was given considerable space. Winnifred subsequently published an entirely "Irish" novel, *The Diary of Delia*, a comic account of a Long Island American family presented from the perspective of their Irish maid. As significant as the abrupt departure from Japanese themes is the fact that Winnifred wanted to publish the novel under the Irish pen name Winnifred Mooney. In the end, however, she gave in to her publishers, who insisted the book be signed Onoto Watanna.

A death in the family may also have played a role in Winnifred's seeking to distance herself from her Japanese persona and the sentimental Japanese stories she had been writing. Her second son, Bertie, died in 1908, at age four. His death affected Winnifred profoundly, and inspired a story, "Other People's Troubles," recounting a similar death, that of a young boy dying of encephalitis. Having always been careful to avoid lapses that might expose her true origins, she named "Canada" as her own place of birth on Bertie's death certificate, later prompting her great-granddaughter to remark that "the poor soul must have been too distraught to lie."[50]

Winnifred did write more "Japanese" stories after Bertie's death, and also two novels with darker themes (*Tama*, 1910, and *The Honorable Miss Moonlight*, 1912), both of which were praised by reviewers for their depiction of "the spirit of Old Japan." But Winnifred, still seeking to break free of her Japanese persona and to find new outlets for her writing, hit upon the idea of embarking on a collaborative undertaking with her sister Sara, who also lived in New York, and who was married to the German artist Karl Bosse.

One product of this collaboration was the *Chinese-Japanese Cookbook*, signed by Sara Bosse and Onoto Watanna, full of recipes for dishes requiring unlikely and hard-to-obtain ingredients as well as elaborate instructions for creating the appropriate atmosphere for presenting them, involving, for example, the removal or concealment of all "American" furniture and the purchasing of Oriental screens and draperies as well as items such as lamps of solid jade.[51] The sisters would later collaborate on a more serious project, namely a quasi-biographical novel about Sara, titled *Marion.*

Winnifred, who since living in the United States had had little to do with those members of her family who had remained in Montreal, travelled there twice, in 1913 and 1914, before and after the deaths of her father and her sister Edith. It may have been the shock of these deaths, particularly Edith's premature passing, and the resurgence of childhood memories evoked by returning to Montreal on these sad occasions, that inspired her to write the autobiographical novel *Me*, published in 1915. Although the book was published anonymously, as was *Marion*, which appeared a year later, it was soon attributed to "Onoto Watanna," as Winnifred may have intended. As Birchall remarks, "By her use of anonymity, Winnifred had created a superbly provocative publicity device."[52] Sales of the books were excellent.

ME: A BOOK OF REMEMBRANCE

Me was presented as an autobiographical account, and the author herself professes, early on, that "this story is frankly of myself."[53] But as Jean Lee Cole has observed, "scholars have been frustrated by how little Eaton actually reveals about herself in the text and, especially, how little she says about her ethnicity."[54] Winnifred's fictionalized (autobiographical) *Me* and *Marion*, which recounts the story of her sister Sara, reveal a darker side to the seemingly playful, capricious persona who authored "Japanese romances" signed Onoto Watanna.

Both novels contain gaps and displacements that can be read as manifestations of repression in the psychoanalytic sense, resulting, at critical junctures, in concealment rather than revelation of the circumstances that determined, in large part, both protagonists' lives: those pertaining to their racial identity. While both *Me*, the story of an aspiring writer, and *Marion*, the story of an aspiring artist, abound with detailed descriptions of the heroines' father's genteel background and antecedents, the mother's origins, although repeatedly alluded to as "foreign," are never explained. The catastrophe of the author's/narrator's/protagonist's race is resolutely withheld, even though such informational omissions mystify the reader. The frequent references to the mother and her (unspecified) origins draw constant attention to these narrative silences, made all the more confounding as it is clear that it is the mother's identity that has been life-determining for both Nora and Marion.

Early on in *Me*, Nora, eager to prove her credentials to her employer in Jamaica, talks about her distinguished antecedents on her father's side, claiming that they are descendants of Sir Isaac Newton: "the greatness of my father's people had been a sort of fairy-story with us all, and we knew that it was his marriage with mama that had cut him off from his kindred."[55]

Equally mysterious references occur when Nora talks about her early writing efforts, inspired by her mother and her "mother's land," never specified but clearly exotic: "I wrote a little story of my mother's land. I had never been there, and yet I wrote easily of that quaint, far country, and of that wonderful troupe of jugglers and tight-rope dancers of which my mother had been one."[56] This quasi-mystical inspiration from her sense of connection to her "mother's land" is enlarged upon when Nora tells Mr Hamilton of the stories she is writing "about my mother's land": "I have an instinctive feeling about that country. A blind man can find his way over paths that he intuitively feels. And so with me. I feel as if I know everything about that land, and when I sit down to write – why things just come pouring to me, and I can write *anything* then."[57]

Her mother's origins come to Nora's mind in non-literary contexts as well. She explains her tender, protective feelings in coming to the rescue of her boss Fred when he has gone on a drunken bender, saying: "I come of a race, on my mother's side, which does not easily forget kindnesses, and somehow I could think of nothing save how Fred had treated me on that first day [at work], and had given me a chance when no one else would."[58]

Towards the end of the book, when Nora gives up her faithful fiancé Robert Bennett, a gifted writer, for the reprehensible Hamilton, by whom she is herself betrayed, a passage invoking her "mother's land" suggests that Hamilton's duplicity is somehow a consequence of Winnifred's own deception of her loyal fiancé: "There is an adage of my mother's land something like this, 'Our actions are followed by their consequences as surely as a body by its shadow.'"[59]

However, any reference that would permit readers to link her "mother's land" to China is studiously avoided in the novel. Nora, on approaching the Chicago stockyards for the first time to seek a job, describes the bustling crowds of workers and the "strong, varied odors" there, feeling reminded of her "father's vivid stories of Old Shanghai,"[60] but providing no explanation as to the circumstances that would have taken her father, proudly presented elsewhere as a cultured Oxford man from a distinguished English family, to that

Chinese metropolis (and of course omitting any mention of her mother, who had come from that city and had met and married her husband there).

This exoticizing of her background, which remains undetermined, is augmented by repeated descriptions of herself as "dark" and "foreign-looking," the opposite of the supposedly quintessential blonde American, the type she so ardently admires. She describes her appearance "at seventeen" (in reality Winnifred was almost twenty-one), departing for Jamaica, self-deprecatingly, although she acknowledges mitigating features: "I was not beautiful to look at, but I had a bright, eager face, black and shining eyes, and black and shining hair. My cheeks were as red as a Canadian apple. I was a little thing, and, like my mother, foreign-looking."[61] Later on in the book she confesses to her fantasy of being blonde: "I myself was dark and foreign-looking, but the blond type I adored. In all my most fanciful imaginings and dreams I had always been golden-haired and blue-eyed."[62]

It is true that filling in these glaring gaps in the autobiographical narrative of the author would have shattered the myth of the famous "Japanese" writer Onoto Watanna, which, after so many years of diligent cultivation, would have exposed her as a fraud and shattered her literary reputation as well. At the same time it can be assumed that the writing of both the (auto)biographical books *Me* and *Marion* was inspired, at least to some degree, by the deaths of several members of her family. Her oldest brother's presumed suicide, her sister Edith's untimely passing, and then the death of her father, all within just a few years, affected Winnifred profoundly. She may have felt remorse at having neglected her family, most of whom she had not seen for years, and at having perpetrated, out of self-interest, the deception regarding her origins even in the face of Edith's death, by alluding to her mother's status as a "Japanese noblewoman" in Edith's obituary. Winnifred may have felt the need to atone, to "come clean," to acknowledge, at least tacitly, her imposture. Hence the references to her mother's "foreignness," and the exoticism of her "mother's land," neither of which, however, she can bring herself to name in the novel.

According to Jean Webster's introduction to *Me*, the book was written in about two weeks, while Winnifred was hospitalized "to undergo an operation," and revised and ready for publication two weeks after that. Webster's quoting Winnifred as to the circumstances that inspired the book supports this assumption: "It seems to me as though these two weeks I have just passed in the hospital have been the first time in which I have had a chance to think in thirteen years. As I lay on my back and looked at the ceiling, the events of my girlhood came before me, rushed back with such overwhelming vividness that I picked up a pencil and began to write."[63] Many of these events of her girlhood that came rushing back "with such overwhelming vividness" would have consisted of instances of social stigmatization due to her Chinese mother. In *Me*, such incidents are not only never mentioned but explicitly denied, most notably in Nora's professed ignorance of "racial prejudice."

In making a mystery out of her "mother's land," and in masking the origins that she herself saw as a defining part of her identity, in a book that she says is "frankly of myself," Winnifred is creating informational gaps that mystify the reader unaware of her true background, as would have been the case with most readers at the time the novel was published. For contemporary readers aware of Winnifred's real biographical history, the dissonance between Winnifred's account (as the protagonist) and her actual life experience is unmistakable. For readers "in the know" who can readily "fill in" the gaps, these silences come to stand at the centre of the narrative insofar as the extra-textual information furnishes motivations crucial for the understanding of the protagonist's feelings and actions, and hence a key to interpreting the entire novel.

Social psychologist Michael Billig maintains that such gaps are a manifestation of "the dialogic unconscious," arguing that in discursive analysis one must "examine the absences, rather than the presences" to identify the elements that are being repressed in an utterance: "the dialogic unconscious comprises utterances which could well have been spoken, but which remain unspoken."[64] This kind of dialogic repression does not originate in the unconscious – Nora/Winnifred had not "forgotten" the fact that she was half Chinese – but represents a strategy of avoidance, sometimes referred to as "narcissistic defense," to protect the image constructed by the ego. Sigmund Freud himself described this avoidance by referring to literature: "even great criminals and humorists, as they are represented in literature, compel our interest by the narcissistic consistency with which they manage to keep away from their ego anything that would diminish it."[65]

In her book on autofiction, Madeleine Ouellette-Michalska proposes a gender-related explanation for such silences, describing their occurrence as feints, discursive strategies that are typical of autofiction writing by women, attributable to the "uncomfortable and ambiguous space" women inhabit between "nature and culture." Elements threatening the perceived integrity of the female narrator/author/protagonist are thus circumvented in the text by leaving them unsaid, by withholding information, or by articulating them in utterances that are "half-truths" or "half-lies."[66]

The trauma of the race shame the Eaton children had experienced throughout their childhood, a shame that went so deep that in Hochelaga their mother tried to keep out of sight of their neighbours, can be seen as the main reason Winnifred cannot bring herself to acknowledge her true origins, even as she resolves to write the story of her (and her sister's) younger years. Both stories are, generically, coming-of-age accounts of the sisters who "made good," in which, however, a salient element of the genre – the true origin of the protagonists – is deliberately obscured and in fact never revealed.

Nora's conviction that she is "exceptional" and destined for greatness is inextricably bound up with overcoming the stigma attached to her family, ostensibly for their poverty, but which even the uninitiated reader by now attributes to their indeterminate "foreignness." As she toils as a secretary in the Chicago stockyards, Nora fantasizes about her future success and fame, and the effects thereof: "Dreams, too, came of the days when I would be famous and rich, and all my dear people would be lifted up from want. My poems would be on every one's tongue, my books in every home. And I saw myself facing a great audience, and bowing in acknowledgement of their praise of my successful play."[67]

If these fantasies of fame and fortune represent one way to achieve the triumphant vanquishing of her family's stigmatization due to their poverty and "foreignness" (code for the racially compromising Chinese mother) in a white, materialistic America, another, more immediately accessible way to attain this goal is to achieve social – and sexual – desirability and acceptance. Nora/Winnifred, the half-caste Chinese, whose origins and appearance deviate so dramatically from the feminine ideal of the age, and who so desperately seeks "to belong," is excessively eager to please: "If as I proceed with this chronicle I shock you with the ease and facility with which I encouraged and accepted and became constantly engaged to men, please set it down to the fact that I always felt an inability to *hurt* by refusing any one who liked me enough to propose to me."[68]

Nora's sexual power helps mitigate the catastrophe of her racial origins, her "otherness." That her affairs with men are determined less by her feelings than by her need for incessant confirmation of her social/sexual desirability, which she equates with the achievement of a socially acceptable image whose main components are a "suitable" family background and a seductive "purity" (implicitly: whiteness), is shrewdly expressed by her friend and roommate Lolly: "She said girls like me [Nora] never really loved a man at all. We loved an image that we ourselves created."[69]

Who the real-life counterpart of Lolly was is unknown. While most of the characters occurring in *Me* have been at least tentatively identified in Winnifred's biography, "Lolly" remains unaccounted for. But she surely had a real-life counterpart, and one who played an important role during Winnifred's years in Chicago. Although she is, like Nora, a "working girl" (she is a reporter), she is "the daughter of a prominent Texas politician," who nevertheless lives an unconventional life and calls herself a "Bohemian." For Nora, she embodies all the attributes of the ideal of American young womanhood, which Nora knows she herself can never attain, given her appearance and her family background. But Lolly is not invulnerable. When Nora, who has the best of intentions, tells her that Lolly's lover has made advances to her, and offers proof of this, Lolly is devastated and demands that Nora move out of their shared lodgings. Nora later learns that she has committed suicide.

The significance of this sequence of events for Nora/Winnifred is unmistakable: the suicide is recounted on the final page of *Me*, constituting one component of a life-changing turning point for Nora, as she separates herself from Mr Hamilton for good and embarks on a new life in New York. That Lolly, a young woman possessed of all the attributes Nora desires and herself lacks, should have been so vulnerable to life's vicissitudes as to commit suicide shocks Nora to the core.

Lolly thus looms large in this autobiographical tale: the book is dedicated to her (as well as to Jean Webster). Self-assured, unconventional, and fearless, with a "prominent Senator" father, she functions as a sort of revered alter ego of the insecure, eager-to-please Nora, daughter of a socially marginalized family. However, it is her appearance, which stands in such striking contrast to Nora's, that attracts Nora to her: "She was tall, with a beautiful figure, which she always showed to advantage in handsome tailor-made suits. Her complexion was fair, and she had laughing blue eyes. She was the wittiest and prettiest and most distinguished-looking girl in the house. [Both girls are staying at the YMCA in Chicago.] I forgot to describe her hair. It was lovely, shining, rippling hair, the color of 'Kansas corn,' as one of her admirers once phrased it."[70]

This image of self-assured blonde, blue-eyed beauty, for Nora an ideal she knows she can never achieve, manifests itself in various contexts in *Marion* as well, where it becomes an object of desire, successfully attained in a resounding happy end in the marriage of Nora's dark, "foreign-looking" sister Marion to a blond, blue-eyed artist.

MARION: THE STORY OF AN ARTIST'S MODEL

Although *Me* contains many of the features of the coming-of-age novel, in that it depicts the heroine leaving her childhood home, bound for new destinations, having crucial life experiences, and acquiring insight and wisdom along the way, it lacks the description of childhood itself. We are not introduced to Nora Ascough until she is a young woman bound for Jamaica, and learn about her childhood only in relatively brief flashbacks. While the book ends with Nora bound for a new destination, leaving her troubled "old life" behind, there is no promise, apart from the fact that she has grown older and wiser, that she will achieve her goals of professional success and personal happiness.

Marion, on the other hand, the real-life Sara Bosse née Eaton, is introduced to the reader as a child. We follow her in her travels and adventures until they culminate in the ultimate romantic ending, a love marriage that seems destined to be happy, although there is no indication that Marion will succeed in her artistic aspirations.

Marion was published in 1916, one year after *Me* appeared, and it is a considerably more complex work. One wonders whether Winnifred was aware of her parodying of a subgenre of the *Bildungsroman*, "a portrait of the artist," or *Künstlerroman*, when she subtitled it *The Story of an Artist's Model*, and of the significance of the deviation, which denies Marion the status of an artist in her own right. The main storyline of *Marion* bears a close resemblance to that of *Me*. Marion, who has artistic ambitions both as a painter and as an actress, is obliged, like Nora, to perform work that she finds uncongenial and even demeaning. The would-be artist becomes a model in order to be able to earn her living.

The fact that in the novel Marion is often used as a model for "Oriental studies" and other racially exoticized subjects, such as a "gypsy girl" (at one point she is also said to look like a "little Indian girl"), underlines the commodification of the protagonist as a model, whose own talent and abilities as an artist are never truly nurtured or acknowledged. It is tempting to interpret the subtitle of the book as a complicated self-referential *jeu de miroirs*, in which the model's poses represent not only a reenactment or simulation of the exotic "other," which she actually is, but also a "pose" assumed by the author, whose true identity can be revealed by examining the "pose" or the mask itself, which coincides with the persona assuming it.

In *Marion*, the body parts of various models are used by the artists to create a composite image, most often that of "American girlhood" epitomized by the famous "Gibson girl," depicted as clean and wholesome, morally irreproachable, and above all white. As Karen E.H. Skinazi points out, while many of the models who posed for commercially used images (and also for public monuments) at that time were in fact at least partially non-white, their "racial differences were massaged into a uniform whiteness."[71] Skinazi also observes that the "all-American girl" illustrations in *Marion* helped erase the racial heritage of the model, just as the Japanese illustrations of Winnifred's "Japanese" novels helped create the racial identity of the heroine and the racial authenticity of the author.[72]

Winnifred uses modelling as a "metaphor to deliberate on the racially ambiguous body,"[73] in which racial differences are obliterated, as is the case in the life of the heroine in the novel itself. Marion (like Nora in *Me*), by attributing her "difference" to her mother's "nationality" rather than to her race, is "passing" to readers who are oblivious to her true origins. According to Skinazi, "by offering a race secret that is *never revealed* … [Winnifred] draws attention to Marion's difference without ever directly attributing a racial component to these issues, giving readers the option of using whiteness as the racial default."[74]

The novel opens with a description of the Ascough family by a French-Canadian grocer, whose interlocutor is an "English" customer. Twelve-year-old Marion has been sent to the corner store on an errand, and the conversation takes place in her presence: "In dat familee are eleven cheeldren, and more – they come! See dat leetle one? She is très jolie! Oui, très jolie, n'est-ce pas? De father he come from EEngland about ten year ago. He was joost young man, mebbe twenty-seven or twenty-eight year ol, and he have one leetle foreign wife and six leetle cheeldren. They were all so cold. They were not use to dis climate of Canada."[75]

Marion is mortified and indignant: "I felt ashamed and humiliated to hear our family thus discussed. Why should we always be pointed out in this way and made to feel conspicuous and freaky? It was horrid that the size of our family and my mother's nationality should be told to everyone by that corner grocer."[76] As a result of the grocer's comments, Marion is "regarded curiously" by the "Englishman" in the store, who agrees that she "*is* pretty – quite remarkably pretty!"[77]

From the outset, Marion is viewed as an object of curiosity due to her "mother's nationality," which is never disclosed, but which reveals itself in the child's own unusual appearance, as can be inferred from the conversation between the grocer and his English customer. That Marion attributes her "conspicuousness" and "freakishness" to the size of her family as well as to her "mother's nationality" is, to the informed reader, a *fausse piste*, as French-Canadians were known to have large families themselves in the period in which the novel is set. It represents, rather, the same kind of discursive displacement that indicates the "dialogic repression" we encounter in *Me*, a form of avoidance, both in direct discourse and in narrative, of the traumatic elements in the subjects' lives. "Unpleasant" feelings or experiences are avoided by dis(re)placement, by drawing the reader's attention to something else.

Although we have observed this phenomenon in *Me*, it is even more pronounced in *Marion*, where it manifests itself in a more explicit form of racial denial. Such strategies of avoidance are well documented in psychoanalysis. In an article titled "Freud and Dora: Repressing an Oppressed Identity,"[78] Michael Billig uses Freud's notes on the famous case of "Dora" to observe that Freud's refusal to acknowledge the role of race and religion ("Dora," like Freud, was Jewish) demonstrated a case of repression on the part of Freud himself. In "Dora," Freud avoids racial and religious elements that are at the centre of Dora's neuroses and replaces them with sexual motivations, resulting, Billig suggests, in a sort of ethnic betrayal.

Like *Me*, *Marion* is generally recognized to be a thinly disguised self-narrative of the author, in which she and her family are re-created as characters who, although they are clearly non-white, remain racially "unmarked" in both novels.[79] Marion's account of her childhood, though it paints a vivid picture of life in the Ascough/Eaton household in Hochelaga, is telescoped into only the first sixteen pages, after which we meet Marion again at age sixteen, seeking to pursue a career as a painter or an actress, but even more preoccupied with her *beaux* and "having a good time." In the course of this latter pursuit, she falls in love with a wealthy law student called Reginald Bertie whose parents are said to be "big nobs" in their native England.

Not surprisingly – "Nora" and "Marion" are sisters – racial concealment is as central to this novel as it is in *Me*. There are numerous references to Marion's being "dark" and "foreign-looking," and the child Marion, having been called "pretty" by a "Frenchman" and an "Englishman," examines herself at home in the mirror, exclaiming: "Oh! If only my hair were gold!"[80] echoing Nora's obsession with this unattainable blonde ideal epitomized by her friend Lolly. Later on in the novel, Marion reiterates her preference of blonds, in particular in her admirers and potential suitors. When she becomes involved with a theatre troupe, she is cast as "Marie Claire" in *Uncle Tom's Cabin*, "in which, to my joy, I wore a gold wig and a lace tea-gown."[81] It is with this performance, wearing a "gold wig," that she first captures Reggie's attention. But she also plays another part in the play, namely that of Cassy, a Black slave, whose spirited rejoinder to Simon Legree expresses defiance and indignation at racial injustice. That Marion (and the author/narrator) identifies with Cassy's outrage is suggested by the fact that Marion relishes speaking the lines: "Simon Legree, you are afraid of me, and you have reason to be, for I have got the devil in me."[82] This is one of the rare, brief passages in which the protagonist openly identifies with victims of racism, the significance of which seems to escape Marion (displaying the strategy of saying something without seeming to say it, according to Ouellette-Michalska). But it suggests that with it Winnifred here was – consciously or unconsciously – introducing a racial subtext into the novel.

The withholding from the reader of any explanation as to why the presence of the protagonist's mother compromises the romantic relationship between Marion and her suitor Reggie has a similar effect to the mysterious, never-explained allusions to the "foreignness" of Nora's mother in *Me*. When Reggie pays his first visit to the family, the heroine's shame is purportedly due to the poverty-stricken, disorderly, prolific household: "Oh, how ashamed I felt that he should see all those dirty, noisy children."[83] However Reggie, smitten as he is, "didn't seem to notice anything except me," and moves to kiss her, but "just then in came mama and Ada, and feeling awfully embarrassed and confused, I had to introduce him."[84] The disastrous visit is partially redeemed by "papa's appearance": "he and Mr. Bertie found much to talk about."[85] That it is the encounter with "mama" that changes everything for Reggie is made clear in the subsequent chapter.

When read through the lens of autofiction, which assumes reader knowledge of the author's background, Marion's unexplained embarrassment at having to introduce "mama" is one manifestation of the narrative silence surrounding a crucial part of Marion's identity, an autofictional counterpart of that of the author. This narrative silence, or *non dit*, poses a problem for the reader in determining the motivation for the plot: the Ascough family's poverty alone cannot be seen to justify the dire predictions that a marriage between Marion and Reggie, whose romantic relationship stands at the thematic centre of the novel, would ruin Reggie's career and cause a break with his family. That the impediment to their marriage is in fact racial is encoded in the dramatic effect (the cause of which is never explained) created by "mama's" appearance in subsequent scenes, and while, as in *Me*, this "blank" in the text can be readily filled in by readers familiar with the author's background, it remains mystifying to those who are not.

In spite of "mama's" embarrassing appearance, after his first visit to meet her family Reggie declares his love for Marion, saying he had fallen in love with her "that first night," at the theatre. Marion replies: "But perhaps that was because I – I looked so nice as Marie Claire."[86] The discontinuity indicated by the dash signals a dialogical movement away from the taboo of Marion's racial identity, the problematic/painful element being "replaced" by the "pleasurable" one of Marion's appearance in the role of the blonde "Marie Claire."[87] The same phenomenon of displacement and discontinuity to create absences that conceal the problematic elements becomes apparent when Reggie explains to Marion the obstacles to their marriage. Although he says he considers himself engaged to her, after the visit to meet the family – after he has seen her mother – he backs off, first under the pretext of her acting ambitions – "Actresses are an immoral lot"[88] – then invoking the fact that Marion is a "working girl": "My people would take a fit if they thought I married a working girl. I've been trying to break it to them gradually about our engagement. I told them I knew very well a girl who was the daughter of Squire Ascough of Macclesfield, but I haven't had the nerve yet to tell them – er –"[89] As in Marion's earlier utterance, the discontinuity indicated by the dash expresses Reggie's embarrassment and reluctance to mention the taboo of Marion's race.

Marion purports to explain the true cause of his confusion: "I knew what he meant. He hadn't told them about us here; how poor we were, of our large family, and how we all had to work."[90] A decoding of the novel as autofiction, however, reveals that it is the mother's race and hence Marion's ethnic/racial origins that constitute the insurmountable obstacle, so catastrophic that they remain unmentioned. Marion's reaction, although it does not explicitly challenge the fiction that Reggie's parents will object to her on grounds of social incompatibility, is one of defiant and impotent rage: "I don't care a snap about your old people … and you don't have to marry me … I'm sick and tired of your old English prejudices and notions, and you can go right now – the sooner the better. I hate you."[91]

Such autofictional encoding through narrative silences or "saying something without seeming to say it" is evident throughout the novel. Even external aspects of the Ascough household are viewed, by the surrounding community, as being determined by the mother's "nationality." The second chapter of the book opens with Marion admiring the neighbours' "opulent and well-kept garden," which she contrasts with their own. "We had an old straggly garden. Everything about it looked 'seedy' and uncared for and wild … It was just like our family, I sometimes treacherously thought – unkempt and wild and 'heathenish.' A neighbor once called us that."[92] It is the mother's "heathenish nationality" that is at the root of the family's stigmatization and the children's shame.

The happy ending of the novel – Marion's desire to find love with a blond, blue-eyed artist is fulfilled — is seen by some critics as the final act of divestment of her true identity. Skinazi remarks:

> Marion's marriage to Bonnat … represents not only her victory in love but also in overcoming the racial barrier that had prevented earlier attempts at marriage. Having crossed the colour line by crossing the borderline away from her family, elided her mother in her verbal construction of her family, and then married a man who resembled her father, Marion succeeds in eliminating her mother and therefore her mother's racial legacy from her family tree and thus herself. Like an artist of American Girlhood, rather than an artist's model, Marion, in her final act of marriage, creates her first truly successful piece of art: a composite whitewashed family out of her father and husband.[93]

MRS FRANK REEVE, CALGARY

With her two (auto)biographical novels, Winnifred had distanced herself from the romantic Japanese tales she had spun as Onoto Watanna. It was the financial success of *Me* and *Marion* that finally led her to go to Reno to obtain a divorce from her husband, taking her three children with her (son Bertie had died in 1908).

Winnifred was still attractive, and with her "decided and instinctive liking for the opposite sex," it did not take long for her to find a suitor. In Reno she met a Calgary rancher and businessman named Frank Reeve, also there to obtain a divorce. She married him about one month after her divorce from Bert was finalized. On the marriage certificate she named her true birthplace, Montreal, a sign that she was now ready to abandon her Japanese imposture and begin a new life, as Mrs Frank Reeve of Calgary.

Although her desire to distance herself from her representations of an idealized, quaint Japan was partly motivated by the growing distrust of that country in North America, there were also motivations in her personal life to shed her Japanese persona. When her mother died, Winnifred travelled to Montreal to be with the family, and was likely involved in writing the obituary, if indeed she did not write it herself. Unlike Edith's obituary, in which her mother is described as a "Japanese noblewoman," this notice refers to her mother as being "Anglo-Chinese," and to some writing in which she reminisced about her early years in Shanghai. Winnifred, it seemed, was no longer concerned about being exposed as a half-caste Chinese.

Winnifred's growing contempt for all things Japanese is reflected in her last "Japanese" novel, *Sunny-San*, which focuses on a half-caste heroine who goes to the United States, where she uses her "Japanese" charm to seduce her American admirers. She reconciles with her wealthy white father, and ultimately marries the most suitable of her (white) suitors.

What is significant about the novel is the depiction of the heroine as calculating and manipulative in her use of her "Japanese" charm, suggesting that she represents an extension of the "poseur" Winnifred (alias Onoto Watanna) herself. The novel marks the abandonment of the exotic refinements of Asiatic culture that had been stressed in Winnifred's previous novels in favour of the inexorable force of white assimilation. As Birchall puts it, "Being Japanese, in this book, is distinctly something to be ashamed of, to minimize; being American is desirable. Sunny's highest aim is to turn herself into an American girl, 'to acquire the American point of view, and in fact to unlearn much of the useless knowledge she had acquired of things Japanese.'"[94] Although Winnifred's abandonment of her Japanese persona coincided with increasing anti-Japanese sentiment, beginning in the 1920s (*Sunny-San* was published in 1922), it was not until the Second World War that she publicly expressed her distaste at her "Japanese" past, from which she vehemently distanced herself. In a piece about her published in Calgary in 1941, she is quoted as saying: "I'm ashamed of having written about the Japanese, I hate them so."[95]

There are other indications that the shift in focus revealed in *Sunny-San* seems to have been opportunistic rather than the result of insights gained from critical self-examination. In an unpublished essay written in 1924 titled "You Can't Run Away from Yourself," when Winnifred appears to be taking stock of her past life, she dissimulates yet again, inflating her literary production, and simultaneously exploiting and diminishing her Asian heritage: "I had written hundreds of short stories and eighteen novels … all concerned with Japan. I was 'labeled' Japanese. The little oriental blood in me did not make me a real 'Jap' any more than the drop of French in me made me a French woman."[96] As Birchall observes, in this piece we see her "in the very act of lying to herself; perpetuating her false identity had become so habitual she did not drop it even in a discourse going on in her own mind."[97]

Winnifred was now determined to make a name for herself as a Canadian writer. In 1921 she founded the Canadian Authors Association chapter in Calgary, becoming its first president (she became vice-president of the national association). She was also writing about Canada, in 1923 publishing an article titled "The Canadian Spirit in Our Literature" in the *Calgary Daily Herald*[98] which she also presented to the Canadian Club of Calgary, stating that "[w]ith a very few and rare exceptions, there has come out of Canada, this far, no important literary production in which a typical Canadian spirit is revealed." For good measure she added that Canadian authors were forced "outside of Canada to find a market for [their] work."[99] Her conclusion seemed calculated to prepare an enthusiastic reception for the "Canadian" novel she was working on, *Cattle*: "Would it not be fine if a Canadian author of great talent should cunningly weave into a tale something of the fascinating glamor, beauty and charm of this land of ours … A strong, hot pen might unfold the epic of our grain fields."[100]

Cattle, set in the Alberta countryside, was just such a novel. It was signed not Onoto Watanna, but Winnifred Eaton. While it cannot be denied that it issued from "a strong, hot pen" – set in a remote ranching area, it centres around a rape, the perpetrator of which ends up being gored by his own bull and hence receives his just deserts, while the long-suffering worthy characters are rewarded with suitable marriages – it was hardly a *chef d'oeuvre*, with its melodramatic plot and stereotypical characters. Reviews were mixed, but Winnifred did manage to sell the film rights, which involved "movie men" visiting the Reeve ranch. Visitors at the Bow View Ranch were welcome, for although it was only forty miles west of Calgary (on the Banff road), in the early 1920s the area was still quite isolated.

It was probably the visit from the "movie men" that made her act upon her growing impulse to leave the remote ranch and return to New York. In "You Can't Run Away from Yourself" she writes: "I am going back East. I am going to come back as a writer, not this time as a writer of fairy-like stories of Japan, but tales of things and people I had known."[101] In the summer of 1924, Winnifred, now age fifty, went to New York hoping to find work as a screen writer, taking her children with her. She soon landed a job at Universal Pictures, which would later take her to Hollywood. She was now Mrs Winnifred Eaton Reeve, protégé of the owners of Universal, Carl Laemmle Jr and Sr. While she was in New York, another novel she had written in Alberta was published. Winnifred cannily dedicated it to her new employer: "To Carl Laemmle / For whom the author has the sincerest admiration."

The novel was titled *His Royal Nibs*, it was signed Winifred (one *n*) Eaton Reeve, and it would be her last. Like *Cattle*, the story is set in Alberta ranch country, but features an Englishman nicknamed Cheerio who is seeking work in Alberta (he turns out to be a war hero and the son of a lord). In spite of his gentle ways, Cheerio gets the better of the western Alberta roughnecks and in the end marries the heroine, the wilful Hilda.

Unlike *Cattle*, *His Royal Nibs* reveals a number of elements that may be read as autofictional inscriptions of the author. As in *Me* and *Marion*, the heroine is repeatedly described as dark-haired and dark-eyed – she has "chocolate-coloured eyes and hair," and her skin is "bronzed"[102] – resembling the author, but as is the case with the two (auto)biographical novels, the heroine remains racially unmarked. Her long-dead mother is never described, and her brother, suitably named Sandy, is "red-haired" and "freckled-faced."[103] Any suggestion of racial "otherness" is thus plausibly obliterated. Like Nora Ascough, the autofictional heroine of *Me*, who repeatedly expresses wistful admiration for blonde-haired young women as the ideal of American girlhood, Hilda admires (and is jealous of) the "yellow-haired" beauty whose photograph Cheerio carries in the precious gold locket he wears. The dark-haired Marion's marriage to a blond, blue-eyed artist for whom she has modelled parallels Hilda's union with the stereotypical upper-class Englishman who turns out to be a gifted artist (for whose work Hilda, unbeknownst to her, has been a model). The fact that Cheerio's real name turns out to be Edward Eaton Charlesmore of Macclesfield and Coventry may be a humorous nod to Winnifred's father Edward Eaton, who came from Macclesfield. But insofar as it also evokes Winnifred's own background, the use of the name can be seen to create a parallel between her (half?) Chinese mother's marriage to Edward and the dark-haired, "bronzed" Hilda's marriage to the British lord, constituting another autofictional element.

In Hollywood, as a protégée of Carl Laemmle, founder of Universal Pictures, Winnifred became one of the film industry's first Asian-American screen writers. She had abandoned the Japanese persona she had cultivated in her earlier years in Chicago and New York, but she did not conceal her Eurasian origins, or that she was the well-known author who had signed her work Onoto Watanna. As Birchall puts it, "this was one time in her career that she did not pretend to be anything other than what she was."[104] She worked hard to prove herself. She was basically providing for her three by now adult children, one of whom (Doris) had eloped but whose marriage was short-lived, another of whom (Perry) became schizophrenic and was institutionalized in California, and the youngest of whom (Paul, known as Charley) wrote poetry but was unemployed and turned to drink. The failed marriages of Doris and Charley had each produced a child.

Due to the long separation from her husband, with no suggestion that Winnifred planned to return to Alberta, the couple were estranged, and in 1928 Frank indicated that he wished to end the marriage. In early 1930, Winnifred was laid off by Universal, and the same year Frank, who had acquired a mistress in Calgary, was seeking a divorce. Winnifred was now desperate to save her marriage, and when Frank, who had gone to Reno to obtain a divorce, came to Hollywood to discuss the terms with Winnifred, she managed a reconciliation.

Returning to Calgary with Frank, who was smitten anew by his wife, the couple successfully outmanoeuvred the mistress, a Mrs Hill, to obtain property and financial documents that Frank had left in her possession. Winnifred used this rather sordid circumstance to write a story about the romantic triangle, the narrative perspective of which was that of the fictionalized Mrs Hill. Titled "Because We Were Lonely," the story was published unsigned in *True Story* magazine.

Ensconced in Calgary with her by now wealthy husband, who had made a fortune from his business interests, Winnifred settled into the conventional married life of a society matron, becoming involved with Calgary's Little Theatre and the Calgary Women's Press Club. Over the last twenty years of her life, she appears to have done no writing. Her daughter Doris, who worked for Frank, was in Calgary, but Perry was still in a mental institution in California, while Charley, estranged from his second wife and the daughter of that marriage, was living a life of alcoholic destitution in New York.

It was on a return trip from California, where Winnifred and Frank had gone to visit Perry, that Winnifred died, suddenly, of a heart attack, on 8 April 1954. Her sons outlived her by only a few years. Her granddaughter, Diana, daughter of Paul (Charley), became a story analyst for a Hollywood film studio, and the biographer of the grandmother she had hardly known.

THE HALF-CASTE LEGACY

Winnifred's two (auto)biographical novels represent perhaps the most painful autofictions examined in this study. The narrative silences surrounding her racial origins, when she had explicitly expressed her intention to be "frank" in her accounts, indicate the depth of repression of a defining component of her identity, one that determined her life and also those of her siblings.

Except for Edith, most of the Eaton children seem to have rejected and concealed their ethnicity. The oldest brother, Edward, "became so English that he belonged to 'whites-only' clubs frequented by the aristocratic English of Montreal."[105] He likely committed suicide. May Darling, a middle Eaton sister, is described (but not identified) by Edith in "Leaves" as a "half Chinese, half white girl … whose face is plastered with a thick white coat of paint" and whose "eyelids and eyebrows [are] blackened so that the shape and whole expression of her face is changed," "a poor child [who] lives in nervous dread of being 'discovered.'"[106] Birchall, who traced the paths of some of Winnifred's descendants, observes: "May's concealment of her Chinese blood was complete; the knowledge was not even passed down to her grandchildren."[107]

These strategies of concealment and displacement deployed by all the Eaton children (except Edith) in their attempts to repress and obliterate their Chinese half-caste origins were replicated in the generation that followed them, depriving their own children of full knowledge of their ethnic identity. In her epilogue, Birchall recalls that growing up, all she knew about her father Paul, Winnifred's son, was that her maternal grandparents, who had raised her, disapproved of her father "because he was a drunk, a poet, and a bum, who never worked."[108] This was the reason given for forbidding her, except on rare occasions, to see him. She grew up having no idea that she was part Chinese. But at Paul's funeral, attended by only a handful of mourners, she perceived two unfamiliar figures, "tiny, teary, elderly, Chinese-looking ladies, in very old-fashioned, long black dresses and hats with veils. They were introduced to me as my father's aunts … 'You didn't even know Paul had any aunts, did you?' they asked smilingly, and all I could do was smile back and admit it, at a loss for words. They were Florence and Beryl, Winnifred's younger sisters."[109]

But in the case of this grandchild, the legacy of her half-caste grandmother was claimed, through a strange coincidence. Diana, in Los Angeles to seek work in a film studio, followed her aunt Doris's advice to use her grandmother's old literary agent to help her find a job. It was this elderly man, who formerly represented the half-caste "Japanese" writer Onoto Watanna, who gave the granddaughter her start.

EDITH MAUDE EATON ALIAS SUI SIN FAR: A SENSE OF "DIFFERENCE"

Although Edith's adoption of the Chinese *nom de plume* Sui Sin Far does not represent a biographical self-reinvention on the order of those undertaken by the other five authors examined in this study, she did to some degree "re-create" herself in her writing. The autofictional elements in her work manifest themselves in her presentation of herself as (full-blooded) Chinese in some of the episodes recounted in her autobiographical essay "Leaves" (although elsewhere in the essay she focuses on her "hybrid" identity), and also in the protagonists and in the narrative voices of many of her stories, some of which also foreground the identitary dysphoria resulting from a mixed-race biography. Her "queer" stories are seen, by most contemporary critics of Sui Sin Far's work, as autofictional inscriptions of her own sexual orientation.

As the eldest daughter of an impoverished mixed-race family with an abundance of children, Edith bore the brunt of the racial harassment encountered by the Eaton children in the community, and of carrying out the many household tasks assigned to the older siblings from a very young age. Once they were old enough to seek employment, they were expected to contribute to the family income. As an aspiring writer, Edith thus faced formidable obstacles in realizing her literary ambitions: the necessity for gainful employment, continuing expectations to help with household tasks, and the resulting lack of the leisure time and privacy so indispensable in a writer's life. Edith met these challenges with astonishing resourcefulness.

At eighteen, she took her first job, working as a typesetter at the *Montreal Daily Star*, most of her modest pay going to the family. Having taught herself shorthand, she began working as a stenographer, eventually setting up her own office as a typist. This allowed her a more flexible work schedule, and by the mid-1880s, Edith's first publications appeared, "humorous articles" published in various American newspapers. But she was also writing stories and "verses," and by 1889 she had published short stories and essays in the *Dominion Illustrated*. These pieces contained no references to Chinese culture or to her own Eurasian heritage, and were signed "Edith Eaton."

The US government had passed the Chinese Exclusion Act in 1882, and while Canada did not enact parallel legislation until much later (1923), it had begun imposing a Chinese head tax in 1885. Thus the Montreal Chinese community in Edith's time consisted almost exclusively of men who had been recruited for manual labour and members of the merchant class who arrived in Canada with the means to start businesses, and who only rarely brought their wives. A chance meeting with a clergyman who solicited Edith and her mother to visit a newly arrived Chinese woman, the bride of a local merchant, was a pivotal event for the aspiring young writer, opening the door to interaction with the Chinese community, to the existence of which Edith had hitherto been entirely oblivious.[110] "From that time," she writes, "I began to go among my mother's people, and it did me a world of good to discover how akin I was to them."[111]

It was a community of which she felt she could be a part, and one with which she identified. She became an engaged advocate for the Chinese cause, and penned an eloquent letter to the *Star* protesting against the Chinese head tax, which she signed not "Edith Eaton" but with the initials "E.E." It was not until her first "Chinese stories" appeared in various American publications that she began to sign with what she took as her Chinese name, "Sui Sin Far," the name she would use in most of her subsequent works.

Another turning point in Edith's career was a brief stint, in 1897, as a journalist in Jamaica, a position in which she succeeded her sister Winnifred. Given the racist attitudes of the dominating white population, she was obliged to pass as white, but her reference to the Jamaican experience as a rebirth clearly indicates that that was where she began unambiguously to identify with all colonized people of colour. In "Leaves" she wrote: "The novelty of life in the West Indian island is not without its charm. The surroundings, people, manner of living, are so entirely different from what I have been accustomed to up North that I feel as if I were 'born again' ... The planters and business men of the island take me as a matter of course and treat me with kindly courtesy. Occasionally an Englishman will warn me against the 'brown boys' of the island, little dreaming that I too am of the 'brown people' of the earth."[112]

Although Edith may not have openly asserted her non-white identity while she was in Jamaica, she seems not to have concealed it, either, as "it begins to be whispered about the place that I am not all white." The rumours, however, had little consequence for her, for people who confronted her with them in the end "retire quite gracefully, leaving me with a few amusing reflections."[113]

Having contracted malaria in Jamaica, and being obliged to return to Montreal, Edith, who had always been sickly, developed inflammatory rheumatism and was advised to seek a west coast climate for medical reasons. In 1898 she moved to San Francisco, where one of her sisters lived. In San Francisco's Chinatown, older, larger, and more established than Montreal's, she openly and consistently acknowledged her Chinese heritage. But it was here that she became fully and painfully aware of the implications of her dual ancestry: she found that she was viewed with suspicion because of her British heritage.

Annette White-Parks maintains that it was likely the double stigmatization she experienced due to her mixed heritage that determined her decision not to marry and have children. Witnessing the pain her mother endured in childbirth and the household chaos resulting from a family of fourteen children probably played a contributing role.

Although in the late nineteenth century being a single woman was in itself stigmatizing, Edith was determined not to marry. In her autobiographical essay she alludes to family pressure to do so, and also to the fact that she had numerous suitors. Winnifred's biographer claims that in 1900, while Edith was in Montreal on a family visit, Sun Yat-Sen, the Chinese revolutionary leader, secretly visited the city, and that Edith "was one of the few who had entrée to his rooms. Family legend holds that they were engaged to be married, but she broke it off because she did not want to live in China."[114] After this visit home, Edith continued to pursue publishing contacts and to work as a stenographer in various American cities. It was with the publication of her autobiographical essay "Leaves from the Mental Portfolio of an Eurasian" in *The Independent* that she achieved a major breakthrough, publishing short stories in various important American publications. In 1912 her first (and only) book, a collection of short stories titled *Mrs. Spring Fragrance*, was published by A.C. McClurg in Chicago.

Sometime after the death of her older brother, in 1911, Edith returned to Montreal in failing health. Although her book was reviewed in both Canada and the United States, and although she published a few more stories after the appearance of *Mrs. Spring Fragrance*, little is known of her last years. She died in the spring of 1914. Her obituary, published in the *Montreal Daily Star* on 8 April 1914, summed up her life and writing career, referring to a "long novel" she had been working on. (This novel was never found.) Another obituary, which appeared in the *New York Times*, identified her as the daughter of "a Japanese noblewoman who had been adopted by Sir Hugh Matheson as a child and educated in England."[115] The latter obituary is generally credited to Edith's sister Winnifred, who had become the acclaimed "Japanese" writer Onoto Watanna, and who would have risked exposure of her own identity had Edith been identified as (half) Chinese.

Although Winnifred paid homage to Edith, both as a sister and a fellow writer, in her autobiography, *Me*, published anonymously in 1915, she could not bring herself to correct the obituary's contrafactual statements about their mother Grace's "Japanese" origins: "I thought of other sisters ... the eldest, a girl with more real talent than I who had been a pitiful invalid all her days. She is dead now, that

Figure 6.2 Edith Eaton monument in Mount Royal Cemetery, Montreal

dear big sister of mine, and a monument marks her grave in commemoration of the work she did *for my mother's country*."[116]

In fact Edith's gravestone, an obelisk in Montreal's Mount Royal Cemetery, identifies her with both her English and her Chinese names, Edith Eaton/Sui Sin Far.[117] Under the Chinese characters at the top of the stone, the approximate translation of which reads "It is right and good that we should remember China," are the lines "Erected By

Her Chinese Friends/In Grateful Memory." According to Edith's biographer, it has never been established who commissioned the monument.

Mary Chapman's retrieval and discovery of a large number of stories and articles by Edith Eaton, of which previous critics and biographical writers had been unaware, throws a new light on the years she spent criss-crossing the continent, and on Edith herself. If previous accounts of Edith's life and work focused on her uncompromising Chinese "authenticity," seen in virtuous counterpoint to her sister's opportunistic posing as a Japanese writer, Chapman's findings indicate that Edith produced and published a wealth of stories and articles on a wide variety of subjects set in a broad range of settings and social *milieux*, and that she was far more successful as a writer than previous portrayals had suggested. As Chapman puts it, this newly discovered corpus "complicate[s] the critical binary that has tended to read Edith Eaton as the 'good sister,' who wrote from an authentic Chinese position, in contrast to the 'bad sister,' Winnifred, who fraudulently assumed the Japanese authorial identity of Onoto Watanna."[118] Many of Edith's newly discovered stories were quite risqué, a far cry from the "dainty stories of Chinese life" for which she had hitherto been known, and some appeared in pulp fiction magazines.[119] Chapman's findings also reveal that Edith published stories set in locales ranging from Jamaica to Alaska, some of them signed not "Sui Sin Far" but "Edith Eaton."[120] She also wrote "Japanese" stories destined for children.[121] A number of stories and articles feature main characters who are white or racially unidentified working women. These stories indicate that Edith was keenly aware of social issues resulting from women entering the working world, as she herself had done, and clear-eyed in identifying their implications, which often resulted in financial and sexual exploitation.[122]

Invoking the newfound stories and articles by Edith Eaton, Chapman argues that focusing on her role as the first writer of Asian–North American fiction, as many critics have done, diminishes the intent revealed in Edith's *oeuvre* to privilege the individual over racial, national, or ethnic affiliation.[123]

In fact, some of Edith's own statements seem to corroborate this view. Towards the end of "Leaves" she writes: "I have no nationality and am not anxious to claim any. Individuality is more than nationality."[124] The fact that Edith, in many of her writings, particularly in those that have only recently been made available, revealed herself to be a proponent of a transnationalism that challenged national, ethnic, and racial categorizations of identity, and that she also called into question gender boundaries as determining sexual identity, has led to a critical revision of Edith's status.[125] The shift in focus that has characterized the reception of her work overall in more recent critical publications, however, is not irreconcilable with her passionate advocacy on behalf of the diasporic Chinese and her equally passionate identification with the Chinese community. For it is also in "Leaves" that she explicitly self-identifies as Chinese, in recounting an incident that took place "in a little town away off on the north shore of a big lake" in the American Midwest, where she was working as a stenographer. She is sharing a meal in a restaurant with several people, among them her employer and her landlady, and records the following conversation:

> Someone makes a remark about the [train] cars full of Chinamen that past [*sic*] that morning … My employer shakes his rugged head. "Somehow or other," says he, "I cannot reconcile myself to the thought that the Chinese are humans like ourselves. They may have immortal souls, but their faces seem to be so utterly devoid of expression that I cannot help but doubt."
>
> "Souls," echoes the town clerk. "Their bodies are enough for me. A Chinaman is, in my eyes, more repulsive than a nigger." …
>
> "I wouldn't have one in my house," declares my landlady.
>
> "Now, the Japanese are different altogether. There is something bright and likeable about those men," continues Mr. K.
>
> A miserable, cowardly feeling keeps me silent …
>
> Mr. K. turns to me with a kindly smile.
>
> "What makes Miss Far so quiet?" he asks.
>
> With a great effort I raise my eyes from my plate. "Mr. K.," I say, addressing my employer, "the Chinese people may have no souls, no expressions on their faces, be altogether beyond the pale of civilization, but whatever they are, I want you to understand that I am – I am a Chinese."[126]

Edith's account of this incident in her autobiographical essay, in which she acknowledges her mixed-race identity as Eurasian and describes the alienating effect of her racial "hybridity," makes it clear that her self-identification as Chinese was a matter of choice. She had travelled unimpeded between the US and Canada, presumably passing as white, and had in fact been denied full acceptance by the Chinese communities in the various cities in which she lived. As Shirley Geok-lin Lim points out, "Edith is received as white, privy to rabid anti-Chinese sentiment, until she chooses to self-identify as Chinese, even as she is never fully accepted into the Chinese community."[127] Nicole Tonkovich also underlines that Edith's self-identification as Chinese was a deliberately made choice: "Sui Sin Far chose to identify as Chinese as a means of exposing, discussing and attempting to mitigate issues stemming from social hierarchy and domination."[128]

Edith chose to self-identify as part of a stigmatized racial-ethnic group rather than to seek acceptance as a member of the dominant and hence desirable racial-ethnic culture. This decision contravenes the conventional definition of "passing" as a means to gain acceptance to the more privileged social group,[129] and represented a visceral response to the anti-Chinese hysteria of her time. Her "passing" represents a subversive strategy to transcend the limitations of an essentialist concept of identity.[130]

The social and ideological background against which Edith was writing was one in which the goal of the dominant culture was to assimilate and "civilize" the Chinese. This goal was to be met by Christianizing them – hence the massive missionary efforts being undertaken in both China and North America. A better alternative, with regard to the Chinese living in North America, was seen to be to send them back to China, once the projects for which Chinese labour had been recruited were completed. The prevailing attitude is summed up in a speech given by John A. Macdonald, prime minister of Canada, in 1882: "I share very much the feeling of the people … against the Mongolian or Chinese population in our country as permanent settlers. I believe they would not be a wholesome element for this country. I believe that it is an alien race in every sense, that would not and could not be expected to assimilate with our Aryan populations … [But] it is a simple question of alternatives – either you must have this labor or you cannot have the railway."[131] In a similar vein, in the United States, a special Congressional Committee of 1876 "underscored popular opinion by reporting that the Chinese were 'loathsome in their habits and vile in their morals … They did not assimilate with whites and never could become an integral and homogeneous part of the population.'"[132] With the completion of the Canadian Pacific Railway, the Chinese were to be made to return to China by the implementation of policies such as the Chinese Head

Tax and the Chinese Exclusion Act, which led to Chinese being "robbed, assaulted, lynched, burned, and entire populations driven out, even murdered, with impunity."[133]

These anti-Chinese policies, which included international travel restrictions, were directed at all persons of Chinese "descent" (a term that was not qualified), and affected Edith directly, as to travel between Canada and the United States, which she did repeatedly, she had to pass as white. There was always the risk of exposure. Indignation and outrage at the inhumanity and injustice of these anti-Chinese policies may well have been factors leading to the Eaton family's becoming involved in human smuggling. It was likely Edith's mother Grace who initiated Edward's connection with a smuggling ring that helped Chinese cross illegally into the US, contravening the Chinese Exclusion Act. Grace had introduced herself to the wives of Chinese merchants Wing Sing and Sang Kee, who both ran smuggling operations. Edward was considered a "kingpin" in Montreal's smuggling rings, and was arrested as such in 1896. Edith may have been involved in the smuggling operations herself, and may also have been involved in helping her father escape from jail in upstate New York.[134]

In California, where Edith lived for a number of years, marriages between whites and Asians had been declared illegal in 1905. Like Blacks, the Chinese were relegated to ghettos and risked violent reprisals if they ventured outside them. There was a spate of "yellow peril" literature, in which the Chinese were depicted as being about to inundate the United States, and Chinatowns were described as being dominated by brothels, gambling houses, and opium dens.[135]

It was against this background of racism, oppression, and violence against the Chinese that Edith, the half-Chinese who could easily have passed as white – and often did – chose to assert her Chinese identity, both in her personal life and in her writing. The pervasiveness and intensity of the hostility towards the Chinese is described in many of Edith's publications.

One remark in "Leaves," cited above, describes the "likeability" of the Japanese as opposed to the Chinese. The Japanese, for various reasons (including the fact that there had been far less immigration from Japan to North America in the nineteenth and twentieth centuries), were viewed much more favourably than the Chinese by the dominant white population. In another incident recounted in "Leaves," it becomes clear that Edith could have passed as Japanese as well as white. It also reveals that she had at least one persistent suitor, a white man, who wanted to marry her. After refusing him nine times (so she claims), she agrees to marry him, giving in to pressure from her mother and married sisters, and "because the world is so cruel and sneering to a single woman – and for no other reason."[136]

The relationship ends when her suitor proposes that she deny her Chinese background: "Everything went smoothly until one day … [He said] 'Wouldn't it be just a little pleasanter for us if, after we are married, you were – er – Japanese? So many of my friends have inquired of me if that is not your nationality. They would be so charmed to meet a Japanese lady.'"[137] Edith responds to her fiancé's suggestion by ending the engagement and, in her diary, she expresses euphoric relief at having done so: "Joy, oh, joy! I'm free once more. Never again shall I be untrue to my own heart. Never again will I allow anyone to 'hound' or 'sneer' me into matrimony."[138]

If in "Leaves" Edith chronicles the humiliations she endured because of her racial identity, it is in her fiction that the traumata of living as a Chinese, or, even worse, as a Chinese half-caste, are fully revealed and expressed. As portrayed in her stories, the racial stigmatization manifests itself in a multiplicity of ways: well-intentioned attempts to "civilize" and "help" the inhabitants of Chinatown, seen as backward and "heathenish"; thoughtless humiliation; cynical exploitation; psychological or even physical cruelty and aggression. It is the half-caste Chinese, however, who suffer the worst fate. In an article on Sui Sin Far's work as a poetics of diaspora, I-Chun Wang observes that "culture constructs identity and hybridity initiates unstable identity," the latter placing the subject in a vulnerable boundary position characterized by alienation and exclusion.[139] Virtually all her stories bear the imprint of Edith's own experiences as autofictional inscriptions, many of them focusing on the trauma of the doubly stigmatized half-caste and the loneliness resulting from this "hybrid" identity, the consequences of which are often catastrophic.

In "Sweet Sin," the main character's name is a homophone of "Sui Sin," suggesting that the protagonist is a sort of double of the author. Sweet Sin is a young half-caste woman who must choose between the white American man she loves (who despises the Chinese) and a marriage with a "Chinaman" arranged by her father. But rather than marrying the American or going to China to marry there, Sweet Sin commits suicide. In a suicide letter addressed to her father, a full-blooded Chinese, she explains that her motive is to spare any children she might bear the suffering she has experienced, suggesting, as Edith herself observes in "Leaves," that even a parent – of either race – cannot begin to comprehend the suffering endured by their half-caste children: "Father, I cannot marry a Chinaman, as you wish, because my heart belongs to an American – an American who loves me and wishes to make me his wife. But Father, though I cannot marry a Chinaman, who would despise me for being an American, I will not marry an American, for the Americans have made me feel so that I will save the children of the man I love from being called 'Chinese! Chinese!'"[140]

Edith's resolve to assert her Chinese identity – and endure the consequences thereof – in a culture that was so openly hostile to the Chinese when she could have passed as white or Japanese, and to remain single in the Victorian era when she had suitors, and when a woman's social status depended on living within a suitable marriage and having children, was determined not by necessity but by deliberate choice.

Her biographer repeatedly describes the defiance Edith manifests in the face of the taunts and the physical attacks from other children and the "curious examination" and deprecating comments she experiences as a child, reinforced by the racism and injustice she sees directed against the Chinese as an adult. This defiance stems as much from the denigration on purely racial grounds of her mother, whom she revered and with whom she seems to have had a very close relationship,[141] as from the fact that she herself identifies with her Chinese heritage more than with her British side.

But the motives underlying her choice to describe herself as Chinese, at times not disclosing that she was half white, were based on more than solidarity with "her mother's people." Claiming the identity of a full-blooded Chinese was a way of becoming a part of a community in which, as a half-caste, her role would always remain ambiguous and marginal. Her autobiography as well as much of her fiction express the yearning for an unambiguous identity as a way to overcome the loneliness of the doubly stigmatized half-caste, which separates her even from her parents: "I do not confide in my father and mother. They would not understand. How could they? He is English, she is Chinese. I am different to both of them – a stranger tho [*sic*] their own child."[142] In a poignant passage in one of her short stories, Sui Sin Far writes: "The flowers … of a kind come up together. The sister violet companions her brother. Only through some mistake in seeding is it otherwise. And the hybrid flower, though beautiful, is the saddest flower of all."[143]

If her ethnic-racial hybridity caused her to articulate her transnationalism in "Leaves," a stance that can be read as emancipatory and that put her ahead of her time, the sense of identitary instability resulting from her hybrid status also gave rise to an intense desire to forge a less problematic identity by privileging her Chinese side. As Shirley Geok-lin Lim remarks, Edith's autobiography "thus presents an intricate hybrid subject: transnational, migratory, and stranger to both Anglo and Chinese communities, yet claiming a Chinese diasporic and political status. This complex identity is problematically related to biology, for the subject is of mixed race, and also problematically related to culture, for the self-identified Chinese subject does not read or speak Chinese and belongs to no Chinese family or community." Lim goes on to point out that far from being determined by her "biology," Edith's claim to a Chinese "insider" status is in fact "a strenuously imagined and worked-out persona – one aimed, in part, at fashioning a Chinese community affiliation in the absence of any. Edith's Chinese persona is therefore as much invented as Winnifred's Japanese persona."[144] Chapman and Ferens, in discussing the long-held critical view that Edith was the racially "authentic" sister and Winnifred a racial impersonator who "performed" her claimed Japanese identity, concur with this assessment.[145]

While Edith never tried to conceal her biracial origins, her assumption of Chinese "insider" status, which she inscribed in most of her writings, including the autobiographical "Leaves," clearly represents an identitary self-reinvention in the sense of autofiction. That Edith herself was keenly aware that the Chinese persona she had created was in fact an autofictional construct is suggested in the title of her autobiographical essay, "Leaves from the Mental Portfolio of an Eurasian."

"Leaves" can be read as a sort of autobiographical collage, consisting of elements of narrative memoir, dramatization of events using direct dialogue, and self-reflective passages, the substance of all of which can be assumed to be authentic and factually accurate. Nicole Tonkovich remarks that the term "Leaves" evokes a family tree as well as denoting a synonym for pages, and reads it as a possible intertextual allusion to Whitman's *Leaves of Grass* and Fanny Fern's collections of journalism.[146] She also observes that the term "portfolio" suggests that the leaves in it are interchangeable, indicating that the autobiographical content can be reconfigured as well as expanded. Tonkovich sees "Leaves" as the textual analogue to a photo album or documentary portfolio, one that creates a "fragmented and always expandable identity" for the writer.[147] In its selectivity and fragmentation, "Leaves" creates textual gaps that are in themselves carriers of meaning, one such significant gap being constituted by the absence of (her identification with) her white English father. Thus, as Tonkovich puts it, "it becomes apparent that her choice of Chinese identity, as well as her femininity, is purposeful rather than instinctive."[148] Its autofictional character manifests itself in the suggestiveness of the title, which evokes a multiplicity of associations that extend the significance of the text as an autobiographical document. In formulating the title that frames what purports to be an autobiographical text that she has herself deliberately assembled, Edith presents identity – or at least the representation of her own identity – as an autofictional construct. The principles of this construct are its virtuality – the possibility of actualizing it in various ways – and the authorial freedom to choose what will be said and what will be withheld. It is in "Leaves" that Edith chooses explicitly to assert her Chinese identity, her identification with her mother, and her consistent privileging of the feminine principle itself, the latter a theme that manifests itself not only in "Leaves" but in the "queer" stories of her fiction corpus as well.

"THE HEART'S DESIRE"

A close reading of Edith's fiction suggests that the existential despair she so eloquently expresses at her hybrid identity conceals another taboo, this one not racial but sexual.

Edith's unconventional life as an unmarried female writer, her sense of difference, which in her autobiography she attributes solely to her half-caste racial status, was partly determined by what Amy Ling labels somewhat tentatively her "lesbian sensibility, which the author herself would not have approved and would have striven to repress."[149] Although Ling hastens to qualify Edith's sexual orientation as latent and unconscious, and we have no biographical evidence to suggest that she lived out her "lesbian sensibility" with same-sex partners, that possibility cannot be excluded. The numerous incidents of gender disguise occurring in Edith's writing can be seen as a form of encoding her ambiguous sexual identity, and the intimacy and complicity between some of her female characters point even more explicitly to the possibility of lesbian inclinations as well as to an emancipatory stance challenging male dominance and superiority.

Commenting on the recently discovered earlier stories by Edith Eaton, Mary Chapman observes that "several stories have lesbian subtexts, anticipating later potentially queer stories such as 'The Story of Tin-A,' 'Chinese Lily,' and 'The Success of a Mistake.'"[150] A number of Edith's stories involve gender performance – cross-dressing, as well as other forms of imposture. Chapman also discusses Edith's exploration of social identity performance involving Eurasians who look European or Black or Europeans who look Asian.[151] As Chapman remarks, these texts, many of them about human smuggling, "use the permeability of national borders as a metaphor for the permeability of other borders, such as race, gender and sexuality."[152] Skinazi, too, underlines the potency of metaphorical (as well as literal) border-crossing in the work of Edith (and Winnifred) Eaton as a way of "rewriting" and constructing new identities.[153]

Notwithstanding the absence of concrete biographical indications as to her sexual orientation, Sui Sin Far's stories can be seen as a vehicle that allowed her to express unmistakably homoerotic feelings. Even Annette White-Parks, Edith's biographer, who categorically dismisses the notion that Edith may have been homosexual, acknowledges that Sui Sin Far's "wry attitude toward marriage ... suggests biographical origins."[154]

A short story titled "Lin John" calls into question the Victorian values of heterosexual marriage as well as those governing patriarchal power, but it also seems to affirm an alternative way of life, determined by female bonding. Lin John is a young Chinese immigrant who has saved his meagre earnings to enable him to buy his only sister free of the man who keeps her as a prostitute and to send her to China to live as an honest woman. The sister herself (she remains nameless in the story) steals the money from Lin John. With it, she luxuriously furnishes a large apartment and buys herself expensive clothing and jewelry. She confides her secret to her female companion, with whom she seems to be living, a "heavy, broad-faced Chinese woman in blouse and trousers of black sateen," saying that she has no wish to give up her present life. "Now, what do I want to be free for? To be poor? To have no one to buy me good dinners and pretty things – to be gay no more?"[155] Lin John, oblivious that it is his sister who has stolen the money, tells the man of whom his sister is the paid mistress that he will work years more to save the sum he has lost to redeem her. While it seems that the reader is meant to empathize with Lin John for his moral values and his willingness to sacrifice, the story's (perhaps inadvertent) effect is to represent a Chinese woman who seeks to exercise her own choices. Her decision to continue the relationship with the man of whom she is the paid lover for the material comforts it offers her indicates that she has no intention of marrying, but seems happy and contented living with her female "companion" and confidante, the brief description of whom suggests a rather masculine appearance.

The subversion of male authority also manifests itself in some of Edith's non-fiction writings, with Edith donning an authorial gender disguise and signing her work as a male, an example of what Annette White-Parks called Sui Sin Far's "trickster authorship."[156]

In 1904, the *Los Angeles Express* published a series of articles in which Edith adopts the voice and persona of a "Chinaman" recounting his travels. In "Wing Sing of Los Angeles on His Travels," Wing Sing, according to the articles, is "the pen name of a well-known Americanized merchant … who recently left Los Angeles to … visit his old home in China, going by way of Montreal."[157] Although the articles are signed "Wing Sing," there can be no doubt that Edith is the author: she herself announced the project in a letter the year the series was published.[158] While the articles can be seen as a mischievous subversion of white stereotypes about the Chinese by reversing the "white" perception of the Chinese as "mysterious" and "inscrutable" (Wing Sing professes to be mystified by white/European customs and attitudes) in order to create empathy for the Chinese protagonist and the Chinese community as a whole, the author's gender disguise clearly represented a subversion of the narrative authority of the male writer as well.

Although it would be a stretch to read the Wing Sing articles as a literary attempt to "become" someone else, they do represent a form of mischievous imposture that allows the author to "speak as a man," and so to break free of two constraints that Edith felt were stigmatizing, that of the half-caste and that of the female spinster writer.

A number of Edith's stories involve gender disguises that seem unmotivated by the plot and that suggest that in them Edith was expressing – consciously or not – her own sexuality.

In "The Smuggling of Tie Co," the handsome and charismatic Jack Fabian, who makes his living smuggling Chinese from Canada to the United States, tells Tie Co, the young Chinese co-owner of a laundry, that he is broke and down on his luck. To Fabian's surprise, Tie Co asks him to smuggle him into the United States. When Fabian asks Tie Co for his motive, pointing out that he has had success in his business and will no doubt soon marry a "little woman," Tie Co says: "I not like woman. I like man." And he adds: "I like you … I like you so much that I want to go to New York, so you make fifty dollars. I no flend in New York." Once underway, Fabian and Tie Co are about to cross a river when they encounter officers patrolling the border area. To protect Fabian, Tie Co throws himself into the river and drowns. When the body is recovered, it is found to have "Tie Co's face" and to be "dressed in Tie Co's clothes," but the body is not that of a young man but that of a young woman.

The story's effect depends upon the fact that the reader is unaware that one of the two male characters in the story is in fact a female in disguise. This circumstance lends the dialogue, which is made highly suggestive due to the withholding of this information, the *frisson* of illicit same-sex love. The tragic ending (the character disguised as a male is drowned in a river that separates the United States and Canada) results in the exposure of the female identity of the supposedly male character, making his (her) romantic interest in the (other) male character socially acceptable.[159]

While smuggling stories such as this one were probably inspired by the Eaton family's participation in human smuggling, they also lend themselves to the metaphorical expression of boundary-crossing and border transgression. Chapman suggests that "smuggling" in Edith's work can be read as a metaphor or trope used not only to "challenge absolute categories of national identity and citizenship and to promote a transnational or even post-national understanding of identity," but also to "call into question … fixed notions of race, gender and sexuality."[160]

It is notable that in many of Sui Sin Far's stories the young female protagonists are half-orphans, usually motherless, and some of these stories suggest a troubled, guilt-ridden relationship with the parents. This sense of guilt often has to do with the girls' refusal to marry, in particular to marry a designated bridegroom. In a number of stories the daughters' disobedience is motivated by their bonding with a beloved female companion. Contextualized by Edith's biography, these stories can be read as autofictional, suggesting the degree to which she was conflicted by her decision to live the unconventional life of an unmarried – and possibly lesbian – female writer.

In "The Story of Tin-A,"[161] a Chinese woman living in America tells the narrator (whose gender is never revealed) the story of her past. Growing up on the island of Formosa, she had a dear friend, A-Ho, who ended up being married to a man living on the other side of the island, depriving the young women of each other's company. When A-Ho does not bear her husband a son, Tin-A is to marry the husband and become a secondary wife. A-Ho begs Tin-A not to acquiesce in this marriage, ostensibly because she loves her husband, and cannot "bear to see another in [her] place." She adds, addressing Tin-A: "My affection for you has never changed, and my eyes long to behold you, but not, oh, as a sharer in him."[162]

When a troupe of actors arrives in Tin-A's area and performs in her father's house, the plays and performances – in which female characters are played by boys – "so excited [her] imagination" that she resolves to become an actor herself. The troupe's chief takes her with him to America, though not as an actor, a profession reserved for men. In America he tries to marry her off, but Tin-A, "remembering A-Ho, [fears] to wed." When the narrator asks Tin-A if she is happy serving as a gardener and companion to the wife of the now former actor, she answers: "Am I happy? ... How can that be when the greatest of all sins is to sin against one's parents? Ah, no. Heaven will surely punish me for my unfilial conduct. And yet – I am not altogether without gladness, for I know that I saved A-Ho much pain."[163]

Another story, "The Success of a Mistake,"[164] features a white journalist, Miss Lund, who inadvertently sabotages a Chinese mother's arrangement of a suitable marriage for her daughter Anna by getting the facts wrong in a report she writes about "a Chinese betrothal." Miss Lund's article, in wrongly asserting that the mother has travelled from Seattle (where the story is set) to San Francisco to find a husband for her daughter (when in fact she has gone there to find a wife for her son, marriageable Chinese women being rare in Seattle), brings shame and disgrace upon the family. Marriageable Chinese men being plentiful in Seattle, the daughters of the family are now considered unmarriageable in the city's Chinese community due to the rumour that the mother had to go all the way to San Francisco to find a husband for Anna. This circumstance, however, enables Anna to become engaged to Wah Lee, the lover she has already chosen and who returns her affection, but whom Anna's mother considers unsuitable because he had been a slave in China.

What has caused the "mistake" in Miss Lund's report is that in interviewing Wah Lee as a Chinatown source on the forthcoming betrothal, she has (subconsciously?) herself assumed Wah Lee's desirous gaze on Anna, as he describes her in a long digression in his account of the son's betrothal that is to be the subject of Miss Lund's article. In fact, owing to Wah Lee's long, detailed, and desirous description of Anna, Miss Lund "misses" the fact that the upcoming engagement she is supposed to write up is about a son and his San Francisco bride and not that of Anna and Wah Lee. Miss Lund subsequently interviews Anna in a tête-à-tête, reinforcing the transferal of feelings of desire from Wah Lee to Anna's female interlocutor, Miss Lund herself. Speaking of "The Success of a Mistake," Kate McCullough remarks that Edith's "cloaking of homosocial desire in overtly heterosexual plots serves as another form of protective passing, passing that here allows for the possibility of the voicing of Othered, marginalized desires."[165]

This homoerotic transfer of desire also occurs on the metanarrative level, so to speak, namely in the flirtatious complicity between Miss Lund and Miss Hastings, a (white) Chinatown missionary, that Jean M. Lutes calls "the queer subtext of the plot, which depends upon the reporter-heroine's sympathetic identification with her source [Wah Lee in his desirous depiction of Anna] and her charged relationship with a female missionary friend [Miss Hastings]."[166] When Miss Lund visits Miss Hastings to report on her meeting with Anna, the "narrative shifts directly from one scene of displaced desire to another."[167] The end of the story does not show the happy ending of Anna and Wah Lee's betrothal, but Miss Lund and Miss Hastings chatting flirtatiously (and suggestively) about Miss Lund's "mistake." As Lutes puts it, "Together, they stand in for the Chinese lovers."[168] It is the omniscient third-person narrator, however, who concludes the story with an ironic and self-referential twist: while Miss Lund and Miss Hastings discuss the happy consequences of Miss Lund's "mistake," "Wah Lee and Mai Gwi Far [Anna] were telling one another that their coming together had surely been ordained by Heaven."[169] As an alter ego of the author[170] Miss Lund represents the autofictional persona of the "queer" writer Edith Eaton, incorporating her Chinese identity into the narrative by way of the "desirous gaze" of the Chinese lover Wah Lee.

Perhaps the most convincing argument that Edith, who unlike Winnifred openly acknowledged her Chinese origins, was concealing the even greater taboo of her sexuality can be found in her stories ostensibly destined for children. Concealed behind the screen of children's innocence and lack of guile are stories that can be read as revelations – whether conscious or not – of the author's sexual identity.

The elevation of female bonding to a status more desirable than heterosexual or indeed any other human relationships is most pronounced in two stories included among the "Tales of Chinese Children." "The Heart's Desire" tells the story of a young princess who secretly desires a "little sister" to mitigate her loneliness. The plausibility of a girl's desire for a sister is undercut by the author's manipulation of characteristic features of the genre in which it is written: "The Heart's Desire," written in the formulaic style of a fairy tale, subverts the (Western) fairy tale paradigm according to which it is a gallant prince who claims and redeems the princess, and explicitly designates a same-sex "Other" as the object of the "heart's desire."

The story is about a lonely princess living on a secluded island whose attendants, to alleviate her loneliness, bring to her first a father, then a mother, and finally a little brother, none of whom prove satisfactory in making the princess less lonely. Finally, the princess dispatches a note attached under the wing of a carrier dove, who delivers the note to a poor little girl called Ku Yum. When Ku Yum arrives at the princess's palace, the two girls find that they complement each other, and the princess announces to her people: "Behold, I have found my heart's desire – a little sister."[171]

Another children's story is striking in its evocation of the physical pleasure of female bonding, which here is associated with a chosen mother/sister figure. The heroine of this story has the same name as the heroine of "The Heart's Desire." In "Ku Yum's Little Sister,"[172] the motherless child Ku Yum, though she has three brothers, desires nothing more than to have a little sister. When reminded that she is blessed with brothers, which is "much better," she says: "But I more badly want what is like myself than what is better." Left alone one day, Ku Yum leaves the house in search of a little sister, but unable to find a suitable candidate close by, she wanders outside Chinatown and gets lost, falling asleep in a garden. When she is found, she is taken into the house where a lady "took Ku Yum in her arms and comforted and petted her as Ku Yum had not been comforted and petted since her mother died two years before." She is finally taken back to her home, where she points to the lady, crying jubilantly: "Behold my little sister!"

Beyond demystifying and "humanizing" Chinese culture for white readers – in the process of which the author readily used common white stereotypes about the Chinese – the Chinese stories signed Sui Sin Far permit their author to construct and assume the insider identity that the author lacked. Edith Eaton had been raised "English," spoke almost no Chinese (although she later tried to learn the language), and, until her immersion in the Chinatowns of San Francisco and Los Angeles, had known little of Chinese culture and society beyond what her Christianized and Westernized mother had told her. In her fiction, however, Edith Eaton could both recreate herself as the "Chinese lily" Sui Sin Far, and, in the persona of a "white" or racially undefined writer, make herself the epitome of the Eurasian transnational in whom she saw a way to overcome the racial binary that stigmatized the Chinese and that excluded her as a white-Chinese half-caste.

In her stories, Edith portrays half-caste identity as a lack, a tragic deficiency, comparing it to a "sad hybrid flower," "a mistake in seeding." She surely felt that these depictions, reflections of the social views of her time, were also seen to apply to her. Hence her repeatedly iterated statements that "the individual" should be privileged over national, racial, or ethnic affiliations. The fact that she was only half Chinese (or half white) she herself perceived as a kind of fragmentation resulting in a constant conflict between her two "sides" that threatened to obliterate what she saw as her true identity. At the conclusion of the autobiographical "Leaves" she writes: "When I am East, my heart is West. When I am West, my heart is East. Before long I hope to be in China. As my life began in my father's country it may end in my mother's ... 'You are you and I am I,' says Confucius. I give my right hand to the Occidentals and my left to the Orientals, hoping that between them they will not utterly destroy the insignificant 'connecting link.' And that's all."[173] Her writing was a way to construct and authenticate a personal identity that made her whole, through which this sense of fragmentation and deficiency could be corrected and overcome.

It was also a way of expressing what Amy Ling calls her "lesbian sensibility." The recurring themes of gender disguise and "female bonding" in so many of her stories suggest that, at the very least, the author was preoccupied with sexual identity and, arguably, vicariously exploring her own.

Both the social and literary conventions of Edith's time dictated that women had to enter into heterosexual relationships, preferably through marriage, to be complete. Nagged at by her "married mother and married sisters" and no doubt others attempting to "hound" or "sneer" her "into matrimony," Edith was made to feel that her single status constituted another lack, another form of deficiency, another kind of "incompleteness." This "incompleteness," too, could be compensated for in her writing, where her female protagonists fulfill their "heart's desire" with an Other of the same sex.

Unlike the "impostor" figures described in previous chapters of this book, Edith, as far as is known, never concealed her true identity (save for using a pen name, and in her playful assumption of the persona of a "Chinaman" in the Wing Sing pieces). Yet her construction of a new identity as Sui Sin Far through her writing was at the heart of her life's work. It was, in a way, a survival strategy, not only to escape the status of a half-caste female but also to escape the fate of the protagonist of one of her stories, Sweet Sin, who ends up committing suicide rather than marrying and subjecting her own children to the treatment she herself had endured as a half-caste.

Becoming a writer gave Edith the freedom to determine the destinies of her characters, some of whom were overwhelmed by the problems arising from their Eurasian identities or from other difficulties, some of whom overcame and triumphed over them by choosing an unconventional path. Almost all of these protagonists can be seen as alter egos of Edith herself. Edith's self-reinvention as Sui Sin Far represented just such an unconventional path, and as a way to claim an alternate identity, it can be seen as her crowning and triumphal achievement. As the tribute inscribed on her gravestone testifies, by the time she died, the proud, self-created persona of the Chinese Sui Sin Far had become as real as the downtrodden half-caste Edith Eaton.

Conclusion

"I contain multitudes"
Walt Whitman

Although the reinventions of the self documented in this book are all set in the early part of the twentieth century, a number of the questions they provoke in the autofictions they generated are essentially postmodern. What constitutes identity, or the self, and how it comes into play, both in writing and in everyday life, is a question that stands in the foreground of works by postmodern writers such as Samuel Beckett, Jorge Luis Borges, Gabriel García Márquez, and Salman Rushdie, all of whom created narrators and central characters whose points of view are often contradictory, indeed whose very (fictive) existence as depicted within the framework of the narrative is ambiguous and open to question. In the Canadian context, the genre is represented by Leonard Cohen, Robert Kroetsch, Hubert Aquin, and Nancy Huston, to mention the most familiar names.

If the autofictional works discussed in this book lack the metatextuality and self-conscious problematization of identity that are typical of postmodern fiction, they still present a series of indicators that reveal how personal identity might be constructed.

LITERARY LEGACIES

Canadian writer Robert Kroetsch in his postmodernist novel *Gone Indian* uses the stories of Archie Belaney/Grey Owl and Felix Paul Greve/Frederick Philip Grove to examine the phenomenon of self-constructed identity. As Canadian icons of literary imposture, Grove and Grey Owl play a central part in the protagonist's self-reinvention. The novel is centred on a character called Jeremy Sadness, a graduate student from New York who goes to Edmonton for a job interview at the university but never shows up for it. Asked by an immigration official about the purpose of his visit to Canada, Jeremy Sadness replies: "I want to be Grey Owl."[1] Instead of keeping his appointment at the university, he disguises himself as a North American Indian, apparently using the items he has found in the suitcase of one Roger Dorck, which he has mistakenly claimed as his at the airport. Using the contents of the suitcase, he proceeds to realize his project of becoming Grey Owl: "I've made a decision. I shall walk out of this place. I shall bravely, recklessly escape from this suffocating dungeon: DISGUISED AS MYSELF."[2]

In describing his self-transformation, Jeremy refers to the items he has found in the suitcase as his own: "Carefully I arrange my two braids … And I slip into my fringed buckskin jacket."[3] Thus attired, he goes to the town of Notikeewin in pursuit of Roger Dorck (the alter ego as which he is disguised), where he ends up taking part in a snowshoe race, which, astonishingly, he wins. A group of local white men take him for an Indian – "You fucking Indian," one of them says – and beat him unconscious. Confused as much by his unlikely triumph in the snowshoe race as by the motives of the men who have attacked him, Jeremy, on waking, finds himself being tended to by a "real" Indian with whom he had become acquainted earlier. Seeing his confusion, the "real" Indian explains: "You look like an Indian … You ran on those snowshoes like a streak of greased lightning."[4]

One critic suggests that Kroetsch, in depicting his character's successful performance of the Indian identity he has assumed, is "questioning the authenticity of ethnic identities,"[5] and by extension the notion of identity itself. Consistent with his postmodernist project of creating a new mythology representing the New World, particularly its western regions, by superimposing New World characters and landscapes on the familiar myths and genres that characterize Western European culture, Kroetsch invokes the transformation of Archie Belaney into Grey Owl as a paradigm of the ancient trope of metamorphosis. Jeremy Sadness re-enacts Archie Belaney's desire to become an Indian, announcing that he has come to Edmonton because he wants to be Grey Owl. If in *Gone Indian* Kroetsch is parodying the well-established quest motif by replacing the "object of value" of the quest with the objective of "becoming" a fake (assuming the identity of an inauthentic Indian), it is to call into question the essentialism of what is traditionally seen as "authentic identity."[6] In a labyrinthine narrative with constantly shifting narrative perspectives, the cast of unlikely characters perform their – sometimes seemingly inadvertent – identitary deceptions, which often involve various forms of personal betrayal.

Embedded in these multiple manifestations of ambiguous identity is the allusion to another impostor figure, that of Frederick Philip Grove. The twice-told tale of purported drowning – that of Roger Dorck and that of Robert Sunderman – occurring in the novel and the mystifying complications that ensue for their "survivors" represent a sustained intertextual allusion to Felix Paul Greve's fake suicide by drowning. Although the repeated references to Greve/Grove are never made explicit, they constitute a subtext that determines the thematic substance of the novel to the same degree as is the case with the Grey Owl story. Thus Jeremy Sadness, "disguised as himself," in going in search of Roger Dorck, whom he has, so to speak, "become," represents a dramatization of Grove's quest as formulated in the title of his "autobiography," *In Search of Myself*.

The plot (to use the term loosely) of *Gone Indian* is driven by allusions to Grove's dual identity, and in particular by his faked suicide by drowning. For example, from Bea Sunderman, the lover of Roger Dorck (owner of the misappropriated piece of luggage), Jeremy learns about Bea Sunderman's dead (or undead) husband who, subsequent to his supposed death by drowning, had "phoned" his wife and then "hung up." The presumed widow's reaction to her husband's purported drowning represents a mischievous parody of Else Endell's imagined reaction to the drowning disappearance of Felix Paul Greve: "She admired him. By God that was obvious and certain: she admired Robert Sunderman for having the courage to leave. To knock a hole in the ice, fake his own death, and disappear. If he hadn't really drowned. If she was right about the phone call. And she went on admiring the sheer will power that had enabled him to stay away."[7]

Bea Sunderman's lover, Roger Dorck, has also "drowned," but (like Grove) has not literally disappeared: he hovers in an undefinable state of being (dead or undead?) in the Notikeewin hospital. At times, the identities of Dorck/Sunderman/Grove are conflated with those of Grey Owl/Jeremy-Sadness-become-Grey-Owl. As Jeremy lies with Bea Sunderman in her bedroom, he dreams that "Robert Sunderman himself was due any moment, sliding as sudden as an owl, through the half-open door."[8] In this labyrinth of alter egos, doubles, and twice-told tales, the name of the man who has disappeared is significant: the literal translation of Sunderman is "man torn asunder," but "Sunder-" can also be related etymologically to "Sonder," meaning "set apart" or "peculiar." Sunderman shares his first name, Robert, with the author who has created him. With this name, the author appears in a sort of self-allusive cameo in his own novel.

Robert Kroetsch had already explored the phenomenon of self-reinvention in an earlier work about Frederick Philip Grove, a poem in which the self-created "new man" is tied to his role as a writer, "a liar" who creates "a world." In "F.P. Grove: The Finding," Kroetsch first questions the veracity of Grove's "autobiographical" accounts. He then introduces numerous allusions to Grove's *Over Prairie Trails* (which consists of the narrator's description of his trips between the remote country school district where he is teaching and his home in an equally remote area of Manitoba, where his wife awaits him). These allusions function as a vehicle to communicate the essence of the writing world, focusing on its loneliness and its existential self-examination, which Kroetsch frames as a sort of self-dialogue, the subject of which is the "finding" of the title. The last four stanzas of the poem read as follows:

> The silence of sight "as if I were not myself
> Who yet am I" riding the drifted snow
> To your own plummeting alone and alone
>
> The *wirklichkeit* of the word itself
> The name under the name the sought
> And calamitous edge of the white earth
>
> The horses pawing the empty fall
> The hot breath on the zero day the man
> Seeing the new man so vainly alone
>
> We say with your waiting wife (but she
> Was the world before you invented it
> Old liar) "You had a hard trip?"[9]

Kroetsch further explores the notion of identitary authenticity in his own memoir, *A Likely Story*, the title itself calling into question the autobiographical accounts contained in the volume as well as the literary personae represented in its (auto)fictional components.[10]

According to Rosalind Jennings, even the photograph of a prairie boy on the cover of the book – which most readers would take to be Kroetsch, as the book presents itself as a memoir – is "inauthentic." In an unpublished letter to Jennings, Kroetsch states that "the photo on the cover ... is not a photo of me. In fact I took the picture – [which is of] ... our hired man."[11] It is presumably the same hired man Kroetsch meets years later in a western bar, who reminds him of his "true" self when he was a boy, and "won't let me change my story."[12]

The episode of the chance encounter with the Kroetschs' hired boy, now a "ragged old man," concludes with what is likely a reference to Frederick Philip Grove's account of riding the rails as a hobo in *In Search of Myself*: "I'll tell you one more thing about Ed Basil [the former hired man]. He caught a freight that night. We drank ourselves foggy, and then we walked over to the train station, and somewhere in the shadowy dark, he let me help him as he gave an awkward jump and roll at the same time, and he lay on his back on the deck of a flatcar. I had wanted to go with him for a ways. I'd wanted to have the experience, but I couldn't do it. I don't know why I'm telling you this."[13]

As Jennings points out, Kroetsch was preoccupied by figures such as Grove and Grey Owl, and felt that Grove might be "paradigmatic of the Canadian artist, uninventing and unwriting his life before imagining himself anew," as Grove had done in *In Search of Myself* and his other "autobiographical" works.[14] Indeed, in a volume of essays published in 1989, by which time details of the Grove story had emerged, Kroetsch, for whom the problem of literary writing about the New World could only be resolved by deconstructing traditional (European) carriers of meaning and "creating them anew," describes Grove as a figure who "comes more and more to represent our [Canadian artists'] predicament."[15]

The assumed identities and autofictional texts discussed in this book have also given rise to a number of other literary works that reflect their authors' fascination with their subjects' autofictional identities.

In "The Ballad of Will James," the well-known Canadian folk and country singer Ian Tyson describes the famous cowboy as his hero. In fact, Tyson's life in some respects resembled that of his hero. Like Will James, Tyson had dreamed of being a cowboy since his early childhood – a dream that was, he says, in fact inspired by his collection of books by Will James – and rode in rodeos while he was (like Will James) attending art school. In the late 1970s, he bought a ranch south of Calgary and became a country and western singer, known for his cowboy ballads.[16] In "The Ballad of Will James" Tyson describes the famous cowboy as his unforgotten childhood hero, elliptically referring to James's assumed identity ("the man *they called* Will James" – my emphasis) and life story (his love of horses, alcohol, and above all the West), indicating that Tyson not only had read James's own books but was also familiar with his "true" biography.[17]

Tyson also figures in the documentary film *Alias Will James*,[18] in which he performs "The Ballad of Will James," and he is interviewed on camera by the director of the film. In the hands of novelist and filmmaker Jacques Godbout, the documentary becomes a multi-faceted exploration not only of Will James's life and art, but of the all-consuming desire of his protagonist to "become" what he "is." Interviewing a modern-day cowboy from Montreal, who has followed the trajectory of Will James (of whom the contemporary cowboy knows little) – leaving Quebec in his teens and going to the western United States to be a cowboy, knowing little or no English – Godbout asks him why he did it. "It was my destiny," replies the cowboy. In Godbout's film, the narrator describes Will James's life in the West and his extraordinary success, for which he paid the price of killing, "little by little," Ernest Dufault. The degree to which Godbout is affected by the Will James story is unmistakable: it manifests itself not only in the probing questions he asks the Montreal cowboy, but also in his depiction of Will James's progressive "killing" of Ernest Dufault as a kind of suicide, which for Godbout stands for the dissolution of Québécois identity.

The story of Grey Owl, too, has inspired not only Robert Kroetsch but also other writers to examine the phenomenon of self-invented identity as undertaken by the famous "apostate Englishman." The Anishinaabe Armand Garnet Ruffo, a descendant of the Espaniel family who took in Grey Owl when his drinking had grown out of control, wrote a book-length poetic biography recounting his subject's dual identity.[19] An extraordinarily sympathetic account of Grey Owl's life, its depiction of his subject's "imposture" also suggests an empathetic understanding of and identification with Grey Owl's self-invention. The poet Ruffo understands the impulse of the writer Grey Owl to "become himself," in the process "killing off" the old self of Archie Belaney, to borrow Jacques Godbout's phrase about Will James.

As we saw in the first two chapters of this book, Felix Paul Greve inspired works written by some of his former European associates.

Two of the most eminent European writers of their time, Thomas Mann and André Gide, portrayed Felix Paul Greve in some of their best-known works, a tribute (if a somewhat dubious one) to a man who had literally re-created himself. These works by Gide and Mann present fascinating accounts of how a gifted literary impostor came to be the real-life protagonist of a fiction he had himself created.

IMPOSTURE NARRATIVES, "PASSING," AND THE ACT OF WRITING

The impostures discussed in this book represent acts of "passing" carried to an extreme: they go far beyond avoiding racial or social stigmatization or identitary role-playing to gain social or financial advantages. They represent a form of "passing" that, as Linda Schlossberg contends, is "about the creation and establishment of an alternative set of narratives. It becomes a way of creating new stories out of unusable ones, or from personal narratives seemingly in conflict with other forms of self-presentation. The passing subject's need to create a coherent, plausible narrative to account for his or her past suggests, on a very basic level, that every subject's history is a work in progress – a set of stories we tell ourselves in order to make sense or coherence out of a frequently confusing and complicated past. The risk and pleasure of narrative thus seems intimately connected to the risk and pleasure of passing."[20] According to Schlossberg, passing "can be experienced as a uniquely pleasurable experience, one that trades on the erotics of secrecy and revelation."[21]

"Passing" in the sense of storytelling, in which the narrator selects which elements should be concealed and which ones revealed, represents the kind of self-invention that also determines the act of writing. The construction of a "new" and coherent identity as seen with the authors discussed in this book is closely linked to the subject's writing, whether the process is initiated through the writing or whether the writing serves to authenticate an already constructed (assumed and claimed) identity. To re-create one's self, to bring into play the "multitudes" that one "contains," may be a universal fantasy, but it is one that is constantly being performed in the process of creating fictive worlds. The seductiveness of such omnipotence, and the temptation to "become" one's own fictive being, underlie all autofictional texts.

The inscription of the writer's personal identity (and the personal attributes and experiences that have formed it) in his or her own works represents the hallmark of autofiction. If, as Linda Schlossberg suggests, identity is primarily a form of storytelling, it follows that the stories are drawn from the storyteller's own repertoire of experience – personal, social, and cultural (the latter including literary works, works of art, travel, etc.). An assumed identity is thus a composite constituted from elements derived from a subject's total repertoire of experience, although, as in the case of Archie Belaney/Grey Owl or Ernest Dufault/Will James, one particular element – the North American Indian or the cowboy – may be dominant or determinant.

In some cases, creating fictive characters becomes a way of vicariously living out the multiplicity of identities authors feel dwell within them, a predisposition which André Gide describes as determining his own work. At his first meeting with Felix Paul Greve, he explains his preference for "causing action," that is, to "live out" his virtual identities by attributing them to various characters in his books, rather than "acting," that is, actually living them out himself in his everyday life. Where such evocations of the author's fictionally constructed identity and experiences occurring in his or her literary works can be linked to his or her own actual biography, we talk about autofiction.

How porous the line that is often drawn between an author's biography and the fiction he or she produces can be is illustrated in the controversy over Canadian writer Joseph Boyden's claims of Aboriginal identity. Boyden's novels, featuring sympathetic Aboriginal characters whose culture and identity clash with and are threatened by the dominant white culture surrounding them, have been critically applauded (the author has been awarded numerous literary prizes). In the promotional publicity accompanying the publication of his novels, and in interviews and articles that followed the awarding of the prizes, Boyden has repeatedly referred to the fact that he has an Indigenous background. On the basis of his self-identifying as a writer of fiction who is (part) Aboriginal, he has become increasingly vocal as a solicited spokesperson (and thus a perceived authority) on Aboriginal issues, even accepting a commission to write a ballet about residential schools in Canada (*Going Home Star – Truth and Reconciliation*).[22] His high public profile as an authority on Aboriginal issues raised questions in First Nations communities about the claims to Native identity of the charismatic novelist who had grown up in North York, Ontario, and now lives mostly in New Orleans, Louisiana. An online article published by APTN (Aboriginal Peoples Television

Network) in December 2016[23] gave rise to heated discussions in the media, in which Native and non-Native voices debated the authenticity of Boyden's Aboriginal identity. Not surprisingly, Grey Owl's imposture was repeatedly invoked in the discussion. The "Grey Owl syndrome," to use Atwood's term for non-Natives passing as Natives, had re-emerged in a controversy that captured national attention.

It would be difficult to argue that Boyden has inscribed his (claimed) Aboriginal identity in his literary writing (nowhere does he claim to be drawing on his own personal experiences in creating his novels) or that he "lived out" this identity, both of which Grey Owl had done. What is noteworthy about the Boyden affair in the context of this study is that Boyden (like Jeremy Sadness in Kroetsch's *Gone Indian*) seems to have constructed his Native identity around a "fake Indian," his uncle, Erl Boyden, who was known as "Injun Joe." Erl König Boyden (named after the Schubert Lied "Erlkönig," which his mother greatly admired), from the day he met Buffalo Bill when the famous Wild West Show appeared on tour in Ottawa, had in a way constructed his own Indian identity. Little Erl, like Archie Belaney/Grey Owl, became a lover of wild animals and all things Indian. According to a *Maclean's* article about him published in 1956 ("The Double Life of Injun Joe"[24]), he "saw himself as a white boy who by his knowledge of hunting and outdoor lore is adopted by an Indian chief and given a place of honor in the tribe." Unlike his nephew, Erl Boyden spent a great deal of time with Indians, learning how to make tepees from the Sioux in South Dakota. He came to be called "Injun Joe" because, "curiously, the boy who dreamed of becoming an Indian [had] grown up to look like one." The purpose of Erl Boyden's Indian impersonation was, however, to commodify his "Indian" appearance: black-haired, dressed in a faded red shirt, rumpled jeans, beaded moccasins, and a feathered headdress, he sold "Indian" souvenir trinkets to tourists from a tepee he had set up near Algonquin Park, Ontario. According to the *Maclean's* article, Erl declared that, as far as he knew, he had not "a drop of Indian blood."

At least some of Joseph Boyden's claims of Aboriginal identity are derived from his kinship with "Injun Joe." The APTN article points out that over the years Joseph referred to his uncle's "Ojibway ways" and once told an interviewer that he saw parallels between himself and his "Indian uncle." The author of the APTN article remarks that Joseph Boyden has at various times claimed Métis, Mi'kmaq, Ojibway, and Nipmuc descent, adding that although he has backed away from some of these claims, he has consistently refused to be interviewed by APTN to respond to questions about his Native identity.

Whether Joseph Boyden is a Native impersonator or actually has hard-to-document Native antecedents is a question that, at the time of writing of this study, has not been conclusively answered. Some of the most sceptical voices from the writing community are non-Native ones. Rick Salutin, for example, alluding to Boyden's somewhat vague assertions that he came to claim his Native identity because of "family stories" he had heard, writes: "What makes you part of a community [are] concrete connections known to you and acknowledged by others. It isn't the stories you hear or tell, pace Boyden ... Any claim that stories are the basis of it all ... is just self-promotion by the writer."[25]

Anishinaabe writer Drew Hayden Taylor, weighing in on the Boyden controversy, takes a less judgmental tone. Like the critics who tended to exonerate Grey Owl's imposture because he chose to "become an Indian" at a time when "the cowboys always won," Taylor points out that claiming Native status is hardly an opportunistic act: "So many people now want to be Native, you have to wonder what the appeal is, what with the number of missing and murdered Indigenous women, high rates of diabetes, bad water, racism, subpar medical care and education."[26] Nevertheless he challenges the legitimacy of Boyden's role as a Native spokesperson: "Still, there's more to writing about the Native community than just having a good imagination – or a few drops of Native blood. To play the Indigenous card you need to have walked the walk and personally dealt with scars left by several hundred years of colonization."

As was the case at the time of the exposure of Grey Owl, however, a consensus seems to be emerging in various Aboriginal quarters to accept Boyden's self-identification as Aboriginal. Taylor concludes his piece on a conciliatory note: "The term 'wannabe' is used a lot in our community to refer to people who wish they were Native. On occasion, though, you meet someone who could be called a 'shouldabeen.'" Anishinaabe writer Wab Kinew writes in a similar vein, in words that evoke Armand Garnet Ruffo's sympathetic portrayal of Grey Owl: "the issue of how Joseph Boyden gained access to our circle does not matter as much as the fact that he is present in our community now. His place among us was built by writing about, giving back to and befriending us ... There is room in our circle for everyone."[27] Taylor's suggestion that Boyden is a "shouldabeen" Native and Kinew's assertion that he "has a place among us" goes to the heart of some of the issues surrounding constructed identity that have been raised throughout this book. Whether Boyden will end up being able to document his identitary claims may turn out to be less significant, in terms of both his personal life and his literary one, than his construction of an identity that represents what he says is his true Self, an identity that Aboriginal writers Taylor and Kinew, at least, seem prepared to acknowledge.

IDENTITY PERFORMANCE, SUBJECTIVITY, AND AUTOFICTION

The recognition that identity – or at least what we refer to as personal identity – is in constant flux did not gain broad currency until the second half of the twentieth century, beginning with Erving Goffman and his work on identity performance.[28] This notion has been further explored by identity theorists such as Sidonie Smith and Susanna Egan, who have applied it to literary texts, including autobiography.[29] Paul John Eakin in his work on autobiography contends that as the individual is constantly constructing and performing his or her (self-constructed) identity, it follows that autobiography is always a process of self-creation.[30]

However, the idea that personal identity is constantly changing is far from new. Raymond Martin and John Barresi, in their study of the history of personal identity, invoke the views expressed by Diotima in Plato's *Symposium* "that the identity over time of every 'mortal' thing is to be understood in terms of a relationship among its ever changing parts." As Martin and Barresi point out, Diotima's statement represents a definition of "the relational view of the identity over time," and observe that this is a view to which virtually all current personal identity theorists subscribe.[31]

In contrast to the shifting and fragmentation that characterize personal identity, the self is also seen as possessing a permanent, unchanging component which the ancient Greeks called the *psyche*, or the soul, and which contemporary theorists call subjectivity, "the world that exists in our heads, the personal life of the soul, one's own private landscape to which no one else has access."[32] This subjective consciousness can be transmitted in the form of metempsychosis (transmigration of souls in ancient Greek philosophy), or, in modern literature, in the numinous relationship between characters (for example that of Leopold Bloom and Stephen Daedelus, both of whom represent incarnations of the epic wanderer Ulysses in James Joyce's novel, and both of whom are generally considered to be alter egos of the author).

In a broader sense, the term *metempsychosis* might be used to describe the relationship that often develops in the writing process between authors and the characters they create. Inventing a world is the essence of being a writer, and the characters created to inhabit this world are often extensions – sometimes manifest, sometimes latent – of aspects of the writer's own identity.

What makes the writers whose lives and works are discussed in this book so extraordinary is not only that they constructed new identities for themselves, which they presented and authenticated in the form of "autobiography," but that they actually lived them out, "becoming," in everyday life, the autofictional selves they had themselves created. In the case of Edith Eaton alias Sui Sin Far, her self-identification as "Chinese" (by implication full-blooded Chinese) represented a favouring of the Chinese part of her heritage that allowed her to overcome the biological and cultural hybridity that she perceived as a kind of identitary incompleteness. Winnifred Eaton's assumption of a Japanese identity, often assumed to be a rejection of the Chinese side of her background, may also have been motivated out of feelings similar to her sister's. Sylvester Clark Long undertook his self-transformation into Chief Buffalo Child Long Lance to escape the confines of life as a "coloured" man in the southern United States, although he came to genuinely identify with the people and the culture of which he had claimed to be a part.

The motivations of Ernest Dufault alias Will James and Archie Belaney alias Grey Owl to construct and assume their new identities were likely determined by a combination of factors: the restrictiveness which they perceived in the lives seemingly prescribed for them by the social and family circumstances in which they had been born, on the one hand, and the appeal of the apparently limitless freedom that the Wild West and the northern wilderness, respectively, seemed to offer. In spite of all they achieved in the lives they had chosen – Will James through his art and above all through his writing, Grey Owl as a writer and world-renowned conservationist – their personal lives were marked by a sense of loss and absence (of their "old" selves?) that they sought to mitigate by drinking and, paradoxically, by their writing in their new personae.

Felix Paul Greve alias Frederick Philip Grove was driven to assume his new identity by the protean impulses described by his friend André

Gide. His was a composite identity that allowed him to assume the paradigmatic roles of the New World without relinquishing the glamorous past he had claimed in Europe. Both of these roles were motivated by a narcissistic desire to belong to the social, intellectual, and artistic elite of an exclusive and cosmopolitan world from which his humble origins and the problematic circumstances of his childhood and early youth (which he seemed to regard as an accident of birth) would have otherwise excluded him.

Autofiction illustrates the complicated relationships between personal identity, assumed identity, and writing, especially autobiography, which is likely the reason that the writers and the works examined in this book have continued to interest writers, identity theorists, and literary critics. For general readers, the self-reinventions documented in the "autobiographical" works written by the subjects discussed in this volume may well be of interest because they so eloquently illustrate – indeed dramatize – the tantalizing possibility of living the "real" lives which, to paraphrase Oscar Wilde, most people cannot – or do not choose to – lead.

Appendix

FPG and the Thomas Mann Connection

The Confessions of Felix Krull, Confidence Man (*Bekenntnisse des Hochstaplers Felix Krull*),[1] the last novel to be published by Thomas Mann, offers a curious and revealing perspective on the figure who was unmistakably one of the main models for the protagonist.[2] What makes it significant in the context of this study is its astonishingly precise mirroring of Greve/Grove's autofiction. Notwithstanding the parodistic inflation with which Mann portrays his "hero," the novel contains many passages characterizing the main figure that coincide with the salient features of Felix Paul Greve. Mann explicitly referred to this novel as a "memoir" of Krull's "early years," calling it "Part 1," and clearly meant to continue Krull's "autobiographical" narrative in a second volume. What direction this continuation of "Krull's" story would have taken, given Mann's awareness of the whereabouts of his real-life model and of the latter's Canadian career, is, of course, not known.

Written in the first person, Mann's novel tells the narrator's story from birth to young manhood, parodically incorporating elements of both the picaresque and the coming-of-age genres. Born to an ineffectual but indulgent father, owner of a champagne firm (whose product is of more than dubious quality), and an equally indulgent and quite uncultured mother, Felix Krull grows up a spoilt child with delusions of grandeur, and develops a decidedly narcissistic personality. The family's high living and mismanagement of the champagne firm ultimately lead to the father's bankruptcy and suicide when Felix is not yet twenty. Felix's godfather settles the family's affairs and arrangements for their future: Felix's mother is to operate a boarding house in Frankfurt, his sister Olympia is to seek a career as an operetta chorus girl,[3] and Felix himself is to be apprenticed to the grand Hotel St James and Albany in Paris.

Due to fortuitous circumstances, his attractive appearance, excellent manners, and generally appealing demeanour (and, to no small degree, his acts of deception), Felix's fortunes are favoured in dramatic ways, culminating in his assumption of the role of the Marquis de Venosta, who has been sent on a world tour by his parents with the aim of separating him from Zaza, his chorus girl lover. Loath to leave Paris and Zaza, the Marquis proposes the role reversal to Felix, who accepts. On the first leg of his journey, in the train from Paris to Lisbon, Felix, as the Marquis, meets a fellow traveller, Professor Kuckuck, an archaeologist and natural scientist who lives in Lisbon and shows him the sights of his city, also inviting him to his home. (One will recall that Greve's heroine Fanny Essler, having run away with her "prince," dies of malaria in Lisbon, the event which constitutes the novel's ending.) Krull's visit to the Kuckucks leads to Felix/Venosta's seduction of both Kuckuck's daughter, Zouzou, and ultimately his wife, Maria. Thus ends what was to be part I of the "memoirs" of Felix Krull.

In an afterword to the novel, Ralph-Reiner Wuthenow, without speculating on possible "models" for the protagonist, sums up the main qualities of Mann's Felix Krull in terms that could not be more applicable to Greve.[4] Wuthenow's observations that Felix Krull is "in love with himself," and that his affirmation of life manifests itself in the desire to be someone else, echo the sentiments expressed by Else in her memoir. Other statements attributed to Krull remind the reader of the qualities Felix Paul Greve presented in defining himself in the "conversation" with André Gide: Krull's assertions that he represents a multiplicity of possible lives, that for him veritable deception is something like an uncompleted truth, and that in his deceptions he is not committing a crime but "acting."

In his analysis of the Felix Krull–Felix Greve connection, Greve/Grove's biographer Klaus Martens, although suggesting that Mann's Felix Krull is a composite and that the novel itself is in the tradition of the "young men's stories" fashionable at the beginning of the twentieth century, nevertheless marshals an impressive number of resemblances between the backgrounds, predispositions, and biographies of Mann's fictitious hero and Felix Paul Greve.[5]

Among the most striking parallels are that Krull's family, like Greve's, disintegrates when Krull is still a child; that Krull's mother, like Greve's, runs a boarding house after the family break-up; and that Krull himself becomes a liftboy and then a waiter at the Hotel St James and Albany in Paris, the very hotel where Greve stayed with Kilian during a romantic trip the two had undertaken in 1902. Martens also points out that "Krull sometimes dreams that he 'were the Emperor.' We recall that young Felix Paul Greve, who must have, not so secretly, thought himself happy indeed [Martens is here alluding to the meaning of the name *Felix*], presided over a banquet in honour of the Emperor."[6]

There are further parallels and coincidental details between Mann's impostor-hero and Greve's fraudulent claimed identity, for instance the correspondence between Krull's assumption of the identity of his rich acquaintance, the Marquis de Venosta, in Mann's novel,[7] and Greve's slipping into Kilian's part-Scots identity and fortune in invoking the "Rutherford" side of the family in *In Search of Myself*.

These resemblances alone between Mann's Felix character and Felix Greve suggest that Mann knew Greve's background and "story," and likely Greve himself. Mann knew a number of Greve's Munich circle; it is almost inevitable that the two had actually come to know each other at the Pension Gisela, an establishment in Schwabing, Munich's bohemian quarter, favoured by homoerotically inclined young men, where Mann's and Greve's respective sojourns in 1902 overlapped by several weeks.[8] It is likely that Mann had, by the time he was writing *Felix Krull*, read Greve's self-revealing German novels (Mann's novel contains a number of plot and character elements that would seem to allude to both *Fanny Essler* – the setting of the finale in Lisbon being only one indicator – and *Maurermeister Ihles Haus*).

However, none of the circumstances surrounding the relationship between Mann and Greve in Europe explain certain references in Mann's novel to Greve/Grove's life in Canada. These references, while oblique, are telling, and the precision with which they evoke certain details related by Greve alias Fredrick Philip Grove in his "autobiographical" *A Search for America* makes it difficult to dismiss them as coincidental. In fact, in 1939 Grove had written to Mann, who was then at Princeton, from Simcoe, and sent him a signed copy of his just-published *Two Generations*.[9] While the letters from Mann to Grove are extant, Grove's side of the correspondence seems to have been lost or destroyed. In 1939, when he wrote to Mann, Grove was also working on another "autobiographical" work that would be published under the title *In Search of Myself*. How much did he tell Mann in his letters? Might Mann have obtained a copy of *A Search for America*? Or, for that matter, of *In Search of Myself*, once the latter had been published?

Martens raises these questions cautiously:

> The question remains whether Greve's Canadian alias had been lifted when he approached Mann ... Had Thomas Mann finally read Grove's "Prologue" to *In Search of Myself*, which was then still an article bearing the title of the purportedly autobiographical novel? Grove's reminiscences, then called "My Life," were being written out in longhand while he was corresponding with Mann. No wonder, then, that he recalled the man who had also stayed at the Pension Gisela. By means of Felix Krull's reminiscences, which Mann calls "memoirs," the author styles the recollections of a gifted climber who, as the narrator, writes down the events of his life in his own idiosyncratic way.[10]

The features of Mann's novel suggesting that Felix Krull was indeed modelled after Felix Greve manifest themselves, first of all, in the physical resemblance and psychological similarities between the two Felixes, but also in their parallel backgrounds. While Martens sees the opening setting of Mann's novel in the Rhineland as a reference to Stefan George's origins (the George family owned vineyards near Bingen, and Greve was associated with the George circle), it could also represent an oblique allusion to Greve's student years in the Rhine city of Bonn. A more immediate parallel, as Martens points out, is that Krull's mother, like Greve's, operates a boarding house in a large German city. What is more, Krull's father, like Greve's, disappears from the scene early on in his life. These similarities, together with the striking parallels in the personal lives, careers, and character predispositions of Felix Krull and Felix Paul Greve, discussed below, let Mann's novel read like a veritable *roman à clef*.

The physical resemblance of Felix Krull to Felix Greve is so close that it suggests an explicitly drawn portrait. Krull is described as conspicuously tall and well-built, his honey-dark complexion a striking contrast to his blond and silky hair and blue eyes.[11] The timbre of his voice, the dignified distance he maintains in social settings, lend this altogether attractive youth an air of mystery. All these features were so conspicuous in Greve that Else was to dwell on them at length in her description of him in her memoirs.[12]

Krull, like Greve, exhibits exquisite taste, and the possession of fine clothes and accessories and the frequenting of elegant and expensive establishments in both cases can be seen to feed their inherent narcissism, the sense that they were destined to a nobler, grander life than the circumstances of their birth would normally have afforded them. Both Felixes manifest a sense of entitlement based on nothing more than their extraordinary good looks, elegant manners, and tastes, and in both cases this sense of superiority and entitlement culminates in the desire to achieve proximity to royalty. Krull's "playing the *Kaiser*" as a child[13] and, in Lisbon, his successful presentations to various royals, ranging from a Romanian prince to the king of Portugal, are in keeping with the parodic tone of Mann's novel, which only makes the parallels to Greve's preoccupation with royal and imperial families all the more striking: his presiding at celebrations in honour of the Emperor's birthday in Bonn, the descriptions of his mother's *soirées* attended by members of the nobility in *In Search of Myself* and *A Search for America*, and, of course, the meeting with the British king and queen of his young hero Leonard Broadus, whose "acknowledgement" and reward by the royal couple is paralleled in Mann's novel by Felix Krull receiving a royal medal from the king of Portugal.

Equally significant indicators that Mann's Felix Krull character was inspired by Greve's story are the multiplicity of allusions that seem to point to Greve's German novels, *Fanny Essler* and *Maurermeister Ihles Haus*. Felix Krull's impressions as he strolls about the bustling streets of Frankfurt, glancing covetously into the display windows of expensive stores,[14] and, later, his first experiences of the elegant streets and shops of Paris[15] closely resemble those of Greve's heroine Fanny Essler when she first arrives in Berlin. What is more, the theatre milieu, in particular that of the operetta and the *variétés*, described in naturalistic detail in *Fanny Essler*, is evoked time and time again in *Felix Krull*. In Krull's description, the employees' dormitory at the Hotel St James and Albany is, like the chorus girls' dressing room in *Fanny Essler*, a site of hectic transformation: in donning their smart uniforms, the dormitory residents, who in private life are indistinguishable from the ragged masses milling on the streets of Paris, dress at the hotel to suit their designated "roles," just as in *Fanny Essler* the quite ordinary and indeed at times vulgar girls, most of them part-time prostitutes, transform themselves to appear as glamorous and seductive figures when they are on stage.

Mann also parodies Greve's sexual prowess, attested to in Else's memoirs. In two of the sexual encounters related in *Felix Krull*, Felix is praised as an exceptional lover, first by the family maid, with whom he has his first affair, then by Madame Houpflé, a hotel guest at the St James and Albany. The latter compares Felix's sexual performance favourably and in ecstatic tones with that of her husband.[16] The reference to her husband's sexual deficiencies can be seen as a specific allusion to both the fictitious Fanny Essler and her model, the biographical Else Endell, both of whose husbands are said to be impotent and for both of whom sexual relations with Greve (in the case of Fanny Essler, Reelen, the Greve figure) are experienced as nothing short of epiphanic.

The repeated references to Felix Krull's predilection for beaches, coasts, and water sports evoke a whole cluster of significant elements associated with Greve's biography. Not only had he grown up near water – first on the Baltic, then in the port city of Hamburg – rowing was one of the main activities of the Rhenus fraternity in Bonn, which Greve had joined soon after enrolling at Bonn University. Martens observes in his biography of Greve that the latter, an excellent rower and swimmer, was a "veritable water creature" and, during his university days, owned a boat called "Nixe," which led to his being given the drinking or club name "Nixe," the German word for mermaid.[17] Martens's book includes a photograph of Greve with his fraternity friends depicting Greve as "Nixe," in which his legs are positioned to resemble a fish tail,[18] an allusion to the famous legendary "Nixe" of the Rhine, the Loreley, whose siren call is said to have seduced sailors and lured them to their death. Greve's fraternity nickname was thus inspired not only as a metonym for water but also because it fit his "androgynous aura"[19] and played on his numerous amorous conquests. A traumatic incident that occurred during this period of Greve's life is linked to Greve's powers of seduction, and it is also associated with water: the mysterious drowning of Greve's fraternity brother Hans Lomberg, who seems to have been attracted to Greve. There is evidence to indicate that Greve's lover Kilian and possibly Greve himself may have been involved in Lomberg's drowning, which occurred during a Rhenus rowing excursion on the Rhine.[20]

Greve personified as "Nixe" is alluded to in *Felix Krull* not only in Felix's affinity for maritime landscapes and pastimes, but also in more specific aquatic contexts. Thus during their chance meeting on the train to Lisbon Professor Kuckuck remarks that Krull reminds him of a *Seelilie* (water lily). The *Seelilie* is a variety of narcissus that has androgynous associations derived from the Greek myth of a beautiful youth who falls in love with his own reflection in a pool of water and drowns. Mann's *Seelilie* slyly references Greve's androgynous attractiveness and narcissistic personality, but it may also be a coded allusion to Greve's faked suicide, said to have been death by drowning. The Loreley, the legendary seductive "Nixe" of the Rhine, figures in a more humorous allusion in Mann's novel in connection with the protagonist: Krull's father's champagne factory produces a product called "Lorley [*sic*] extra cuvée."[21]

While the aquatic predilections of the protagonist and water images associated with him in *Felix Krull* evoke significant elements in Greve's background (the Baltic, the North Sea), personal life (the drowning incident on the Rhine, the faked suicide by drowning), and personality (his "androgynous aura" and narcissistic tendencies), water also figures as a theme in the literary works of both the fictional Felix Krull and his autofictional counterpart, Felix Paul Greve alias Frederick Philip Grove. Felix Krull's remark that the literary works he was later to produce often had maritime settings echoes Grove's narrator in *A Search for America*, who declares: "All my life I have been a lover of water – rivers, lakes, the sea."[22] The reference to Krull's literary use of "maritime settings" evokes not only the Baltic setting of the author's "ancestral estate" but also the sailing escapades and water mishaps described in Grove's *In Search of Myself* and *The Adventure of Leonard Broadus*. The maritime setting is particularly significant in the extended aquatic images in *A Search for America*, in one of which the protagonist Phil Branden compares his shattered life to the empty sea shells that have been thrown up by the waves.[23]

Many more oblique references to Greve and his literary works can be found in *Felix Krull*, some of them occurring in the most trivial of contexts. The (true) Marquis de Venosta's lover, a chorus girl called Zaza (a shortening of Suzanne or Susanne), in Felix Krull's mind is a "sister" to Zouzou (Suzanne), Professor Kuckuck's daughter: Mann seems to be conflating Fanny the chorus girl in *Fanny Essler* and the heroine of *Maurermeister Ihles Haus*, whose real name is Susanne but who is called Suse. Another parallel in this context: in *Felix Krull* the (real) Marquis de Venosta plans to take Zaza to live in a "Paris suburb" – "Boulogne" or "Sèvres"[24] – while Felix (posturing as the Marquis) is on his travels, a possible allusion to Felix Greve's sojourn with his mistress Else not far from Paris at Étaples, also known as Paris-Plage.

Mann's choice of the rather uncommon name of Kilian in listing the men with names beginning with the letter K called up for military service (in the scene in which Krull is ultimately declared unfit) is hardly coincidental. The same is true of the name of a wealthy Scottish St James and Albany hotel guest called Lord Kilmarnock,[25] whose amorous advances Felix (at this point a dining-room waiter re-christened "Armand") spurns, evoking the relationship between Felix Greve and his fraternity brother Herman Kilian as well as the latter's Scottish ancestry.

While references to Greve's prison term and subsequent life in America occur in passing, so to speak, and although they appear in contexts not central to Krull's "memoir," they are, like the seemingly random occurrence of the name "Kilian," significant in our context due to the specificity with which they evoke elements in Greve's story. At times, these elements are displaced onto different contexts and characters. Thus Stanko, a kitchen helper in the Hotel St James and Albany (and also a small-time thief) with whom Krull becomes friendly, admits to Krull that he has served a year's prison term "in his home country."[26] In a similarly elliptical allusion to Greve, one of Krull's conversations with the Marquis de Venosta leads to the latter observing that in America, Europeans can be identified by differences in customs, such as the way they manipulate knife and fork. Venosta asks Krull if he has been to America, to which Krull answers no, he knows it only "from pictures."[27] In the passage that follows, Venosta speculates on Krull's past and family background, summing up his impression with the statement: "Somehow there's a mystery about you."[28] An allusion to Greve's "mysterious" disappearance from Europe and his "mysterious" and concealed identity in America?

Another evocation of Greve/Grove's life in America can be found in a passage describing Krull/Armand's performance as a waiter in the Hotel St James and Albany dining-room, where he describes his own attentive yet discreet way of serving guests, anticipating their need for "extras" such as "English mustard," "Worcestershire sauce," or "tomato ketchup" to accompany their dishes.[29] In a corresponding passage in *A Search for America*, the manager of Johnson's café in Toronto, where Phil Branden is being interviewed for a job as a waiter, the latter recommends himself by saying that he knows exactly what dishes should be accompanied by "Lea and Perrin's or H.P. Sauce."[30]

The manager, in replying, points out that dining customs in America are different from those in Europe, and that for cost reasons, "Lea and Perrin's Sauce" and "tomato-catsup" should not be offered by a waiter unless the customer specifically requests them.[31] And like Krull in his initial interview at the hotel in Paris, Branden is asked if he speaks French.[32]

The parallels outlined above can hardly be seen as coincidental. They suggest that Mann had read Grove's "autobiographical" novels (or parts thereof) and that Grove, in the letters he wrote to Mann from Simcoe, may have described in some detail the life he had lived since leaving Europe. But what is most striking of all in Mann's depiction of Felix Krull are his psychological insights into the chameleon nature of his "hero," insights that coincide with observations made earlier by Else in her memoirs and also by André Gide in his journal and indirectly in his novels *Les Caves du Vatican* and *Les Faux-monnayeurs*.

Here is Krull as a young boy, feigning pathological symptoms, which he himself describes as one of his first acts of self-engenderment, an act of creation: "I had improved upon nature, realized a dream; and only he who has succeeded in creating a compelling and effective reality out of nothing, out of sheer inward knowledge and contemplation – in short, out of nothing more than imagination and the daring exploitation of his own body – he alone understands the strange and dreamlike satisfaction with which I rested from my creative task."[33] This quotation, and particularly the final phrase, echoes, in its tone and in some of its very formulations, a passage from *A Search for America*: "To master nothing less than all human knowledge was for my ambition – or, had I better say, for my conceit? – no more than the preliminary to swinging the earth out of its orbit and readjusting, while improving upon, the creator's work."[34] These strikingly similar formulations describe the narcissism inherent in the ambitions of both Mann's and Grove's protagonists, to achieve the ultimate act of creation, to "improve upon the creator's work" by (re)creating their own lives.

Mann also parodies Greve/Grove's narrative strategy of shifting time frames and re-contextualizing events relating to the protagonists, all the while claiming their authenticity. In confessional tones, Mann's narrator points out, early on in the novel, that the chronology of events as he depicts them in his memoir are not chronologically faithful[35] in a passage that evokes Grove's "Author's Note" to *A Search for America*: "every event in the story was lived through [but] only a very few events ... had taken place in the years with which this book deals."[36]

In another allusion to Greve's propensity to re-invent himself, Mann invokes gender norms that come into play in the socially sanctioned "identity change" women undergo upon marriage, implied by a name change. That such an "identity change" represents a "prohibition" when undertaken in other circumstances (such as homosexual relationships?) is presented as a "danger" to the protagonist as he reinvents himself and assumes a new identity. In Mann's novel, the identity change is implicitly associated with assuming a new gender role. Felix Krull explains the envy he felt as a young boy at the fact that his sister, soon to be married, would acquire a new name, observing that a name change and the resulting change in identity has an energizing effect. The reference to his sister's name change due to marriage prefaces his allusions to the numerous and diverse identities that he, Krull, himself assumed in his later years: "I have often disregarded a prohibition that ran counter to both my safety and my dislike of the humdrum and everyday. In doing so I have displayed a very considerable gift of invention and I mention now, by way of anticipation, the peculiar charm of that place in my notes where I first speak of the occasion on which I laid aside like a soiled and worn-out garment the name to which I was born, to assume another."[37]

Mann also references the circumstances of Greve's departure from Germany, ascribing to Krull, who has gone abroad, the impulse Greve/Grove must have felt to return in triumph, as a successful writer, to his homeland, which he had been forced to leave in shame and disgrace. One passage captures with singular perceptiveness the desire of the "youth" who, like Frederick Philip Grove in his European life, has felt unjustly and unsympathetically treated and misunderstood in his earlier surroundings, to present himself as endowed with the glamour and success of what he has subsequently become in a foreign land. Krull observes:

> How lightly, how impatiently does youth, bent on taking the wide world by storm, turn its back, contemptuous and unfeeling, on its little homeland ... And yet, however much a man may have outgrown it and may continue to outgrow it, its ridiculous, too familiar image still remains in the background of his consciousness, or emerges from it strangely after years of complete

> forgetfulness: what was absurd becomes estimable; among the actions, impressions, successes of one's life abroad, at every juncture, one takes secret thought for that small world, at every increase in one's fortunes one asks inwardly what it may be saying or what it might say, and this is true especially when one's homeland has behaved unkindly, unjustly, and obtusely toward one.[38]

Krull's ruminations on his past and his life abroad, where he has made good, also contain what may be a veiled allusion to Greve/Grove's desire to "reveal himself," as he had done in taking up contact with Mann: "While he is dependent on [the homeland], the youth defies it; but when it has released him and may long since have forgotten him, of his own free will he gives it the authority to pass judgment on his life. Yes, some day, after many years rich in excitement and in change, he will probably be drawn back to his birthplace, *he will yield to the temptation, conscious or unconscious, to show himself to its narrow view in all the glitter he has gained abroad*, and with mixed anxiety and derision in his heart he will feast upon its astonishment – *just as, in due course, I shall report of myself.*"[39] (My emphasis.)

In this passage, particularly in the phrases I have emphasized, Mann offers an intriguing clue that Grove may have revealed himself to him in his letters. The passage suggests the psychological motivation that drove Grove to reveal himself, albeit in encoded form, in his two "autobiographical" novels, a decision which was motivated, in the case of *In Search of Myself*, by learning of his old associate Gide's success in Europe. Grove's discovery that the eminent writer Thomas Mann, whose literary milieu in Germany had been bound up, at least indirectly, with his own, was now in America, likely also played a role in shaping Grove's "autobiography," the purported aim of which was to "explain" himself to his now famous former associates.

Mann's novel also captures Greve/Grove's inherent disposition to disguise himself. Felix Krull repeatedly expresses his delight at his own deceptions in his role-playing, perceiving the prescribed name change (from Felix to Armand) as an enhancement rather than an impoverishment or deprivation of his true identity. Felix sees the uniforms he wears as an employee of the Hotel St James and Albany as a possibility to become someone else, just as delightful as the "costumes" his godfather, ridden by pedophile fantasies, had dressed him in as a child: "My secret wealth ... transformed my uniform and my job into a role, a simple extension of my talent for 'dressing up.' Although later on I achieved dazzling success in passing myself off for more than I was, for the time being I passed myself off for less, and it is an open question which deception gave me the greater inner amusement, the greater delight in this fairy-tale magic."[40]

Felix Paul Greve's sense of entitlement and his passing himself off as a wealthy heir apparent from his university days on are evoked in Krull's ruminations on social class. While in the employ of the hotel, Felix develops a theory about the reversibility of roles between the elegantly uniformed, impeccably mannered waiters and the monied guests they serve: "It was the idea of *interchangeability*. With a change of clothes and make-up, the servitors might often just as well have been the masters, and many of those who lounged in the deep wicker chairs, smoking their cigarettes, might have played the waiter. It was pure accident that the reverse was the fact, an accident of wealth; for an aristocracy of money is an accidental and interchangeable aristocracy."[41]

This notion of the reversibility of roles feeds Krull's sense of entitlement and reinforces his feeling that the fact that he is a poor waiter rather than a rich guest is a whim of fate. Indeed, thanks to a considerable savings account, a consequence of the theft of Madame Houpflé's jewels and also of her largesse after their sexual adventure, the waiter Krull, on his days off, retires to a room he has rented for the express purpose of transforming himself into an elegant gentleman. In the rented room, he dons the appropriate attire for visiting the city's nobler establishments. It is on one of these sorties to a fine Paris restaurant, dressed as an elegant rich gentleman, that he encounters the Marquis de Venosta, who is a regular lunch guest at the St James and Albany. It is when Venosta recognizes Felix as his lunchtime waiter in disguise, so to speak, that he proposes to Felix that the latter should "become" the Marquis and undertake the world tour prescribed by his parents in his place. And it is in describing this encounter that Venosta, paraphrasing a statement made by Suse in *Maurermeister Ihles Haus*, asks Krull: "Can one wish to be a different person from the one he is?"[42] To which Felix offers the following reply: "Consider … that if you should become another person, you would not feel the lack of your present self or regret it, simply because it would no longer be you."[43]

On the train to Lisbon, Krull, now impersonating the Marquis, muses on the difficulty of creating a new personal past and the consequences, in doing so, of obliterating the old one. Although he welcomes the new, elegant identity he has acquired, he remarks, albeit quite unemotionally, that the change leaves him "empty in his inner self" and results in a kind of amnesia: "No, it was the change and renewal of my worn-out self, the fact that I had been able to put off the old Adam and slip on a new, that gave me such a sense of fulfilment and happiness. I was struck, though, by the fact that in this change of existence there was not simply delightful refreshment but also a sort of emptying out of my inmost being – that is, I had to banish from my soul all memories that belonged to my no longer valid past ... It gave me a strange feeling of faulty memory, of emptiness of memory."[44]

In the train carrying him to Lisbon, Krull/Venosta meets Professor Kuckuck in the dining-car, as we have already recounted. But the professor is not only a paleontologist and archaeologist, he is also a genealogist and, when Krull introduces himself as Venosta, Kuckuck turns out to be well informed of Venosta's circumstances and antecedents, all the while remaining oblivious to the fact that he is chatting with an impostor. One is tempted to attribute his self-satisfied comment to Krull/Venosta that "he knows all about him"[45] to the novel's author, and to read it as a playful metafictional reference to the fact that Mann, indeed, "knew all about" Greve alias Grove and his turbulent life.

Mann's strategy is to manipulate Greve/Grove's heterogeneous personae to create an equivalent cast of heterogeneous characters in *Felix Krull*, creating a fictional mirror that reflects Grove's autofictions. That Mann makes Greve/Grove, in his various autofictional incarnations, the (anti-)hero of his novel endows the biographical Greve/Grove figure with a kind of metatextual status.

Frederick Philip Grove died years before *Felix Krull* was published. How he would have reacted to Mann's parodistic account of his dubious and peripatetic "career" remains a matter of conjecture. Although in *Confessions of Felix Krull, Confidence Man, Part I* the protagonist is portrayed as an out-and-out fraud and a subject of parody, Frederick Philip Grove might have derived some satisfaction from Mann's unsympathetic rendering of the "elites" whom Felix Krull exploits, but also from Mann's sympathetic understanding (expressed in the voice of Felix Krull after he has gone abroad) of the ambiguous relationship to his "homeland" that has treated its son "unkindly, unjustly, and obtusely." What also remains unknown is how Mann would have continued his chronicle in part 2. That he would have vindicated Felix's youthful impostures by depicting him as achieving success in his ultimate incarnation as a North American writer is unlikely. But it is not entirely inconceivable.

Notes

INTRODUCTION

1 Ginsberg, "Introduction," in *Passing and the Fictions of Identity*, 3.
2 For a discussion of identity as performance see, for example, Sidonie Smith, "Performativity, Autobiographical Practice, Resistance"; Eakin, *Living Autobiographically*; Egan, *Burdens of Proof*.
3 Gray, *Flint and Feather*.
4 Adams, *Howard Adams*.
5 See Buckley, "Rampa, T. Lobsang."
6 See Yanofsky, "Who Is Andreas Karavis?" and Homel, "Le mystérieux poète grec."
7 See Sheppard, *HA!*
8 I have used the term *Indian* throughout this book, to avoid anachronism, as the word was in current usage during the time of Grey Owl and Long Lance.
9 The Croatans were originally one of the Algonquin peoples, and are also believed to be connected to the Lumbees and other mixed-race groups that included African-Americans in their genealogies. See Raymond D. Fogelson, *The Handbook of North American Indians*, vol. 14, 323–6.
10 Grove, *In Search of Myself*, 452.
11 Régine Robin discusses this premise in *Le Golem de l'écriture*.
12 Ibid., 121.
13 Joseph Roth (1894–1939) was born into a Jewish family in Brody, Galicia (Austria-Hungary). In Vienna, where he launched his career as a writer, he concealed his provincial Jewish background and presented several versions of his origins, one being that he was the illegitimate son of an Austrian officer. In his self-created persona as a member of Austria's venerated

military establishment – at one point he claimed to be an Austrian officer himself – he adopted the culture of a Viennese society defined by the benevolent patriarchy of the Emperor. His devastation at the fall of the Austrian Empire after World War I inspired his most famous novel, the autofictional *Radetzkymarsch*, in which the Emperor appears as a father figure of the protagonist. Roth later emigrated to Paris, where he died in 1939. Even in death, his double identity was a source of controversy. At his funeral, Catholic and Jewish mourners almost came to blows in a dispute over the rites by which he was to be buried. Although Roth had professed to be a Catholic, the Jewish community claimed he was Jewish.

Romain Gary (1914–1980) was born Roman Kacew in Vilna, now Vilnius, Lithuania, into a Jewish family. He moved to Nice as a teenager. During the Second World War he changed his name to Romain Gary, subsequently making various claims as to his family origins and introducing suitable adjustments to his own past. After the war he became famous as a novelist, at one point posing as an unknown writer called Émile Ajar, author of *La Vie devant soi*, which won the Prix Goncourt in 1975. No one in the French literary establishment was aware of the hoax. He is the only author to have been awarded the Prix Goncourt twice, as he had already received it for a previous novel (signed Romain Gary). Gary committed suicide in 1980. Both Roth and Gary are discussed at length in Robin, *Le Golem de l'écriture*.

14 Robin, *Le Golem de l'écriture*, 16–17. My translation. The original reads: "Occuper toutes les places est bien le rêve de tout romancier, de tout poète, de tout artiste, voire de tout un chacun. Faire jouer tous les autres qui sont en moi, me transformer en autre, laisser libre cours à tout processus de devenir-autre, devenir son propre être fictif ou, plus exactement, s'attacher à expérimenter dans le texte le fictif de l'identité; autant de tentations fortes, presque à notre portée et qui sortent à l'heure actuelle du domaine de la fiction."

15 For a full discussion of the significance of the flawed will, see chapter 4.

16 See, for example, Robin, *Le Golem de l'écriture*, and Hildenbrock, *Das andere Ich*.

17 Doubrovsky, *Fils*.

18 See Hornung, "Introduction," in *Auto/Biography and Mediation*, xi–xviii, and, in the same volume, Howes, "Mediating between Life Writing Studies and Lives," 3–13.

19 See for example Browder, *Slippery Characters*; Powell, ed., *Beyond the Binary*; Rak, ed., *Auto/Biography in Canada*.

20 Doubrovsky, *Le livre brisé*, 212. My translation.

21 Lejeune, *Le Pacte autobiographique.*
22 Genon, *Autofiction.*
23 Colonna, *Autofiction et autres mythomanies.*
24 Vilain, *Défense de Narcisse.*
25 Delaume, *La règle du je*. Delaume's notion of autofictional self-reinvention as a kind of suicide of the Self can also be found in some theoretical works on "passing" which, as Judith Butler has pointed out, can be seen as a kind of pun, signifying the "ultimate turning away," or death. See Butler, *Bodies That Matter*, 183.
26 Robin, *Le Golem de l'écriture.*
27 Grove, "Thoughts and Reflections," 307.

CHAPTER ONE

1 In spite of his cultivated English accent and obvious familiarity with English literature and culture, and despite the fact that he claimed Scottish-Swedish ancestry, questions as to his true identity emerged long before the doubts first expressed by D.O. Spettigue in his *Frederick Philip Grove*, published in 1969. At that point Spettigue could only speculate that "[Grove] probably was not Swedish [as he had claimed] but German, that he may not have been as old as he claimed when he arrived [in Canada], and that his name was perhaps not Frederick Philip Grove" (22). Margaret Stobie, citing taped interviews with Grove's former pupils and other people who knew him when he was a teacher in rural Manitoba, suggests that "it is not at all unlikely that Grove went to Manitoba because he knew of the Mennonite settlements and the bilingual English-German schools there" (Stobie, *Frederick Philip Grove*, 26). According to Elisabeth Peters, who taught in rural Manitoba in the 1940s, a colleague of hers, Agnes Wiebe, who had been a pupil of Grove's in Winkler, told her that Grove spoke excellent German, and that in the Mennonite community he was assumed to be German. (Interview with Elisabeth Peters, Winnipeg, 25 March 2006.)
2 Spettigue, *FPG: The European Years.*
3 See for example Eggleston, "F.P.G.: The Ottawa Interlude," 104, 109.
4 I borrow this term from Andrew Hunter, who uses it to describe the Thomson myth in his splendid essay "Mapping Tom," in *Thomson* (the catalogue to the Tom Thomson exhibition), 44.
5 Grove, *In Search of Myself*, 16.
6 Martens, *F.P. Grove in Europe and Canada*, 55ff. For biographical information on Grove's European years, I have relied mainly on Martens's biography.

7 Ibid., 22.
8 Robin, *Le Golem de l'écriture*, 18.
9 Felix Paul Greve served the prison sentence for fraud, in connection with the debt he owed Herman Kilian. According to Else Endell, however, the debt was not fraudulently incurred, and it was Kilian who was behind Greve's arrest as the latter stepped off the train in Bonn. She maintained that Kilian had lured Greve back to Bonn on a pretext, motivated by jealousy over Greve's liaison with her. See Hjartarson and Spettigue, eds., *Baroness Elsa*, 103ff.
10 Blodgett, "Foreword," xii.
11 I borrow this term from Robin, *Le Golem de l'écriture*, 28.
12 Grove, *In Search of Myself*, 226–7.
13 Pache, "'Greek to us, Grove.'"
14 Grove, *Over Prairie Trails*, 50–1.
15 Ibid., 51.
16 Ibid.
17 Gide, "Conversation," 143–4.
18 Ibid., 143.
19 Ibid. Emphasis in the original. My translation. The original reads: "'L'action ... c'est cela que je veux; oui, l'action la plus intense ... intense ... jusqu'au meurtre.' 'Non, dis-je enfin, désireux de bien prendre position, l'action ne m'intéresse point tant par la sensation qu'elle donne que par ses suites, son retentissement. Voilà pourquoi, si elle m'intéresse passionnément, je crois qu'elle m'intéresse advantage encore commise par un autre. J'ai peur, comprenez-moi, de m'y compromettre. Je veux dire, de limiter par ce que je fais, ce que je pourrais faire. De penser que parce que j'ai fait *ceci*, je ne pourrais plus faire *cela*, voilà qui devient intolérable. J'aime mieux *faire agir* que d'agir."
20 Gide, *Fruits of the Earth*, 136. The original reads: "Jette mon livre; dis-toi bien que ce n'est là *qu'une* des milles postures possibles en face de la vie. Cherche la tienne" (Gide, *Les Nourritures terrestres*, 182).
21 Gide, "Conversation," 143–4.
22 Wilde, "The Decay of Lying."
23 Gide, "Conversation," 141.
24 See Ernst and Martens, eds., "*Je vous écris.*"
25 Mann, *Bekenntnisse des Hochstaplers Felix Krull*. In quotations from this work elsewhere in this chapter, I have used Denver Lindley's translation, *The Confessions of Felix Krull, Confidence Man (The Early Years)*.
26 Greve/Grove's complicated connections with André Gide and Thomas Mann are further discussed in chapter 2 and in the appendix.

27 Hjartarson and Spettigue, eds., *Baroness Elsa*, 70.
28 Ibid., 93. Emphasis in the original.
29 Ibid., 109.
30 Ibid., 120. Emphasis in the original.
31 See Gammel, *Baroness Elsa*, 64–120. See also Martens, *Translated Lives*, 94–5.
32 Letter from Elsa von Freytag-Loringhofen to Djuna Barnes, Spring 1924, "Djuna Sweet – if you would know," cited in Gammel, *Baroness Elsa*, 118.
33 Cited in Gammel, *Baroness Elsa*, 123.
34 Ibid.
35 Grove, *Settlers of the Marsh*, 161–2.
36 Gammel, *Baroness Elsa*, 126.
37 Ibid., 120.
38 Ernst and Martens, eds., *"Je vous écris"*, 125. Letter dated 1 July 1905. My translation. The original reads: "La méthode c'est moi: et c'est une méthode sans commentaire; édition du texte sans annotations." The translated sentence appears in Gammel, *Baroness Elsa*, 138.
39 Hjartarson and Spettigue, *Baroness Elsa*, 65. Emphasis in the original.
40 Ernst and Martens, eds., *"Je vous écris"*, 74–5. Letter dated 17 October 1904. Emphasis in the original. The original reads as follows: "Je ne suis plus une personne, j'en sommes trois: je suis 1.) M. Felix Paul Greve; 2.) Mme Else Greve; 3.) Mme Fanny Essler." The translated passage appears in Gammel, *Baroness Elsa*, 139.
41 See Divay, "Felix Paul Greve's & Else von Freytag-Loringhoven's 1904/5 'Fanny Essler' Poems: His or Hers?"
42 See Martens, *Translated Lives*, 226.
43 Essler [pseud.], "Gedichte/Drei Sonnette."
44 Grove, *Fanny Essler*, 47. The original reads: "Und jene Sehnsucht nach dem Überallsein kam über sie, die die Menschen meist, wie jetzt auch sie, befriedigen zu können meinen, indem sie anders wohin gehen."
45 Ibid., 283. The original passage reads: "Fern, ganz fern tauchte noch einmal wieder eine Vision auf: die des Befreiers, der wie vom Himmel hernieder kam: des Prinzen, der sie erlösen sollte und musste."
46 Ibid., 19. The original passage reads: "gelang der Schritt, so wusste sie, dass sie zu den Künstlern gehörte, dass sie dort den Prinzen zu suchen hatte, und gelingen musste er: sie wollte schon zäh genug daran festhalten! Und schliesslich sagte sie sich beinhahe übermütig, wenn ich nur plötzlich Geld genug hätte, um davon zu leben, so ginge ich überallhin." (295) As E.D. Blodgett has pointed out, "It would appear that Fanny is a kind of artist, a character at least striving to be an artist, who fails by straying into

reality. The motif of the novel – to find a prince – is apparently beyond realization" (Blodgett, "*Alias* Grove," 128).

47 Ibid., 208–9. The original reads: "das alles hat sein müssen, damit du wurdest, was du bist ... und es ist gut, das es so gewesen ist: weil du dadurch du geworden bist."

48 Ibid., 209. Emphasis in the original. The original reads: "Du brauchst dich nicht vor *dir* ekeln, aber vor dem *Weg*, den du gegangen bist ... Du verwechselst immer dich mit deiner Vergangenheit."

49 Ibid., 211. The original reads: "Plötzlich sah sie sich mit den Augen von früher, den Augen der Zeit, da sie noch das 'kleine Mädchen' war, hier sitzen als das, was sie jetzt war ... Und sie wurde beinahe neidisch auf sich selber" (536).

50 Ernst and Martens, eds., *"Je vous écris"*, 125. The original reads: "après l'avoir relu, j'ai vu avec beaucoup d'étonnement que c'était Moi qui l'ai écrit."

51 Greve, *Maurermeister Ihles Haus*, 38–9. My translation. The original reads: "Maurermeister Ihle sprach selten von sich. Suse hatte von je eine ungeheure Vorstellung von seiner Kraft, Grösse und Macht. Bis etwa zu ihrem neunten Jahr war für sie ihr Vater der Vater: alle Väter, glaubte sie, seien wie er, nur vielleicht nicht so mächtig als Fürsten. Stolz auf den Vater, in seiner Abwesenheit, Furcht vor ihm, sobald er zugegen war; das waren die beiden Empfindungsmomente, die für sie das Verhältnis zum Vater bezeichneten. Sie wusste, ihr Vater war in der Stadt mächtig und auch wohl beliebt, und Untergebene, Maurer, Fuhrleute usw. drängten sich zu seinem Dienst. Ihr Papa kam gleich nach dem König."

52 Ibid., 122. My translation. The original reads: "nach Ems war der alte Kaiser oft gegangen ... Am nächsten Tag wusste es die ganze Schule: Herr Ihle geriet dadurch in einen gewissen, fast persönlichen Zusammenhang mit dem toten Landesherrn: man rechnete ihm die Reise fast wie einen Akt der Pietät als Verdienst an: Suse stieg gewaltig in der Achtung aller."

53 Ibid., 123. My translation. The original reads: "Suse wie Lotte freuten sich, als der Abschied vorüber war. Aber Suses Freude war stark mit Rührung untermischt. Sie hatte den Eindruck, als habe ihr Vater es einmal mit Güte versuchen wollen und schäme sich dessen. – Ja, wenn du so wärst! dachte sie ... Es befriedigte sie, dass er Wert auf Briefe von ihnen legte."

54 Ibid., 88. My translation. The original reads: "ihr schien, der Kaiser trage den Bart wie ihr Vater ... auf jeden Fall erhielt er für Suse etwas Väterliches, nur ohne die Schrecken eines wirklichen Vaters."

55 Gammel, *Baroness Elsa*, 135.

56 Anton Kippenberg to Mrs Else Greve, 21 September 1909, in Desmond Pacey, ed., *The Letters of Frederick Philip Grove*, 550. Also cited in Gammel, *Baroness Elsa*, 146.
57 See Divay, "About FPG (Greve/Grove)"; and Martens, *Translated Lives*, 240–7.
58 Gammel, *Baroness Elsa*, 151.
59 Martens, *Translated Lives*, 264.
60 Cited in Gammel, *Baroness Elsa*, 3.
61 Louis Bouché, "Autobiography," roll 688, frame 702, cited in Gammel, *Baroness Elsa*, 170.
62 Gammel, *Baroness Elsa*, 199.
63 Ibid., 197.
64 Cited in Gammel, *Baroness Elsa*, 242. Biddle also described Else's living quarters: "[The Baroness's apartment] was in an unheated loft on 14th Street. It was crowded and reeking with the strange relics which she had purloined over a period of years from the New York gutters. Old bits of ironware, automobile tires, gilded vegetables, a dozen starved dogs, celluloid paintings, ash cans, every conceivable horror, which to her tortured, yet highly sensitized perception, became objects of formal beauty. And, except for the sinister and tragic setting, it had to me quite as much authenticity as, for instance, Brancusi's studio in Paris, that of Picabia, or the many exhibitions of children's work, lunatics' work, or dadaist and surrealist shows, which in their turn absorb the New York and Paris intellectuals." George Biddle, *An American Artist's Story*, 140, cited in Gammel, *Baroness Elsa*, 220–1.
65 Cited in Gammel, *Baroness Elsa*, 250.
66 Ibid., 267–8.
67 Ibid., 286.
68 Blodgett observes that it is the protagonists' hubris that makes romance, in Grove's works, notably in Len Sterner's relationship with Lydia, "come perilously close to pathology" (Blodgett, "*Alias* Grove: Variations in Disguise," 113). Blodgett also points out, again alluding mainly to Len Sterner, that "the heroic stature that Grove's male figures may be said to possess, a stature characterized by innocence, is in fact their flaw" (113).
69 Grove, *The Yoke of Life*, 141.
70 Ibid., 148.
71 Ibid., 139–41.
72 Ibid., 222.
73 Ibid.
74 Ibid., 284.

75 Ibid., 223.
76 Ibid., 224.
77 Ibid., 216.
78 Ibid.
79 Ibid., 247.

CHAPTER TWO

1 Spettigue, *FPG: The European Years*, 200ff.
2 Martens, *Translated Lives*, 15.
3 Grove, *In Search of Myself*, 58–61.
4 Grove, "Rebels All," 67–8.
5 Martens, *Translated Lives*, 16.
6 Ibid., 26, 31.
7 Grove, *In Search of Myself*, 28–9.
8 Martens, *Translated Lives*, 29–30.
9 Grove, *In Search of Myself*, 21–2, 24–5.
10 Rubio, ed., *The Genesis*.
11 Martens, *Translated Lives*, 259ff.
12 Letter to Lorne Pierce dated 24 May 1939, in Pacey, ed., *The Letters of Frederick Philip Grove*, 354.
13 Ibid., 355–6.
14 Martens, *Translated Lives*, 52.
15 Ibid.
16 Grove, *Leonard Broadus*, 124–5.
17 McMullin, "Introduction," ix.
18 Grove, "Author's Note to the Fourth Edition," in *A Search for America*, n.p.
19 For more detailed analysis of the biographical features encoded in the journey metaphor, see Heidenreich, "The Search for FPG," 63–70.
20 Grove, *In Search of Myself*, 4.
21 Ibid., 11.
22 Ibid., 3.
23 Ibid.
24 Ibid., 4.
25 Martens, *Translated Lives*, 40–1.
26 Gide, "Conversation," 142. The original reads: "Je m'avançais incertain dans le hall [de l'hotel]. – Je vis aussitôt cette figure glabre, comme passée au chlore, ce corps trop grand pour qui tous les sièges sont bas … Je souhaitai ardemment que ce fût lui. C'était lui." For a detailed discussion

of the relationship between Felix Paul Greve and André Gide, see Heidenreich, "André Gide et Felix Paul Greve," 27–43.

27 Gide, *Journal 1889–1939*, 1104. My translation. The original reads: "'J'aime mieux faire agir que d'agir'. Non, cette phrase ne m'a pas 'échappée' … L'étonnant, c'est que Grève, en me répondant, ne faisait que réciter l'enseignement de mes *Nourritures*. En s'emparant de mon rôle, il me précipitait à droite. Somme toute, je me défilais."

28 Painter, *André Gide*, 105–6.

29 Grove, *In Search of Myself*, 82.

30 Gide, *Les Caves du Vatican*, 56. My translation. The original reads: "un beau jeune homme blond qui l'observait en souriant."

31 Gide, *Journal des Faux-monnayeurs*, 11. My translation. The original reads: "J'hésite depuis deux jours si je ne ferai pas Lafcadio raconter mon roman."

32 Claude Martin, *André Gide par lui-même*, 138.

33 Ernst Robert Curtius, "Les Faux-Monnayeurs," 652. My translation. The original passage reads: "Für Edouard [sic] hat das Wort 'Aufrichtigkeit' seinen Sinn verloren, weil sein Ich beständig variiert. Es kann ihm geschehen, dass er abends das Wesen nicht wiedererkennt, das er am Morgen war."

34 Grove, *A Search for America*, 125.

35 See the appendix, "FPG: The Thomas Mann Connection," in this volume.

36 Letter to Lorne Pierce dated 5 April 1940, and 20 May 1940, in Pacey, ed., *Letters*, 386, 390, 391.

37 Letter to Desmond Pacey dated 30 January 1945, in Pacey, ed., *Letters*, 462.

38 See the editor's note to the letter to Lorne Pierce dated 5 April 1940, in Pacey, ed., *Letters*, 386.

39 Letter to Desmond Pacey dated 30 January 1945, in Pacey, ed., *Letters*, 462.

40 Grove, *A Search for America*, 72.

41 Ibid., 103.

42 Ibid.

43 Ibid., 137.

44 Ibid., 191.

45 Ibid., 217.

46 Ibid., 218.

47 Ibid., 219.

48 Ibid., 225.

49 Ibid., 229.

50 Ibid., 322.

51 Ibid., 323.

52 Ibid., 342.

53 Bizouard, *Le cinquième fantasme*, 21–2. My translation. The original reads: "La totipentialité concerne des être dont la souffrance est de ne pas se sentir exister. L'objet de leur fantasme totipotentiel est de s'auto-créer afin de naître. Ils deviennent tour à tour ce qu'ils investissent."
54 Grove, *A Search for America*, 5.
55 Ibid., 30.
56 Ibid., 99.
57 Ibid., 108.
58 Quoted in Spettigue, *FPG: The European Years*, 114.
59 Grove, *A Search for America*, 91.
60 Ibid., 136.
61 Grove, *In Search of Myself*, 452.
62 Robin, *Le Golem de l'écriture*, 29. My translation. The original reads: "Toute l'autofiction est là: dire 'je' et ne pouvoir le dire, dire 'je' sans savoir ce que cette instance enonciative recoupe exactement."
63 Malcolm Ross, "Introduction," x.
64 Grove, *Over Prairie Trails*, 118.
65 Ibid., 35.
66 Ibid., 29.
67 See Heidenreich, "The Search for FPG," 63–70.
68 Grove, *Over Prairie Trails*, 86.
69 Ibid., 147.
70 Ibid., 121.
71 Hjartarson and Spettigue, eds., *Baroness Elsa*, 64–5. Emphasis in the original.
72 Ibid., 111.
73 In Ferret, *Le bateau de Thésée*, 17. Quoted in Robin, *Le Golem de l'écriture*, 16. My translation. The original reads as follows: "Le vaisseau sur lequel Thésée alla et retourna était une galiote à trente rames, que les Athéniens gardèrent jusqu'au temps de Démétrius le Phalérien, en ôtant toujours les vieilles pièces de bois, à mesure qu'elles se pourrissaient, et y en mettant des neuves en leurs places: tellement que depuis, dans les disputes des philosophes touchant les choses qui s'augmentent, à savoir si elles demeurent une, ou si elles se font autres, cette galiote était toujours alléguée pour l'exemple de doute, parce que les uns maintenaient que c'était un même vaisseau, les autres, au contraire, que non."
74 Grove, "Rebels All," 67.
75 Grove, *Settlers of the Marsh*, 166.
76 Grove, "Thoughts and Reflections," 307.
77 Grove, *In Search of Myself*, 457.
78 Ibid.

CHAPTER THREE

1 Rosenthal, "'The Wish to Be a Red Indian," 46.
2 Among those who voiced doubts concerning Grey Owl's Native identity before his death were the English professor W.T. Allison, who reviewed Grey Owl's *The Men of the Last Frontier;* literary critic William Arthur Deacon; the writer Barry Callaghan; and possibly even his employers at the National Parks Branch. See Braz, *Apostate Englishman*, 43, 56, 126, 113.
3 David Chapin, cited in Braz, "The Modern Hiawatha," 54.
4 Colin Ross, "The Story of Grey Owl," 79–83. Cited in Braz, *Apostate Englishman*, 138.
5 McKenzie, "Chasing Tales," 150. Also cited in Braz, *Apostate Englishman*, 90–1.
6 See Braz, "The Modern Hiawatha," 53.
7 Taylor, "Pretending to Be an Impostor," 229.
8 Ruffo, *Grey Owl.*
9 Birkle, "Mediation and Appropriation," 149.
10 Ibid.
11 Ginsberg, *Passing and the Fictions of Identity*, 11.
12 Birkle, "Mediation and Appropriation," 150.
13 Egan, *Burdens of Proof*, 64.
14 Rosenthal, "'The Wish to Be a Red Indian,'" 56.
15 Atwood, "The Grey Owl Syndrome," 72.
16 Ibid., 37.
17 See definitions of passing in Dawkins, *Clearly Invisible*, xi, and Rosenthal, "Introduction," in *Fake Identity?* 19.
18 Billinghurst, *Grey Owl*, 2.
19 Braz, *Apostate Englishman*, xiv.
20 Ibid., 170.
21 Prose, "Going Native," 41–8. Cited in Braz, *Apostate Englishman*, 14.
22 Anahareo, *Devil in Deerskins.*
23 Dickson, *Wilderness Man*, 20.
24 Smith, *From the Land of Shadows*, 14. For biographical information on Grey Owl, I have relied mainly on Smith's biography.
25 Ibid., 15.
26 Anahareo, *Devil in Deerskins*, 177.
27 Eakin, *Living Autobiographically.*
28 Smith, *From the Land of Shadows*, 12.
29 Ibid., 13.
30 Anahareo, *Devil in Deerskins*, 177–8.

31 Ibid., 178.
32 Ibid., 29–30.
33 Smith, *From the Land of Shadows*, 8.
34 Dickson, *Wilderness Man*, 9.
35 Smith, *From the Land of Shadows*, 38–9.
36 Dickson, *Wilderness Man*, 57–8.
37 Smith, *From the Land of Shadows*, 41.
38 In *Country Life*, 6 May 1929, quoted in "A Bookman's Diary," *John O'London's Weekly*, 29 April 1938. Cited in Smith, *From the Land of Shadows*, 42.
39 Grey Owl to Ellen Elliott, dated 20 July 1934, McMaster Archives. Cited in Smith, *From the Land of Shadows*, 44.
40 Dickson, *Wilderness Man*, 64.
41 Cited in Smith, *From the Land of Shadows*, 49.
42 Cited in ibid., 51.
43 Browder, *Slippery Characters*, 10.
44 Smith, *From the Land of Shadows*, 56.
45 Cited in ibid., 57.
46 Cited in ibid., 58.
47 Dickson, *Wilderness Man*, 105.
48 Ibid., 107.
49 Cited in Smith, *From the Land of Shadows*, 68.
50 Dickson, *Wilderness Man*, 111.
51 Cited in Smith, *From the Land of Shadows*, 71.
52 Dickson, *Wilderness Man*, 114.
53 Rosenthal, "'The Wish to Be a Red Indian,'" 50–1.
54 Braz, *Apostate Englishman*, 93.
55 Smith, *From the Land of Shadows*, 81–2.
56 Cited in ibid., 83.
57 Dickson, *Wilderness Man*, 202.
58 Smith, *From the Land of Shadows*, 86.
59 Cited in ibid., 88.
60 According to the National Film Board web site, the 8-minute silent film *Beaver People* was made in 1928, not 1930, as indicated by Smith. National Film Board, "Beaver People," and Smith, *From the Land of Shadows*, 299.
61 Cited in Smith, *From the Land of Shadows*, 91.
62 Grey Owl, *The Men of the Last Frontier*, 154.
63 See Smith, *From the Land of Shadows*, 105–7.
64 Grey Owl, "Prologue," in *The Men of the Last Frontier*, n.p.
65 Grey Owl, *The Men of the Last Frontier*, 7.

66 Ibid., 145.
67 Ibid., 151.
68 Ibid., 199.
69 Ibid., 31.
70 Ibid., 32–3.
71 Ibid., 206. Regarding Long Lance, see chapter 5 in this volume.
72 Grey Owl, *The Men of the Last Frontier*, 225.
73 Dickson, *Wilderness Man*, 68–9.
74 Grey Owl, *The Men of the Last Frontier*, 227.
75 Ibid., 225–6.
76 Ibid., 240.
77 Ibid., 243.
78 Braz, *Apostate Englishman*, 36.
79 Grey Owl, *The Men of the Last Frontier*, 250–3.
80 Ibid., 252.
81 Grey Owl, *Pilgrims of the Wild*, 15.
82 Ibid., 14–15.
83 Ibid., 138.
84 Ibid., 149.
85 Ibid.
86 Ibid., 150.
87 Ibid., 10.
88 Ibid., 12.
89 Ibid.
90 Ibid., 49–50.
91 Ibid., 113.
92 Ibid., 139.
93 Ibid., 210.
94 Ibid., 11.
95 Ibid., 250–1.
96 Ibid., 58–9.
97 Ibid., 177.
98 Ibid., 177–8.
99 See for example Anahareo, *Devil in Deerskins*.
100 Grey Owl, *Sajo and the Beaver People*, 8.
101 Ibid., 124.
102 Ibid., 180.
103 Smith, *From the Land of Shadows*, 123. The book was published in Canada by Macmillan in 1935, and a year later it appeared in the United States under the title *Sajo and the Beaver People*, published by Charles Scribner's Sons.

104 Ibid., 121.
105 Dickson, *Wilderness Man*, 3.
106 Dickson, "Grey Owl, Man of the Wilderness," 64, 73–4. Part of the article read:

> The story has its beginnings in an Indian village in Mexico more than forty years ago. In the house of a white man and an Apache woman a child is born into a world of frontier warfare and Indian fights. It is a world of strife of every kind. Family feuds are waged incessantly and never allowed to die, for the need for vengeance renews them from generation to generation. This is true especially of the Apaches, the most merciless of all Indian tribes.
>
> The white man who has married an Apache is killed in a feud, and in revenging him his eldest son is also killed. The little boy who has been born in the Mexican village is left alone with his Indian mother. Though he is part white, he never remembers this. He grows up an Indian in mentality and physique. The Indians teach him their way of life, and from his earliest youth he is hunting and trapping with the braves.
>
> In this way Grey Owl passed his youth. But in him, strongly welded and waiting the moment that should reveal them, are the steel of endurance and the idealism given him by his mixed blood.

Also cited in Smith, *From the Land of Shadows*, 122–3.
107 Smith, *From the Land of Shadows*, 1.
108 Ibid.
109 Ibid.
110 Cited in ibid., 125.
111 Cited in ibid., 148.
112 Cited in ibid., 145.
113 Cited in ibid., 154.
114 Ibid., 158.
115 Grey Owl, *Tales of an Empty Cabin*, viii.
116 Ibid., ix.
117 Ibid., x.
118 See Smith, *From the Land of Shadows*, 60.
119 Grey Owl, *Tales*, 91.
120 Smith, *From the Land of Shadows*, 160.
121 Cited in ibid.
122 Cited in ibid., 161–2. Emphasis in the original.
123 Part of her account reads as follows:

> His father's name was George McNeil, a third generation Scot in the United States, and an Apache Indian woman of Arizona was his mother.

> Shortly before Grey Owl was born the mother and father travelled to Mexico to see an aunt of Grey Owl, a Mrs. Blenay [Belaney], school teacher who lived near the Rio Grande. That is the history of Grey Owl being born in Mexico, otherwise he would have been born in Arizona.
>
> Grey Owl's mother was a near relative of the great Indian, Chief Geronimo, famed in the western border history, and she died in 1921. The only education Grey Owl got was from his aunt, Mrs. Belaney, and that was little."

Cited in Smith, *From the Land of Shadows*, 170–1.

124 In all, nine films featuring Grey Owl were produced between 1928 and 1937. They range in length from approximately 8 to 15 minutes. For the earlier films, the dates cited by Donald Smith diverge from those indicated by the National Film Board. See Smith, *From the Land of Shadows*, 299, and https://www.nfb.ca/film/beaver_people/, and also https://www.nfb.ca/film/beaver_family/.

125 Smith, *From the Land of Shadows*, 178.

126 Cited in ibid., 189.

127 Cited in ibid., 187.

128 See Braz, *Apostate Englishman*, 130–2, 168–9.

129 Cited in Smith, *From the Land of Shadows*, 214.

130 Anahareo, *Devil in Deerskins*, 184.

131 Ruffo, *Grey Owl*.

132 Ibid., 14.

133 Ibid., 2.

134 Rosenthal, "'The Wish to Be a Red Indian,'" 58.

135 Ruffo, *Grey Owl*, 110.

136 Ibid., 2.

137 Grey Owl, *Tales*, 79–90.

138 Anahareo, *Devil in Deerskins*, 134.

139 Dickson, *Wilderness Man*, 202.

140 Dickson, ed., *The Green Leaf. A Tribute to Grey Owl*, 85. Possibly a misquotation of the concluding lines of the poem "Invictus" by William Ernest Henley (1849–1903): "I am the master of my fate:/I am the captain of my soul." See https://www.poetryfoundation.org/poems/51642/invictus (accessed 5 December 2017).

CHAPTER FOUR

1 For biographical information on Will James, I have relied mainly on Amaral, *The Gilt Edged Cowboy*, as well as his subsequent *The Last*

Cowboy Legend; Bell, *Will James*; and Bramlett, *Ride for the High Points*.

2 Quoted in Bell, *Will James*, 81. Santee also expressed his annoyance at James's vagueness in his correspondence with Anthony Amaral. See Amaral, *The Gilt Edged Cowboy*, xv.

3 Dudar, "The West d'un Cow-boy Solitaire," 8–9.

4 Cardinal, "L'oblitération du nom." My translation. The original reads: "[Ce fantasme serait comme] la mise en acte d'un transfert massif sur l'autre comme lieu de vérité du désir du sujet."

5 Grescoe, *Sacré Blues*, 50.

6 Although many of them originally came from the East or Midwest, and some wrote under pseudonyms, unlike Will James, none of them seem to have actually assumed a false identity.

7 Fleischhauer, "Germany's Best-Loved Cowboy."

8 Published by Alfred Mâme and later by Flammarion in Paris. See Anon., "Livres de Karl May traduits en français." See also Galchen, "Wild West Germany."

9 Bell, *Will James*, 11.

10 Amaral, *The Gilt Edged Cowboy*, 68.

11 James, *Lone Cowboy*, 268.

12 Bell, *Will James*, 9.

13 Ibid., 108.

14 This point is made by James's biographers as well as in an article by Laurier Gareau, "Ernest Dufault, Alias Will James." Grescoe (*Sacré Blues*, 50), however, claims James had entirely lost his French accent.

15 James, *Lone Cowboy*, 1–3.

16 Bell, *Will James*, 12.

17 The size of the ranch is given on the *Montana Kids* website: Anon., "Will James." In Jacques Godbout's film about James (*Alias Will James*), however, the size of the ranch is referred to as being 8,000 acres.

18 Buell, "New Books for Boys and Girls," BR 12.

19 Duffus, "The Long Trail of the Cowboy," BR 5.

20 Bell, *Will James*, 104.

21 Quoted in ibid., 107.

22 Quoted in Bramlett, *Ride for the High Points*, 11.

23 Amaral, *The Gilt Edged Cowboy*, 185.

24 Bell, *Will James*, 107.

25 See Millar, "Ernest Dufault, alias Will James," 15–28, 181n.

26 Given his sojourn of several years in Val Marie, Saskatchewan, Will James's choice of his purported mentor's surname, Beaupré, may be a nod

to Édouard Beaupré (1881–1904) of Willow Bunch, Saskatchewan. Of Métis extraction, the "Beaupré Giant," at the time of his death at twenty-three, was 8 feet 3 inches tall. He had worked as a cowboy and, like Will James, had been kicked in the face by a horse, which put an end to his cowboy career. He subsequently toured the country with the Barnum and Bailey Circus, and became known for his feats of strength. See Lalonde, "Beaupré, Édouard," and Anon., "Édouard Beaupré."

27 James, *Lone Cowboy*, 17–18.
28 Quoted in Bell, *Will James*, 6.
29 James, *Lone Cowboy*, 140.
30 See Bell, *Will James*, 14. Will James uses the term "mustangeer" in a novel titled *The Three Mustangeers*, in which the adventures of three cowboys bound together by friendship and loyalty are recounted. *The Three Mustangeers* would seem to be a take-off on Alexandre Dumas's *The Three Musketeers*.
31 James, *Lone Cowboy*, 40.
32 Ibid., 158.
33 Ibid.
34 Ibid., 98.
35 Ibid., 258.
36 Ibid., 70.
37 Ibid., 72.
38 Ibid.
39 Ibid., 73.
40 See Bell, *Will James*, 27.
41 Hildenbrock, *Das andere Ich*, 272–3. My translation. The original reads as follows: "Indem der Doppelgänger diejenigen Eigenschaften repräsentiert, die das Urbild entweder schmerzlich an sich vermisst oder aber als 'unerlaubt' zensiert und deshalb verdrängt hat, kommt ihm gewissermassen eine Ersatzfunktion zu … (Wie der Traum) ist auch der Doppelgänger insofern eine Wunscherfüllung als er in die Tat umsetzt, was sein Urbild aus was für Gründen auch immer unterlässt."
42 Bell, *Will James*, 27.
43 Quoted in ibid., 44.
44 Ibid., xvi.
45 James, *The American Cowboy*, 273.
46 Bell, *Will James*, 67.
47 Ibid., 91.
48 Quoted in Bell, *Will James*, 81.
49 Ibid., 82.

50 James, *Lone Cowboy*, 119–20.
51 Quoted in Bell, *Will James*, 89.
52 Hildenbrock, *Das andere Ich*, 272.
53 James, *Lone Cowboy*, 311.

CHAPTER FIVE

1 See Browder, "'One Hundred Percent American,'" 107.
2 Ibid. See also, by the same author, the introduction to *Slippery Characters*, 2. See also Rosenthal, "Introduction," in *Fake Identity?* 16.
3 Browder, *Slippery Characters*, 3–4.
4 Kroeger, *Passing*, 8.
5 Excerpts from this letter are cited later in this chapter.
6 Smith, *Chief Buffalo Child Long Lance*, 36. For biographical information on Long Lance, I have relied on Smith's splendid biography.
7 Winston and Salem were originally two separate towns, but the agglomeration became known as Winston-Salem in the 1890s.
8 Smith, *Chief Buffalo Child Long Lance*, 23.
9 Lutz, "Receptions of Indigenous Canadian Literature in Germany," 36–63.
10 Cited in Smith, *Chief Buffalo Child Long Lance*, 321.
11 Ibid.
12 Mooney, "Croatan Indians," 365.
13 Long Lance, "Valedictory Address," 73–4.
14 Long Lance, "My Trail Upward," 72.
15 Ibid.
16 Browder, "'One Hundred Percent American,'" 111.
17 Ibid., 112.
18 Long Lance, "My Trail Upward," 72.
19 See Abley, *Conversations with a Dead Man*, 33, and Pratt, *Battlefield & Classroom*, 215.
20 Long Lance, "Princes Go West, but What of the Young Man without Money?" 53.
21 Browder, *Slippery Characters*, 58.
22 Browder, "'One Hundred Percent American,'" 118.
23 See Smith, *Chief Buffalo Child Long Lance*, 47–9, 55.
24 Handley and Lewis, eds., *True West*, 12.
25 Owens, *Mixedblood Messages*, 12–13. Cited in Cook, "The Only Real Indians Are Western Ones," 152.
26 Browder, *Slippery Characters*, 5.

27 Micco, "Tribal Re-Creations," 76.
28 Rak, "Translocal Representation," 177. See also Cook, "The Only Real Indians Are Western Ones," 152.
29 Cook, "The Only Real Indians Are Western Ones," 140–54.
30 Smith, *Chief Buffalo Child Long Lance*, 66.
31 Cited in ibid., 69.
32 Ibid.
33 Ibid., 70.
34 Long Lance, "West Point's Predicament," 375–83.
35 Smith, *Chief Buffalo Child Long Lance*, 75.
36 Cited in ibid., 76.
37 Ibid.
38 Cited in ibid., 79.
39 Ibid., 82.
40 Ibid., 86–7.
41 Ibid., 88.
42 Beverly Smith, "One Hundred Percent American," *New York Herald Tribune* (19 January 1930). Cited in Browder, "'One Hundred Percent American,'" 122.
43 Cited in Smith, *Chief Buffalo Child Long Lance*, 342.
44 Ibid., 93.
45 See ibid., 103.
46 Ibid., 41.
47 Cited in ibid., 118.
48 Micco, "Tribal Re-Creations," 76.
49 See Abley, *Conversations with a Dead Man*, 204.
50 See Smith, *Chief Buffalo Child Long Lance*, 131–2.
51 Long Lance, "Squamish," cited in Smith, *Chief Buffalo Child Long Lance*, 132.
52 Smith, *Chief Buffalo Child Long Lance*, 135.
53 Ibid.
54 Cited in ibid., 146.
55 Ibid., 147.
56 Ibid., 148.
57 Ibid., 153.
58 See Abley, *Conversations with a Dead Man*, 198–200.
59 Long Lance, "Indians of the Northwest and West Canada," 22.
60 See Abley, *Conversations with a Dead Man*, 199. See also Spiritalk Gathering, "Sun Dance."
61 Cited in Smith, *Chief Buffalo Child Long Lance*, 163.

62 See Anon., "Almighty Voice."
63 Long Lance, "How Canada's Last Frontier Outlaw Died," 19–20, 42, 44.
64 Rak, "Translocal Representation," 196.
65 Long Lance, "How Canada's Last Frontier Outlaw Died," 19–20, 42, 44.
66 See Smith, *Chief Buffalo Child Long Lance*, 176.
67 Long Lance, in (mis)translating Chief Big Plume's words, said that the original Bull's Head (the name the Sarcees were giving to Haig) had died in 1825, whereas he had not died until 1911. See Smith, *Chief Buffalo Child Long Lance*, 178.
68 Long Lance, "My Trail Upward," 138.
69 Ibid., 72.
70 Cited in Smith, *Chief Buffalo Child Long Lance*, 185–6.
71 Long Lance, "My Trail Upward," 72.
72 Ibid., 138.
73 See the account of Long Lance's behaviour in Banff in *On the Old Trail: Through British Columbia after Forty Years* by English novelist and journalist Morley Roberts. Cited in Smith, *Chief Buffalo Child Long Lance*, 188–9.
74 Long Lance, "The Secret of the Sioux," 41.
75 Long Lance, "Indians of the Northwest," 1–24, esp. 9.
76 Browder, "'One Hundred Percent American,'" 123.
77 Long Lance, *Long Lance*, 2.
78 Smith, *Chief Buffalo Child Long Lance*, 292.
79 See Browder, "'One Hundred Percent American,'" 112.
80 Long Lance, *Long Lance*, 47–8.
81 Ibid., 213.
82 Ibid., 215–16.
83 See ibid., 217.
84 See ibid., 220.
85 Ibid., 4.
86 Vernon, "The First Black Prairie Novel," 41.
87 Ibid., 42–3.
88 Ibid., 45.
89 Long Lance, *Long Lance*, 11, 38.
90 Ibid., 40.
91 Scott's role in determining the fortunes of Aboriginal Canadians is the main subject of Abley's *Conversations with a Dead Man: The Legacy of Duncan Campbell Scott*.
92 Cobb, "Foreword," in Long Lance, *Long Lance*, viii.
93 Smith, *Chief Buffalo Child Long Lance*, 215.

94 Browder, "'One Hundred Percent American,'" 125.
95 Cited in Smith, *Chief Buffalo Child Long Lance*, 214. Long Lance had already pronounced himself on this issue, basing his views on a four-year study he claimed was undertaken at the University of Wisconsin. See his "History of and Agricultural Work among Indians in Western Canada," 25–7, esp. 25.
96 See Smith, *Chief Buffalo Child Long Lance*, 224–6.
97 Ibid., 225.
98 Cited in ibid., 226.
99 Cited in Anon., "Indian Writer Faces Big Thrills," 80.
100 See Smith, *Chief Buffalo Child Long Lance*, 235.
101 Ibid., 237.
102 Cited in ibid., 238–9.
103 Ibid., 240.
104 Ibid.
105 Ibid., 241.
106 Laurence, "How *The Silent Enemy* Was Made," 83.
107 Anon., "Facts About The Silent Enemy," in *Redman Echoes*, 91.
108 Cited in Smith, *Chief Buffalo Child Long Lance*, 246.
109 Ibid., 260.
110 Ibid., 264.
111 Ibid., 266.
112 Ibid.
113 Cited in Laurence, "How *The Silent Enemy* Was Made," 83.
114 Smith, *Chief Buffalo Child Long Lance*, 267.
115 Ibid., 271.
116 Ibid., 273.
117 Ibid., 274.
118 Browder, "'One Hundred Percent American,'" 125.
119 Ibid., 264.
120 Cited in Smith, *Chief Buffalo Child Long Lance*, 289.
121 Ibid., 291–2.
122 Ibid., 292.
123 Ibid., 303.
124 Newashe McAllister, "Preface," n.p.
125 Cited in Smith, *Chief Buffalo Child Long Lance*, 319.
126 Forsberg, ed., *Redman Echoes*, 69, 70, 218–19.
127 Foster, "An Appreciation," 71.
128 Newashe McAllister, "Preface," n.p.
129 Middleton, "Foreword to Book IV," 184.

CHAPTER SIX

1 Chapman, ed., *Becoming Sui Sin Far*, xvi. According to another source, Grace's mother's name is recorded as Ah Cheun and her father's as A. Trefusis. See Tonkovich, "Genealogy, Genre, Gender," 238–9.
2 Ling, *Between Worlds*, 26.
3 White-Parks, *Sui Sin Far/Edith Maude Eaton*, 17–18, 54n31.
4 Sui Sin Far, "Leaves," 125.
5 White-Parks, *Sui Sin Far/Edith Maude Eaton*, 16.
6 Sui Sin Far, "Leaves," 128.
7 Ibid., 127.
8 Ibid., 126.
9 White-Parks, *Sui Sin Far/Edith Maude Eaton*, 50. According to Chapman (*Becoming Sui Sin Far*, xvi), Edward "earned his living as a commissioner merchant, clerk, bookkeeper, and artist."
10 Anon. [Onoto Watanna/Winnifred Eaton], *Marion*, 145.
11 Sui Sin Far, "Leaves," 128.
12 Ibid., 127.
13 Ibid., 126.
14 Anon. [Onoto Watanna], *Me*, 4.
15 For biographical information on Edith Eaton, I have relied mainly on Chapman, *Becoming Sui Sin Far*, and White-Parks, *Sui Sin Far/Edith Maude Eaton.* For biographical information on Winnifred Eaton I have relied mainly on Birchall, *Onoto Watanna.*
16 Anon., *Marion*, 31.
17 Ibid., 173.
18 See Doyle, "The Devil and Dame Chance," 15–30.
19 Anon., *Me*, 3.
20 Ibid., 19–20.
21 Ibid., 41.
22 Ibid., 55.
23 Lim, "Sibling Hybridities," 89.
24 See Birchall, *Onoto Watanna*, 39, and Anon., *Me*, 87.
25 Birchall, *Onoto Watanna*, 18.
26 Ferens, *Edith and Winnifred Eaton*, 119.
27 Ibid.
28 Anon., *Marion*, 257.
29 Cited in Birchall, *Onoto Watanna*, 44.
30 Matsukawa, "Cross-Dressing and Cross-Naming," 107.
31 Birchall, *Onoto Watanna*, 58.

32 With the exception of *The Wooing of Wistaria*, a historical novel, replete with battle scenes, that focuses on Commodore Perry's expedition to Japan in the mid-nineteenth century, opening up that country to the West. Although so different from Winnifred's previous writing, the novel was a success mainly due to the love intrigue it contained, one review referring to it as a "Japanese Romeo and Juliet." See Birchall, *Onoto Watanna*, 77–9.
33 Onoto Watanna, "The Half Caste." Cited in Birchall, *Onoto Watanna*, 61.
34 Ibid.
35 Ibid., 75.
36 Rosenthal, "Introduction," in Rosenthal and Schäfer, eds., *Fake Identity?* 12.
37 Anon., "Onoto Watanna," 236.
38 Ferens, *Edith and Winnifred Eaton*, 138.
39 Ibid.
40 Cited in Birchall, *Onoto Watanna*, 76.
41 Ibid.
42 Ibid., 76–7.
43 Ibid., 95.
44 Cited in ibid., 58.
45 Cited in ibid., 74.
46 Cited in ibid., 92.
47 Ibid., 96.
48 Cited in ibid., 93.
49 Cited in ibid.
50 Ibid., 102.
51 Ibid., 108.
52 Ibid., 117.
53 Anon., *Me*, 4.
54 Cole, *The Literary Voices of Winnifred Eaton*, 79–80.
55 Anon., *Me*, 26.
56 Ibid., 125.
57 Ibid., 176.
58 Ibid., 189.
59 Ibid., 314.
60 Ibid., 138.
61 Ibid., 6.
62 Ibid., 41.
63 Cited in Webster, "Introduction," n.p.
64 Billig, "The Dialogic Unconscious," 140–1.

65 Freud, "On Narcissism," 405.
66 Ouellette-Michalska, *Autofiction et dévoilement de soi*, 81.
67 Anon., *Me*, 153.
68 Ibid., 149–50. Emphasis in the original.
69 Ibid., 217.
70 Ibid., 129–30.
71 Skinazi, "Introduction," xlvi, xlix.
72 Ibid., lxxv.
73 Ibid., i.
74 Ibid., lvii. Emphasis in the original.
75 Anon., *Marion*, 1.
76 Ibid., 2.
77 Ibid.
78 Billig, "Freud and Dora." See also Billig, *Freudian Repression*.
79 See Skinazi, "Introduction," 31–2.
80 Anon., *Marion*, 3.
81 Ibid., 47.
82 Ibid.
83 Ibid., 58.
84 Ibid., 59.
85 Ibid., 60.
86 Ibid., 63.
87 Cf. Billig, *Freudian Repression*, 64.
88 Anon., *Marion*, 64.
89 Ibid., 76.
90 Ibid., 77.
91 Ibid.
92 Ibid., 7–8.
93 Skinazi, "Introduction," lxxv, lxxvii.
94 Birchall, *Onoto Watanna*, 138.
95 Naomi Lang, "Alberta Women Who Make News Include Noted Novelist, Scenarist," *Calgary Herald* (6 September 1941), cited in Ferens, *Edith and Winnifred Eaton*, 140.
96 Cited in Birchall, *Onoto Watanna*, 140.
97 Ibid.
98 Ibid., 146.
99 Ibid.
100 Cited in ibid., 146.
101 Cited in ibid., 145.
102 Onoto Watanna, *His Royal Nibs*, 20.

103 Ibid., 11.
104 Birchall, *Onoto Watanna*, 160.
105 Ibid., 19–20.
106 Sui Sin Far, "Leaves," 131.
107 Birchall, *Onoto Watanna*, 19.
108 Ibid., 206.
109 Ibid.
110 Sui Sin Far, "Leaves," 128.
111 Sui Sin Far, "Sui Sin Far, the Half Chinese Writer, Tells of Her Career."
112 Sui Sin Far, "Leaves," 130.
113 Ibid.
114 See Birchall, *Onoto Watanna*, 112.
115 "Edith Eaton Dead: Author of Chinese Stories under the Name of Sui Sin Far," *New York Times* (9 April 1914). Cited in White-Parks, *Sui Sin Far/ Edith Maude Eaton*, 50.
116 Anon., *Me*, 194. My emphasis.
117 Edith's Chinese name is misspelt in the monument inscription. It reads "Sui Sun [*sic*] Far."
118 Chapman, *Becoming Sui Sin Far*, xxiv.
119 Ibid., xxii.
120 Ibid., xx.
121 Ibid., xxiv.
122 Ibid., xxii.
123 Ibid., xviii.
124 Sui Sin Far, "Leaves," 132.
125 Chapman, *Becoming Sui Sin Far*, xviii–xxiv.
126 Sui Sin Far, "Leaves," 129.
127 Lim, "Sibling Hybridities," 83–4.
128 Tonkovich, "Genealogy, Genre, Gender," 239.
129 See Rosenthal, "Introduction," in *Fake Identity?* 12, and Dawkins, "Introduction," in *Clearly Invisible*, xi.
130 See Ginsberg, ed., *Passing and the Fictions of Identity*, 11.
131 Sir John A. Macdonald speaking to the House of Commons, 1882, file on Chinese Canadians, Canadian Pacific Railway Archives, Montreal. Cited in White-Parks, *Sui Sin Far/Edith Maude Eaton*, 73.
132 Roy Garis, *Immigration Restriction: A Study of the Opposition to and Regulation of Immigration into the U.S.* (1928), 291–2. Cited in Ling, *Between Worlds*, 23.
133 Ibid., 24.

134 Chapman, *Becoming Sui Sin Far*, xxvi. According to Chapman, newspaper accounts describe one of Edward's daughters "as a bright young lady who speaks English and Chinese with equal fluency." A subsequent article talks about "clever women ... who invented, perfected and carried out the plans for [Edward Eaton and his partner's] escape from the Plattsburgh jail and brought them the necessary tools" (cited in Chapman, *Becoming Sui Sin Far*, xxvi).

135 White-Parks, *Sui Sin Far/Edith Maude Eaton*, 106.

136 Sui Sin Far, "Leaves," 128.

137 Ibid., 131–2.

138 Ibid.

139 Wang, "Space and Identity," 275.

140 Sui Sin Far, "Sweet Sin," 226.

141 See White-Parks, *Sui Sin Far/Edith Maude Eaton*, 16, 28, 48, 49, 155, 200–1.

142 Sui Sin Far, "Leaves," 128.

143 Sui Sin Far, "Chan Hen Yen, Chinese Student," 462–6.

144 Lim, "Sibling Hybridities," 87.

145 See Ferens, *Edith and Winnifred Eaton*, 6, 15, and Chapman, *Becoming Sui Sin Far*, xxiv.

146 Tonkovich, "Genealogy, Genre, Gender," 243.

147 Ibid.

148 Ibid., 249.

149 Ling, *Between Worlds*, 48.

150 Chapman, *Becoming Sui Sin Far*, xlviii.

151 Ibid.

152 Ibid., xxvii.

153 Skinazi, "'As to her race,'" 47.

154 White-Parks, *Sui Sin Far/Edith Maude Eaton*, 64. While White-Parks allows that there is "intimate bonding" between women in Sui Sin Far's stories, she sees this not as sexual but as "essentially psychological and spiritual, a bonding envisioned by the author as springing from women's common experience – as mothers, victims of the patriarchal system, preservers of culture – and with roots in both sides of her heritage." She associates this bonding with *nushu*, "the secret language that Chinese women created and used to communicate both orally and in writing, for more than ten centuries. Relationships as *laotongs*, or 'sames,' allowed women to become best friends forever, bonding not only with each other but to a network that crossed generations and could include all

female family members." See White-Parks, *Sui Sin Far/Edith Maude Eaton*, 233n47.

155 Sui Sin Far, "Lin John," 223. The word "gay" did not have the sexual connotations until the twentieth century, although it did imply "carefree and uninhibited," "a willingness to disregard conventional or respectable sexual mores," as early as the seventeenth century.

156 White-Parks, "We Wear the Mask," 1–20.

157 Anon. [Sui Sin Far], "Wing Sing of Los Angeles on His Travels."

158 White-Parks, *Sui Sin Far/Edith Maude Eaton*, 143.

159 Sui Sin Far, "The Smuggling of Tie Co," 184–92.

160 Chapman, *Becoming Sui Sin Far*, xxvii.

161 Sui Sin Far, "The Story of Tin-A," 101–3.

162 Ibid., 102.

163 Ibid., 103.

164 Sui Sin Far, "The Success of a Mistake," 270–9.

165 McCullough, *Regions of Identity*, 274. Cited in Lutes, "The Queer Newspaperwoman," 283.

166 Lutes, "The Queer Newspaperwoman," 280.

167 Ibid., 293.

168 Ibid.

169 Sui Sin Far, "Mistake," 279.

170 Lutes, "The Queer Newspaperwoman," 293.

171 Sui Sin Far, "The Heart's Desire," 302.

172 Sui Sin Far, "Ku Yum's Little Sister."

173 Sui Sin Far, "Leaves," 132.

CONCLUSION

1 Kroetsch, *Gone Indian*, 6.

2 Ibid., 11. Emphasis in the original.

3 Ibid.

4 Ibid., 93.

5 Edwards, "Going Native in Robert Kroetsch's *Gone Indian*."

6 Ibid.

7 Kroetsch, *Gone Indian*, 33.

8 Ibid., 34.

9 Kroetsch, *The Stone Hammer Poems*, 47.

10 Kroetsch, *A Likely Story*. See for example the section "The Poetics of Rita Kleinhart," 171–216.

11 Jennings, "Disappearing Doubles," 24.
12 Kroetsch, *A Likely Story*, 56.
13 Ibid., 56–7.
14 Jennings, "Disappearing Doubles," 26.
15 Kroetsch, *The Lovely Treachery of Words*. Cited in Jennings, "Disappearing Doubles," 26.
16 See "Ian Tyson Is More than a Music Legend – He Gives Voice to the West," http://www.ctvnews.ca/w5/ian-tyson-is-more-tha-a-music-legend-he-gives-voice-to-the-west-/.2658092 (accessed 17 June 2016).
17 Tyson, "The Ballad of Will James."
18 Godbout, *Alias Will James*.
19 Ruffo, *Grey Owl*.
20 Schlossberg, "Introduction," in Schlossberg and Sanchez, eds., *Passing*, 4.
21 Ibid., 3.
22 *Going Home Star – Truth and Reconciliation* was commissioned by the Royal Winnipeg Ballet and premiered in Winnipeg in 2014.
23 Barrera, "Author Joseph Boyden's Shape-Shifting Indigenous Identity."
24 Sangster, "The Double Life of Injun Joe."
25 Salutin, "The Boyden Affair Just Got Murkier."
26 Taylor, "Is Joseph Boyden 'Grey Owling'?"
27 Kinew, "There Is Room in Our Circle for Joseph Boyden," A11.
28 Goffman, *The Presentation of Self in Everyday Life*.
29 See Smith, "Performativity, Autobiographical Practice, Resistence," and Egan, *Burdens of Proof*.
30 Eakin, *Living Autobiographically* and *Fictions in Autobiography*.
31 Martin and Barresi, *The Rise and Fall of Soul and Self*, 13.
32 Quotation taken from an interview with David Gelernter, "Computer träumen nicht," 118. My translation. The original reads: "die Welt in unserem Kopf, ein eigenes Seelenleben, eine eigene private geistige Landschaft, durch die kein anderer wandern kann." David Gelernter is the author of *The Tides of the Mind: Uncovering the Spectrum of Consciousness*.

APPENDIX

1 In quotations from this work in the text that follows, I have used Denver Lindley's translation, *The Confessions of Felix Krull, Confidence Man (The Early Years)*.
2 Mann's early plans (beginning around 1911) for the novel were based on the autobiographies of the Romanian con artist Georges Manolescu.

Although Mann scholars have identified Manolescu as the initial inspiration for *Felix Krull*, most acknowledge that the Manolescu-like figure disappears after the first few chapters. See Mindin, "Mann's Literary Techniques," 58.

3 Felix Paul Greve had an older sister called Henny, who left home at fifteen. It is not known what became of her, although Klaus Martens speculates that she might have become a domestic servant and/or an actress/chorus girl. There is also some evidence to suggest that she later emigrated to the United States. See Martens, *Translated Lives*, 1, 3–5.

4 See Wuthenow, "Nachwort," n.p.

5 Martens also discusses two other novels of the early twentieth century whose heroes seem to have been modelled, to a greater or lesser extent, on Greve: O.J. Bierbaum's *Prinz Kuckuck* and Franziska von Reventlow's *Von Paul zu Pedro*. See Martens, *Translated Lives*, 268–9.

6 Ibid.

7 Ibid., 269–70.

8 Ibid., 228–29.

9 Letter from Thomas Mann to Frederick Philip Grove, 5 June 1939 (Spettigue Collection, Mss 57, University of Manitoba Libraries, Archives and Special Collections).

10 Martens, *Translated Lives*, 270.

11 Mann, *Confessions*, 69.

12 One is also reminded of Gide's description of Greve at their first meeting: what strikes Gide is Greve's conspicuously tall figure and fair complexion.

13 Mann, *Confessions,* 13.

14 Ibid., 81–2.

15 Ibid., 132–3.

16 Ibid., 183.

17 Martens, *Translated Lives*, 40–1.

18 Ibid., 41. This photograph is reproduced in chapter 1 of this volume.

19 Ibid.

20 See chapter 1 in this volume.

21 See Mann, *Bekenntnisse*, 10 and elsewhere.

22 Grove, *A Search for America*, 237.

23 See chapter 2 in this volume.

24 Mann, *Confessions*, 160.

25 Mann's choice of the name "Kilmarnock" would seem to have been determined by the fact that the first syllable is the same as that in the name of Greve's one-time lover, Kilian, whose antecedents included Scottish nobility. The Earl of Kilmarnock, a historical figure who was executed in 1746

for his role in the Jacobite uprising, is sympathetically portrayed in Sir Walter Scott's "Scottish History." Mann, as a highly cultured and educated literary author and an anglophile, would have been familiar with Scott's works.

26 Mann, *Confessions*, 204.

27 Ibid., 243.

28 "Irgendwie ist es ein Geheimnis mit Ihnen." (Mann, *Bekenntnisse*, 244.)

29 Ibid., 211.

30 Grove, *A Search for America*, 35.

31 Ibid., 36–7.

32 See Mann, *Bekenntnisse*, 154, and Grove, *A Search for America*, 32.

33 Mann, *Confessions*, 34. Unless otherwise indicated, the quotations from *Felix Krull* are from the translation by Denver Lindley. The original reads: "Ich hatte die Natur verbessert, einen Traum verwirklicht,– und wer je aus dem Nichts, aus der blossen inneren Kenntnis und Anschauung der Dinge, kurz: aus der Phantasie, unter kühner Einsetzung seiner Person eine zwingende, wirksame Wirklichkeit zu schaffen vermochte, der kennt die wundersame und träumerische Zufriedenheit, mit der ich damals von meiner Schöpfung ausruhte." (Mann, *Bekenntnisse*, 43.)

34 Grove, *A Search for America*, 5.

35 See Mann, *Confessions*, 21, and *Bekenntnisse*, 27.

36 Grove, "Author's Note to the Fourth Edition," in *A Search for America*, n.p.

37 Mann, *Confessions*, 48. The original reads: "so habe ich mich später, nicht ohne Erfindungsgabe zu bekunden, sehr oft über ein Verbot hinweggesetzt, das sowohl meiner Sicherheit wie meinem Unterhaltungsbedürfnis zuwiderlief, und schon hier verweise ich auf die eigentümlich leichte Schönheit jener Stelle in meinen Aufzeichnungen, wo ich zum erstenmal meinen amtlichen Namen wie ein abgetragenes und verschwitztes Kleidungsstück von mir tue, um mir—sogar mit einer gewissen Befugnis — einen neuen angedeihen zu lassen." (Mann, *Bekenntnisse*, 58.)

38 Mann, *Confessions*, 66. The original reads: "Wie leicht, wie ungeduldig, geringschätzig und unbewegt lässt der ins Weite stürmende Jüngling die kleine Heimat in seinem Rücken ... Und doch, wie sehr er ihr auch entwachsen sein und ferner entwachsen möge, doch bleibt ihr lächerlich-übervertrautes Bild in den Hintergründen seines Bewusstseins stehen oder taucht nach Jahren tiefer Vergessenheit wunderlich wieder daraus hervor: Das Abgeschmackte wird ehrwürdig, der Mensch nimmt unter den Taten, Wirkungen, Erfolgen seines Lebens dort draussen geheime Rücksicht auf jene Kleinwelt, an jedem Wendepunkt, bei der Erhöhung seines Daseins

fragt er im stillen, was sie wohl dazu sagen werde oder würde, und zwar gerade dann ist dies der Fall, wenn die Heimat sich misswollend, ungerecht, unverständig gegen den besonderen Jüngling verhielt." (Mann, *Bekenntnisse*, 76.)

39 Mann, *Confessions*, 66. The original reads: "Da er von ihr abhing, bot er ihr Trotz; da sie ihn entlassen musste und vielleicht längst vergessen hat, räumt er ihr freiwillig Urteil und Stimme über sein Leben ein. Ja, eines Tages, nach Ablauf vieler für ihn ereignisreicher, veränderungsvoller Jahre, zieht es ihn wohl persönlich an jenen Ausgangspunkt zurück, *er widersteht nicht der Versuchung, erkannt oder unerkannt, sich im erlangten fremden und glänzenden Zustande der Beschränktheit zu zeigen* und, viel ängstlichen Spott im Herzen, sich an ihrem Staunen zu weiden—wie *ich an seinem Orte von mir zu berichten haben werde.*" (Mann, *Bekenntnisse*, 76.)

40 Mann, *Confessions*, 180–1. The original reads: "Mein heimlicher Reichtum ... machte diese Tracht, nebst dem Dienst, den ich darin versah, zu einer Vorspiegelung, einer blossen Bewährung meines "Kostümkopfes"; ja, wenn ich mich später mit verblendendem Erfolge für mehr ausgab, als ich war, so gab ich mich vorläufig für weniger aus, und es ist noch die Frage, welchem Truge ich mehr innere Erheiterung, mehr Freude am Verzaubert-Märchenhaften abgewann." (Mann, *Bekenntnisse*, 193.)

41 Mann, *Confessions*, 218. The original reads: "Es war der Gedanke der *Vertauschbarkeit*. Den Anzug, die Aufmachung gewechselt, hätten sehr vielfach die Bedienenden ebensogut Herrschaft sein und hätte so mancher von denen, welche, die Zigarette im Mundwinkel, in den tiefen Korbstühlen sich rekelten — den Kellner abgeben können. Es war der reine Zufall des Reichtums; denn eine Aristokratie des Geldes ist eine vertauschbare Zufallsaristokratie." (Mann, *Bekenntnisse*, 231.)

42 Mann, *Confessions*, 233. The original reads: "Könnten Sie sich wünschen, ein anderer Mensch zu werden, als der Sie sind?" (Mann, *Felix Krull*, 247.) Cf. Suse in *Maurermeister Ihles Haus*: "I wish I were someone else!" My translation. The original reads: "Ich wollt, ich wär jemand anders!" (Grove, *Maurermeister Ihles Haus*, 18.)

43 Mann, *Confessions*, 233. The original reads: "Bedenken Sie immerhin ... dass Sie, sollten Sie ein anderer geworden sein, Ihr früheres Selbst, das gegenwärtige, nicht vermissen und ihm nicht nachtrauern würden, einfach weil Sie es nicht mehr sind." (Mann, *Bekenntnisse*, 248.)

44 Mann, *Confessions*, 252. The original reads: "Nein, die Veränderung und Erneuerung meines abgetragenen Ich überhaupt, dass ich den alten Adam hatte ausziehen und in einen anderen hatte schlüpfen können, dies eigentlich war es, wa mich erfüllte und beglückte. Nur fiel mir auf, dass

mit dem Existenzwechsel nicht allein köstliche Erfrischung, sondern auch eine gewisse Ausgeblasenheit meines Inneren verbunden war, – insofern nämlich, als ich alle Erinnerungen, welche meinem ungültig gewordenen Dasein angehörten, aus meiner Seele zu verbannen hatte … Ein eigentümliches Gefühl von Gedächtnisschwäche, ja Gedächtnisleere wollte mich ankommen." (Mann, *Bekenntnisse*, 267.)

45 My translation. The original reads: "Sehen Sie, ich bin im Bilde." (Mann, *Bekenntnisse*, 274.)

Bibliography

Abley, Mark. *Conversations with a Dead Man: The Legacy of Duncan Campbell Scott*. Vancouver: Douglas & McIntyre, 2013.

Adams, Howard. *Howard Adams: Otapawy*! Edited by Hartmut Lutz with Murray Hamilton and Donna Heimbecker. Saskatoon, SK: Gabriel Dumont Institute, 2005.

Amaral, Anthony. *Will James, the Gilt Edged Cowboy*. Los Angeles: Westernlore Press, 1967.

– *Will James, the Last Cowboy Legend*. Reno: University of Nevada Press, 1980.

Anahareo. *Devil in Deerskins: My Life with Grey Owl*. Edited and with an introduction by Sophie McCall. Winnipeg: University of Manitoba Press, 2014 [1972].

Anon. [Edith Eaton/Sui Sin Far]. "Wing Sing of Los Angeles on His Travels." *The Los Angeles Express* (4, 5, 6, 10, and 24 February and 9 March 1904).

Anon. [Onoto Watanna/Winnifred Eaton]. *Me: A Book of Remembrance*. New York: The Century, 1915.

– *Marion: The Study of an Artist's Model* (Critical edition, with an introduction by Karen E.H. Skinazi). Montreal, QC, and Kingston, ON: McGill-Queen's University Press, 2012. (Originally published under the same title in New York by W.J. Watt, 1916.)

Anon. "Almighty Voice." *Saskatchewan Indian* 3, no. 6 (1973). http://www.sicc.sk.ca/archive/saskindian/a73aug06.htm.

Anon. "Édouard Beaupré." *Le Musée virtuel de la Saskatchewan*. http://musee.societehisto.com/edouard-beaupre-n372-t210.html (accessed 20 June 2016).

Anon. "Facts about *The Silent Enemy*." In Forsberg, *Redman Echoes*, 91–3.

Anon. "Grey Owl: Trapper, Conservationist, Author, Fraud." Television story narrated by Lister Sinclair, with Gertrude Bernard, Lovat Dickson, John Diefenbaker. CBC Digital Archives. Broadcast 11 December 1972.

Anon. "Indian Writer Faces Big Thrills in Far North before Completing Movies." *Oklahoma City Times* (1929). In Forsberg, *Redman Echoes*, 80–1.

Anon. "Livres de Karl May traduits en français." https://winnetou.fr/documents/livres_français.pdf (accessed 14 June 2016).

Anon. "Onoto Watanna." *Current Literature* 32 (February 1902): 236.

Anon. "Will James." *Montana Kids*. 2007. http://montanakids.com/cool_stories/Famous_Montanans/james.htm (accessed 18 November 2017).

Aquin, Hubert. *Prochain episode*. Montreal, QC: Le Cercle du Livre de France, 1965.

Arribert-Narce, Fabien, and Alain Ausoni. *L'Autobiographie entre autres: Écrire la vie aujourd'hui*. Bern, Switzerland: Peter Lang, 2013.

Atwood, Margaret. "The Grey Owl Syndrome." In *Strange Things: The Malevolent North in Canadian Literature*, 35–61. Oxford, UK: Clarendon Press, 1995.

Barrera, Jorge. "Author Joseph Boyden's Shape-shifting Indigenous Identity." *APTN*, 23 December 2016. http://aptnnews.ca/2016/12/23/author-joseph-boydens-shape-shifting-indigenous-identity/.

Beckwourth, James. *The Life and Adventures of James P. Beckwourth, Mountaineer, Scout and Pioneer, and Chief of the Crow Nation*. New York: Harper and Brothers, 1856.

Bell, William Gardner. *Will James: The Life and Works of a Lone Cowboy*. Flagstaff, AZ: Northland Press, 1987.

Billig, Michael. "Freud and Dora: Repressing a Repressed Identity." *The Virtual Faculty*. Palmerston North, NZ: Department of Psychology, Massey University. http://www.massey.ac.nz/~alock/virtual/dora4.htm (accessed 13 November 2014).

– "The Dialogic Unconscious: Psychoanalysis, Discursive Psychology and the Nature of Repression." *British Journal of Social Psychology* 36, no. 2 (June 1997): 140–1.

– *Freudian Repression: Conversation Creating the Unconscious*. Cambridge: Cambridge University Press, 1999.

Billinghurst, Jane. *Grey Owl: The Many Faces of Archie Belaney*. Vancouver and Toronto: Greystone Books, 1999.

Birchall, Diana. *Onoto Watanna: The Story of Winnifred Eaton*. Urbana and Chicago: University of Illinois Press, 2001.

Birkle, Carmen. "Mediation and Appropriation: Imaginary Indians and the Grey Owl Syndrome." In *Auto/Biography and Mediation*, edited by Alfred Hornung, 139–59. Heidelberg, Germany: Universitätsverlag Winter, 2006.

Bizouard, Élisabeth. *Le cinquième fantasme: auto-engendrement et impulsion créatrice*. Paris: Presses Universitaires de France, 1995.

Blodgett, E.D. "*Alias* Grove: Variations on a Disguise." In *Configuration: Essays on the Canadian Literatures*, 112–53. Downsview, ON: ECW Press, 1982.

– "Foreword." In Klaus Martens, *F.P. Grove in Europe and Canada: Translated Lives*, ix–xv. Edmonton: University of Alberta Press, 2001.

Bramlett, Jim. *Ride for the High Points: The Real Story of Will James*. Missoula, MT: Mountain Press, 1998.

Braz, Albert. "The Modern Hiawatha: Grey Owl's Construction of His Aboriginal Self." In *Auto/biography in Canada: Critical Directions*, edited by Julie Eak, 53–68. Waterloo, ON: Wilfrid Laurier University Press, 2005.

– *Apostate Englishman: Grey Owl the Writer and the Myths*. Winnipeg: University of Manitoba Press, 2015.

Browder, Laura. "'One Hundred Percent American': How a Slave, a Janitor, and a Former Klansman Escaped Racial Categories by Becoming Indians." In *Beyond the Binary: Reconstructing Cultural Identity in a Multicultural Context*, edited by Timothy B. Powell, 107–38. New Brunswick, NJ, and London: Rutgers University Press, 1999.

– *Slippery Characters: Ethnic Impersonators and American Identities*. Chapel Hill and London: University of North Carolina Press, 2000.

Buckley, Michael. "Rampa, T. Lobsang." 2009. http://www.abcbookworld.com/view_author.php?id=9746 (accessed 11 November 2015).

Buell, Ellen Lewis. "New Books for Boys and Girls." *The New York Times Book Review*, 24 March 1935, BR 12.

But, Juanita. "The Making of a Eurasian: Writing, Miscegenation, and Redemption." *Asian American Literature: Discourses and Pedagogies* 3 (2012): 14–26.

Butler, Judith. "Performative Acts and Gender Constitution: An Essay in Phenomenology and Feminist Theory." *Theatre Journal* 40, no. 4 (December 1988): 519–31.

– *Bodies That Matter: On the Discursive Limits of "Sex."* New York: Routledge, 1993.

Cardinal, Jacques. "L'oblitération du nom. Considérations sur le romanesque aquinien et sur le sujet-nation québécois." *Surfaces* 3 (1993). Montreal, QC: Presses de l'Université de Montréal, 27 July 2013. http://www.pum.umontreal.ca/revues/surfaces/vol3TdM.html.

Chapman, Mary, ed. *Becoming Sui Sin Far: Early Fiction, Journalism and Travel Writing by Edith Maude Eaton.* Montreal, QC, and Kingston, ON: McGill-Queen's University Press, 2016.

Cobb, Irvin S. "Foreword." In Chief Buffalo Child Long Lance, *Long Lance*, xiii–xv. New York: Cosmopolitan Book Corporation, 1928.

Cole, Jean Lee. *The Literary Voices of Winnifred Eaton.* New Brunswick, NJ, and London: Rutgers University Press, 2002.

Colonna, Vincent. *Autofiction et autres mythomanies.* Paris: Éditions Tristram, 2004.

Cook, Nancy. "The Only Real Indians Are Western Ones: Authenticity, Regionalism, and Chief Buffalo Child Long Lance, or Sylvester Long." In *True West: Authenticity and the American West*, edited by William R. Handley and Nathaniel Lewis, 140–54. Lincoln and London: University of Nebraska Press, 2004.

Curtius, Ernst Robert. "Les Faux-Monnayeurs." *Neue Rundschau* (December 1926): 652.

Dawkins, Marcia Aleson. *Clearly Invisible: Racial Passing and the Color of Identity.* Waco, TX: Baylor University Press, 2012.

Dawson, Carrie. "Never Cry Fraud: Remembering Grey Owl, Rethinking Imposture." *Essays in Canadian Writing* 65 (Fall 1999): 120–40.

Delaume, Chloé. *La règle du je.* Paris: Presses Universitaires de France, 2010.

De Lauretis, Teresa. *Technologies of Gender: Essays on Theory, Film and Fiction.* Bloomington: Indiana University Press, 1987.

Dichek, Bernie. *Long Lance* [film]. National Film Board of Canada, 1986.

Dickson, Lovat. "Grey Owl, Man of the Wilderness." *Strand Magazine*, May 1936: 73–4.

– ed. *The Green Leaf: A Tribute to Grey Owl.* London: Lovat Dickson, 1938.

– "Grey Owl's Confidante Speaks." Radio interview with Warren Davis. Broadcast 21 September 1971. CBC Digital Archives.

– *Wilderness Man: The Strange Story of Grey Owl.* Toronto: General Paperbacks, 1991 [1973].

Divay, Gaby. "Felix Paul Greve's & Else von Freytag-Loringhoven's 1904/5 'Fanny Essler' Poems: His or Hers?" 2005. https://home.cc.umanitoba.ca/~divay/FEArt/.

– "Felix Paul Greve's & Else von Freytag-Loringhoven's 1904/5 'Fanny Essler' Poems." 2005. http://home.cc.umanitoba.ca/~divay/FEPoems05/.

– "About FPG (Greve/Grove): A Biographical Sketch." 2005. http://home.cc.umanitoba.ca/~fgrove/bio/bionarr.html.

Doubrovsky, Serge. *Fils*. Paris: Galilée, 1977.

– *Le livre brisé*. Paris: Grasset, 1989.

Doyle, James. "Sui Sin Far and Onoto Watanna: Two Early Chinese-Canadian Authors." *Canadian Literature* 140 (Spring 1994): 50–8.

– "The Devil and Dame Chance: The Life and Writings of Walter Blackburn Harte." *Canadian Review of American Studies* 16, no. 1: 15–30. http://www.utpjournals.press/doi/10.3138/CRAS-016-01-02.

Dudar, Judith Ann. "Feint of Heart and Sleight of Hand: Autobiographical Art and Artifice in the Life-Stories of Will James, Grey Owl, and Frederick Philip Grove." Dissertation, Dalhousie University, 1994.

– "The West d'un Cow-boy Solitaire." In *Literature of Region and Nation: Proceedings of the 6th International Literature of Region and Nation Conference*, edited by Winnifred M. Bogaards, 1, 8–16. Saint John: University of New Brunswick in Saint John, 1998.

Duffus, R.L. "The Long Trail of the Cowboy: Will James Rounds Up His History in Fictional Form." *The New York Times Book Review*, 15 March 1942, BR 5.

Eakin, Paul John. *Fictions in Autobiography: Studies in the Art of Self-Invention*. Princeton, NJ: Princeton University Press, 1985.

– *Touching the World: Reference in Autobiography*. Princeton, NJ: Princeton University Press, 1992.

– *The Ethics of Life Writing*. Ithaca, NY: Cornell University Press, 2004.

– *Living Autobiographically: How We Create Identity in Narrative*. Ithaca, NY: Cornell University Press, 2008.

Edwards, Justin D. "Going Native in Robert Kroetsch's *Gone Indian*." *Studies in Canadian Literature* 26, no. 1 (2001). http://journals.lib.unb.ca/index.php/scl/article/view/12874/13930.

Egan, Susanna. *Burdens of Proof: Faith, Doubt and Identity in Autobiography*. Waterloo, ON: Wilfrid Laurier University Press, 2011.

Eggleston, Wilfrid. "F.P.G.: The Ottawa Interlude." In *The Grove Symposium*, edited by John Nause, 101–10. Ottawa: University of Ottawa Press, 1974.

Ernst, Jutta, and Klaus Martens, eds. *"Je vous écris, en hâte et fiévreusement": Felix Paul Greve-André Gide: Korrespondenz und Dokumentation.* St Ingbert, Germany: Röhrig Universitätsverlag, 1999.

Essler, Fanny [pseud.]. "Gedichte/Drei Sonnette: Ein Porträt/Gedichte." Translated by Jan Horner and Gaby Divay. 2005. http://home.cc.umanitoba.ca/~divay/FEPoems05/feSonnFacs.html.

Ferens, Dominika. *Edith and Winnifred Eaton: Chinatown Missions and Japanese Romances.* Urbana and Chicago: University of Illinois Press, 2002.

Ferret, Stéphane. *Le bateau de Thésée: Le problème de l'identité à travers le temps.* Paris: Minuit, 1996.

Fleischauer, Jan. "Germany's Best-Loved Cowboy: The Fantastical World of Cult Novelist Karl May." *Spiegel Online*, 30 March 2012. http://www.spiegel.de/international/germany/marking-the-100th-anniversary-of-german-cult-author-karl-may-s-death-a-824566.html.

Fogelson, Raymond D. *The Handbook of North American Indians*, vol. 14. Washington, DC: United States Government Printing, 2004.

Forsberg, Roberta, ed. *Redman Echoes. Comprising the Writings of Chief Buffalo Child Long Lance and Biographical Sketches by His Friends.* Los Angeles: Frank Wiggins Trade School, Department of Printing, 1933.

Foster, E.H. "An Appreciation." In Forsberg, *Redman Echoes*, 71–2.

Francis, Daniel. *The Imaginary Indian: The Image of the Indian in Canadian Culture.* Vancouver: Arsenal Pulp, 1992.

Freud, Sigmund. "On Narcissism." In *The Major Works of Sigmund Freud*, 405. Chicago, London, and Toronto: Encyclopaedia Britannica, 1952.

Galchen, Rivka. "Wild West Germany. Why Do Cowboys and Indians So Captivate the Country?" *The New Yorker*, 2012. https://www.newyorker.com/magazine/2012/04/09wild-west-germany.

Gammel, Irene. *Baroness Elsa: Gender, Dada, and Everyday Modernity – A Cultural Biography.* Boston: MIT Press, 2002.

Gareau, Laurier. "Ernest Dufault, Alias Will James." *Le Musée virtuel francophone de la Saskatchewan* 2, no. 4 (May 1992). Société historique de la Saskatchewan. http://musee.societehisto.com/ernest-dufault-alias-will-james-n151-t940.html.

Gasparini, Philippe. *Est-il je? Roman autobiographique et autofiction.* Paris: Seuil, 2004.

Gelernter, David. "Computer träumen nicht." Interview in *Der Spiegel* (Nr. 21/21.5.2016, 117–19), 118.

– *The Tides of the Mind: Uncovering the Spectrum of Consciousness.* New York: Liveright, 2016.

Genette, Gérard. *Fiction et Diction*. Paris: Seuil, 1991.
Genon, Arnaud. *Autofictions: pratiques et théories*. Paris: Mon petit éditeur, 2013.
Gide, André. *Les Caves du Vatican*. Paris: Gallimard, 1914.
– "Conversation avec un Allemand quelques années avant la guerre." In *Incidences*, 135–45. Paris: NRF, 1924.
– *Fruits of the Earth*. Translated by Dorothy Bussy. Penguin, 1970.
– *Journal 1889–1939*. Paris: La Pléiade, 1951.
– *Journal des Faux-monnayeurs*. Paris: Gallimard, 1975 [1927].
– *Les Nourritures terrestres*. Paris: Bordas, 1970 [1917].
Ginsberg, Elaine K., ed. *Passing and the Fictions of Identity*. Durham, NC, and London: Duke University Press, 1996.
Godbout, Jacques, dir. *Alias Will James* [film]. National Film Board of Canada, 1987. https://www.nfb.ca.alias_will_james-en.
Goffman, Erving. *The Presentation of Self in Everyday Life*. New York: Anchor Books, 1959.
– *Stigma: Notes on the Management of Spoiled Identity*. New York: Prentice Hall, 1963.
Gray, Charlotte. *Flint and Feather: The Life and Times of E. Pauline Johnson, Tekahionwake*. Toronto: HarperCollins, 2002.
Grescoe, Taras. *Sacré Blues: An Unsentimental Journey through Quebec*. Toronto: Macfarlane Walter & Ross, 2000.
Greve, Felix Paul. *Fanny Essler: Ein Berliner Roman*. Stuttgart, Germany: Axel Juncker, 1905.
– *Maurermeister Ihles Haus*. Berlin: Karl Schnabel, 1906.
– *Randarabesken zu Oscar Wilde*. Minden, Germany: J.C.C. Bruns, 1903.
Grey Owl. *The Men of the Last Frontier*. London: Country Life, 1931.
– *Pilgrims of the Wild*. Toronto: Macmillan, 1968 [1935].
– *Sajo and the Beaver People*. Toronto: General Paperbacks, 1991 [1935].
– *Tales of an Empty Cabin*. Toronto: Macmillan, 1936.
Grove, Frederick Philip. *The Adventure of Leonard Broadus*. Serialized in twelve weekly installments as "The Adventure of Leonard Broadus" in *The Canadian Boy* from 7 April 1940 to 23 June 1940.
– *Fanny Essler*. Translated by A.W. Riley and Douglas O. Spettigue. Ottawa: Oberon, 1984.
– *In Search of Myself*. Toronto: McClelland and Stewart, 1974 [1946].
– *Over Prairie Trails*. Toronto: McClelland and Stewart, 1957 [1922].
– "Rebels All." In *A Stranger to My Time: Essays by and about Frederick Philip Grove*, edited by Paul Hjartarson, 67–82. Edmonton: NeWest Press, 1986.

– *A Search for America*. Toronto: McClelland and Stewart, 1974 [1927].

– *Settlers of the Marsh*. Toronto: Ryerson Press, 1925.

– "Thoughts and Reflections." In *A Stranger to My Time: Essays by and about Frederick Philip Grove*, edited by Paul Hjartarson, 302–40. Edmonton: NeWest Press, 1986.

– *The Yoke of Life*. Toronto and New York: Macmillan, 1930.

Handley, William R., and Nathaniel Lewis, eds. *True West: Authenticity and the American West*. Lincoln and London: University of Nebraska Press, 2004.

Heidenreich, Rosmarin. "André Gide et Felix Paul Greve: le Soi dans l'autre." In *L'Autre en mémoire*, edited by Dominique Laporte, 27–43. Quebec: Les Presses de l'Université Laval, 2006.

– "FPG and André Gide: Life, Art and *Rifacimento*." In *American and Canadian Literature and Culture: Across a Latitudinal Line*, edited by Klaus Martens and Paul Morris, 40–54. Saarbrücken, Germany: Centre for Canadian and Anglo-American Culture, Amarant Presse, 2008.

– "Inventions of the Self: Canadian Palimpsests." In *New Worlds: Discovering and Constructing the Unknown in Anglophone Literature*, edited by Martin Kuester, Gabriele Christ, and Rudolf Beck, 217–38. Munich, Germany: Verlag Ernst Vögel, 2000.

– "The Search for FPG." *Canadian Literature* 80 (Spring 1979): 63–70.

Hildenbrock, Aglaja. *Das andere Ich: Künstlicher Mensch und Doppelgänger in der deutsch- und englischsprachigen Literatur*. Tübingen, Germany: Stauffenberg Verlag, 1986.

Hjartarson, Paul. "Staking a Claim: Settler Culture and the Canonization of 'Frederick Philip Grove' as a Canadian Writer." In *Pioneering North America: Mediators of European Literature and Culture*, edited by Klaus Martens, 19–29. Würzburg, Germany: Königshausen & Neumann, 2000.

Hjartarson, Paul I., and Douglas O. Spettigue, eds. *Baroness Elsa*. Ottawa: Oberon Press, 1992.

Homel, David. "Le mystérieux poète grec." *La Presse* [Montreal], 26 November 2000.

Hornung, Alfred. "Introduction." In *Auto/Biography and Mediation*, edited by Alfred Hornung, xi–xviii. Heidelberg, Germany: Universitätsverlag Winter, 2006.

Howes, Craig. "Mediating between Life Writing Studies and Lives." In *Auto/Biography and Mediation*, edited by Alfred Hornung, 3–13. Heidelberg, Germany: Universitätsverlag Winter, 2006.

Hubier, Sébastien. *Littératures intimes: les expressions du moi, de l'autobiographie à l'autofiction*. Paris: Armand Collin, 2003.

Hunter, Andrew. "Mapping Tom." In *Tom Thomson*, edited by Dennis Reid, 19–45. Ottawa, Toronto, and Vancouver: National Gallery of Canada/Douglas & McIntyre, 2002.

James, Will. *The American Cowboy*. New York: Charles Scribner's Sons, 1942.

– *Big Enough*. New York: Charles Scribner's Sons, 1931.

– *Cowboys North and South*. New York: Charles Scribner's Sons, 1924.

– *Lone Cowboy: My Life Story*. New York and London: Charles Scribner's Sons, 1930.

– *Smoky the Cowhorse*. New York: Charles Scribner's Sons, 1926.

Jennings, Rosalind. "Disappearing Doubles and Deceptive Landscapes in the Writings of Robert Kroetsch." *The London Journal of Canadian Studies* 12 (1996): 20–34.

Kadar, Marlene, Linda Warley, Jeanne Perreault, and Susanna Egan, eds. *Tracing the Autobiographical*. Waterloo, ON: Wilfrid Laurier University Press, 2005.

Karpinski, Eva C. *Borrowed Tongues: Life Writing, Migration, and Translation*. Waterloo, ON: Wilfrid Laurier University Press, 2012.

Kinew, Wab. "There Is Room in Our Circle for Joseph Boyden." *The Toronto Globe and Mail*, 3 January 2017, A11.

Kroeger, Brooke. *Passing: When People Can't Be Who They Are*. New York: Public Affairs, 2003.

Kroetsch, Robert. *Gone Indian*. Toronto: New Press, 1973.

– *The Stone Hammer Poems*. Lantzville, BC: Oolichan Books, 1975.

– *The Lovely Treachery of Words: Essays New and Selected*. Toronto: Oxford University Press, 1989.

– *A Likely Story: The Writing Life*. Red Deer, AB: Red Deer College Press, 1995.

Lalonde, André. "Beaupré, Édouard." In *Dictionary of Canadian Biography*, vol. 13. University of Toronto/Université Laval, 2003. http://www.biographi.ca/en/bio/beaupre_edouard_13E.html.

Laurence, William D. "How *The Silent Enemy* Was Made." In Forsberg, *Redman Echoes*, 83–5.

Lejeune, Philippe. *Le Pacte autobiographique*. Paris: Seuil, coll. "Poétique," 1975.

Lim, Shirley Geok-lin. "Sibling Hybridities: The Case of Edith Eaton/Sui Sin Far and Winnifred Eaton/Onoto Watanna." *Life Writing* 4, no. 1: 81–99.

Ling, Amy. *Between Worlds: Women Writers of Chinese Ancestry*. New York: Pergamon Press, 1990.

Long Lance. "History of and Agricultural Work among Indians in Western Canada." *Proceedings of the Eighteenth Annual Meeting of the American Railway Association* (1926): 25–7.

– "How Canada's Last Frontier Outlaw Died." *Maclean's*, 1 January 1924, 19–20, 42, 44.

– "Indians of the Northwest and West Canada." *The Mentor*, March 1924, 1–40.

– *Long Lance*. New York: Cosmopolitan Book Corporation, 1928.

– "My Trail Upward." *Hearst's International-Cosmopolitan*, June 1926, 70–3, 138.

– "Princes Go West, but What of the Young Man without Money?" In Forsberg, *Redman Echoes*, 49–57. (Originally published in *McClure's*, 1927.)

– "The Secret of the Sioux." *Hearst's International-Cosmopolitan*, June 1927, 41.

– "Squamish." *Vancouver Sun*, 21 May 1922.

– "Valedictory Address." In Forsberg, *Redman Echoes*, 73–4.

– "West Point's Predicament: Why There Are Two Hundred Vacancies." *The Century Monthly Magazine* 117 (January 1929): 375–83.

Lutes, Jean Marie. "The Queer Newspaperwoman in Edith Eaton's 'The Success of a Mistake.'" *Legacy: A Journal of American Women Writers* 29, no. 2 (2012): 280–99.

Lutz, Hartmut. "Canadian Multicultural Literatures: Ethnic Minorities and 'AlterNatives.'" In *The Canadian Alternative*, edited by Klaus Martens, 37–51. Würzburg, Germany: Königshausen & Neumann, 2003.

– "Receptions of Indigenous Canadian Literature in Germany." In *Reflections of Canada: The Reception of Canadian Literature in Germany*, edited by Martin Kuester and Andrea Wolff, 36–63. Marburg, Germany: Schriften der Universitätsbibliothek Marburg, 2000.

Mann, Thomas. *Bekenntnisse des Hochstaplers Felix Krull (Erster Teil)*. Frankfurt am Main, Germany: S. Fischer, 1954.

– *The Confessions of Felix Krull, Confidence Man (The Early Years)*. Translated by Denver Lindley. New York: Vintage Books, 1969.

Martens, Klaus. "Canada's First Bohemian." In *The Canadian Alternative*, edited by Klaus Martens, 77–91. Würzburg, Germany: Königshausen & Neumann, 2003.

– *Felix Paul Greves Karriere. Frederick Philip Grove in Deutschland*. St Ingbert, Germany: Rohrig Universitatsverlag, 1997.

– *F.P. Grove in Europe and Canada: Translated Lives*. Edmonton: University of Alberta Press, 2001.

Martin, Claude. *André Gide par lui-même*. Paris: Seuil, 1963.

Martin, Raymond, and John Barresi. *The Rise and Fall of Soul and Self: An Intellectual History of Personal Identity*. New York: Columbia University Press, 2013.

Matsukawa, Yuko. "Cross-Dressing and Cross-Naming: Decoding Onoto Watanna." In *Tricksterism in Turn-of-the-Century American Literature*, edited by Elizabeth Ammons and Annette White-Parks, 106–25. Hanover, NH, and London: University Press of New England, 1994.

McCullough, Kate. *Regions of Identity: The Construction of America in Women's Fiction 1885–1914*. Stanford, CA: Stanford University Press, 1999.

McKenzie, Stephanie. "Chasing Tales: Review of *Tales of an Empty Cabin* by Grey Owl and *Grey Owl* by Armand Garnet Ruffo." *Canadian Literature* 177 (Summer 2003): 150–1.

McMullin, Stanley. "Introduction." In Frederick Philip Grove, *A Search for Myself*, ix–xv. Toronto: McClelland and Stewart, 1974 [1946].

Micco, Melinda. "Tribal Re-Creations: Chief Buffalo Child Long Lance and Black Seminole Narratives." In *Re-placing America: Conversations and Contestations*, edited by Ruth Hus, Cynthia Franklin, and Suzanne Kosanke, 74–81. Honolulu: University of Hawai'i and the East-West Center, 2000.

Middleton, S.H. "Foreword to Book IV." In Forsberg, *Redman Echoes*, 184–6.

Millar, Ruth. "Ernest Dufault, alias Will James." In *Saskatchewan Heroes and Rogues*, 15–28. Regina: Coteau Books, 2004.

Mindin, Michael. "Mann's Literary Techniques." In *The Cambridge Companion to Thomas Mann*, edited by Ritchie Robertson, 43–63. Cambridge: Cambridge University Press, 2001.

Mooney, James. "Croatan Indians." In *Handbook of American Indians North of Mexico*, vol. 1, edited by Frederick Webb Hodge, 365. 2 vols. Washington, DC: Government Printing Press Office, 1907.

Moser, Linda Trinh. "Afterword." In *Me: A Book of Remembrance* [Onoto Watanna], 357–72. Jackson: University of Mississippi/Jackson and Banner Books, 1997.

National Film Board of Canada. "Beaver People." 1928. https://www.nfb.ca/film/beaver_people.

Newashe McAllister, Emma (Hankasheota). "Preface." In Forsberg, *Redman Echoes*, n.p.

Ouellette-Michalska, Madeleine. *Autofiction et dévoilement*. Montreal, QC: XYZ éditeur, 2007.

Owens, Louis. *Mixedblood Messages: Literature, Film, Family, Place*. Norman: University of Oklahoma Press, 1990.

Pacey, Desmond. *Frederick Philip Grove*. Toronto: Ryerson, 1945.

– ed. *The Letters of Frederick Philip Grove*. Toronto: University of Toronto Press, 1996.

Pache, Walter. "Der Fall Greve – Vorleben und Nachleben des Schriftstellers Felix Paul Greve." *Deutschkanadisches Jahrbuch* 5 (1979): 121–36.

– "The Dilettante in Exile: Grove at the Centenary of his Birth." *Canadian Literature* 90 (1981): 187–91.

– "'Greek to us, Grove': *Over Prairie Trails* as Odyssey." *International Symposium on the 50th Anniversary of the Death of Frederick Philip Grove/Felix Paul Greve*. Winnipeg: University of Manitoba, 30 September–2 October 1998. https://home.cc.umanitoba.ca/~fgrove/symp98/videos/index.html.

Painter, George D. *André Gide*. London: Arthur Barker, 1951.

Poletti, Anna, and Julie Rak, eds. *Identity Technologies: Constructing the Self Online*. Madison: University of Wisconsin Press, 2014.

Powell, Timothy B., ed. *Beyond the Binary: Reconstructing Identity in a Multicultural Context*. New Brunswick, NJ, and London: Rutgers University Press, 1999.

Pratt, Richard Henry. *Battlefield & Classroom*. Norman: University of Oklahoma Press, 2003.

Prose, Francine. "Going Native." *Creative Nonfiction* 19 (2002): 41–8.

Rak, Julie. *Auto/Biography in Canada: Critical Directions*. Waterloo, ON: Wilfrid Laurier University Press, 2005.

– "Translocal Representation: Chief Buffalo Child Long Lance, Nello 'Tex' Vernon-Wood, and Canlit." In *Critical Collaborations: Indigeneity, Diaspora and Ecology*, edited by Smaro Kamboureli and Christl Verduyn, 175–98. Waterloo, ON: Wilfrid Laurier University Press, 2014.

Rampa, Tuesday Lobsang. *The Third Eye*. London: Secker and Warburg, 1956.

Riley, Anthony W. "The German Novels of Frederick Philip Grove." In *The Grove Symposium*, edited by John Nause, 55–66. Ottawa: University of Ottawa Press, 1974.

Robin, Régine. *Le Golem de l'écriture: De l'autofiction au Cybersoi*. Montreal, QC: XYZ éditeur, 1997.

Rosenthal, Caroline. "'The Wish to Be a Red Indian': The Canadian Dream of Grey Owl." In *Fake Identity? The Impostor Narrative in*

North American Culture, edited by Caroline Rosenthal and Stefanie Schäfer, 46. Frankfurt, Germany, and New York: Campus Verlag, 2014.

Rosenthal, Caroline, and Stefanie Schäfer, eds. *Fake Identity? The Impostor Narrative in North American Culture*. Frankfurt, Germany, and New York: Campus Verlag, 2014.

Ross, Colin. "The Story of Grey Owl." *Compass: A Provincial Review* 5 (1979): 79–83.

Ross, Malcolm. "Introduction." In Frederick Philip Grove, *Over Prairie Trails*, v–x. Toronto: McClelland and Stewart, 1957 [1922].

Rubio, Mary, ed. *The Genesis of Grove's "The Adventure of Leonard Broadus": A Text and Commentary.* Guelph, ON: Canadian Children's Press, 1983.

Ruffo, Garnet Armand. *Grey Owl: The Mystery of Archie Belaney*. Regina: Coteau Books, 1997.

Salutin, Rick. "The Boyden Affair Just Got Murkier." *The Toronto Star*, 13 January 2017. http://www.thestar.com/opinion/commentary/2017/01/13/the-boyden-affair-just-got-murkier-salutin.html.

Sangster, Dorothy. "The Double Life of Injun Joe." *Maclean's*, 21 July 1956. http://www.macleans.ca/archives/the-double-life-of-injun-joe/.

Schlossberg, Linda, and Maria Carla Sanchez, eds. *Passing: Identity and Interpretation in Sexuality, Race, and Religion*. New York and London: New York University Press, 2001.

Sheppard, Gordon. *HA! A Self-Murder Mystery*. Montreal, QC: McGill-Queen's University Press, 2003.

Shih, David. "The Self and Generic Convention: Winifred Eaton's *Me, A Book of Remembrance*." In *Recovered Legacies: Authority and Identity in Early Asian American Literature*, edited by Keith Lawrence and Floyd Cheung, 41–59. Philadelphia, PA: Temple University Press, 2005.

Skinazi, Karen E.H. "'As to her race, her secret is loudly revealed': Winnifred Eaton's Revision of North American Identity." MELUS 32, no. 2 (Summer 2007): 31–53.

– "Introduction." In *Marion: The Study of an Artist's Model* [Onoto Watanna], i–xciv. Montreal, QC, and Kingston, ON: McGill-Queen's University Press, 2012.

Smith, Donald B. *Chief Buffalo Child Long Lance: The Glorious Impostor*. Red Deer, AB: Red Deer Press, 1999.

– *From the Land of Shadows: The Making of Grey Owl*. Saskatoon, SK: Western Producer Prairie Books, 1990.

Smith, Sidonie. "Performativity, Autobiographical Practice, Resistance." *a/b: Auto/Biography Studies* 10, no. 1 (Spring 1995): 17–33.

Spettigue, Douglas O. *FPG: The European Years*. Ottawa: Oberon, 1973.
– *Frederick Philip Grove*. Toronto: Copp Clark, 1969.
Spiritalk Gathering. "Sun Dance." http://www.native-americans-online.com/native-american-sun-dance.html (accessed 22 August 2016).
Stich, K.P. "Grove's New World Bluff." *Canadian Literature* 90 (1981): 111–23.
Stobie, Margaret R. *Frederick Philip Grove*. New York: Twayne, 1973.
Sui Sin Far [Edith Eaton]. "Chan Hen Yen, Chinese Student." *New England Magazine* 45 (June 1912): 462–6.
– "The Heart's Desire." In *Mrs. Spring Fragrance*, 300–3. Chicago: A.C. McClurg, 1912.
– "Ku Yum's Little Sister." *Chicago Evening Post*, 13 October 1900.
– "Leaves from the Mental Portfolio of an Eurasian." *The Independent* 66 (21 January 1909): 125–32.
– "Lin John." In *Mrs. Spring Fragrance*, 220–3. Chicago: A.C. McClurg, 1912.
– *Mrs. Spring Fragrance*. Chicago: A.C. McClurg, 1911.
– "The Smuggling of Tie Co." In *Mrs. Spring Fragrance*, 184–92. Chicago: A.C. McClurg, 1912.
– "The Story of Tin-A." *Land of Sunshine* 12 (December 1899), 101–3.
– "The Success of a Mistake." *Legacy: A Journal of American Women Writers* 29, no. 2 (2012): 270–9.
– "Sui Sin Far, the Half Chinese Writer, Tells of Her Career." *The Boston Globe*, 5 May 1912. Archived at http://suisinfar.omeka.net (accessed 12 April 2016).
– "Sweet Sin." *Land of Sunshine* 3 (April 1898): 223–6.
Taylor, Drew Hayden. "Is Joseph Boyden 'Grey Owling'?" *Now* online. https://nowtoronto.com/news/in-defense-of-joseph-boyden/ (accessed 22 February 2017).
– "Pretending to Be an Impostor." In *Fake Identity? The Impostor Narrative in North American Culture*, edited by Caroline Rosenthal and Stefanie Schäfer, 227–30. Frankfurt, Germany, and New York: Campus Verlag, 2014.
Tonkovich, Nicole. "Genealogy, Genre, Gender: Sui Sin Far's 'Leaves from the Mental Portfolio of an Eurasian.'" In *Beyond the Binary: Reconstructing Identity in a Multicultural Context*, edited by Timothy B. Powell, 236–60. New Brunswick, NJ, and London: Rutgers University Press, 1999.
Turkle, Sherry. *Life on the Screen: Identity in the Age of the Internet*. New York: Simon and Schuster, 1995.

Tyson, Ian. "The Ballad of Will James." http://www.cowboylyrics.com/tabs/tyson-ian/will-james-1018.html (accessed 18 June 2016).

Vernon, Karina. "The First Black Prairie Novel: Chief Buffalo Child Long Lance's Autobiography and the Repression of Prairie Blackness." *Journal of Canadian Studies/Revue d'études canadiennes* 45, no. 2 (Spring 2011): 31–57.

Vilain, Philippe. *Défense de Narcisse*. Paris: Grasset, 2005.

Wang, I-Chun. "Space and Identity: Hybridization and Boundary Crossing in Sui Sin Far's Poetics of Diaspora." *Canadian Review of Comparative Literature* 36, no. 3 (2009): 274–88.

Warken, Arlette. "Frederick Philip Grove and Knut Hamsun: Northern European Perceptions of the New World." In *American and Canadian Literature and Culture: Across a Latitudinal Line*, edited by Klaus Martens and Paul Morris, 28–39. Saarbrücken, Germany: Centre for Canadian and Anglo-American Culture and Amarant Presse, 2008.

Watanna, Onoto. "The Half Caste." *Conkey's Home Journal*, November 1898.

– *A Japanese Nightingale*. New York: Harper and Brothers, 1901.

– *Miss Numè of Japan*. Chicago: Rand, McNally, 1898.

– *Sunny-San*. New York: George H. Doran, 1922.

– *The Wooing of Wistaria*. New York: Macmillan, 1902.

– [published anonymously]. *Me: A Book of Remembrance*. New York: The Century, 1915.

– [published anonymously]. *Marion: The Study of an Artist's Model*. Critical edition, with an introduction by Karen E.H. Skinazi. Montreal, QC, and Kingston, ON: McGill-Queen's University Press, 2012. [New York: W.J. Watt, 1916.]

– [Winnifred Eaton Reeve]. *Cattle*. New York: W.J. Watt, 1924.

– [Winnifred Eaton]. *His Royal Nibs*. New York: W.J. Watt, 1925.

Webster, Jean. "Introduction." In *Marion: The Study of an Artist's Model* [Onoto Watanna], n.p. New York: W.J. Watt, 1916.

White-Parks, Annette. "We Wear the Mask: Sui Sin Far as One Example of Trickster Authorship." In *Tricksterism in Turn-of-the-Century American Literature: A Multicultural Perspective*, edited by Elizabeth Ammons and Annette White-Parks, 1–20. Hanover, NH, and London: University Press of New England, 1994.

– *Sui Sin Far/Edith Maude Eaton: A Literary Biography*. Urbana and Chicago: University of Illinois Press, 1995.

Wilde, Oscar. "The Decay of Lying." In *The Complete Writings of Oscar Wilde*, vol. 7. New York: The Nottingham Society, 1909. At *The*

Victorian Web, edited by George P. Landow, 13 November 2014, http://www.victorianweb.org/authors/wilde/decay.html.

Wuthenow, Ralph-Rainer. "Nachwort." In Thomas Mann, *Bekenntnisse des Hochstaplers Felix Krull (Erster Teil)*, n.p. Frankfurt am Main, Germany: S. Fischer, 1994.

Yanovsky, Joel. "Who Is Andreas Karavis?" *The Montreal Gazette*, 20 November 2000.

Index